# THE ORIGINS OF
# THE COLD WAR IN
# EUROPE

# THE ORIGINS OF THE COLD WAR IN EUROPE

*International perspectives*

---

*Edited by*
DAVID REYNOLDS

YALE UNIVERSITY PRESS
*New Haven & London*

Designed by John Trevitt

Set in Linotron Ehrhardt by Best-set Typesetter Ltd, Hong Kong
Printed in Great Britain by St Edmundsbury Press

ISBN 0–300–05892–6

Library of Congress Catalog Number 93–61583

With the defeat of the Reich and pending the emergence of the Asiatic, the African and, perhaps, the South American nationalisms, there will remain in the world only two Great Powers capable of confronting each other – the United States and Soviet Russia. The laws of both history and geography will compel these two Powers to a trial of strength, either military or in the fields of economics and ideology. These same laws make it inevitable that both Powers should become enemies of Europe. And it is equally certain that both these Powers will sooner or later find it desirable to seek the support of the sole surviving great nation in Europe, the German people.

The 'Testament' of Adolf Hitler
2 April 1945

My statement 'we will bury you' was misconstrued. . . . I meant that capitalism would be buried and that Communism would come to replace it.

Nikita Khrushchev, Washington D.C.,
16 September 1959

. . . the biggest thing that has happened in the world in my life – in our lives – is this: By the grace of God, America won the Cold War.

George Bush, State of the Union Address
28 January 1992

It is not given to human beings . . . to foresee or to predict to any large extent the unfolding course of events. In one phase men seem to have been right, in another they seem to have been wrong. Then again, a few years later, when the perspective of time has lengthened, all stands in a different setting. There is a new proportion. There is another scale of values. History with its flickering lamp stumbles along the trail of the past, trying to reconstruct its scenes, to revive its echoes, and kindle with pale gleams the passion of former days.

Winston S. Churchill, House of Commons
12 November 1940

# Contents

# *Acknowledgements*

This book was conceived in 1989 as the iron curtain started to crumble. The ending of the Cold War in Europe seemed a good moment to take stock of its beginnings. Moving from conception to birth has been a long process – finding appropriate contributors, accommodating their busy schedules, taking account of readers' comments, and allowing time for revisions in the wake of the upheavals of 1989–91. Two of the eight essays went through their first incarnation at a small one-day colloquium arranged by the Centre of International Studies at Cambridge, and I appreciate the support of Jonathan Haslam and Richard Langhorne in organizing that event. John Nicoll of Yale University Press in London has taken a keen and constructive interest in the project from the start. I am grateful to Lloyd Gardner, Jonathan Haslam, Zara Steiner and John Thompson for helpful comments. Above all, I should like to thank the other contributors for their willingness to work against tight deadlines, in a language that is not their native tongue, and for their patience with the editor's letters, faxes and phone calls!

*Cambridge*                                                                     DAVID REYNOLDS
*January 1993*

# Contributors

WOLFGANG KRIEGER (b. 1947) is Senior Research Fellow at the Stiftung Wissenschaft und Politik at Ebenhausen in Germany and also teaches modern history at the University of Munich. Educated at Munich and Oxford, he was a Kennedy Fellow at Harvard University in 1983–4 and Dulles Visiting Professor of International Affairs at Princeton University in 1991–2. He is the author of *Labour Party und Weimarer Republik, 1918–1924* (1978) and *General Lucius D. Clay und die amerikanische Deutschlandpolitik, 1945–1949* (1988), as well as numerous articles on American, British and German history. He is the European Co-ordinator of the multinational Nuclear History Program, and among his current projects is a study of nuclear weapons in international relations.

HELGE Ø. PHARO (b. 1943) is a graduate of the University of Oslo, where he is now Professor of International History. He is a frequent visitor to the United States and Britain, and has been a visiting fellow at the University of Wisconsin at Madison in 1987–8 and at the London School of Economics in 1990. A specialist on the Cold War and on Norwegian history, he has published several articles in English, in addition to *USA og den kalde krigen* (1972) and three other books in Norwegian on Norway's political, economic and diplomatic history. He is working on a study of Norway, the Marshall Plan and European integration, a volume in the *History of Norwegian Foreign Relations* and an account of the origins of EFTA.

CONSTANTINE PLESHAKOV (b. 1959) was educated at Moscow State University and the National University of Singapore. He gained his Ph.D. in 1987 from the Institute of the U.S.A. and Canada, Russian Academy of Sciences, Moscow, where he is currently a Head of Section, and he has also been a visiting lecturer at the University of Hong Kong. In 1990–2 he was the recipient of a John D. and Catherine T. MacArthur Writing and Research Grant. A specialist on the Cold War and current Russian foreign policy, he is currently engaged with Vladislav Zubok on a comprehensive study of the Soviet leadership in the Cold War, based on archives and oral history.

ILARIA POGGIOLINI (b. 1958) received her undergraduate and graduate degrees from the University of Florence where she teaches in the Faculty of Political

Science. She has been a Fulbright Scholar in Washington, a NATO Fellow at the London School of Economics and a Visiting Fellow at the Center of International Studies at Princeton. She is the author of *Diplomazia della transizione: Gli alleati e il problema del trattato italiano* (1990) and various articles on Italian foreign policy and American-Italian relations in the post-war period.

DAVID REYNOLDS (b. 1952) is a Fellow of Christ's College, Cambridge University. He has researched and lectured extensively in the United States, including several periods as a visiting fellow at Harvard. His works include *The Creation of the Anglo-American Alliance, 1937–1941: a Study in Competitive Co-operation* (1981), which was awarded the Bernath Prize; *An Ocean Apart: the Relationship between Britain and America in the Twentieth Century* (co-author, 1988); *Britannia Overruled: British Policy and World Power in the Twentieth Century* (1991); *Allies at War: the Soviet, American and British Experience, 1939–45* (co-editor, 1994) and various articles on the diplomacy of the Second World War and the Cold War.

GEORGES-HENRI SOUTOU (b. 1943) is Professor of History at the Sorbonne. He is the author of *L'Or et le Sang: les buts de guerre économiques de la première guerre mondiale* (1989), as well as numerous articles on international relations during the First World War, the 1920s and the post-1945 era. He has served on the Editors Group in Bonn for the series *Documents on German Foreign Policy* and is a member of the Nuclear History Group, for which he wrote *The French Military Program for Nuclear Energy, 1945–1981* (1989). His current research is directed towards a study of France and the Cold War.

ANDERS STEPHANSON (b. 1950) is Assistant Professor of History at Columbia University. Educated there and at the Universities of Gothenburg and Oxford, he has also been a visiting fellow at the University of Southern California and the University of California at Los Angeles, as well as an Assistant Professor at Rutgers University. His book on *Kennan and the Art of Foreign Policy* (1989) was joint winner of the Bernath Prize in 1990. Among his current projects is a study of William Appleman Williams and the Wisconsin 'school' of historians of US foreign relations.

CEES WIEBES (b. 1950) is Lecturer in the Department of International Relations and International Public Law at the University of Amsterdam. He published *Indonesische dagboeknotities van dr H. N. Boon* (1986, with Bert Zeeman), *Affärer till varje pris* (Stockholm, 1989, with Gerard Aalders), and *Towards the North Atlantic Treaty: Belgium, the Netherlands and Alliances, 1940–1949* (1993, with Bert Zeeman). He has contributed to *International Affairs*, *International History Review*, *Review of International Studies*, *Scandinavian Economic History Review* and *Vierteljahrshefte für Zeitgeschichte*.

BERT ZEEMAN (b. 1958) is Reference and Acquisitions Librarian at the University Library of the University of Amsterdam. He published, with Cees Wiebes, *Indonesische dagboeknotities van dr H. N. Boon* (1986) and *Towards the North Atlan-*

*tic Treaty: Belgium, the Netherlands and Alliances, 1940–1949* (1993). He has contributed to the *European History Quarterly*, *Review of International Studies*, *International Affairs*, *International History Review*, *Vierteljahrshefte für Zeitgeschichte* and the *Bulletin of Bibliography*.

VLADISLAV ZUBOK (b. 1958) gained his BA and MA from Moscow State University and his Ph.D. in 1985 from the Institute for the U.S.A. and Canada, Russian Academy of Sciences, Moscow. He has spent ten years at the Institute, latterly as a senior scholar and Secretary of the Advanced School for International Security and Disarmament. The author of two books and numerous articles in Russian, he is currently engaged with Constantine Pleshakov on a comprehensive study of the Soviet leadership in the Cold War, based on archives and oral history. He has taught in the United States at the Universities of Massachusetts (Amherst) and Michigan (Ann Arbor) and in 1993 was an international guest scholar at the Kennan Institute in Washington and the Norwegian Nobel Institute in Oslo.

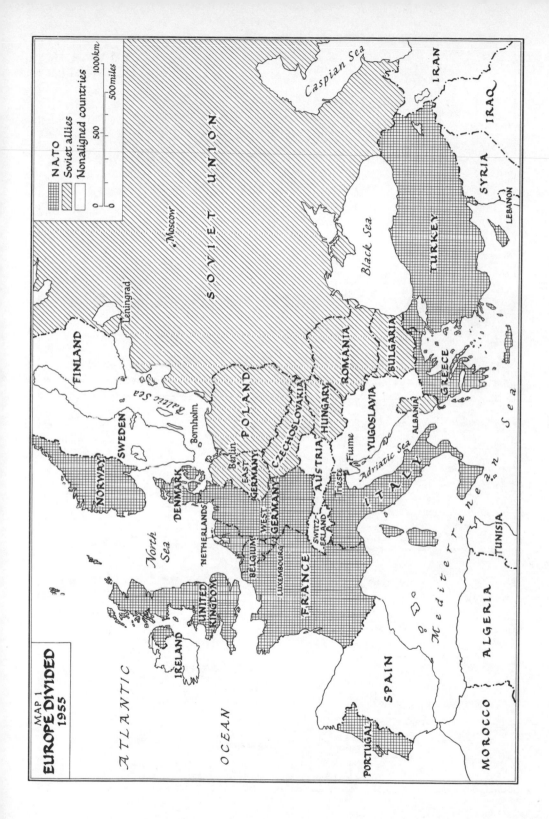

MAP 1
EUROPE DIVIDED
1955

NATO
Soviet allies
Nonaligned countries

1000km
500miles
500
0
0

ATLANTIC

OCEAN

IRELAND

UNITED
KINGDOM

North
Sea

NORWAY

SWEDEN

FINLAND

Leningrad

Baltic Sea

Bornholm

Moscow

SOVIET UNION

Caspian Sea

DENMARK

NETHERLANDS

BELGIUM

LUXEMBOURG

Berlin

EAST
GERMANY

WEST
GERMANY

POLAND

SWITZ-
ERLAND

CZECHOSLOVAKIA

AUSTRIA

HUNGARY

ROMANIA

FRANCE

ITALY

Trieste

Fiume

YUGOSLAVIA

Adriatic Sea

ALBANIA

BULGARIA

Black Sea

GREECE

TURKEY

IRAN

SYRIA

IRAQ

LEBANON

PORTUGAL

SPAIN

Mediterranean Sea

MOROCCO

ALGERIA

TUNISIA

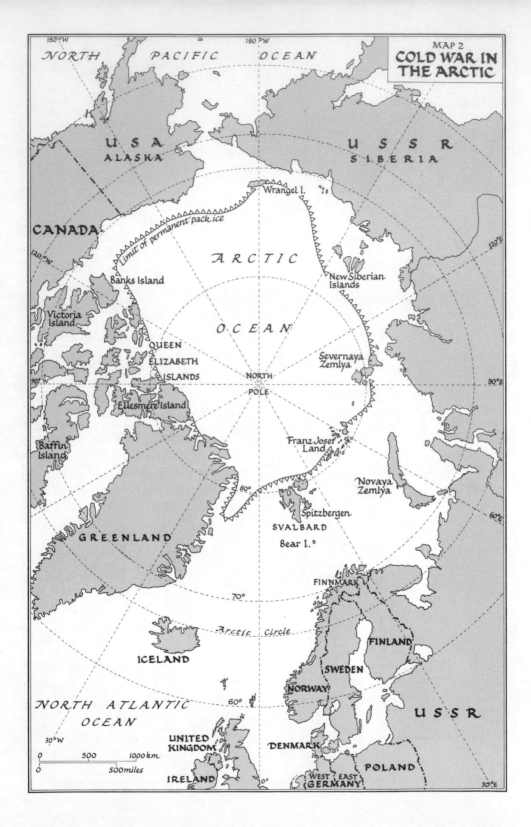

MAP 2
COLD WAR IN
THE ARCTIC

150°W

180°W

NORTH    PACIFIC    OCEAN

USA
ALASKA

USSR
SIBERIA

Wrangel I.

CANADA

Limit of permanent pack ice

120°W

ARCTIC

Banks Island

New Siberian
Islands

Victoria
Island

OCEAN

QUEEN
ELIZABETH
ISLANDS

90°W

Severnaya
Zemlya

NORTH
POLE

90°E

Ellesmere Island

Baffin
Island

Franz Josef
Land

80°

Novaya
Zemlya

GREENLAND

60°E

Spitzbergen
SVALBARD
Bear I.

120°E

FINNMARK

70°

Arctic Circle

FINLAND

ICELAND

SWEDEN
NORWAY

60°

USSR

NORTH ATLANTIC
OCEAN

30°W

UNITED
KINGDOM

DENMARK

POLAND

0    500    1000 km

0    500 miles

IRELAND

0°

WEST EAST
GERMANY

30°E

# Introduction

## DAVID REYNOLDS

In the light of history the Soviet revolution of 1989–91 promises to be every bit as significant as the French revolution of two centuries before. In three breathless years the Cold War came to a dramatic end. 1988 saw radical superpower arms control agreements, in 1989 the Soviet bloc in Eastern Europe disintegrated, the two Germanies were reunited in October 1990, and finally, at the end of 1991, the Soviet Union itself crumbled into separate, feuding republics. In the wake of these *bouleversements*, politicians and pundits pondered the shape of the new international order. Such futurology is understandable, indeed essential; yet there is merit in looking back as well as forward. For the end of the Cold War enables historians to look afresh at its origins, aided by the new perspective offered thanks to recent events and also by the new evidence that the demise of the Soviet bloc is making available. Such a task is not mere antiquarianism. The origins of the Cold War are entangled with problems that still beset us today. In fact the Cold-War order in Europe was a temporary resolution of those problems, and the collapse of that order has brought them to the surface anew, particularly the so-called 'German question'.

The term 'Cold War' has ancient roots. It has been traced back to the German socialist, Eduard Bernstein, writing of the arms race of the 1890s, and even to the fourteenth-century Castilian political commentator, Don Juan Manuel.[1] Its application to the Soviet-American confrontation after 1945 owes most to *The Cold War* by the American journalist Walter Lippmann, which appeared in 1947. Yet one might also note its use in the same way by the British author, George Orwell, as early as October 1945 when he pondered the implications of the atomic bomb and predicted ' "a peace that is no peace" . . . an epoch as horribly stable as the slave empires of antiquity' in which a great power could at once be '*unconquerable* and in a permanent state of "cold war" with its neighbours'.[2]

Whoever coined the term, it quickly entered common currency – in the process becoming seriously debased. Often it has been taken loosely to define the whole post-war period, as in the catchphrase a 'post-Cold-War era'. Historians and political scientists, however, have inclined to a more specific definition, identifying several Cold Wars punctuated by periods of détente. Thus, one might postulate a First Cold War dating roughly from the enunciation of the Truman Doctrine and the Marshall Plan in the spring of 1947 and lasting until the thaw following Stalin's death in March 1953, which led up to the Geneva summit in July 1955. A second phase is discerned by some historians between the onset of the second Berlin crisis in November 1958 and the signing of the Test Ban treaty in August 1963, with its culmination in the Cuban missile crisis of October 1962. And a third can be dated from the Soviet invasion of Afghanistan in December 1979 until the Gorbachev-led revolution in Soviet policy signalled by the Geneva summit of November 1985. In between these phases of cold war were periods of reduced antagonism, especially the era of détente associated with the arms-control agreements of the early 1970s, and they were followed by a genuine superpower entente in the late 1980s before the Soviet Union's final downfall.[3]

These frameworks remain a matter of debate.[4] The point is that in this volume the 'Cold War' refers to the decade from 1945 – sometimes called the First Cold War. It is on this period and its antecedents that these essays focus. They examine the reshaping of Europe after the Second World War. The first two chapters deal with the superpowers; the remainder explore the reactions of West European states to the growing bipolar order, especially the division of Germany between the two blocs, and also consider how these issues have been handled in national historiographies. Central to the story are the international responses to the Marshall Plan for European economic recovery, announced in June 1947, to the North Atlantic Treaty of April 1949, and to the American demand for German rearmament following the outbreak of the Korean War in June 1950 which cul-minated in West Germany's admission to NATO in May 1955, exactly ten years after the Nazi surrender.

These events posed tough choices for the Western Europeans. Was it possible and/or desirable to avoid siding with one or other superpower? Who constituted the real threat in the long-term – Russia or Germany? How far did anti-commu-nism and fear of the Soviet Union necessitate acceptance of American financial and military help? Could the United States, notorious in Europe for its 'isolationism' between the two world wars, now be relied upon as an ally? What did the Cold War mean for the status of the two defeated and discredited Axis powers, Germany and Italy, in post-war Europe? How far would their neighbours tolerate their rapid rehabilitation? In particular, would France and the Benelux countries (Belgium, the Netherlands and Luxembourg) – victims of aggression from Germany twice in a quarter-century – accept its economic recovery and, from 1950, its rearmament? Why did countries so closely linked by history and economics, such as those in Scandinavia, answer these questions so differently? (Norway and Denmark joined the Atlantic Alliance while Sweden remained neutral.) Why did Britain's alacrity in working with the United States contrast so strikingly with France's suspicious hesitation? And what part did these European countries play in shaping American Cold-War policy?

These are some of the questions addressed in this book. Possible answers are offered by specialists on the foreign policy of the countries they describe, who have drawn on their own research and that of other scholars to offer overviews of the post-war decade. Their essays provide novel analytical introductions to the mass of new work on these countries, much of it unavailable in the English language.[5] They are also arranged in pairs to highlight certain broader themes about the structure of post-war international politics.

The first pair of essays examines the superpower context – *The Big Two*. Their rivalry formed the crucible in which post-war Europe was forged. What stand out in the 1990s, of course, are the differences as much as the similarities in their situation – not merely the familiar contrasts of ideology (capitalism and communism) and of political systems (liberal democracy and authoritarian bureaucracy) but also the basic difference in the nature of their power. Although Soviet economic capability should not be dismissed (victory over Hitler was not a matter of mere numbers), essentially American international leadership after 1945 was *because of* its economic position, whereas Soviet hegemony was *in spite of* its economic position. More precisely, only the diversion of a large proportion of gross domestic product (perhaps one-fifth) into the military-industrial sector enabled the semi-modernized Soviets to keep up in the Cold War;[6] and that diversion, in turn, was possible only because of the repressive political system which controlled consumer aspirations and extinguished sparks of dissent. This relationship between the Cold War and the Soviet political economy was both central and symbiotic: international tension legitimized domestic repression, Stalinism at home made possible expansion abroad. When Gorbachev tried to end the Cold War in order to reform the economy, he brought the whole shaky edifice crumbling down.

From the angle of Cold-War scholarship, there is another striking difference between the two superpowers. Stated baldly: Cold-War America has a history, the Soviet Union does not. As Vladislav Zubok and Constantine Pleshakov show in the first part of chapter 2, very little of pre-1990 Soviet writing is of value. Occasional (and quickly silenced) independent voices, such as Alexander M. Nekrich on the German invasion in 1941, had no echoes for postwar foreign policy.[7] Most so-called diplomatic 'history' was ammunition for official propaganda against the United States. Self-styled 'revisionists' of the late 1980s, in the main, simply turned the tables and blamed everything on Stalin. Only the opening of the archives and the collapse of communism created preconditions for 'history' according to Western canons.

What this confirms is the centrality of American writing of the Cold War for that of all other nations. As Anders Stephanson reminds us, in the opening essay of this collection, the Cold War obsessed Americans for two generations, notably in the traumas of McCarthyism and Vietnam. Consequently the history of the Cold War mattered to American society and, moreover, it was available. US archives, both in print and in the raw, were opened years ahead of those elsewhere and they were devoured, digested and disgorged by the uniquely vast army of American Cold-War scholars.[8] The sometimes vitriolic debates among these historians have shaped research and writing the world over. It is for this reason that Stephanson's essay concentrates on the historiography rather than the history of US Cold-War policy, which in any case has been detailed extensively elsewhere and, in outline, is now familiar.[9] (Summaries can found in his essay and in appendix one at the end of the volume.)

With reservations, Stephanson adopts the typology of 'traditionalists' (who focused on Soviet territorial expansion), 'revisionists' (who pointed to American economic expansion) and 'post-revisionists' (eclectic in explanation, though leaning to the first). But he analyzes their work in novel ways and also pays particular attention to recent developments. These include the so-called 'corporatist' school, with its ambition to offer a synthesis of American international policy over the century as a whole, and, more recently, the 'geopoliticians' – scholars whose work centres on American conceptions of global security in the context of a changing international system. The latter he finds particularly fruitful but not in any way sufficient, and his essay concludes with a provocative return to the *mentalités* of Cold-War America.

The critical, yet unanswered, question running through this American debate was whether US Cold-War policy was correct. Answers to that depended on assessments of Soviet aims, objectives and reactions – assessments which, in the absence of hard evidence, remained a matter of speculation, prejudice or contemporary politics.[10] In 1949 Soviet policy was still, in Churchill's words from a decade before, 'a riddle wrapped in a mystery inside an enigma'.[11] Zubok and Pleshakov, two younger Russian scholars energetically exploring the newly-opened archives, offer their own evaluation of what motivated Soviet foreign policy. The central 'enigma' remains Stalin. Like biographers such as Robert C. Tucker and Dmitri Volkogonov, they emphasize Stalin's neurotic insecurity, his xenophobia and his psychological need to outdo Lenin.[12] In line with post-communist Russian historiography, they stress also his preoccupation with tsarist precedents, particularly Alexander I, victor over Napoleon. Stalin's world, in their view, revolved around two suns: (communist) revolution and (tsarist) imperialism. The two were not incompatible since communism was ultimately a vision of universal empire. Yet that does not make Stalin the crude megalomaniac of some Cold-War caricature. His main concerns were geographically specific – East Asia always came far behind Eastern Europe – and wartime cooperation with Roosevelt and Churchill was not only welcome recognition psychologically but also suggested that he could secure his political aims by diplomatic agreement.

Why, then, the ensuing confrontation? To understand this, Zubok and Pleshakov examine the interaction of Stalin's tortured psyche with the international and domestic context. They set out three imperatives: the demands of 'state' politics, of normal international relations; the pressures of running a revolutionary party at home and abroad; and the burdens of occupying vast tracts of conquered or liberated territory. In 1945–7 Stalin thought he could get what he want by state politics: America appeared to be withdrawing into itself, Western Europe teetered on the edge of economic collapse and strong communist parties seemed poised to assume power by political means across the continent. But the firm US stand in 1947 forced a radical change of policy, with party imperatives now dominant. Communist revolution was implemented in Eastern Europe and encouraged in the West. Stalin felt confident that American self-assertion would soon falter in the inevitable crisis of capitalism and his own hubris was centrally responsible for the disastrous miscalculations over Berlin in 1948 and Korea in 1950. After his death in 1953, Soviet policy tried to move back towards 'state politics'. Yet the burdens of occupation and party were too great. The former is best seen in the case of East Germany, an increasing liability which Beria and Malenkov would have abandoned, given a free hand, in 1953. The imperatives of party leadership were evident in Khrushchev's expansion of ideological rivalry with the United States, particularly into the Middle East. For Zubok and Pleshakov, the Stalin phenomenon, coupled with the pressures of ideological leadership and imperial occupation, makes it difficult to envisage real missed opportunities for a 'normal' relationship with the West.

Such observations about the origins of the Cold War, though tentative, complement general Western verdicts about why it came to an end. These emphasize the impact of the Gorbachev revolution, both in removing communist controls at home and loosening Soviet rule in Eastern Europe. In particular, Gorbachev's failure to intervene in 1989, in contrast with his predecessors over Hungary in 1956 or Czechoslovakia in 1968, was the critical factor in the collapse of the Warsaw Pact.[13] Thus, the beginning and the end of the Cold War both appear to be explained by primary reference to Moscow.

This casts a new light on the debate about US policy in the 1940s. The language of containment now has a different resonance from the way it sounded during the Vietnam furore of the late 1960s. Take, for instance, George F. Kennan's classics of 1946–7, the 'Long Telegram' and the 'Mr X' article. Both of these advocated a policy of containment not to provoke war but 'to promote tendencies [in the Soviet Union] which must eventually find their outlet in either the break-up or the gradual mellowing of Soviet power'.[14] Or one might ponder the remarks of Andrei Vishinsky, the Soviet deputy Foreign Minister, in London in February 1946 when he told Sir Stafford Cripps that it was historically impossible for Soviet policy to accord with British ideas of democracy and human rights. As Cripps paraphrased Vishinsky: 'Perhaps in 50–100 years they would have reached the stage when they could hold our view. They could understand what our views were but they could not [now] share them or practise them.'[15] Vishinsky had been Stalin's chief prosecutor during the notorious purge trials of the late 1930s and the Foreign Office did not take his observations seriously. Half a century on, however, his words take on a new meaning.

These developments appear to give enhanced credibility to the 'traditionalist' and 'post-revisionist' American views of the origins of the Cold War – which identified as its root cause Soviet expansion. To quote John L. Gaddis, for instance: containment 'proved remarkably successful in maintaining the post-World War II balance of power without war and without appeasement until the Soviet Union, confronting the illogic of its own system and its own position in the world, simply gave up'.[16] Where, then, do the historical and historiographical revolutions of 1989–91 leave the revisionist critique of US foreign policy – with its focus on *American* self-assertion?

One possible response is to develop the argument advanced at the beginning of Anders Stephanson's essay and to distinguish between the first bout of Soviet-American Cold War, on the one hand, and the larger post-war order of a bipolar, two-bloc Europe, on the other. The Soviet presence or influence in East and East-Central Europe was indeed the most striking novelty of the European situation in

1945 – a projection of Russian power farther west than at any time since 1814, when the Tsar's armies paraded in triumph through Paris. But, if we remember that the First Cold War was also the beginning of a longer era, then that helps to remind us that it takes two to make hot war, cold war, or bipolarity. Zubok and Pleshakov end their essay in similar vein by noting that, while the Stalin phenomenon was unique, the Soviet propensity for ideological expansion and military over-commitment had its parallels in the United States and that this helps to explain, if not the origins and outcome of the Cold War, then at least 'its dynamics and exhausting durability'. In other words, an equally important question for historians is why Soviet expansion evoked such a strong reaction in the United States, given the latter's abhorrence of political and military entanglements in Europe in the 1920s and 1930s.

Here the recent scholarship examined by Stephanson offers important clues. The Second World War prompted new globalist (rather than purely continental or hemispheric) definitions of American national security, encompassing the European balance, a global economy shaped in America's image and interests, and the widespread projection of US bases to ensure extended defence in the new age of air power. Europe (and the wider world) seemed to matter to America more than ever before, and this was reflected in the simultaneous cartographic revolution whereby the prevalent image of a separate, self-contained western hemisphere protected by oceans on either side was replaced by maps highlighting North America's proximity to Europe and, focusing on the North Pole, to the Soviet Union.[17] More profound still, if less tangible, was the heady sense of national self-confidence and mission generated by America's role in the war, which stood in marked contrast with the mood of national self-doubt so pervasive in the Depression. As Roosevelt's confidant, Harry Hopkins, put it in 1945:

I have often been asked what interests we have in Poland, Greece, Iran, or Korea. Well I think we have the most important business in the world – and indeed, the only business worthy of our traditions. And that is this – to do everything within our diplomatic power to foster and encourage democratic government throughout the world. We should not be timid about blazoning to the world our desire for the right of all peoples to have a genuine civil liberty. We believe our dynamic democracy is the best in the world. . . .[18]

This points us to what Stephanson notes at the end of his essay – the cultural and social roots of American Cold-War policy which have still to be properly explored because of the previous preoccupation with political ideology and military power.[19]

Understanding the 'Big Two' relationship will be a central task of Cold-War historiography as the archives become available, requiring collaborative projects and the careful cross-referencing of American and Russian policies, as has already been done in microcosm for the so-called 'long telegrams' of 1946.[20] But both these essays on the Big Two point us also to another theme for investigation: the superpowers' clients.

Much of the American research, especially in the 1960s and 1970s, when the archives were being assimilated, was understandably preoccupied with American-Soviet relations. It was as if the post-war world, in Senator J. William Fulbright's words of 1945, was a matter of 'two big dogs chewing on a bone', or, to quote the eminent political scientist, Hans Morgenthau, in 1954, 'two giants eyeing each other with watchful suspicion'.[21] But, as Stephanson notes, several American historians of the 1980s produced monographs on Anglo–American relations which sought to 'depolarize these years'.[22] At the same time, scholars across the Atlantic called for closer examination of the 'European dimension' of the Cold War. Norwegian historian Geir Lundestad argued in a particularly influential article that if, to follow the revisionists, the late 1940s saw the establishment of an informal American empire in Europe, then it was 'empire by invitation' – solicited and even manipulated by the Europeans.[23] For their part, Zubok and Pleshakov, adapting such ideas, draw attention to the leverage exerted by Soviet clients, notably East Germany, over their superpower master – the so-called 'tyranny of the weak'.[24] Alliances, in short, are two-way streets.

Of America's international allies, Britain and France were the most significant in the postwar decade. They were *the other two* members of the Big Four – great, if declining, powers. Today, it is their decline that seems the most obvious fact of the post-war era, a decline that was masked by often hubristic illusions of grandeur. General de Gaulle, France's first post-war leader, claimed in September 1945 that 'in the world England and France are the two principal nations, whose task is to guide the others towards more prosperous material development, greater political maturity and a higher level of civilization.'[25] Yet the risibility of such pronouncements today should not blind us to post-war realities. Both Britain and France were still major empires with large armed forces, each occupied a permanent seat on the UN Security Council, they shared with America and Russia in the occupation of Germany, and they were runners-up to the two superpowers in the race to join the nuclear club: Britain in 1952 and France in 1960. Above all, each had decided views about the future of Europe in 1945–55. While their role in the actual division of the continent was limited, compared with that of the superpowers in 1947, they *were* of considerable importance in shaping the basic institutions of the new Western Europe that emerged from the division – notably the Organization of European Economic Cooperation, the North Atlantic Alliance and the embryo European Community.

To date, the process of 'depolarization' has centred on Great Britain. As my own essay emphasizes, this is a reflection of the continued importance of British power in the post-war world, a theme often slighted by earlier American writers in their pre-occupation with bipolarity. Although Britain's decline was rapid from the mid-1950s, in the initial post-war decade the country was still the leading military and economic power of Western Europe, whose bases around the world were of considerable value to American containment and whose political stability stood in striking contrast to the chaos in France and most of the continent. It is worth remembering that when the American political scientist William T.R. Fox coined the term 'superpower' in 1944 to refer to states with 'great power and great mobility of power', he included Great Britain with the United States and the Soviet Union in that exalted category.[26] Recent work has argued that the British forced the pace over German recovery in 1946, helped to turn Marshall's offer of

American financial aid into a viable European recovery plan in 1947, and were more hawkish than the Americans in the early stages of the Berlin blockade in 1948. They also acted as catalysts for the North Atlantic treaty of 1949 and crafted a distinctive framework for German rearmament in 1954. Outside Europe in the early 1950s they tried to restrain American anti-Soviet globalism, especially in confrontation with China, and were co-architects of the Indo-China settlement of 1954, which was much resented in Washington. As with any revisionist work, this line of argument has been pushed too far and now needs integrating with research on the United States and other allied countries in a mature synthesis, but it has enlarged the America-centred focus of some earlier US scholarship.

If Britain used to be written off, France's foreign policy was the subject of caricature in English-language literature. In April 1954 President Dwight D. Eisenhower complained: 'Ever since 1945 France has been unable to decide whether she most fears Russia or Germany. As a consequence, her policies in Europe have been nothing but confusion. . . .'[27] In his essay, Georges-Henri Soutou makes this confusion explicable. France had been the victim of German aggression on three occasions in the previous 75 years; hence its concern to restrain German recovery. Moreover, the communists were polling some 25 per cent of the vote in the post-war decade and were members of coalition governments in 1945–7. Persistent French hopes of avoiding a complete rift with Moscow and of acting as a 'third force' between the big two make more sense if we bear this in mind. Although, under Foreign Minister Georges Bidault, France shifted definitively westward in the spring of 1947, encouraged by the Truman Doctrine speech, Soutou shows how the process of realignment had begun much earlier. As in Britain, the French military had identified a Soviet threat at the end of the war and, among politicians such as Bidault, their anti-Germanism was more precisely a fear of the Soviet Union gaining control of the resources of Germany.

Even so, France's new policy was more cautious than Britain's. It took the shock caused by the coup in Czechoslovakia in February 1948 – a country with third-force aspirations like those in France – to reconcile France to an Atlantic alliance. Although Soutou notes France's contribution to shaping the new Western order in 1947–9, his essay devotes particular attention to the period after 1950. Faced with a new West German state in 1949 and, from autumn 1950, with American insistence on German rearmament, the French took the lead in European integration as a way to tame the new Germany. The Schuman Plan for a coal and steel community and the Pleven Plan for an integrated European army (the European Defence Community (EDC)) were both attempts in 1950 to harness German power for the benefit of Western Europe and prevent German economic recovery becoming the base for renewed military power. Soutou explores the debate over the EDC, its defeat in the French Assembly in 1954 and the renewed bout of neutralist feeling surrounding the debacle. By 1955 the latter had abated, but Soutou's account shows that French support for the Atlantic alliance was based on shakier foundations than Britain's – as became clear in the 1960s when, as President, de Gaulle extricated France painfully from NATO's integrated command structure. On the other hand, French proposals for European integration, masterminded by Jean

Monnet, laid the foundations for one of the most durable products of Cold-War Europe – the European Community.

America, Russia, Britain and France were all, to varying degrees and in different ways, active participants in the reordering of post-war Europe. They took diplomatic initiatives, forged alliances and created new European institutions. This reflected their position as the victors of the Second World War. For those they defeated, by contrast, the Cold War was a very different experience, tied up with the struggle for rehabilitation abroad and reform at home, above all with the effort to recover national sovereignty in the face of Allied occupation. Italy and Germany were both *the vanquished* of the Second World War. Their experience of the Cold War exhibits similarities but also striking contrasts.

Italy had jumped on Hitler's apparently unstoppable bandwagon in 1940, only to take a tumble very soon afterwards, and its alliance with Berlin proved tenuous. As Ilaria Poggiolini's essay reveals, its subsequent evolution was significantly different from that of Germany. Italy surrendered in September 1943 to the invading Anglo-American forces and then proclaimed itself their 'co-belligerent' against continued Nazi occupation of the north. The Soviet Union was never allowed a significant say in Italy, and the country was therefore not formally divided, as was Germany, though the negotiation of its peace treaty did become a pawn in larger Cold-War power-plays in 1945–6. Nevertheless, Italy's rehabilitation was gradual and complicated. Britain and America differed over major policy issues, such as the future of the Italian monarchy, and the United States gradually displaced Britain as 'senior partner' in the occupation. Equally important was the swing to the left in Italian politics, with the communists prominent partners in successive coalition governments from 1944 until their exclusion in May 1947 and their determined bid for power in the April 1948 elections.

Italy made its overt 'western choice' in the spring of 1947, joining enthusiastically in the Marshall Plan, but Poggiolini (like Soutou for France) shows that the new alignment had been prefigured since 1945 in the Anglo-American hegemony and the growing influence of the Christian Democrats under Alcide De Gasperi.[28] But, as Poggiolini also emphasizes, the Cold War did not immediately expunge the stain of world war. Italy's acceptance back into international society was slow and painful. The peace treaty was delayed until 1946 and its provisions were deeply resented by Italians, in particular the loss of Trieste – another Cold War pawn, temporarily divided between the Anglo-American occupying forces and the Yugoslavs, then close allies of Moscow. Only France's keen desire that the North Atlantic Treaty have a Mediterranean dimension – to include France's North African colonies – ensured Italian membership over strong British objections. Furthermore, at that stage, in 1949, Italy was still restricted by the peace treaty as to its military forces and yet was *not* covered by the Atlantic treaty's guarantees – an intolerable predicament for Italian leaders.[29] Italy's attitude to the EDC after 1950 was therefore closely bound up with the issues of its own rearmament and of full NATO membership; these were not resolved until 1954–5, together with the return of Trieste. Thus, Italy was a major political arena for the Cold War and it did not eliminate its wartime stigma until a full decade after 1945.

It was Germany, however, which was the main Cold-War battleground for the great powers. The challenges posed by Soviet power and militant communism intertwined with the issue of who would control the vast resources of Germany. On this the four major powers were unable to agree and the eventual division of the continent into two armed blocs represented a (temporary) de facto settlement of this issue. The border between the two Europes ran through Germany itself, divided in 1949 into the Federal Republic of Germany (FRG) in the West and the German Democratic Republic (GDR) in the East. Germans often depicted that as a fault line of global importance.[30]

Since the German question was so central to all the wartime 'Big Four' and since their policies have already been described at length in this book, it would have been otiose for Wolfgang Krieger to narrate that story yet again from the German angle. While summarizing the international history, Krieger therefore concentrates on the *domestic* impact of the Cold War and on the way this has been treated in German scholarship. Utilising the catchphrase popularized by Soviet historians in the glasnost era, he describes the Cold War as a 'blank spot' for many years in German historiography. Instead emphasis was placed on earlier periods of Germany's apparently 'unmasterable past',[31] especially the Nazi era, and on the questions of whether Germany had a uniquely militaristic and anti-democratic history – the so-called *Sonderweg*. More generally, social history proved much more appealing than diplomatic history in a country disenchanted with international power politics following its defeat and division. Yet what Krieger demonstrates is how the gradually emerging domestic debate about Cold-War Germany linked up with those long-standing arguments about the continuity or discontinuity of Germany's development during this century. The classic 'German question' always had two aspects – external and internal. In British historian A.J.P. Taylor's formulation in 1945: 'How can the peoples of Europe be secured against repeated bouts of German aggression? And how can the German people discover a settled, peaceful form of political existence?'[32] The European Cold War revolved around the German question in both those facets. Peace in Europe would come when Germany was at peace with its neighbours *and* at peace with itself.

Krieger detects three main themes in German political and scholarly debate. The first was a controversy about the legitimacy of the West German state – was it simply imposed by the Allies? While acknowledging that after the war all Germans were 'mere objects of Allied policy', he notes marked differences between the democratic legitimacy that did emerge in the Federal Republic and the lack of genuine popular support enjoyed by its artificial neighbour to the east. Krieger is particularly doubtful about claims that the Allies destroyed the German left, noting that the latter had already been a victim of Nazism. A second theme has been the desirability of West Germany's integration with the United States and its Western European allies, both economically and militarily, and the prospects in the post-war decade for a bridging role between East and West. On the latter point Krieger is deeply sceptical. He stresses the *political* importance of the Marshall Plan for German and European stability and, like Zubok and Pleshakov, casts doubt on supposed 'lost opportunities' such as the Stalin note of March 1952 proposing

German unification in return for non-alignment. Thirdly, West German historians have debated the degree of continuity in their national elites from the Nazi era into the Cold War. Krieger shows how all three Western occupying powers allowed denazification to be overriden by anti-communism. Yet he also underlines the transformation of German values since 1945 – militarism eradicated and democracy taken root – although he acknowledges the problem of domesticating the orphans of the old GDR's more authoritarian culture. By the time Germany transcended its division in 1990, (west) Germans, in Krieger's view, had mastered their past to a degree unimaginable in 1945.

Europe's collapse into bipolarity forced all its states to make choices – whether to take sides, how far to assume military burdens. Major powers like Britain and France had some leverage over the superpowers; even defeated but potentially weighty states such as Germany and Italy were not impotent. But what of the position of *small states among big powers*?

The cases of the Benelux and Scandinavian countries are explored in the last two chapters of the book, written respectively by Cees Wiebes and Bert Zeeman of Amsterdam and Helge Pharo of Oslo. Two themes stand out. One is the way these countries, building on precedents from the 1930s,[33] were willing to make some sacrifice of national sovereignty in order to ensure prosperity and security. Sovereignty, after all, had profited them little in the war. Despite their professed neutrality, Denmark, Norway, Belgium, Luxembourg and the Netherlands had all been victims of Nazi aggression. After the war, all were drawn into the NATO alliance and the last three formed the Benelux customs union of 1948, which was a precursor of the European Community of the 1950s. Yet, secondly, these countries cannot be crudely lumped together, as has sometimes been suggested.[34] Among the 'Scandinavians', Sweden continued to follow its own form of neutrality, while the image of Benelux unity, not to say uniformity, does not survive close scrutiny of the frequent differences between the Dutch and the Belgians.

The creation of the Benelux customs union in January 1948 was in one sense a reflection of similar interests and common wartime experience (it had been agreed in principle back in 1944, when the three governments were exiled in London). It was also hoped that Benelux would form the basis of more extensive post-war European co-operation. But the Belgian and Dutch visions of the larger framework tended to diverge. The Belgians, animated by long-time foreign minister Paul-Henri Spaak, aspired to a Western European entente, hoping that Britain or, increasingly, France would play a leading role. Dutch policymakers, on the other hand, notably Eelco van Kleffens and Dirk Stikker, were consistently keener about a transatlantic framework. They looked much more to the United States, as befitted a state with substantial global interests, especially in trying to retain the vast Dutch empire in the East Indies (which became Indonesia from 1949).

Benelux unity was most apparent in the Brussels Pact negotiations of early 1948. The partners' common stance ensured a multilateral treaty and not, as Britain and France would have preferred, a series of bilateral agreements on the lines of the Anglo-French treaty of Dunkirk in 1947. This reflected the Benelux aspiration for intensive Western integration. But over the Atlantic treaty in 1948–9, Benelux did not operate as a single delegation. The Belgians (like the French) were reserved and reluctant passengers, whereas the Dutch saw an Atlantic alliance as vital to their larger interests and played a much more active part in shaping the negotiations. On the movement for European integration in the 1950s, the roles were reversed, with Belgium taking the lead. Over both the Schuman and Pleven plans the Dutch were wary of supranationalism and French domination, though they participated for fear of being left out. Only when the more Europeanist Jan-Willem Beyen succeeded Stikker as Dutch foreign minister was there a renewed convergence of Belgian and Dutch policy, and in 1955–6 Benelux took the lead in laying the foundations of the new European Economic Community.

The Benelux approach to integration grew out of geography: the three small states were effectively trapped between France and Germany. The three Scandinavian countries (Norway, Denmark and Sweden) had a different geopolitical stimulus, lying as they did on the northern flank of that other great axis of modern European history – Germany and Russia. Helge Pharo shows how the Scandinavians, despite their interwoven histories and common social-democratic tendencies after the Second World War, reacted very differently to the progressive polarization of Europe. He concentrates on the crucial period 1947–9, when their post-war alignments were determined and no Scandinavian equivalent of Benelux emerged.

Norway had long looked towards Britain for security, while the much more powerful Sweden had traditionally relied on a posture of heavily-armed neutrality. Denmark, on the mainland of Europe and adjacent to Germany, was the most vulnerable of the three and therefore the most non-militaristic. Efforts to concert a common Scandinavian policy ('bridge-building') foundered in 1947–8 amid the growing international crisis. Marshall's offer of aid, Bevin's Western Union speech of January 1948 and especially the Czech coup the following month convinced the Norwegians to throw in their lot unequivocally with the West. The Swedish attempt to prevent this by proposing a non-aligned Scandinavian defence union set in motion intense negotiations, but these foundered in January 1949 over the issue of an explicit Western security guarantee, which the Norwegians deemed essential and the Swedes wished to avoid. Norway, followed more reluctantly by Denmark, then joined the negotiations for the North Atlantic Treaty.

Yet both these countries took a distinctive view of their NATO membership in at least two respects, reflecting their geopolitical position. First, they did not have such grave reservations as France or the Benelux states about German rearmament. In fact, this seemed to them the only way to ensure that America and Britain had enough resources free to defend Scandinavia. On the other hand, as close neighbours of the Soviet Union and its satellites, they did not want to seem gratuitously provocative. This (together with a desire to maximize national independence) explains their declarations that they would not host American or any other foreign military bases in peacetime. This dual policy of 'deterrence and reassurance' – of trying to 'nail' the Western powers to Northern Europe without inviting Soviet retaliation – became an abiding theme of Norwegian and Danish defence policy.[35]

Thus, not only big states such as Gaullist France, but even small states like Norway and Denmark, found some liberty to enjoy NATO 'à la carte'.[36]

By setting the new Russian history against the old American historiography, our first two essays advance the cause of Cold-War scholarship. Our other six essays contribute in a different way by exposing the European dimension of the Cold War – taking seriously the concrete European problems and issues around which Soviet-American rivalry took shape. Several over-arching themes emerge.

Most significant was the struggle for mastery of Germany, which lay at the heart of both the wartime alliance and also its disintegration into Cold War.[37] The Soviet Union and France, the powers most devastated by two great German wars in three decades, favoured a punitive peace. The Soviets wanted to rape Germany through massive reparations to rebuild their shattered economy, while the predominant French inclination was to castrate Germany, amputating its vital parts – the Ruhr, Rhineland and Saar – to make it militarily impotent. These strategies were blocked by the British and Americans, who quickly concurred on the need to revive the German economy, in order to release themselves from an enormous relief burden and also to head off the danger of communism thriving amid depression. As countries much less damaged by German aggression than France and the Soviet Union, their fears about Germany derived as much from the 1920s as from the War: the collapse of the international economic system around German debts, hyperinflation and recession.

What made France's dilemma, and that of its small Benelux neighbours, more acute was that they all shared the Anglo-American view to some extent. Germany was a potential threat to their security but also the key to their economic recovery, particularly through its vast capacity in coal, iron and steel. US policy was formulated as an answer to the vexatious complexities of the German question. The Marshall Plan had as its central aim the economic rehabilitation of Germany; the development of NATO conventional forces after 1950 centred on German rearmament. Both of these *démarches* – particularly the second – engendered intense debate in Western Europe, with successive French governments of the early 1950s desperately seeking a politically acceptable formula. Britain also had reservations and only Norway and Denmark readily welcomed German rearmament. Thus, to think of NATO simply as an anti-Soviet military alliance is too simple. There is much truth in the quip of Lord Ismay, NATO's first Secretary-General, in 1949, that the organization's purpose was 'to keep the Russians out, the Americans in, and the Germans down'.[38]

The German question was also central to the process of European integration, as several essays make clear. Undoubtedly pan-Europeanism and supranationalism were prevalent in the wake of the war, which was widely attributed to unbridled nationalism. Yet the more pragmatic motive was Germany and the need to harness its power and moderate its militarism in peaceful, prosperous co-operation with its neighbours. That was a major reason why the Americans placed such emphasis on a joint European recovery program, aiming at greater integration. Jean Monnet drew a similar morale from France's pyrrhic victories of two world wars. In his plan for a fusion of French and German heavy industry the warlike symbiosis of blood and iron would be replaced by a new and peaceful pact of steel.[39]

A full understanding of American containment policies in the Cold War cannot, therefore, neglect the German question. In fact, to quote historian Thomas A. Schwartz:

The United States pursued a 'dual containment' policy in Europe, designed to keep both the Soviet Union and Germany from dominating the Continent. . . . The two policies, which were inextricably linked, were always in a delicate balance; the United States could not contain the Soviet Union in Europe without German strength, and it could not maintain its hold over the Federal Republic without the Soviet threat.[40]

It has even been suggested that there was a third aspect of containment: Konrad Adenauer's desire for German 'self-containment'. Hans Buchheim argues that 'to protect the Germans from themselves, he considered it necessary that Germany be irrevocably integrated in a European community'. This echoes Wilhelm Röpke's classic formulation of the 'German question' in 1945, 'the protection of Europe against Germany and of Germany against herself'.[41]

From the other side of the 'Iron Curtain', Western actions taken over Germany stimulated the evolution of Soviet Cold-War policy. The Marshall Plan was seen as endangering Stalin's sphere of influence in Eastern Europe (hence his warnings in July 1947 to interested East European countries such as Poland, Hungary and Czechoslovakia not to participate, followed by the progressive Stalinization of these and other Soviet satellites). Indeed, *pace* Churchill, one might legitimately argue that the Iron Curtain came down in the second half of 1947 rather than in 1945–6. Likewise, in 1948 it was the Anglo–American–French policy of creating a West German state which induced the Soviet blockade of Berlin, in a desperate effort to deflect the West and intimidate the Germans. In September 1949 the birth of the Federal Republic was followed in October by the creation of the German Democratic Republic. Similarly, in 1955 German rearmament and admission to NATO prompted consolidation of the Soviet satellites into the Warsaw Pact.

Soviet-American rivalry in Europe did not therefore take place in a vacuum. The German question was one central issue at stake. A second, which, in contrast to Germany, may be harder to take seriously in the 1990s, is the remarkable strength of socialism and communism throughout much of Western Europe immediately after 1945. This was in part a reflection of the role of the left, particularly the communists, in wartime resistance to Nazi occupation, but it also testified to the conviction, widespread throughout Europe, that such an appalling war *must* result in a better life for its survivors. The Labour victory in Britain in July 1945 and the Social Democratic predominance in Norway, Sweden and, from 1947, Denmark are evidence of this mood. The natural orientation of these parties was not pro-American. The comment of Norwegian Foreign Ministry adviser Arne Ording – 'We wanted socialism plus civil liberties, the American liberals were thinking only of civil liberties' – was echoed in 1946 even by such a staunch advocate of co-operation with the United States as Labour's Foreign Secretary Ernest Bevin.[42] And one of the major rifts between Britain and America over policy towards

Germany was the Labour Government's desire to place the Ruhr coal mines under state control, as it was doing in Britain.

In continental Europe, the old political right had been discredited by association with fascism and enemy occupation. Central to the French and Italian Cold-War stories (as Soutou and Poggiolini both insist) was the appeal of communism in national politics in the post-war decade, averaging a quarter of the vote in France and 20 per cent in Italy. Similarly, in the Belgian elections of 1946, the communists were supported by nearly 13 per cent of the electorate. Thus the dynamics of European politics were totally novel, and the alarm this induced in Washington and among non-left Europeans is fundamental to the story of what happened. In those days the Eurocommunism of the 1970s did not exist – most communist parties were tightly controlled by Moscow – and the fear in 1946–7 was not so much of the Red Army sweeping across the plains of Germany as of Moscow-directed communism sweeping to electoral victory through much of impoverished Europe. The exclusion of communists from coalition governments in France, Italy and Belgium in the spring of 1947 was therefore a critical stage in the Cold War and the ideological polarization of Europe. These actions have often been blamed on the United States, who supposedly made them a condition for economic aid. Soutou, Poggiolini and Wiebes/Zeeman show that in each case communist exclusion grew out of internal politics as much as external pressures and was often expected to be temporary rather than permanent. All this is indicative of the need to pay much more attention to the domestic political character of the European participants in the Cold War. As Alfred Grosser asserted, 1945 was not 'Year Zero' and the Europeans were not merely blank slates on which America could write a new history.[43]

Attention to the importance of the German question and of Europe's swing to the left after 1945 suggests a third theme: just how important were American initiatives in the reshaping of post-war Europe? Even a moment's thought will indicate the magnitude of Washington's contribution. The fundamental contrast between American economic aid in the two post-war eras was that in the 1920s this took the form of private finance, loaned by Wall Street, whereas in the 1940s it was public money from the American Treasury. In the first case, the withdrawal of speculative capital after 1929 was a major precipitant of the European slump; whereas in 1948–52 American government aid helped to bridge the dollar gap and sustain West European recovery.[44] Likewise, Washington's acceptance of a permanent peacetime alliance and substantial military commitments in Europe was totally unprecedented in American history. America's successful insistence on the liberalization of international trade provided Germany (and Japan) with the opportunity to achieve by peaceful means the access to markets and raw materials that, in the 1930s, they had felt impelled to seek through war. And the American provision of a security framework for Franco-German rapprochement and, less celebrated but also important, for Greco-Turkish co-existence, merits Josef Joffe's characterization of America as Europe's 'pacifier'.[45]

And yet this argument can be pushed too far. In a controversial but important study, Alan Milward has indicated the *European* roots of European economic recovery and downplayed the role of the Marshall Plan.[46] The same line can be pursued from the political angle. Although the spring of 1947 – with the Truman Doctrine and Marshall's Harvard speech – obliged several European governments to abandon 'third-force' aspirations and make explicit decisions about their future orientation, Soutou and Poggiolini have shown that, for France and Italy, the 'western choice' had its roots in the prior evolution of policy and politics. Moreover, both Britain and France played significant roles in turning Marshall's offer into a viable recovery plan, by orchestrating a concerted Western European response.

Likewise, in 1948–9, NATO took shape in response to European as well as American concerns. America's security guarantee and its military commitment in return for German rearmament were crucial determinants of the Alliance. The Senate arguments in 1948 about the terms of the treaty and the 'Great Debate' in 1950–1 about sending forces to Europe have rightly been closely analyzed by American historians. But Ernest Bevin's contribution to the North Atlantic Treaty has been underlined in recent American and British scholarship. Furthermore, the precise character of NATO emerged from diplomatic interplay among the founder members. The debate about Italian membership was in part a battle between British conceptions of a alliance centred on the Anglo-American axis and France's desire to include its own North African colonies and ensure that the alliance's centre of gravity lay in Paris. At the same time, the Norwegians and Danes tried to stretch NATO northwards, while securing for themselves special conditions, such as the no-foreign-bases policy, to avoid provoking the Soviet Union. And the Dutch backed the Canadians in giving NATO an economic and social dimension through article two of the treaty. Moreover, American military commitments were always predicated on German rearmament. It is worth remembering that, in the early 1950s, some leading US policymakers did not envisage a long-standing American military presence in Europe. Eisenhower observed on several occasions that if this lasted more than a decade it would have failed in its purpose of galvanizing Western Europeans to organize their own defence.[47]

All this casts doubt on the impression that there ever was a 'golden age' of NATO, when wise Americans led and docile Europeans followed (in contrast to subsequent Alliance bickering as the transatlantic balance evened up).[48] In reality, to borrow the title of Dean Acheson's memoirs, inter-alliance bargaining was 'present at the creation'. In its early years the Alliance was not an impressive military force; one British MP joked in 1952 that NATO was 'like the Venus de Milo, plenty of SHAPE, but no arms'.[49] The acute economic strains caused by US demands for rearmament in 1950–1 were followed in Western Europe by growing diplomatic tensions. Soutou and Poggiolini note the appeal of neutralism and nationalism in France and Italy. Wiebes and Zeeman discuss the ambivalance about America in Belgium and, at times, the Netherlands. Even America's closest ally, Britain, took a different line over China, Indo-China and, under no less an exponent of the special relationship than Churchill himself, détente with the Soviet Union. In other words, the Europeans, though weakened by war and reliant on American assistance, were at times still significant international actors, whose concerns blurred the sharp pattern of bipolarity. British exertions as a still-global power are the most striking indication of this. Likewise, France's unease with

American policy in the post-war decade, though overcome in public, prefigures the Gaullism of the 1960s, marked by withdrawal from NATO and renewed 'third force' aspirations. The great American initiatives of mid-century, the Marshall Plan and NATO, therefore have to be set in their European context.

These essays go some way to establishing that context. Yet they deal mainly with the countries of Western Europe.[50] That is partly for reasons of space, but mainly because the countries of the old Soviet bloc are only just beginning to develop a free and critical historiography and to investigate the contents of government archives. For their scholars to research the documents and write a coherent narrative will take years. The opening section of the Soviet essay and the end of that on Germany show how patchy and politically sensitive will be archival access throughout the former Warsaw Pact.[51]

Nevertheless, it is clear that the European dimension of the Cold War can and must be pushed east beyond the boundaries of NATO. This has already been done in some places and the conclusions are both interesting and suggestive. Take Austria, for instance.[52] The country was annexed to Hitler's Reich in 1938, fought with the Germans in the war and was then placed under four-power occupation in 1945. Unlike Germany or Italy, however, Austria was much more adroit in shrugging off the full burden of complicity in the Axis war effort. Active diplomacy spearheaded by the young and energetic Foreign Minister Karl Gruber promoted the theory of Austria's 'forced occupation' in 1938, conveniently ignoring half-a-million Austrian members of the Nazi party and over one million Austrians who fought in the *Wehrmacht*. The Austrians were also far more successful than Germany in terminating the occupation of their country. Under the Austrian State Treaty of May 1955, all the occupying powers withdrew in return for an Austrian posture of armed neutrality between the two blocs. (The term 'state treaty' rather than 'peace treaty' was further testimony to Austria's successful dissemination of 'the occupation theory' whereby a peace treaty was deemed inappropriate since Austria itself had never been at war with the Allied powers.)

Precisely why the USSR agreed to withdraw from Austria remains a matter of speculation. Assiduous Austrian diplomacy, the new atmosphere in Moscow after Stalin's death and a Soviet desire to prevent another Anschluss with the rearmed Germany are among the possible reasons. But more relevant here than the precise motivation is the evidence the Austrian case provides to illustrate some of the larger themes of this book. For one thing it shows the influence that a small but well-placed and determined country could exert over great-power policies. Under Gruber and Julius Raab (Chancellor from 1953) Austrian diplomacy was both persistent and subtle, exerting successful leverage over the great powers. The Austrian case also offers some suggestive pointers to Soviet policy. Not only does it show that Moscow *could* be flexible, it also highlights a central obsession of Soviet diplomacy in the post-war years – reparations. In 1947 the USSR extracted perhaps as much as $100 million in current production from its zone of Austria; in 1949 still around $50 million. Between 1948–52 it has been estimated that while the United States put some $13 billion in aid into Western Europe, the Soviet Union *took out* approximately the same amount from the far more backward and impoverished countries of Eastern Europe.[53] For years we have had some idea of the enormity of Soviet human and physical losses during the war, but recent research pushes the figures up and not down, with 28 million or even 38 million 'premature deaths' among the current estimates (roughly one-seventh or even one-fifth of the prewar population).[54] What glasnost has also revealed about the primitiveness of the Soviet economy and its technology gives added meaning to Stalin's insistence to Secretary of State Marshall during the fateful Moscow meetings of April 1947: 'The United States and England might be willing to give up reparations; the Soviet Union could not.'[55]

Another intriguing case-study of Cold War dynamics is that of Finland,[56] where one might have expected Stalin to adopt a ruthlessly annexationist line. Finland had been a semi-autonomous part of the Tsarist Russian empire from 1809 to 1917. During the Second World War it was engaged in two bitter conflicts with the Soviet Union: the 'Winter War' of 1939–40 and the so-called 'Continuation War' from June 1941 until September 1944. Under the Armistice terms the Soviets gained parcels of Finnish territory, including the Karelian peninsula, which lay within shelling distance of Leningrad; a lease on the naval base of Porkkala, west of Helsinki; and the pledge of some $300 million in reparations. The Soviets were also the dominant presence on the Allied Control Commission (ACC) in Finland, set up to implement the armistice terms – a mirror image of the Anglo-American dominance in Italy. Meanwhile, the Finnish People's Democratic League, the communist front, was building up its political position. A member of the coalition governments from 1944, it had six Cabinet posts and a quarter of the seats in Parliament by the end of 1945. The eventual peace treaty, signed in February 1947, was worked out in parallel with those for the other Axis satellites. It came into force in September 1947 and, soon after the ACC left at the end of the year, Stalin issued a request in February 1948 for a treaty of mutual assistance on the lines of the close military pacts binding key countries of Eastern Europe to Moscow.

The story so far therefore seems to bear striking resemblance to that noted elsewhere – mounting communist strength within Finland and growing Soviet pressure from outside. Yet the eventual treaty of friendship concluded in April 1948 did not bind the Finns to the emerging Soviet bloc, but was only a general treaty of mutual assistance in wartime. Finland, despite its proximity and strategic importance, did not become a Soviet satellite. And in July 1948, after elections run on an explicitly anti-communist platform, the communists were excluded from the coalition government by the President, J.K. Paasikivi.

How do we explain Stalin's circumspection? Perhaps he had secured the essentials of what he wanted in territory and Finnish alignment under the armistice and the treaties of 1947 and 1948? Perhaps Finland did not lie on the central axis of Soviet concern, the line from Moscow to Berlin? But questions – as yet unanswered – remain and it is striking that recent scholarship, based on available Finnish and Western archives, surmises that Stalin was actually satisfied with a Finnish posture of independent co-operation. One of the leading Finnish diplomatic historians, Tuomo Polvinen, concludes that the ACC was probably not intended to create conditions for a communist takeover but, 'following the instructions of the Soviet leadership, *sought to smooth the way for the new Finnish foreign policy that was emerging* and that was later to be associated with the name of Paasikivi'.[57]

The contrast with Soviet heavy-handedness in Romania is instructive. Anglo-American arrogation of Italy in 1943 and Churchill's 'percentages' diplomacy in 1944 probably left Stalin with the conviction that both Finland and Romania were acknowledged to be within his sphere of influence. In Finland the potential existed for a semi-independent but friendly neighbour – not least political stability and a tradition of more than a century of autonomy within the Tsarist empire. In Romania neither of these conditions existed. Moreover, Iuliu Maniu's pro-Western line in Romania contrasts strikingly with Paasikivi's pragmatic awareness that Helsinki had to make its own accommodation with Moscow.[58] The same point can be made about Poland. Antony Polonsky has argued that the Poles might have done better had they accepted from an early stage in the War that they would have to exist within a Soviet sphere and that what mattered was establishing the best possible terms for co-existence. This would have meant conceding the issue of borders, on which they haggled for most of the War, and concentrating on the complexion of the post-war government, which in the long run proved the decisive issue.[59]

None of this is to deny that Stalin's tolerance of political pluralism was notoriously thin, as the appalling internal history of the Soviet Union under his rule demonstrates. Perhaps his restraint in some parts of Eastern Europe immediately after the war was purely tactical – he was biding his time for appropriate opportunities. But these examples from Eastern Europe do offer evidence that his policies were influenced by local circumstances. And, as the need for reparations suggests, he did have compelling reasons for not egregiously offending the West. In Greece, for instance, though the evidence remains fragmentary, he seems to have honoured his 'percentages' deal with Churchill and kept out of the civil war. Outside support for the Greek communists came mainly from Yugoslavia and was a cause of the Tito-Stalin rift of 1948.[60] But perhaps the most important test-case for the thesis than Stalin might have tolerated a looser sphere of influence – where local conditions threw up governments that were sympathetic to Soviet security concerns – is Czechoslovakia.

Like Paasikivi, Eduard Beneš understood his country's geopolitical realities. During and after the war he accepted Western support while doing nothing to offend Soviet sensitivities. The collapse of the coalition government and the communist takeover in Prague in February 1948, together with the suspicious death of Jan Masaryk, was therefore a red light throughout Western Europe. It seemed to prove that Stalin's ambitions were far greater than optimists had believed. Yet the current evidence suggests that the communist takeover was not masterminded by Stalin. Although Czech coalition politics became increasingly fraught in 1947 amid the polarization of Europe, the political crisis was precipitated not by the communists but by the decision of the National Socialist, Catholic People's and Slovak Democrat parties to resign from the coalition government on 20 February, in advance of the May elections. This attempt to outmanoeuvre and undermine the communists in the struggle for control of the police failed dismally because the National Socialists and their allies sat back and did nothing to mobilize popular support, whereas the communists, led by Klement Gottwald, moved quickly through strikes and demonstrations to press Beneš to form a new communist-dominated government on 25 February. Stalin undoubtedly exploited the communist takeover – especially given his growing fears about US economic penetration of his sphere – but he does not seem to have precipitated it.[61] The communists were more deeply entrenched in Czechoslovakia than in Finland, for instance (picking up 40 per cent of the vote as against 20 per cent), and were much more successful than in France at mobilizing support among the workers.[62] As one historian of Eastern Europe has observed, 'only the interrelation of local circumstances and international events can fully explain the communization of Eastern Europe after the Second World War'.[63]

In East as in West, the Cold War therefore had a European dimension. These essays try to expose it for the West. Uncovering it in the East is a major task for the new post-1989 historiography. In each case what matters is not merely archives but a new vantage point. As Churchill said, in words used as one of the epigraphs to this volume, 'when the perspective of time has lengthened, all stands in a different setting'.[64] The crux here, above all, is that the era of Cold Wars, of almost global bipolarity, now appears to be a thing of the past. From the 1950s to the 1980s bipolarity had seemed almost the goal of history. Following the anticipations of nineteenth-century German theorists such as Konstantin Frantz or even the philosopher G.W.F. Hegel, it seemed that a division of the world between America and Russia was inevitable. Hitler gave those clichés lurid expression as he dictated his final testament in the bombed-out ruins of Berlin.[65] By 1945 the pre-war European states system had totally collapsed and a divided Europe seemed to be its 'firmly established and probably longlived successor', to quote Alexander DePorte in his 1979 study *Europe between the Superpowers: The Enduring Balance.*[66] Today, however, it is no longer axiomatic that the old world was buried in the new, that the Cold-War bipolarity was the inevitable order of things. It was but another phase, albeit momentous, of modern international history, to be evaluated as history rather than experienced as a fact of contemporary life.

What will probably become clearer as the Cold War slides from present into past is the enormity of the World War from which it grew.[67] Hitler's remarkable and unexpected victories in 1940 left him effectively in control of most of Europe, from the Bay of Biscay to the Black Sea. It meant that his defeat, if it came, could only be achieved by the two great extra-European powers, the United States and the Soviet Union. Hitler pulled Europe down in ruins around him and left the two new superpowers straddling a continent from which they had kept aloof for much of the inter-war period. That somewhat artificial hegemony took decades to wane, when (Western) Europe at last recovered its economic vitality and transcended some of its nationalist rivalries. The discrediting of the political right with the defeat of fascism produced a marked swing leftwards after 1945, with socialists and communists in power in much of Europe. The post-war left, in its various Eastern and Western mutations, survived for nearly half a century on the political capital earned as resistance fighters against 'fascism' during the war. And the inability of the wartime Allies to agree on the future of Germany resulted in the division of that country in the context of two increasingly militarized blocs. For a generation, security was seen as a zero–sum game, conducted through an unrestrained arms race which subsided only when it had broken the backward Soviet economy. In many ways, then, the Cold War, at least in Europe, was a series of reactions to the fallout from the Second World War. It was not so much the inevitable goal of history as one of Adolf Hitler's most durable legacies.

# PART ONE

# THE BIG TWO

---

I     *The United States*

## ANDERS STEPHANSON

It was the appearance in fall 1947 of a slim but powerful book by the columnist Walter Lippmann that popularized the 'Cold War' as a term. Lippmann's work was a critique of George F. Kennan's anonymous 'X-Article' of that same year, an article whose theme of containment had been taken by the informed public to articulate Washington's new policy toward the Soviet Union. Kennan had assumed that expansionism was inherent in the very nature of the Soviet regime, and containment thus signalled, among other things, a general intention to do whatever was necessary to stop the Russians from expanding in places of vital importance to the west. Since the Russians were thought to be fanatics, alien to western traditions, they were impossible to talk with; doing whatever was necessary therefore meant a period of *no real diplomacy*, in effect a period of deep freeze coupled with tit-for-tat moves until frustration, presumably, had either broken the Soviet regime or mellowed it to the point where it could be made to see Western reason.[1]

Lippmann took Kennan severely to task for this, most saliently for not understanding that diplomacy – the negotiated resolution of issues of mutual concern – does not require 'intimacy' and common views among the parties concerned. Containment, in other words, seemed to Lippmann a negative concept, strategically leaving the crucial aspect of the postwar situation undealt with: namely the presence of the Red Army in the middle of Europe. Clearly, said Lippmann, we should try to get these troops out of Europe by means of negotiation. Since the Russians had agreed to talk about it, the West should undertake to find out what the price was and whether it could be paid. By mid-1948, Kennan had swung around towards this view, and, in sharp contrast to the Administration he was serving, began to argue for a diplomatic resolution of the pivotal German problem.

The Eastern European events of 1989–91 lend to this debate a certain contemporary resonance. For the question immediately arises whether containment has been instrumental in bringing about the collapse of the Soviet empire and the transformation of the regime itself, or if it has merely served to maintain existing conditions far longer than might otherwise have been the case. Arguably, a more Lippmannesque policy might have facilitated these astonishing changes much earlier. Whatever one's view, there is now room for renewed debate on the origins of the Cold War, whereas a decade ago historians were wont to talk about it as a largely settled issue.

Although Lippmann's critique was entitled *The Cold War*, he never actually explicated the phrase itself, which seems to have been added as an afterthought. It is a peculiarity of almost all American historiography on the subject (including my own) that it shares this missing feature with Lippmann: to a remarkable degree there is a failure to specify what it is one wants to explain, if indeed explanation is the desired end. The concept is used promiscuously, designating a whole host of possible periods, events and relationships.[2] At present, public and cognoscenti alike appear convinced that the Cold War has just ended, a view which would seem to equate the term with the entire post-war, possibly even post-1917, relationship between the United States and the Soviet Union. Let us recall, however, the sentiment of the early 1970s, especially after President Richard M. Nixon's trips to Moscow and Beijing, that the Cold War was over; and similar talk during the thaw that followed the Cuban missile crisis in the 1960s.

For the sake of clarity, it may be useful therefore to begin these reflections with an outline of my own (unoriginal) conception and periodization.[3] I consider the Cold War, largely in effect as a system by the end of 1947, to have been marked by these characteristics:

(a) warlike hostility, carried on by means short of war;

(b) diplomacy, consequently, being turned into militarized thinking and a kind of warfare itself;

(c) denial of the opponent's legitimacy as a regime, resulting in intense propaganda attacks;

(d) an increasingly bipolar structure of international politics through the superimposition of the conflict on the rest of the world;

(e) intense military build-up in the arms race;

(f) suppression of internal dissidents.

The Cold War thus differed in important ways from the classical balance of power structure of the eighteenth and nineteenth centuries. It was bipolar and static rather than multipolar and shifting. It had no place for any 'balancer' to 'equilibrate' the balance, such as Great Britain had traditionally done. It also tended, by being ideologically charged, to deny the other party's right to exist and participate in the comity of nations. In that sense it was a return to the absolute enmity and hatred, the manicheism, typical of the religious wars before the European state system evolved in the seventeenth century.[4] Along Clausewitzian lines, it became an extreme polarity in which victory meant total annihilation of the opponent. The conflictual element inscribed in the very separation between states hence assumed the *antagonistic* nature traditionally reserved for moments of war, as distinct from 'peace'.

This is why it makes sense to call the period in question a Cold *War*. This is also why it makes much less sense to use it, in the now commonly accepted manner, as a description of the whole post-war era. Soviet-American relations were generally strained after 1917, but in very different ways and with different effect. The Cold War, as conceived here, actually underwent in the 1950s a series of changes that turned it into something else after 1962; and we need a way to describe this without diluting the usefulness of the cold war as a concept, without losing its specificity.

What were these changes? The Cuban missile crisis in 1962 was, apart from Berlin Blockade of 1948, perhaps the single most dangerous moment in the entire post-war era, but in its aftermath was ushered in a new stage in the superpower relationship. The features of this phase have been described by many and are not in themselves very controversial. Among them are:

(a) de facto recognition of the other's legitimacy and consequently de-emphasis of the irreconcilable ideological differences;

(b) mutually, if tacitly, agreed spheres of influence, the American sphere being both far looser and far larger;

(c) no direct military conflict between NATO and Warsaw Pact forces in Europe or elsewhere, so that the major wars involving the two (Korea, Vietnam and Afghanistan), were fought indirectly or by means of proxies;

(d) agreement, again tacit, not to use nuclear weapons except as ultimate resort on the vital assumption of MAD (mutually assured destruction).[5]

Elements of this rapprochement had been present ever since Stalin's death, in some instances even before, but had not dominated the relationship. It took the (apparently) final division of Germany in 1961 and the near hit of the missile crisis of 1962 to achieve that. The new situation then found very clear expression the following year in the limited Nuclear Test Ban treaty. The dialectic had been transformed into a non-antagonistic one, a mutually profitable system, to put it bluntly, of hegemonic control over the two halves of Europe, competition narrowed down to the arms race and manoeuvres in the third world. The Cold War proper was thus over in its European context, though it experienced a phantasmagorical and brief return during the late 1970s and early 1980s. What has come to an end now, according to this periodization, is *the whole post-war order itself*, an international order dominated in the last instance by the relationship between the United States and the Soviet Union but not to be conflated with any Cold War.

### Diplomatic history in the American academy

I must now also make some 'sociological' remarks about American historiography which is incomparable in size and production, particularly in the field under consideration here. This is partly a consequence of the sheer size of the country; but it is also a result of the university system, which combines college education as a direct extension of high school with the advanced research customary for seats of higher learning. The institutional result is a mass of historians working in considerable social autonomy. The Society for the Historians of American Foreign Relations, as the sub-discipline cumbersomely calls its organization, has by itself more than a thousand members, most of them working on the twentieth century.[6] Their outpourings on the 1943–50 period have been particularly massive, since that moment has rightly been seen as a watershed and, more prosaically, the relevant archives were opened fairly early.

Two other institutional oddities should be mentioned. First, history departments tend to be rigidly separated into various sub-fields, and here the historians of foreign relations have come to fall under *American* history. There is consequently no 'international history' in its own right. This is to some extent the effect of parochialism, a certain reluctance, for example, to learn foreign languages.[7] A British historian has described the end product uncharitably as a 'paradigm which places the United States at the centre and draws out from there simply a series of bilateral links, like the spokes of a rimless wheel'.[8] The image is not wholly inaccurate. Relatedly, as Charles Maier has underlined, the Americanist preponderance has forced historians of other areas to stick more to the company of foreign colleagues.[9]

The second oddity is the additional separation from the discipline of 'international relations', which in the United States became a sub-field of political science and thus pre-eminently concerned with theoretical model-building or providing policy advice to various administrations.[10] This demarcation between history and international relations has been quite sharp in the case of the Americanists, much less so for, say historians of East Asia, the Middle East, the Soviet Union, or any other field that falls within what is known as 'area studies'. It was in fact the Cold War and the global commitments it entailed that gave rise in the 1950s and 1960s to the huge growth in such policy-oriented and partly interdisciplinary institutions within the university. Sovietology, for obvious reasons, became especially tightly tied to the state and its need for knowledge and intelligence.

From that angle, the Americanist tilt among historians has not been an unmitigated ill. For it freed the profession from any too onerous imperative to serve the powers that be and allowed, in the 1960s and 1970s, a critical edge seldom found in international relations. However, the trend towards the right in the 1980s has signalled a move away from this will to dissent. In recent years diplomatic history has also opened up a bit towards international relations, though this development has been marked by a simple importation of neo-realist and geopolitical theories, which in the 1980s have actually been subjected to sharp critiques within their own discipline of origin.[11] International relations is itself largely parasitical on outside theory and experiences periodic moments of identity crisis; but it is ultimately too connected to the functionality of policymaking to cultivate quite the same penchant for self-flagellation as diplomatic history, acutely aware as the latter is of its provincialism, conceptual backwardness, and obvious limitations as a discipline apparently devoted to the study of something that is becoming historically less and less important. Recent moments of introspection indicate nevertheless the possibility of a qualitative leap in sophistication, and towards something wider than merely diplomacy as traditionally conceived.[12]

A final note is necessary about political commitment. American history is a politicized field and nowhere more so than in the subfield of foreign relations and the Cold War. Writing history has often been both a conscious intervention and a way of coming to terms with one's place in American society and the world. This is true not only for leftist historiography. Indeed, numerous of the earlier, mainstream historians participated in the events they described and thus had an irreducible existential stake in their histories. Virtually all the present generation of active historians, from left to right, have in some way been deeply marked by the experience of Vietnam. From that traumatic, extended and divisive war there was no personal escape, and though it now seems as distant as the 1960s, its shadows are still inescapable. Sovietology, meanwhile, included on its side a good number of emigrés, with all the passions and interests attached to that difficult position. This political 'presentism' has, again, been both good and bad: good in the sense that it sometimes acknowledges the uses to which history is put, bad in the sense that it can, or at least did, sometimes degenerate into pure polemic.

### A note on Hegel

The story of cold-war historiography is often told in the form of a Hegelian triptych. First there were the traditionalist or orthodox accounts of the 1950s and 1960s which on the whole supported the official American position: the totalitarian Soviet Union started the Cold War by its expansionism while the democratic United States, initially reactive, eventually moved to stop this and so defended the free world. Then, antithetically, came along the revisionists of the 1960s and 1970s, for whom the all-powerful United States initiated the Cold War for ideological and economic reasons, and the Soviet Union was cautious, reactive and nationalistic, restrictive in its security claims rather than messianically ideological and expansionist. Finally, the disciplinary resolution arrived with the post-revisionists of the 1970s and 1980s, emerging from the preceding confrontation to create a superior synthesis by choosing the best elements of both schools: a transcending *Aufhebung* in other words.

This caricature is not without heuristic value. The labels it employs cannot of course be created except ex post facto. The traditionalists did not know that they were writing traditionalist work; only when the revisionists appeared was this slightly derogatory term invented. And the post-revisionist imprint is in some ways a self-serving construct by post-revisionists themselves; they might just as well be dubbed anti-revisionist or neo-realist. Finally, the whole picture was complicated by the emergence in the late 1970s and early 1980s of a seemingly rival school of 'corporatism'. For this new antithesis cast itself in the form of a critique of the new post-revisionist orthodoxy and considered the Cold-War problematic of the preceding schools, if not a dead end, at least something whose terms should be sharply revised. Consequently, it had very little to say about the origins of the Cold War as such. With the passing of the passion there has indeed been a diffusion of perspectives, such that one can no longer distinguish schools with the same clarity as a decade ago. Nonetheless, with all due misgivings about excessive crudity, my analysis here will follow, critically, the general contours of the Hegelian story, with suitable additions. The emphasis will be on interpretation and explanation, not on empirical detail and exhaustive lists of names.

### Traditionalism

The traditionalist historians of the 1950s and 1960s actually ranged from straight-forward apologists to critical realists.[13] Most of them agreed, however, that the

Stalinist regime was exceptional and not just an ordinary Great Power. Co-operation (a supposedly neutral concept seldom investigated) was therefore doomed. The genesis of, and hence blame for, the cold war lay in the unilateral moves of the Soviet Union, initiated even before the end of the Second World War, to impose its rule on the areas of Eastern Europe liberated from Nazi occupation: 'Thus the cold war grew out of the interactions between traditional power politics and the nature of the Soviet regime. The power vacuum created by Germany's defeat provided the opening for Soviet power to fill, and Communist ideology made a clash inevitable.'[14]

Traditionalists disagreed over how important communist ideology was in Moscow's expansionism, but not about the moves of the Kremlin blatantly to disregard the established consensus of the wartime coalition. The Polish question is often brought forth as an egregious example: Stalin broke the Yalta accords on free elections, ruthlessly rolling on to centre stage his stooges, the Lublin regime, to the exclusion of other forces. By the fall of 1945, continues the argument, it was abundantly clear that Moscow would allow no democratic, free states in Eastern Europe, as had been implied in the Atlantic Charter of 1941 and agreed upon at Yalta in the Declaration of Liberated Europe.

The United States, according to this account, played a comparatively passive role, preoccupied during the war with military affairs and assuming post-war cooperation with the Soviet Union within the future United Nations. Still, in the months immediately before the German collapse in May 1945, events in Eastern Europe were beginning to cause serious alarm. Washington, having expected to play the modest role of mediating between the imperial Britain and the radical Soviet Union, found the former tottering and the latter hostile. The Russians proved intransigent in the Council of Foreign Ministers, the periodically convened forum for negotiations about the post-war order. There followed, even more ominously, Soviet thrusts in 1945–6 into the Near East: the resurgence of communist-instigated civil war in Greece, imperious demands on Turkey, and the refusal to leave northern Iran as previously agreed. The appearance, meanwhile, of illegitimate communist regimes in Eastern Europe continued apace, a progression reaching its brutal end with the Prague Coup of February 1948 which eliminated the last non-communist vestiges in Czechoslovakia.

Under the impact of these ever-more evident Soviet transgressions, the Americans finally began vigorous counteraction. Eastern Europe was more or less lost, but Washington was able to shore up the threatened Iran in 1946, to shoulder Britain's responsibilities in the eastern Mediterranean through the Truman Doctrine in the spring of 1947 (offering primarily military assistance to Greece and Turkey on grounds of universal defence of freedom), and, most important, to prop up the vital Western European area by economic assistance (the Marshall Plan, announced in summer 1947), supplanted by military ties through the establishment of NATO in 1949. In occupied Germany, where co-operation had broken down as a result of Moscow's obstinacy, the United States found it necessary in 1946 to cease the eastward flow of reparations from its occupation zone and to merge it with the British zone into the so-called Bizonia. In the absence of agreement with the Russians, the Western powers announced plans in June 1948 for a new Western German state and an immediate currency reform. The Soviet Union responded with an illegal blockade of divided Berlin but was thwarted by an immense Western air lift; and in 1949 a democratic West Germany came into being that would serve as an engine for European recovery. Thus Western Europe was saved from Soviet expansionism and domestic communism. A somewhat similar turn took place in Japan.

These, then, were the chief ingredients in the traditionalist histories. The predominant theme is an ideological one: the democratic, hitherto isolationist United States reluctantly assumes its objective responsibilities as leader of the free world and major opponent of the totalitarian and ruthless Soviet Union. Traditionalists of a more realist bent, however, typically made much less of a morality tale out of it. For the realists (as distinct, in their own eyes, from idealists), the world of international relations is a Hobbesian jungle, a space unlike the domestic one in featuring few common norms and no ultimate sanction of force for those that do exist, a field in which every state does whatever it can to keep up with the competition for power, a world defined by the might-makes-right logic of Thrasymachus. Accordingly, it may well prove a fatal mistake to project one's own standards of morality on the outside. On the contrary, argues the realist, one will have to violate those internal standards when engaged with the outside world. The role of ideology/morality is thus characteristically given short shrift in realist explanations of international events. In our context, Louis Halle is exemplary of this tendency. In a now famous formulation he compared (1967) the Cold War to putting a 'scorpion and a tarantula together in a bottle'.[15]

For the realists, in short, the question was chiefly one of re-establishing a workable balance of power: a naive and inexperienced American regime comes to understand the realities of power and act with suitable acumen. At this point, however, the realists began to differ. Some considered the increasing ideological fervour that accompanied the new activism as necessary to break the isolationism once and for all; they also defended much of the expanded American role. Others, notably Kennan, thought the universalist discourse disastrous in the long run because it confused the issues, thus clearing the way for the limitless and ultimately impossible American commitments that were to follow. Indeed, for Kennan the realistic period lasted only until 1948, after which the rhetoric took over and there was a growing gap between means and ends.[16]

The ideologically charged apologia is of mostly archeological interest now, but the realist narrative survives in pristine form in various post-revisionist accounts. This future connection is already evident in what is often taken to be a quintessentially traditionalist piece, Arthur M. Schlesinger, Jr's 'Origins of the Cold War' (1967). To the extent that it is the first serious attempt to rethink the traditionalist position after the revisionist onslaught, it is in fact a precursor of post-revisionism. Schlesinger seems willing at the outset to do away with orthodox villainy: what is crucial for him is instead the conflict over spheres of influence. Whereas the Soviet Union doggedly pursued an exclusive sphere in the East, the United States was committed to one-world universalism. Both misunderstood the other's moves as an offensive against vital interests, the Soviet Union in Eastern Europe, the United States in the Western parts. A clash was inevitable, for 'each side believed with a passion that future international stability depended on the success of its own conception of world order.' However, Schlesinger then reverts in the final part of his article to the ideological explanation: the Soviet Union was not a normal nation-state but a totalitarian one, run by an intermittently paranoid dictator. The American reaction was consequently legitimate and understandable.[17] The contours of this analysis were to reappear in post-revisionism.

### Revisionism

The 1950s had been placidly quietist. A high degree of agreement had reigned between historian and officialdom; historiographical debate on foreign policy was correspondingly narrow.[18] A measure of this is what happened to Kennan in 1957–8 when he ventured forth to argue for American-Soviet disengagement in Europe and the neutralization of Germany. He was vilified by the very establishment of which he himself was a member (though admittedly a marginalized one). Revisionism, to paraphrase Walter Benjamin, would blast this serried conformism apart.

Several moments in American historiography have earned the label revisionist: the debunking attacks after each of the World Wars on the official accounts of the American entry are two instances.[19] In the 1950s, very much in the spirit of the times, there was something called 'business revisionism', whose basic claim was that the robber barons of the late nineteenth century, in their exemplary capitalist greed, had been essential producers of the material wealth which now enabled the United States to lead and fund the free world against the totalitarian danger; thus they were not robber barons at all.[20] By revisionism today, however, we usually mean that extraordinary reversal of conventional cold-war wisdom that took place in the 1960s and 70s.

This reversal should not be considered simply a result of the 'new left' of that period. The inestimable importance of Vietnam has already been alluded to. Yet, reinforced as they were in their views by the burgeoning anti-war (and civil rights) movements, most revisionist historians were products of the late 1950s and early 1960s, the first new left by contrast to the second, counter-cultural left that followed. The historians of the latter generation, though also mainly Americanists, inclined towards social rather than diplomatic history, towards E.P. Thompson rather than William Appleman Williams.[21]

It is indeed with Williams and his Wisconsin group that any delineation of revisionism must begin.[22] The prevalent interpretation of American history in the 1950s was the so-called consensus school. Against the older 'Progressive' thematic of clashing interests and upheaval, these historians emphasized basic pragmatic continuity and integration: conflict there was, but chiefly over status, not economic interest. The United States was portrayed as one big middle-class society with a minimum of ideological dissension; the very term ideology became itself badly tainted.[23] Progressive history survived chiefly at the University of Wisconsin under the auspices of Merle Curti, Fred Harvey Harrington and others. Williams, who had done his graduate work at Wisconsin, returned there in the fall of 1957 to teach. Several eminent revisionists would come out of Williams's circle. His first teaching assistants, Lloyd Gardner, Walter LaFeber and Thomas McCormick, are all now among the leading diplomatic historians in the United States.

Williams was actually a deeply patriotic man, a Navy graduate outraged late in life by the misdeeds of his fellow midshipmen North, McFarlane and Poindexter. He possessed a midwesterner's suspicion of the eastern elite but combined this populist sensibility with wide-ranging intellectual pursuits outside his field. He was anything but parochial theoretically.[24] Unlike his followers, he never wrote a monograph on the Cold War; his forte was the extended interpretative essay, a narrative framework in which the Cold War typically became a phase of a longer trend.[25] Here, effectively, Williams tried to wed the insights of the consensus analysis to the older Progressive emphasis on economic interests. Thus he saw consensual continuity, but a consensual continuity of economic expansionism: there had always been a constructed identity between expansion and well-being in American history, first in the form of the westward-moving frontier, then, after 1900, through the increasing globalism of corporate capitalism, resolving internal problems by means of external expansion. It was this general interpretation that came to be known as the Open Door thesis.

Launched in his now classic but then largely ignored *Tragedy of American Diplomacy* (1959), the Open Door thesis essentially maintained that Americans had replaced territorial notions of national interest with a market conception, propagating unfettered international competition, an Open Door for capitalist penetration. In theory this would then be beneficial to all but in fact it would reward the economically strong, in this case the United States. Such a self-interested approach, or *Weltanschauung* as Williams preferred to think of it, was not a product of ruling-class manipulation but expressed honestly felt views. The tragedy, then, lay in the fundamental divergence between ideal and reality, or rather in the dialectical irony that realizing the ideal subverted the ideal. Pragmatic and tolerant encouragement of self-determination everywhere, for instance, was in reality an attempt to impose the American system and ideology on others:

The tragedy of American diplomacy is not that it is evil, but that it denies and subverts American ideas and ideals. The result is a most realistic failure, as well as an ideological and a moral one; for in being unable to make the American system function satisfactorily without recourse to open-door expansion (and by no means perfectly, even then), American diplomacy suffers by comparison with its own claims and ideals, as well as with other approaches.[26]

This was an immanent critique, a critique from the inside, using the given ideals to show that reality did not live up to them. The Cold War, specifically, was seen as a result of the American move after 1944 to replace co-operation with the basically defensive Soviet Union with an imperial Open Door system. The frost that followed was, so to speak, the icy condensation of this move. The original utopian ideal of American democracy had mutated into global counter-revolution.

Williams's account suffered, as many observers have noted, from a basic indistinction between system and ideology.[27] It was not clear if American corporate capitalism actually needed economic expansion for its survival as a system (which, at any rate, was hard to demonstrate historically), or if it merely *tended* to expand, or if expansionism was an ideological misconception, false consciousness, on the part of its representatives. To a degree this confusion had to do with Williams's reliance on the concept of *Weltanschauung*, which he appropriated from Wilhelm Dilthey and German idealism. There is on the whole more of the latter than of Marxist materialism in Williams. A world-view, a *Weltanschauung*, forms a totality in which any given part expresses the truth of the totality, and vice versa. The *Weltanschauung* of the Open Door expresses such a total truth in the sense that, in Williams's words, '[it] integrates economic theory and practice, abstract ideas, past, present, and future politics, anticipations of utopia, messianic idealism, social-psychological imperatives, historical consciousness, and military strategy'.[28] In short, everything.

This epistemological manoeuvre made possible a characteristic tendency to concentrate, not on actual economic systems and processes, but on economic ideology (as a partial yet simultaneously total truth). The field thereby opened up for his followers to move into ideological research. The result could be outstanding, as for instance Lloyd Gardner's symptomatically entitled *Architects of Illusion* (1970). In this collective biography of early-Cold-War figures, Gardner argued that the American disagreement with Moscow over Eastern Europe was the result of an Open-Door-inspired opposition to exclusive spheres and blocs:

Against the fear of revolution, the United States erected a barricade built upon the Bretton Woods system and anchored by the British loan. Economic opportunity in Eastern Europe was not essential to American capitalists, but an open world was – especially after twelve years of depression and war. The world could not be divided without being closed to someone, so it had better not be divided.[29]

The USA, then, was held more responsible than the Soviet Union for the manner in which the Cold War developed. There had been alternatives. Washington could have avoided playing politics with economic aid; it could have offered Moscow an agreement in 1945 on German disarmament and a security treaty; and it could have tried to approach Moscow directly on the control of atomic energy instead of pushing through an unworkable plan in the UN. This, argues Gardner, might not have eliminated the conflict itself but its 'worst moments'.[30]

If the systemic problem was partly evaded by the 'Wisconsin school', the other major vein of revisionism, Gabriel Kolko's, dealt with it simply by postulating a direct causal link between economic interest and policy. The Wisconsin school had revised traditionalism chiefly by focusing on the United States and its early activism: instead of naive but decent Americans operating on the assumption of co-operation, there were self-conscious capitalist expansionists meddling with cautiously formulated and on the whole understandable Soviet security concerns. In believing this sort of Open-Door expansionism necessary these capitalist ideologues may or may not have been mistaken; but expansionism was nevertheless a fact. For Gabriel Kolko and his sometime collaborator Joyce Kolko, however, capitalism as a whole had been not only counter-revolutionary ever since the Bolshevik Revolution but also systemically rapacious and expansionist. By the Second World War, the United States was the leading power within this constellation. Afterwards, having suffered no devastation, it was ready to impose its will 'to restructure the world so that American business could trade, operate, and profit without restrictions everywhere'.

Yet Washington was clearer on its economic goals than on how to achieve them politically. And, here, in addition to the problems of the Soviet Union and Britain, the United States found itself confronted by a more serious threat in the form of the left, emerging out of 'the disintegration of the prewar social systems and the growth of revolutionary movements and potential upheaval everywhere in the world'. This had nothing to do with Moscow which 'had long since abandoned revolution elsewhere in Europe on behalf of national security, and had embarked on a policy of minimizing political risks'. In Eastern Europe, for example, the Russians followed a 'conservative and cautious line wherever they could find local non-Communist groups willing to abjure the traditional diplomacy of the cordon sanitaire and anti-Bolshevism'. Far from simply Sovietizing the region, Moscow's order reflected to no little degree existing social forces, though none of the three Great Powers would generally allow 'democracy to run its course anywhere in Europe at the cost of damaging their vital strategic and economic interests'. In Western Europe, Moscow gave 'capitalism the critical breathing spell' by making the communist parties follow a policy of class collaboration. For Kolko, on the contrary, the Left denotes a radicalized European working class distinct from both communists and social democrats, as well as the rising anticolonial movement. The Second World War, in short, had unleashed a crisis of the old order and the emergence of powerfully anti-systemic forces. The reaction came in the form of American-led global counter-revolution, 'vast quantities of violence' as Kolko puts it.[31]

In light of his concern with the third world and the forces outside the basically conservative framework of Great Power politics, it is logical for Kolko to refuse the whole Cold-War problematic as too centred on the bipolar conflict between the United States and the Soviet Union. For him and Joyce Kolko, the term is actually 'egregious' because

that static concept conditions us not to probe further the real character of the forces of intervention and expansion – therefore violence – in our times. It minimizes the nature and causes of mankind's fate today, leading us to believe that conflict and violence are accidental rather than inevitable consequences of the objectives of American foreign policy and the imperatives it has imposed on movements of social transformation throughout the world.[32]

We have come a very long way from traditionalism here. It is almost a case of incommensurability: events are analysed in radically different frameworks which allow no empirical adjudication between rival claims. The Marshall Plan, in the orthodox view the saviour of Western European democracy, becomes for the Kolkos a tactical American move to subordinate European capitalism and destroy any tendency towards autarky. What seemed good turns out, on closer inspection, to have been bad. But the Kolkos also deviate from other revisionists in finding the determinant factors of the post-war epoch to have little to do with the emerging Cold War, which is nothing but a side issue, an obfuscation. They face a problem, nevertheless, in explaining it. For if the Soviet Union was in reality a conservative and appeasing (if not outright counter-revolutionary) power, the American-induced freeze would seem incomprehensible or at least illogical, except possibly as a kind of shield for the overall US drive towards open markets. And the Kolkos do indeed tend to resort to the quasi-conspiratorial notion of the cold war as *expedi-ence*: the usefulness of crisis diplomacy would thus explain why the Soviet Union was not allowed its security zone.

In the new remarks that frame his republished *The Politics of War* (1968, 1990), Gabriel Kolko tones down his views considerably, now claiming that the United States 'missed comprehending the richly textured, infinitely complicated web of factors that had gone into producing the postwar international order' and, in the ensuing frustration, mistakenly blamed Moscow: hence the confrontation. But then we seem to back in the realm of false consciousness, the distance to the Wisconsin school correspondingly reduced.[33]

The notion of a systemic conflict between revolution and counter-revolution after the Bolshevik revolution is also problematic in that it is never clarified when and why the Soviet Union ceased to be part of the anti-systemic left, an abstraction which functions symbolically in Kolko's narrative as a concept of moral foundation and means of regeneration. The threat posed by the left is also considerably exaggerated, at least in the European context.[34] However, it is almost too easy to be critical of Kolko: the apocalyptic tone, the absolute certitude, the often crude determinism are immediately suspect, while the claims are often empirically questionable or one-sided. Yet he and Joyce Kolko attempted something highly unusual. Much of the preceding historiography, traditionalist or revisionist, had been locked into a bilateral fixation, centred affirmatively or negatively on American policy. Other actors often seemed to be plastic matter or did not exist, except of course the Soviet Union in the early parts of traditionalist histories. There was very little context. The Kolkos transcended this and actually dealt with the local circumstances, the constraints, in which intervention and policy took place. The attempt was in that respect far more dialectical and complete than any other. Few have tried to emulate its scope.[35]

There were other early revisionist works, of which should be mentioned D.F. Fleming's *The Cold War and Its Origins* (1961). This pioneering narrative focused on 'crisis-events' as told by an old Wilsonian internationalist for whom Truman represented a sharply negative break with Roosevelt's co-operative policies.[36] Fleming thereby encouraged interest in what has proved an endless question: was there in fact a basic change between the two presidents and would things have been different if Roosevelt had lived? This question is not without interest. In its simple form, however, it is unanswerable. The material precondition for it is of course the accidental fact of history that Roosevelt's death virtually coincided with the end of the war, with the end of an obvious 'period'. There could, accordingly, be both a traditionalist and a revisionist case for either side. Both could take the position that (a) there was no fundamental change (Roosevelt and Truman were of the same cloth, the differences being only tactical shifts depending on the demands of moment) or (b) there was such a change (Roosevelt was naïve and Truman realistic, alternatively Roosevelt was far-sighted and Truman was the cold warrior incarnate).

A later and more scholarly work which in some ways extended Fleming's thread (without its Wilsonian streak) is Daniel Yergin's *Shattered Peace* (1977, 1990). Also featuring events and personalities, it elaborates the thesis of a qualitative break by delineating two sets of competing American axioms about the Soviet Union: a co-operative one dominant during Roosevelt and a non-co-operative one during Truman, resulting during the latter's reign in the 'national security state'. This has rightly been criticized as altogether too neat and symmetrical an account. The most recent authoritative treatment of Roosevelt, Warren Kimball's, argues that his style and substance differed essentially from that of such close advisers as Averell Harriman, advisers who would later not only advise Truman but *make his policies*. Roosevelt's non-confrontational style might, in Kimball's view, have led to a less acute kind of conflict with the Soviet Union.[37]

The revisionist critique, then, did not suggest a single argument, except insofar as it saw the general causes of the cold war in American actions.[38] The internal diversity can best be seen in the reception of what became perhaps the most notorious revisionist work, *Atomic Diplomacy* (1965), written by a former under-graduate from Wisconsin, Gar Alperovitz. The standard traditionalist on the subject, Herbert Feis, had argued that the atomic bomb had been deployed, justifiably, at the end of the war in August 1945 because it saved lives, though he acknowledged that Japan probably would have surrendered anyway shortly thereafter. Alperovitz put forth, by contrast, the scandalous view that the bomb had been dropped to impress the Russians. Truman, knowing that the bomb would be militarily unnec-essary, had reversed Roosevelt's co-operative policy but delayed confrontation with Moscow until the bomb had been tested, thus making possible a tougher line against the Russians in Eastern Europe and conceivably an end of the war against Japan before Stalin could enter it as agreed. This tactic also rendered existing alternatives to deploying the bomb meaningless. After Potsdam, then, the atomic monopoly became the foundation for a harsh posture versus Moscow. The bomb, in short, was central to American manoeuvres in 1945, ipso facto also in the emergence of the Cold War.[39]

Alperovitz's view was contested not only by traditionalists but also by some revisionists. Thus Kolko, agreeing here with the traditionalists, argued that the tactical changes on the American side could not be tied directly to the bomb and that the atmosphere was simply not conducive to restraint. Hence he minimized the political aspect of the question. Gardner also criticized Alperovitz, on somewhat similar grounds. The historiographical debate since then has been intermittently vigorous and the issue refuses to die, for the bomb is a fascinating subject and the available empirical evidence is open to speculation. In an excellent overview, J. Samuel Walker summarizes the present consensus as follows: 'the bomb was used primarily for military reasons and secondarily for diplomatic ones'. This is obvi-ously not Alperovitz's argument but it concedes an important part of it, above all the very posing of the question.[40]

### Post-revisionism

As the archives progressively opened and the political atmosphere cooled, there was a clearing for a new historiographical moment – an empirical reconsideration of the whole Cold-War problematic in light of revisionism but without its political com-mitment. This has been labelled post-revisionism. It is not an altogether happy choice of term. Strictly speaking, it merely implies that one is writing *after* the revisionists, a purely temporal as opposed to substantial designation. Some historians included in this category would perhaps have difficulty recognizing what precisely it is that has earned them their membership. The concept owes its strength chiefly to John Lewis Gaddis, its most eminent exponent and the most visible American historian of the cold war. Post-revisionism is for this and other reasons now an accepted concept. What does it entail?

In its early stages post-revisionism can be seen as an attempt to come to terms with revisionism while remaining within the political mainstream. Hence its deliberately neutral tone and apparent impartiality. It tries to determine the validity of traditionalist and revisionist claims by empirical means, while preserving a pro-Western realist version of the traditionalist narrative. The best taxonomy of post-revisionism has been made by one of its most solid proponents, Geir Lundestad.[41]

Post-revisionism, for him, is first of all not interested in the question of war guilt which so exercised both traditionalists and revisionists. If anything, Americans and Russians were both to blame. Post-revisionism agrees with revisionism that the United States had an active policy much earlier than 1947 and indeed showed hostility towards the Soviet Union as early as 1944. Nevertheless, the revisionist picture of compact anti-Sovietism is considered overdrawn. As Lundestad's own research reveals, Washington had no coherent policy in Eastern Europe. The United States worked here with inconsistent energy for democracy and free trade, in effect to gain power in the region at the expense of the Soviet Union, but without ever resolving how much to sacrifice for these aims. Eventually the Soviet-controlled regimes were recognized: Poland in June 1945, Romania and Bulgaria the following December. Contradictory impulses and policies thus render any single model along the lines of the Open Door inadequate as an explanation for the American posture.

There is further agreement with revisionists that there was a hostile element in the abrupt stop in Lend-Lease aid at the end of the War, but post-revisionists also emphasize the constraints of congressional law and domestic politics. Gaddis, in particular, is wont to criticize revisionists for having a reductionist view of domestic politics and not understanding the internal limitations. Post-revisionists concede, however, that the Truman Administration sometimes consciously exaggerated the Soviet threat to get certain legislation through Congress. The contours of the Marshall Plan, moreover, had been visible for a while and this famous move was therefore not the sharp break postulated in orthodox accounts. And, as the revisionists had argued, the United States did establish a kind of sphere of influence of its own by excluding the Soviet Union (and Britain) from the occupation of Japan and the Philippines. Finally, there were also early plans for a global chain of overseas military bases. In short, the United States was not innocently naive; it moved to defend its own interests and it did so long before 1947.[42]

On the other hand, revisionism was found to have exaggerated the uniformity and universality of American expansionism. Some areas were more important than others. Washington refused, for example, to offer massive support to the Nationalist regime in China, and interests in Eastern Europe were given up de facto in exchange for a free hand elsewhere. The Soviet actions in its zone were therefore not the result of any American meddling. Stalin acted unilaterally, not on account of any messianic ideology but chiefly for security reasons. Nevertheless, these moves were expansionist when measured against the status quo ante 1941 and certainly cause for legitimate western concern. Nor, continue the post-revisionists, can capitalism be the privileged explanatory device, as revisionists believed; economics was merely one factor among many. For one thing, the United States did not depend on external trade. In explaining American policy, much more emphasis should instead be put on geopolitical concerns of security. Post-revisionists underline, therefore, that the United States frequently acted with the complicity and encouragement of the various overseas regimes with which it dealt. Thus, in Lundestad's now celebrated phrase, the 'empire by invitation'.[43]

Many of these arguments, sustained by extensive archival research, represented decisive advances. Epistemologically, however, the post-revisionist theme of a bundle of complex circumstances and motivations lent itself to accusations of eclecticism: presenting simple aggregations of factors without any explanatory power. Over time, partly as a response, there has been less eclecticism and more of a reversion to traditionalism in its realist form. This has been particularly discernible in the trajectory of John Lewis Gaddis. His early, much acclaimed work *The United States and the Origins of the Cold War* (1972) had concluded that the Cold War was unavoidable because domestic political constraints would not allow deals with such dictators as Stalin. This was rather a lame ending to an otherwise nuanced book which had paid proper attention to revisionist arguments. During the following decade, Gaddis was to develop a more sophisticated neo-realist understanding of the issue and rework the traditionalist standpoint into a plausible geopolitical narrative centred on the concept of security.[44]

Relying mainly on Vojtech Mastny's work *Russia's Road to the Cold War* (1979), he began to argue that Stalin was never actually interested in basic co-operation with the west, at least not co-operation on grounds acceptable to any reasonable westerner (which had been the unspoken revisionist assumption). Roosevelt had pursued a kind of 'containment of integration', an attempt to bring the Soviet regime by means of sticks and carrots into the American project for a new international order. The attempt failed because of 'the Soviet Union's imperviousness to external influences'. When in doubt, Moscow always relied for its security on unilateral action.[45] Truman understood this:

Repeated demonstrations of Moscow's callousness to the priorities and sensibilities of its former allies had by this time virtually drained the reservoir of good will towards the Russians that had built up during the war. American leaders had been inclined, for many months, to give the Kremlin the benefit of the doubt: to assume, despite accumulating evidence to the contrary, that difficulties with Moscow had arisen out of misunderstandings rather than fundamental conflicts of interest. But such charitableness could not continue indefinitely . . .[46]

So the United States got going after the strategic uncertainty that had originated in the novel sense of vulnerability induced by Pearl Harbor. The old continentalist sense of security had given way to a more expansive view according to which the chief objective now was the 'preservation of a global balance of power'. However,

this notion emerged before any identifiable 'challenges to that balance had manifested themselves'. It remained an abstraction in search of concretion: the Russians
were not yet there to fill the role of an enemy. But 'Soviet unilateralism, together
with the conclusions about the roots of Soviet behavior that unilateralism provoked, had by 1947 created a credible source of danger, with the result that
American strategy now took on a clearer and more purposeful aspect.'[47] The
structural void had been filled.

Gaddis's functionalism here is peculiarly reminiscent of Kolko's notion of the
Cold War as an instrumental invention; though for the former Washington was
really right anyway about not wanting co-operation on Stalin's conditions. More
elementarily, however, Gaddis is proposing a geopolitical reading. He envisions the
genesis of the Cold War in terms of improperly scaled and executed security moves
by the Soviet Union, the mammoth 'heartland' power, against the European
'rimland' powers. The logic of Soviet expansionism was neither ideological nor
totalitarian but imperial. Nevertheless, Moscow's security needs were expansive
and ill-defined and the manner in which it tried to satisfy them was nasty. This
impropriety caused alarm in the west and eventually vigorous counter-moves
ensued, quite rightly, in the form of containment. If anything, the implementation
of containment had been rather late. The object was not American hegemony but
resurrection of Western Europe as one of a series of 'independent centres of power'.
Indeed the Europeans themselves were desperately eager to prevent the United
States from leaving the region to its fate. The means to achieve Western aims were
in 1947 economic as opposed to military, but economics was precisely a means to a
geopolitical end, not the other way around. Capitalism was secondary and strategy
primary.[48] Propriety, it seems, had been restored by a new version of the old
balance-of-power system, the difference being that the United States replaced
Britain not as balancer but as permanent supporter of one side.

To reinstate the geopolitical in this manner is a healthy corrective both to
ideologically primitive forms of traditionalism and to the economic determinism of
some revisionism. It is to insist that geopolitics is a discrete sphere with its own
logic. But to identify American policy-making in the early Cold War with strict
balance-of-power thinking is in my view to superimpose an altogether too clear
vision on the events, in some ways as reductionist an operation as the systemic
capitalist expansionism in Kolko's account. Like all realist stories it tends to
downplay ideology, for example the visceral anti-communism that permeated
much of the American policy-making elite. Like all realist stories it tends to
subordinate objective economic processes to voluntarist moves of more or less deft
strategists. Ideology (anti-Sovietism, Wilsonianism) is for Gaddis something that
serves chiefly as an ex-post-facto rationalization and legitimation for geopolitical
directions already in place. Soviet ideology is similarly displaced by the reference to
the imperial.

There is in fact a basic tension here in Gaddis's causal reasoning. The geopolitical is a realm which takes as its premise unified states and polities, territorialized
entities inherently in more or less overt conflict: the system determines. Yet
Gaddis, following Kennan, has also been apt to underline the constraints of domestic politics, the seemingly unending difficulties of the American polity in getting

things across at home; in brief, the impossibility of letting the geopolitical logic run its course. Thus, at the very end of his fine survey of post-war American *Strategies of Containment* (1982), Gaddis suddenly reintroduces, much along the lines of his 1972 work, the 'remarkable degree' to which 'containment has been the product, not so much of what the Russians have done, or of what has happened elsewhere in the world, but of internal forces operating within the United States'. And he is further surprised by how much strategy has been determined by domestic considerations of economy (problems, to be sure, of a fiscal nature and not the revisionist economics of surplus capital and markets).[49] Whither then the causal effectivity of the international system? It has to be specified.

Gaddis's narrative is also less critical than Kennan's original, its source of inspiration. In Kennan's periodization there is a golden moment between the twin errors of naiveté and anti-communist crusades, a period between 1946 and 1948 when Washington actually manages to conduct policy intelligently and in the national interest. Ideological fog and Cold-War fixation then take over. In point of fact, Kennan had had a deeply disheartening experience with the limits of clever American policy-making precisely when he had tried in 1948 to implement the idea of 'independent balancing centres' in Germany and Japan. He found that by then the world was supposed to be manichean, black or white. It was actually the American refusal to construct a decentred balance of power system that made Kennan by 1949 an alienated and marginalized presence in the Administration. For Gaddis, on the contrary, the defensive strategy of containment was outstandingly successful in Europe and Japan, and vis-à-vis the Soviet Union. That no third force actually developed was really a good thing: the Europeans did not want it, and the system that evolved proved remarkably stable. The period might then better be understood as a long peace than a Cold War. On the negative side, there was in the fullness of time a tendency, as in other imperial systems, to lose the critical distinction between vital and peripheral areas. The result was over-commitment and serious setbacks, exemplified most graphically by the Vietnamese debacle.[50]

It is characteristic that Gaddis should think of this loss of discrimination as a product of some transhistorical imperial tendency and not, in Kennan's terms, as the result of American universalism. At this stage one might enquire, as Gaddis rhetorically does himself,

just how postrevisionism differs from traditional accounts of the origins of the Cold War written before New Left revisionism came into fashion. What is new, after all, about the view that American officials worried more about the Soviet Union than about the fate of capitalism in designing the policy of containment, about the assertion that Soviet expansionism was the primary cause of the Cold War, about the argument the American allies welcomed the expansion of U.S. influence as a counterweight to the Russians, about the charge that the government responded to as well as manipulated public opinion?[51]

In responding he points principally to the recognition of an American empire as the distinguishing mark. But it is of course an empire by invitation and so implicitly benevolent.[52] And the kinds of Europeans that actually do the inviting are rarely subjected to systematic scrutiny. When all is said and done, we are essentially back to blaming Stalin, not necessarily for being an evil totalitarian but for lacking imperial competence. Gaddis's post-revisionist synthesis can thus itself be grasped as a kind of strategy of containment: it contained the revisionist critique within the overall boundaries of a realist form of traditionalism.

This, as such, does not diminish its validity or interest, and it remains a powerful analysis. Yet it is worth pointing out that Gaddis has increasingly been writing history inside the operative sphere of policy-making, writing history for the purpose of providing guidelines for American officialdom by answering relevant questions about 'what is to be done?' Here, since the Cold War for Gaddis turned out in the end to have been a long peace in the European theatre, the question naturally arises what could possibly follow – except something worse. From there it is but a short step to look back on the Cold War as rather a good thing.[53]

In view of the sharp rightwards trend of the 1980s, it is not surprising that some postrevisionists would reinvent the revisionist inversions of the 1960s. In no case is this as evident as in Robert Pollard's *Economic Security and the Origins of the Cold War, 1945–1950* (1985). Revisionism had confronted traditionalism head-on, setting out methodically to revise ('invert') what was perceived as an omnipresent, asphyxiating mythology. The scope of their findings was therefore shaped by the nature of the target. Still, revisionism had given an economic flavour to the proceedings that was distinctly it own. Pollard appropriated this element straightforwardly and turned it around.

Calling his book the 'first synthetic, "post-revisionist" interpretation of Truman's foreign economic and security policies', Pollard essentially accepts the Open Door argument and adds a strategic twist. The difference is that he thinks the resultant policy 'one of the great success stories of the twentieth century, not just for the United States but for the Western world as a whole'. The basic American goal, long before the Cold War, had been an 'interdependent economic system'. Then, after the War, bearing 'the long-term need of American business for an open worldwide economic environment' clearly in mind, the United States 'captured, for itself and its allies, control over the most important sources of strategic minerals in the non-Communist world'. Particularly helpful here in sustaining the West was 'the vast expansion of cheap overseas oil supplies'. The policy pursued was good since the alternative was protectionism and the system served the West as a whole (if not the third world) exceedingly well for a long time. Hence we are not dealing with any 'imperialist elite bent upon aggrandizing power in the service of world capitalism or narrow U.S. interests', but with a 'largely enlightened and responsible' polity, 'willing to sacrifice short-term national advantage to long-term gains in Western stability and security'.[54]

Yet Pollard refuses to link this US quest for multilateralism causally to the Cold War. The Truman Doctrine was certainly meant 'to reduce American inhibitions about establishing a sphere of influence in Western Europe to counterbalance the Red Army's presence in Eastern Europe'. But multilateralism had not been incompatible with Soviet security earlier on: 'agreements with Moscow, a reconstruction loan, and Lend-Lease were all possible before the Soviet crackdown in Poland'. Alas, Moscow refused to play along, opting instead for 'extreme hardship'. The Cold War, then, was a conflict over Europe and geopolitical security, induced by the Soviet actions.[55]

The disagreement with revisionism here seems mainly of a normative kind. The facts, aside from the strategic aspect, are not so much in dispute as is the way of approaching them. Williams might have found much to agree with empirically in this quite illuminating work. If strategy is seen as part of a *Weltanschauung*, he might even have concurred in privileging that as a more comprehensive totality than economics. In a certain sense Pollard's work represents the highest stage of post-revisionism, the point indeed at which the whole concept of post-revisionism ceases to be meaningful.[56]

### Corporatism

At the very moment that the new synthesis was being celebrated in the early 1980s, it was challenged by a school or approach called corporatism. This set itself consciously apart from the state-centric neorealism of post-revisionism by arguing for a socio-economic or decentred approach. A central theme in the corporatist manifestos was the need for a truly new synthesis, by which was meant, of course, not the kind of simple aggregations that post-revisionism put forth but a genuinely synoptic way of looking at the periodization of American foreign policy, beyond the limits of the immediate post-war moment. Talk of the need for 'synthesis', for some all-embracing agreement on interpretation, fact and method, is strangely popular in Amerian diplomatic history. What is really needed instead is more and sharper competition between *different*, explicitly theorized syntheses, or frameworks of explanation.[57]

Corporatism, in a historiographical context, has two separate but partly overlapping origins. On the one hand, it comes out of the work of a series of economic historians with a particular interest in organization and modernization. They are politically, if not always conservative, at least far from radical. On the other hand, it has roots in Williams's Wisconsin seminar, in his own periodization of American history on the basis of the emergence of corporate capitaliam, as well as in his student Martin Sklar's analysis of Wilsonian Progressivism (1960). This odd genealogy is in fact not so odd: behind each will eventually be found the imposing figure of Max Weber and the problematic of rationalization, stability and order.[58]

In social theory, corporatism has been a conceptual rival to 'pluralism' as a way of describing capitalist societies. Rather than a plurality of individual actors competing on the neutral arena of the state, there is a determinate set of embodied interests, associations or 'corporations'. These seek representation before and within the state, a state that is consequently an actor in its own right. This development is generally seen as the result of the transition from competitive, preindustrial capitalism to the corporate age, usually dated to around the turn of this century. To bring order and regulation into these new conditions, liberalism thus responded in the American case by trying to find a golden mean between the alternatives of laissez-faire and welfare statism. One paradigmatic solution here was the voluntarism of the associative state attempted by Herbert Hoover in the 1920s, bringing interests 'voluntarily' together in co-operation for the elimination of waste and inefficiency. In the realm of foreign relations, this period was not as commonly believed one of isolationism; instead it featured an activist, corporatist policy aimed at an international order in the American image.[59]

This American image is then said to have pivoted increasingly around the concept of 'productionism': escaping the traditional nature of politics as necessity/scarcity by means of constant growth. The originator of this notion of productionism was Charles Maier, also the first to rethink the two post-war epochs within a single conceptual framework. As a Europeanist, however, his work was situated at a certain remove from the internal debates on corporatism, a concept he did not in fact feature. For Maier, productionism was the essential element in American post-war strategy to eliminate ideology from politics, since it turned the latter into a question of economic growth. In short, politics was reduced to a problem of output and efficiency. It is in this light, he argues, that one must understand the American restoration of Germany and Japan as geo-economic rather than geopolitical powerhouses, a transformation facilitated to no little degree in the German case by the pre-war fascist destruction of working-class organization.

The Cold War fits into Maier's scheme only in a secondary manner. While it 'had a decided influence on internal outcomes' and 'imposed a framework on international politics', it 'did not exhaust the issues'. On the contrary, 'viewed over the whole half century, the US international economic effort of the era of stabilization centred on overcoming British, Japanese, and especially German alternatives to a pluralist, market-economy liberalism'. The state of Soviet-American relations, in short, is not the best place to find out what the post-war era was chiefly about.[60]

This perspective has been highly influential; parts of it, for example, appear in more celebratory form in Pollard. To understand its implications for corporatism, however, we must turn to the most consistent member of that tendency, Michael Hogan. Like most historians of this persuasion, he began by doing work on the 1920s, but it is his magnum opus, *The Marshall Plan* (1987), that is of interest to us. Here he seeks 'to cast the Marshall Plan in the context of America's twentieth-century search for a new economic order at home and abroad'; and, 'viewed from this perspective rather than in the context of the Cold War, the Marshall Plan can be seen as a logical extension of domestic- and foreign-policy developments going back to the first-American effort to reconstruct war-torn Europe'. The domestic origin, according to Hogan, lay in the 'New Deal coalition' and its combination of 'the technocorporative formulations of the 1920s with the ideological adaptations of the 1930s in a policy synthesis that envisioned a neo-capitalist reorganization of the American and world systems'. Marshall Aid, then, aimed at 'economic growth, modest social programs, and a more equitable distribution of production' which 'would immunize participating countries against Communist subversion while generating the resources and mobilizing the public support necessary to sustain a major rearmament program'.

In this project the United States was enormously successful. Though clearly a vast self-interested expansion of power into Western Europe, the Marshall Plan was also 'far less heavy-handed than the concurrent interventions in Greece or the subsequent interventions in Central America, Southeast Asia, and other parts of the globe'. It was 'a reasonable defense of American interests, one in which the means used were largely positive, largely scaled to the interests involved, and largely applied in collaboration with reliable local elites'. Foreign policy, then, was brought into line with the systemic shifts of the preceding decades in the United States.[61]

Hogan's massive study has been criticized empirically by the British historian Alan Milward, whose earlier, equally massive study had maintained that the Marshall Plan was never the critical intervention it is almost always considered to have been. In his later critique of Hogan, Milward argued that the models for the Marshall Plan did not originate so much in the inter-war period as in the wartime system, and that the expansive policies pursued by the European governments were in large measure a product of political expectations from below. Western Europe, as William Diebold had pointed out, also had closer traditional ties between state, capital and class than the United States, which renders dubious the notion that the neo-corporatist solution was simply an export item.[62]

The debate is of the greatest factual interest; and it may be said in passing that Roosevelt always enthused about schemes to internationalize the New Deal. What is important to note, however, is that the Cold War is virtually non-existent as a problem in Hogan's account. This is what separates him from Gaddis and post-revisionism. For there is nothing, surely, in the analysis of the Marshall Plan itself that Gaddis would seriously disagree with; the disagreement concerns mostly the corporatist tendency to disregard geopolitics (i.e. the international system) in favor of domestic derivation of policy.[63] For corporatism, as a scholarly inquiry, is typically more interested in the complexities of economy and society than in geopolitics.

Despite high early hopes, the corporatist thrust has fizzled out as a coherent methodological movement, although not in terms of individual research. In part this has to do with the extravagant claims that were made for the concept at the outset. The desire to establish an explicit approach of some sort was laudable. The extent to which it led to enquiries into the social origins of policy, investigations of clashes and compromises of interests inside and outside the state was also laudable. The danger was a certain lack of demarcation and a subsequent open-endedness in potential research topics, detrimental to the conceptual rigour of the problematic. More seriously, corporatism was taken to be an explanatory category. In fact, it is merely descriptive, on par, say, with expansionism. As description it is not without its uses, though the United States strikes me as singularly devoid of corporatist elements in any traditional sense: disorganized and heterogeneous, a porous state machinery marked historically by complete domination of various sections of capital, lacking the strong working-class organizations that are a precondition for a truly reformist (as opposed to fascist) corporatism, the state is therefore not at all the relatively autonomous entity implied by the concept. Moments of corporatist class strategies, notably in the New Deal, do not to my mind outweigh the over-powering mastery historically of the bourgeoisie and its entirely rational way of treating the state as its possession, as an administrative shell to be populated and put to good uses.[64]

These problems can be followed in Thomas McCormick's work of the 1980s. McCormick welcomed corporatism enthusiastically as a way of rejuvenating revisionism, assuming that it would allow a kind of social history of foreign relations, a move away from narratives of crisis-events towards questions of power and domination over the *longue durée*. He stressed the ecumenical virtues of corporatism, but his agenda, as befitted a veteran of the Wisconsin school, was unapologetically left-wing. What he wanted to analyze under the umbrella of this new synthesis was really corporatism as an American form of hegemony and social imperialism. By the mid-1980s, however, McCormick was already having difficulties in defending the concept against an attack from another leftist, John Rossi, who argued that corporatism covered up the dominance of capital over labor and was confused with ordinary state/capital interaction. And in *America's Half-Century* (1989), McCormick's recent survey of the post-war epoch, he has completely abandoned corporatism in favour of a more congenial world-systems model, inspired by Braudel and Wallerstein.[65]

This work tells, with regard to the Cold War, a familiar story in somewhat new language. The United States, notes McCormick, finished the Second World War determined to accomplish the 'hegemonic goals, awesomely global and omnipresent in nature' of integrating the periphery (the Pacific rim, the Mediterranean and Latin America) into an American-led global market economy and to prevent any other core power form dominating 'the Eurasian heartland'. The Cold War (left undefined) was caused by the Soviet refusal to go along with the implementation of these goals, though there were also great problems with the Europeans right after the war. Eventually, there was 'bipolarization between Russia and America' over the future of Europe and Middle Eastern periphery. Stalin, more of a Peter the Great than a Marx, had been faced with the choice of integration into the world system or isolation and had not surprisingly chosen the latter. The Iron Curtain then closed off Poland, Bulgaria and Romania, but the domination was one of expediency rather than doctrine, much in the manner of the United States in the Caribbean. The ensuing American offensive McCormick sees, ingeniously, in three stages: the short-, medium- and long-term moves of, respectively, the Truman Doctrine, the Marshall Plan and NATO. The fundamental link, however, in his causal chain is constituted by the particularist class interests of a domestic elite orientated towards 'long-term globalism', an elite apart in this regard from congressional opinion as well as from large sections of the business community.[66]

This causal aspect is the corporatist residue, an attempt to retain some notion of policy as a mediation between the inside and the outside. For McCormick seems otherwise to be joining what I think is the dominant trend of the 1980s, the shift towards geopolitics (in his case with a geo-economic emphasis) as *the* explanatory category. This shift was by no means unique for diplomatic history. Between 1945 and 1975, there appeared not a single work with the word geopolitics in the title; since then they have been numerous. There was thus widespread renewal of interest in geopolitical discourse, especially on the new right.[67] Corporatism, by contrast, was largely alien to geopolitical notions of territorialized balances since these presuppose the very unified state actors that it wanted conceptually to discard.[68]

McCormick's slide towards strategy was in part influenced by Melvyn Leffler, a historian sometimes also billed a corporatist but actually more interested in geopolitics. When the postrevisionist synthesis was being declared, he too was in the process of challenging it.

### Reaching for Security

In 1984, Leffler originated an intensely polemical exchange with Gaddis and Bruce Kuniholm. At stake was Leffler's unequivocal claim that 'the American conception of national security' involved a unilateral desire already in 1943–4 to establish a globalist system of defence; and that that move had little to do with any projected Soviet actions. Pearl Harbor, new air technology, and the rising popularity of geopolitical commonplaces about the Eurasian landmass and its importance combined to create a sense of vulnerability, which eventually would express itself in a grandiose strategic vision:

This conception included a strategic sphere of influence within the Western Hemisphere, domination of the Atlantic and Pacific oceans, an extensive system of outlying bases to enlarge the strategic frontier and project American power, an even more extensive system of transit rights to facilitate the conversion of commercial air bases to military use, access to the resources and markets of most of Eurasia, denial of those resources to a prospective enemy, and the maintenance of nuclear superiority.[69]

Meanwhile, the American assessment of Soviet strategy underwent a basic change in 1945–6. Initially, security as opposed to ideology was presumed the central concern. Soviet expansionism was noted but so were the difficulties it faced and the potential for agreement. These notions then altered so that, while immediate aggression was still ruled out, the long-term Soviet goal was now assumed to be a communist world. But the cluster of American moves initiated in late 1946 had less to do with this change of perception than with 'appraisals of economic and political conditions throughout Europe and Asia', more specifically the 'prospects of famine, disease, anarchy, and revolution'. The possibility seemed great that the Soviet Union might come to dominate vital areas without having to do very much. Hence 'the Truman administration assumed the initiative by creating German Bizonia, providing military assistance to Greece and Turkey, allocating massive economic aid to Western Europe, and reassessing economic policy toward Japan'.[70]

The Marshall Plan, as Leffler argues in a later piece, was the decisive factor 'that brought about the final division of Germany and Europe and institutionalized a stable balance of power in the Old World'. It also extended American interests to the periphery, since these areas were deemed crucial to the European core powers and therefore

encouraged American officials to look beyond Europe to safeguard markets, raw materials, and investment earnings in the Third World. Revolutionary nationalism had to be thwarted outside Europe, just as the fight against indigenous communism had to be sustained inside Europe. In this interconnected attempt to grapple with the forces of the left and the potential power of the Kremlin resides much of the international history, strategy, and geopolitics of the Cold War era.[71]

This was not, Leffler argues against Gaddis, an initially sensible effort to bring about an end to the Cold War that eventually lost sight of its objective; on the contrary, it was intended to accomplish the goals of national security unilaterally, 'regardless of the impact on the Cold War or on the Soviet Union'. Indeed, one was aware at the time that these initiatives would increase Soviet insecurity and thereby hence also the risk of war.[72] As he puts it in his *magnum opus* on the Turman Administration, 'the cold war and division of Europe were regrettable prospects but not nearly so ominous as the dangers that inhered in economic contraction, autarkical trends, Communist gains, and the prospective erosion of American influence throughout the industrial core of Western Eurasia'. It would have been better, concludes the Leffler of 1984, to have raised the question if there were other ways of defending one's interests that diminished 'Soviet perception of threat, aligned the United States with popular nationalist movements, curtailed the dependency on nuclear weapons and air power, and circumscribed American commitments'.[73]

Leffler was criticized by Gaddis and Kuniholm – by the former for confusing hypothetical military contingency plans with real national policy, by the latter for underestimating the initial Soviet thrust into the Near East and hence not giving proper credit to the Truman Administration for its judicious response of containment. For Kuniholm, the aims of the Soviet Union in the Near East, though in the tradition of Russian geopolitics, were 'far in excess of its reasonable security requirements'. To have caved in to Stalin's intimidation might have put the area within his sphere, and the American response was consequently a legitimate restoration of the balance of power. Because 'the mood of the American public was uncertain', continues Kuniholm, it may indeed have been necessary to couch containment in the admittedly less than perfect form of the Truman Doctrine.[74]

The disagreement between Leffler and Kuniholm hinges largely on the empirical question of Soviet behaviour in the Near East (especially towards Turkey) and the related problem of what in fact constitutes legitimate security concerns. Leffler maintains forcefully that Soviet pressure on Turkey was negligible, to the point where it was eminently difficult for American officialdom to find any justification at all for aid; and, consequently, that it was the far-reaching strategic interests of the United States rather than Moscow's moves that put bombers in Turkey. The issues of this most interesting exchange remain open.[75]

In 1984, Leffler, as Gaddis rightly pointed out, was rather circumspect about the Soviet side of things.[76] To remedy this Leffler later (1992) offered what is effectively a geopolitical reading of the Kremlin. Co-operation in the manner that was offered by the West would have run counter to the most crucial security needs of the Soviet Union. Moscow could not 'accept popular elections, self-determination, open trade, and the free flow of capital in the countries on their immediate periphery' or 'defer payments and provide raw materials and foodstuffs to the western zones of Germany'. Hence 'it was unreasonable to expect any Russian leaders to comply with such priorities'.[77]

Soviet actions during 1945–6 did not fit into a uniform picture, but in Leffler's judgement of 1992 the moderate element was not sufficient to quell American apprehension. For at the same time there was serious erosion in the western position: the strong position of communist parties in France and Italy, the civil wars in Greece and China, economic distress in Western Europe, and surging third-world nationalism. While the Kremlin was not responsible for these developments, the United States felt obliged to act. There followed the Truman Doctrine, the Marshall Plan and the decision to divide Germany. The Kremlin, broadly speaking, was on the receiving end. The central question for Leffler is therefore 'not whether American actions exacerbated Soviet-US relations, but whether they were intelligent responses to real and perceived dangers'. Here, on balance, he now thinks Washington could not have avoided 'provoking the Soviets' in 1946–7 if a 'tolerable configuration of power' was to be achieved. The risks were too great. Hence, 'prudently conceived and skilfully implemented', American initiatives 'were of decisive importance in fueling the cold war'. Still, the Soviet response to these was not such as to warrant the enormous follow-on in the form of rapidly expanding arsenals and perpetual interventionism in the third world.[78]

This, then, is Leffler's general answer to the query he posed so powerfully in 1984: was there an alternative? Apparently not in the first phases, he seems now to be saying. Only after the initial successes do things get out of hand. There is nothing fundamental here that deviates from Gaddis's standard account. The convergence between the two was indeed facilitated by the similarity of perspective that, polemics notwithstanding, pertained from the beginning: both views are geopolitical in nature, with emphasis on security as a total concept. Leffler, like Gaddis, is also writing from the subject-position of an ersatz policy-maker. The question is the instrumental one: what the United States should and should not do. His actual viewpoints, however, especially in 1984, are more critical of the American side. Gaddis is not particularly interested in counter-revolution; Leffler is quite explicit about it.[79] For Leffler, who has looked beyond the State Department, especially beyond Kennan, the case is closed: the United States initiated the Cold War, the Soviet Union did not. This is what makes his account something other than 'Gaddis plus archives': his is not a story about restoration of any independent centres. It is largely about an American game. The question, then, is whether the game was a good thing.

### Brief note on other contributions

To speak of schools and tendencies, as I have, marginalizes a whole host of significant contributions and developments which do not quite fit. One thinks, for example, of Ronald Steel's work in the 1960s: deeply critical of Wilsonian internationalism and American globalism, unmistakably isolationist in tone, yet influenced not by Wisconsin revisionism but by the appearance of Gaullism and, later, the folly in Vietnam. One thinks, too, of Thomas Paterson's contributions, from the early revisionist works to the centrist ones of late. His and Les Adler's essay (1970) on the American conflation of Nazi Germany and the Soviet Union under the sign of totalitarianism was especially influential.[80]

With the exception of a few remarks on Vojtech Mastny, I have also ignored Sovietology. Something more must now be said of it. As a subfield it was marked by its many emigré scholars, its role as a virtual service organ to the state, and the paucity of archival sources for the Soviet side. These were not propitious conditions for wide-ranging debate. Stephen Cohen's verdict is telling: 'the profession lost the purpose, vigor, and scope' because of 'scholarly consensus on virtually all major questions of interpretation'. More precisely, the totalitarianism school became totally dominant. A revisionism of sorts began to appear in the late 1960s that challenged notions of an unchanging monolithic essence marching through history; but this concerned mainly the nature of the domestic Soviet system and the discipline seems to have remained largely untouched by the continuing revisionist controversy in American historiography on the cold war itself.[81]

The result earlier, however, was not always American apologia. Marshall Shulman's work in the 1960s, for example, was in certain respects *compatible* with erstwhile revisionist notions of Soviet defensiveness and caution. Adam Ulam, in the same period, while sharply critical (as Mastny would be in the 1970s) of revisionism as well as of the ineptitude of American policy-making in 1944–5, also underscored how the emerging conflict gave rise to such simplistic and unfruitful questions as 'Was Soviet Russia out to conquer the world or was Stalin going to abide faithfully by the charter and spirit of the United Nations?' The ensuing 'grandiose rhetoric' would, in Ulam's realist view, form the background both for 'would-be magic solutions' (massive retaliation) and for revisionist evocations of American guilt.[82]

A more recent feature of Cold-War historiography, hitherto also neglected, must now be acknowledged. For in recent years there have been several excellent studies which transcend the bipolar fixation on American-Soviet relations, studies of areas and countries not as mere objects of action but, so to speak, as live matter. Thus there is now a better picture of the concrete context and effects of the cold war in such diverse places as Latin America, Italy, Scandinavia, Britain, the Near and Middle East, and East Asia (a particularly vibrant area of scholarly inquiry).[83] A central theme in the literature has indeed been the extent to which local forces (classes, elites, parties and individuals) played an active and in some cases crucial role in the unfolding events. As a result, the Western European part in NATO's genesis is now much better understood – as can be seen in chapters three to eight of this volume. Fraser Harbutt, in the same vein, has quite properly restored the trilateral aspect, Britain's position as a Great Power in the wartime coalition and immediately after. In emphasizing this he has corrected distorted back projections of exclusive bipolarity (a motif also explored in David Reynolds' essay in this work), though Harbutt then goes on to exaggerate the importance of Britain and especially Churchill in the immediate post-war period.[84]

## Conclusion: The ends of geopolitics

If there has been a geopolitical turn in recent historiography, it is only proper to conclude with a (speculative) elaboration of my earlier remarks. I have suggested, in brief, that the Cold War and its origins are not reducible to geopolitics, much less to questions of security. Geopolitics can give an account of the military-political but has little or nothing to say about the ideologico-cultural and socio-economic spheres, which typically become auxiliary functions of strategy, or generalship. The totalizing nature of the Cold War, however, is inexplicable without elucidation of the other two domains. This is not to say that geopolitics was irrelevant, so let us determine what such a framework can and cannot explain.

Social theory (and this is true both of marxism and liberalism) tends to centre on time and society, internally conceived, rather than on space and societies.[85] Yet states and the polities that govern them function in a geopolitical realm and employ the tactical and strategic technologies appropriate to it. The privileged domain of interstate conflict has in fact been the military-political: states historically have been organizations of war and the preparation for war, though perhaps less for negative reasons of security than for profitable aggrandizement of one kind or another.[86] Seen from that angle, the initial postwar confrontation was clearly *played out* on geopolitical terrain. That there would be antagonism of this spatial, potentially violent kind between the United States and the Soviet Union after the war is hardly startling. Two huge and hitherto peripheral powers took centre stage and, finding themselves on unfamiliar ground, failed to establish a modus vivendi, each probing for security in its own decisive manner. Acute conflict ensued, creating a situation short of war and more reminiscent of a truce than peace: the Cold War, in other words.

The 'radical' Soviet Union was indeed far more traditional in that regard than the United States, a fact often noted but with considerable puzzlement: was this *Realpolitik* as opposed to marxism? The either/or form of the question is misconceived, for the Leninist tradition sees no contradiction. Politics here has always been conceived in military-strategic terms, leading one's forces from territory won against the opposition by means of tactical and strategic moves. With the Bolshevik Revolution, this class perspective necessarily became a state logic which was to reach its apotheosis under Stalin. For Stalin combined an internal concept of progressive time and transformation ('stages') with an external sense of spatial control ('geopolitics'). It is another matter that by 1935 (certainly by 1945), his class and state logic had become prudently non-revolutionary, while remaining marxist (of a sort) and military-strategic. The object was to secure what had been won, not to jeopardize it with any adventurism.

The United States, meanwhile, vastly better off, vastly better positioned, enjoyed the peculiar privilege of the dominant of being able to follow its inclinations without any too precise calculation of interest.[87] *In pure form*, the American conception of the national interest, couched in universal terms, was heavily suffused with Wilsonian notions that open markets and self-determination should replace the shady balance-of-power politics of archaic Europe and thus ensure peace and prosperity throughout. It was a market as opposed to a territorial conception of interest, positing not a strong state acting forcefully in the geopolitical arena but a weak, negative state. This amounted to an impossible strategy of depoliticization, a way of evading political antagonism by means of models of economic competition and law.[88] And ultimately, of course, the whole project was laced with a subterranean streak of Rooseveltian power politics.

When Moscow declined this opening gambit as too unpredictable and risky, Washington did two things. It escalated already existing efforts to open up a capitalist world system outside the boundaries of Soviet control, and it broke with tradition in moving vigorously to secure this system geopolitically by asserting its military-strategic presence wherever possible (an embryonic project already during the war). Against that offensive Moscow had very few options except fortress vigilance, coupled with mostly empty 'peace' alliances of the most diluted kind. Eventually the Soviet position did improve as a result of independently anti-Western movements in the third world and herculean internal efforts to achieve military parity with the United States. Not coincidentally, that is also the moment, roughly speaking, when the relationship with Washington was transformed. The world, geopolitically, turned into two superstates with sharply diverging internal systems and a third heterogeneous area in which contradictions could be played out in the extreme direct form that was otherwise impossible.

So far, geopolitical categories are of explanatory value, but they are not altogether sufficient. Neither the American nor the Soviet position of 1945 can be understood, for instance, without reference to ideology and class. Neither strategy can be grasped outside the discursive framework within which it was formulated. More basically, however, what must be explained here is not just an ordinary state conflict, however globalized, but the anomaly of annihilation of the Other in a period of ostensible peace. That there would be antagonism between the US and the USSR in a geopolitical sense after the War is scarcely surprising. What must be explained is why it took the extraordinarily nasty form it did, why it became a Cold War, why indeed it came to transcend the geopolitical.

An obvious initial answer would be to refer to the systemic aspect, for the cold war was at once a socio-economic, ideological-cultural and military-political conflict. Neither side, one might then argue, could tolerate the other because its very existence meant the inversion of one's own system. This, if my original periodization is correct, is mistaken: the two systems continued to exist after the end of the Cold War in the early 1960s. They could do this because they were not locked into any vertical master/slave or capital/labour dialectic. Their relationship, on the contrary, was a *horizontal* one across space. From a functional viewpoint, neither side needed for its own survival the destruction of the other. Each could, in theory, have gone on indefinitely without having to change its system as a result of the other's existence.[89] The fact that the Soviet side has now actually disappeared on what amounts to Western conditions has less to do with any systemic conflict and more to do with its internal dynamic. In particular, it has to do with the historical limits of the model of accumulation that Stalin introduced in the 1930s and with the ruling technocracy he thereby created; the descendants of that system would eventually, amidst stagnation, look across the border for more advanced models of efficiency and so, more or less unwittingly, destroy the system itself. Marx would have appreciated the historical irony, if not the actual result.

Yet if the Cold War was not systemic in this sense, it was clearly so in another. For it remains that it was launched in fiercely ideological terms as an invasion or delegitimization of the Other's social order, a demonology combined of course with a mythology of the everlasting virtues of one's own domain. This is not surprising, considering the universalism of the respective ideologies. Ideology, once unleashed, allowed little leeway. The rigid territorialization of ideology and economy catapulted to the forefront the only thing that could move, namely the mutually exclusive ideological aspect. *Everything* was thereby put on the table. Henceforth, the domestic social order could not be taken for granted as an unproblematic spatial whole. One could no longer view international politics simply as a function of some spatially set and largely atemporal realities (e.g. the size and location of states, their resources and organization), supposedly outside ideology and discourse.[90] From the moment that it was obvious that the two powers would not be able to work out a bargain in areas of common interest, the geopolitical boundaries had automatically been transgressed. The unique systemic aspects of each side to be given free play.

I think this occurred symbolically around 1947–8, when the Munich analogy became the prevalent model of abuse on both sides. From then on, there were no intrinsic limit to the proceedings except that imposed by the other's military threat.

What ensued was not a normal diplomatic dialogue but the simultaneous declamation of two monologues, separated in space. This dominance of the ideological was possible – indeed necessary – precisely because of the project of securing, in different ways, one's own socio-economic systems in the two halves of Europe and anchoring the whole thing in a military deadlock. Elsewhere, the effects were lethal. The Cold War was a conflict of total symbolic annihilation, its millions of casualties primarily suffered by the third would.[91]

To raise the matter in such a way is to raise questions of class, culture and ideology. It is also to transcend the absolute border between the inside and outside, to hold together in tension the domestic and the foreign. Meanwhile, the collapse of the Second World in 1989–91 has dislodged us from our received wisdom and turned what used to be obvious, normal and necessary into something that need not have been so. Any rigid focus on national security seems, for one thing, decidedly passé. All kinds of new histories should thus be possible. Ideology will no doubt reappear. But will this return of the repressed be nothing more than a reinvention of full-blown traditionalism?

### Bibliographical note

American works on the early Cold War are staggeringly numerous and the following suggestions are only a minimal starting point. References mentioned in the notes are generally excluded.

Good historiographical points of departure are Richard Dean Burns, *Guide to American Foreign Relations Since 1700* (1983); Michael J. Hogan & Thomas G. Paterson, eds., *Explaining the History of American Foreign Relations* (Cambridge, 1991); J.L. Black, *Origins, Evolution, and the Nature of the Cold War: an Annotated Bibliography* (1985); J. Samuel Walker, 'Historians and Cold War Origins: the New Consensus'; and Mark Stoler, 'World War II Diplomacy in Historical Writing: Prelude to Cold War', both in Gerald K. Haines & J. Samuel Walker, eds., *American Foreign Relations* (Westport, CT, 1981). The initial historiographical chapter in Geir Lundestad, *America, Scandinavia and the Cold War 1945–1949* (New York, 1980) has influenced my conception of the problem. Surveys nowadays tend to be about more specific areas, e.g. atomic diplomacy or East Asia. The best place to find these is in the professional journal par excellence, *Diplomatic History*.

For a handy collection of primary materials, see Thomas H. Etzold & John Lewis Gaddis, *Containment: Documents on American Policy and Strategy, 1945–1950* (New York, 1978). Otherwise the fundamental source of primary sources is U.S. Department of State, *Foreign Relations of the United States*.

Few traditionalist accounts can still be read for their intrinsic value. An early work of considerable nuance is William H. McNeill's *America, Britain and Russia* (New York, 1953). The rhetorical style of Herbert Feis's oeuvre has, on the whole, not aged well, but he can still be read for the empirical detail and as an archetype. A latish example of traditionalism is Lynn Etheridge Davis, *The Cold War Begins: Soviet-American Conflict over Eastern Europe* (Princeton, 1974).

I mention George Kennan, Walter Lippmann, Louis Halle and Norman Graebner among the critical realists. One should also have a look at the realists outside the profession, such as Hans Morgenthau: see his *In Defense of the National Interest* (New York, 1951).

Classic revisionist works, aside from those mentioned, include Richard M. Freeland, *The Truman Doctrine and the Origins of McCarthyism* (New York, 1972) and Bruce Kuklick, *American Policy and the Division of Germany* (Ithaca, 1972). Later revisionist efforts should be mentioned since the tradition carries on: Lawrence S. Wittner, *American Intervention in Greece* (New York, 1982), Bruce Cumings, *Origins of the Korean War* (Princeton, 1981) and Howard B. Schonberger, *The Aftermath of War* (Kent, OH, 1989). Books on the United States and the third world tend to be more critical and may thus be mentioned in the present context. For two significant examples, see Robert J. McMahon, *Colonialism and Cold War: the United States and the Struggle for Indonesian Independence* (Ithaca, N.Y., 1981); and outside our period but relevant, Richard Immerman, *The C.I.A. in Guatemala* (Austin, 1982).

A very good introduction to the problem of atomic diplomacy is J. Samuel Walker, 'The Decision to Drop the Bomb', *Diplomatic History*, 14 (winter 1990). Other recent contributions are Martin J. Sherwin, *A World Destroyed* (New York, 1975), Gregg Herken, *The Winning Weapon* (New York, 1980) and Michael S. Sherry, *The Rise of American Air Power* (New Haven, 1987).

Exploration of post-revisionism should begin with John Lewis Gaddis's 'The Emerging Post-Revisionist Synthesis on the Origins of the Cold War', *Diplomatic History*, 7 (summer 1983). Works by other authors include Lundestad's *The American Non-Policy Towards Eastern Europe 1943–1947* (Tromsø, 1978), George C. Herring, *Aid to Russia 1941–1946* (New York, 1973) and Bruce Kuniholm, *The Origins of the Cold War in the Near East* (Princeton, N.J., 1980). Perhaps Thomas G. Paterson, *On Every Front* (New York, 1992), could be included here as well, though the author comes out of a more revisionist framework. Corporatism is best understood after reading the corporate manifestos mentioned in note 57. *Informal Entente* (Columbia, MO, 1977), Hogan's earlier work on the 1920s, is of interest in view of his later periodization.

Biography, collective and individual, has been a lively area. On the State Department, see Hugh DeSantis, *The Diplomacy of Silence* (Chicago, 1980) and Martin Weil, *A Pretty Good Club* (New York, 1978). On Kennan, see Walter Hixson, *George F. Kennan: Cold War Iconoclast* (New York, 1989) and David Mayers, *George Kennan and the Dilemmas of Foreign Policy* (New York, 1989). Kennan's fellow Soviet expert Charles Bohlen is depicted by T. Martin Ruddy, *Cautious Diplomat* (Kent, 1986). A journalistically composed but nonetheless interesting account of the Cold-War generation of policy-makers is Walter Isaacson & Evan Thomas, *The Wise Men* (New York, 1986). James Byrnes is the chief subject of Robert L. Messer's important *The End of An Alliance* (Chapel Hill, 1982). We still await an up-to-date work on Acheson as Secretary of State.

(Thanks to Lars Bildt and Anders Jansson for logistical support during the initial writing of this essay.)

# 2  *The Soviet Union*

## VLADISLAV ZUBOK AND
## CONSTANTINE PLESHAKOV

### *Historiography: new sources, new questions*

There is no proper historiography of the Cold War in Russia and today historians
and political scientists, working on the subject, draw little on research under the
ancien regime. An absolute control over intellectual life in the Soviet Union
guaranteed that all writings on the origins and phases of the Cold War had to reflect
official legend. The latter, however, was not merely a propaganda myth designed to
present Soviet foreign policy in the best possible light. It inherited, to a large
degree, some original assessments that the Soviet leadership made about the causes
and nature of the Cold War, the motives and plans of their opponents, the dynamics of arms race, and so on. In other words, the official version was not
intentionally invented by the propaganda masters of the Kremlin, but grew from
the process of estimates and policy-making. Diplomats at the Soviet embassy in
Washington were among the first historians of the subject, when they wrote in
September 1948:

A frustration of the designs of American reactionaries aimed at weakening the Soviet state,
a successful recovery and further development of economic and military power of the USSR
after the war, achievements by the countries of the new democracy [in Eastern Europe] and
the continuing struggle of colonized and dependent countries [together] brought about a
situation, in which . . . the American reactionaries set out on the path of open support for
and imposition of reactionary regimes in Europe, Asia and Latin America, . . . of aggravating
relations with the Soviet Union and countries of the new democracy. This policy, by the
logic of things, is pushing the USA toward an adventurist road of preparation for a new
world war.[1]

That was exactly what Stalin wanted to hear in the Kremlin. Dogmatic and
completely self-serving, this explanation became the rationale for assessments and
activities of Soviet diplomacy for several decades. By laying all the blame on the
imperialists, it discouraged any discussion of Soviet foreign policy, since the latter
was supposed to remain perennially good and peace-loving. Once the ground was
laid and the façade erected, the task of later writers – some of them former
diplomatic officials and government experts – remained to embellish it with details,
to paper over most embarrassing failures and put a touch of formal logic on this

edifice. The official history of diplomacy was edited by Valerian Zorin, Molotov's deputy, in the Foreign Ministry, and then by Andrei Gromyko.[2] It used some Soviet archival materials (without citing them) and classified histories; other writings referred to selected Western historiography, and were sometimes based on exclusive access to selected documents or personal experience in government.[3] Two momentous developments – a rise of 'revisionism' and 'post-revisionism' in the United States, and declassification of some Western archives – evoked a response among the Soviets, but did not change their schemes and conclusions. Soviet historians of the Cold War were allowed to glean new archival findings only to prove the official viewpoint.[4] Soviet authors never mentioned actions by the USSR that had triggered tension and Western response; nor did they refer to Soviet archives, which remained completely closed to researchers.[5]

What were the main arguments of official mythology of the Cold War? First, as we already mentioned, it was unleashed by the 'imperialist circles', which, according to Lenin's 'theory of imperialism' included groups with dominant positions in society, primarily financiers and industrialists, who – in pursuit of their class interests – promoted an aggressive and world-wide expansion of American influence. Lenin had borrowed much of his theory of imperialism from the concepts of Austrian Marxists. Soviet writers kept borrowing most of their arguments from American revisionist historians and social scientists, in pursuit of more sophisticated approaches than just Wall Street conspiracy.[6]

Second, at the core of the cold war lay the class concept of the two camps, democratic and imperialist. This concept was enunciated by Andrei Zhdanov in September 1947 at the founding meeting of the international Communist Information Bureau (Cominform). It presented the Soviet Union as a major, democratic, peaceful power and, until its renunciation in 1988, exonerated the Soviet Union from all blame for the Cold War and justified its role in arms race, wars by proxy, and so on.

The Soviet myth, while stressing the 'logic of things' in history, still left much room for certain missed opportunities and for the personal factor (*lychnostni faktor*). It implied that a group of leaders or a leader in the United States and other Western countries might accept a peaceful coexistence, that is to say, a balance of power between the two camps. Eventually the Soviet military-industrial mobilization and the growing nuclear force had to persuade even the most arrogant hard-liners in the United States, revanchists in West Germany and other 'evil forces' to become realists. The gallery of realists included Franklin D. Roosevelt, John F. Kennedy, and sometimes Richard M. Nixon.

In the years of glasnost, this myth was first challenged and then swept away by a series of pamphlets and articles. In a famous split in the Politburo on the basics of foreign policy, Edward Shevardnadze and Alexander Yakovlev, both Mikhail Gorbachev's comrades-in-arms, repudiated the concept of the two camps and acknowledged partial responsibility of the Soviet Union for the Cold War and the arms race.[7] Yet a new crop of revisionists, using mass media, went beyond 'equal responsibility': they blamed the Cold War unequivocally and solely on the Stalin's totalitarian regime. Not unlike the Vietnam-era revisionism in the United States, the Soviet revisionism was deeply rooted in domestic soul-searching. However, the

Soviet revisionists were not original: in their conclusions they referred not to Soviet archives, but to Western historians – curiously enough, those who stood at the opposite pole from the American revisionism – the admirers of American containment of Soviet expansion and militarism.[8] This explained why, for all its democratic merits, Soviet revisionism could not become a foundation of Cold-War historiography in the new Russia. Its iconoclastic fervour could not substitute for new issues and questions, which required the injection of materials from the classified archives of the Soviet party and the state. Thus, unwittingly, revisionists discouraged historiographic discussion, since they eliminated both the issue of blame for the origins of the Cold War (Stalin and the communist regime were obvious culprits), as well as that of missed opportunities in terminating it (coexistence with the totalitarian regime was impossible).

With the collapse of the Soviet Union came a gradual opening of the Soviet archives[9] and, potentially, the emergence of a Cold-War history with a genuine Russian imprint. Will the influx of new data give rise to a post-revisionism? It is likely that a new set of issues will come to the forefront, issues overlooked by revisionists but which are strongly suggested by the newly available sources on the Soviet part of the Cold War. It is also likely that Russian Cold-War historians will be influenced by Western methodological diversity, including studies on interaction among great powers and between domestic and foreign interests; the microanalysis of leadership and bureaucratic factors, involving the role of strategic planning, intelligence, spiral of misperceptions, collective learning, and so on.[10]

Future debates among historians will be above all determined by available sources. These present an ambiguous landscape, alternatively frustrating or promising for researchers. Soviet memoirs are notably fewer and scantier than Western recollections. Some authors, like Gromyko, simply restate the old mythology.[11] Others, like those by Sergei Khrushchev, Fyodor Burlatsky and Georgy Arbatov, are full of insight; but their authors were not part of decision-making.[12] Nobody among Stalin's successors did any writing, except Nikita S. Khrushchev, whose memoirs remain an unrivalled source.[13] Recently Felix Chuyev published his interviews with V.M. Molotov, containing valuable information on the mentality and motives, if not the decisions, of the Soviet leadership in the early the cold war years.[14] As to specific events of the Cold War, the best witness accounts are available on the Cuban missile crisis,[15] but various morsels have appeared in periodicals.[16] Also memoirs of Soviet defectors give more controversial, but still useful insights.[17] Some titbits can be culled from oral history interviews with living participants. Such personal reminiscences still can give many clues to Soviet perceptions, motives and decisions and they often make sense of what can be found in the now-opening archives.

Together, the archives, memoirs and oral history help understand the Party-State system of decision-making, information and implementation that constituted a backbone for Soviet cold war behaviour. In the Russian archives researchers are finding new evidence on interaction between the Foreign Ministry and the Party's international departments, on the role Soviet embassies played and particularly channels to the communist and other 'progressive' networks in Eastern and Western Europe, as well as in the United States.[18] However, declassified documentation still does not provide detailed description of the process of decision-making. Typical files contain memoranda to the Foreign Ministry, Party Secretariat and the Politburo from diplomatic sources: records of conversations, quarterly and annual reports from embassies and consulates and initiative reports from embassy officials. There are some files on negotiations, including atomic energy, disarmament, test bans, and the like. Many decisions on personnel, intelligence operations, secret communications and financial aid are kept closed in the top-secret, very sensitive special files (*osobyie papki*) of the Central Committee.[19] And much of the day-to-day communication (encoded cables), with few exceptions, are still not available.[20] There is almost no access to transcripts of Stalin's and Khrushchev's conversations, Communist Party of the Soviet Union (CPSU) Politburo and Plenary meetings on foreign policy, or the personal archives of leaders. These materials are in the Kremlin archives, tightly controlled by the office of the President.[21] Another huge collection of files on Cold-War decision-making still lies unclaimed in the Central State Archives of Russia (former TsGAOR). It includes the archives of state ministries and committees and the Presidium of the Council of Ministers (more important than the Politburo in 1945–53). The KGB files, too, may soon be found there in the near future.

On the basis of these limited new sources, however, one can return to some old issues of the Cold War, long explored by Western historians and political scientists. First, what was in the minds of Stalin and his closest subordinates in 1945–6 and later, when confrontation became more and more likely? How did they understand Western conduct and motives, and which Western reactions did they miscalculate? Among the cases often mentioned in this regard are the Baruch plan on atomic energy, Churchill's Iron Curtain speech, the Truman Doctrine, the Marshall Plan, and the Berlin blockade.

Second, were there missed opportunities for accommodation with Stalin and his successors? Did the West over-react – or under-react – to Soviet attempts to consolidate their war gains? Several episodes come to mind here: Soviet policies in Iran and Manchuria (1946), Stalin's plans for Eastern Europe (1945–6), the Moscow meeting of foreign ministers (March 1947), Stalin's proposals to reunify Germany (spring 1952) and the Malenkov-Beria peace initiative (spring–summer 1953).

Third, was Soviet conduct in the Cold War a result of the monolithic totalitarian drive, involving ideology and the leader's whims, or was it shaped by diverse forces and interests, for instance party ideologues vs. technocrats, security vs. army, and the like? Some authors believed Stalin chose the wrong policy in 1945–6; others argue that he, and Khrushchev in the years of crises, reacted to domestic challenges.[22]

Besides, new sources suggest a set of new issues, that had not attracted enough attention from Western historiography, mostly for lack of evidence. Among these issues are:

  1. The effectiveness of US and Western actions in the early Cold War. Did they help to curb Soviet expansion, or did they rather contribute to siege mentality, in other words helping to prolong the totalitarian regime and the cold war? How

exactly did American policies (containment, psychological warfare, 'secret wars' in the third world) affect the Kremlin's conduct?

2. The consequences of the Soviet Union's dual communist/imperial commitments. To what extent were Soviet policies in the Cold War a product of the Kremlin's hegemony in the communist movement? Or were they a reflection of the tyranny of the weak, that is pressures from near-to-collapse satellites like East Germany?[23]

3. The totalitarian state and its policies in the Cold War. Were the Soviets inefficient in the cold war, as in the economy, or had they certain advantages (such as 'party', as well as 'state', means of foreign policy, superior intelligence and total secrecy, ruthless military administration in satellite countries), that helped them wage it for so long? How comparable were the Cold-War structures in Western democracies and the totalitarian Soviet state?

Before we begin our analysis, however, a few words of definition are required. The Cold War was unique as an international confrontation that was not merely bipolar but also global, in which nuclear weapons played a distinctive role as both the potentially explosive and ultimately stabilizing force. The *Cold War* should be distinguished from the *Cold-War Era*. The former lasted roughly from 1948 to 1962 and was characterized by its intense military fever, culminating in the Cuban missile crisis. What ensued was a prolonged armistice in which, at the same time, both sides extended their tentacles, particularly into Latin America and Africa. But neither Vietnam nor Afghanistan provoked a military stand-off on the scale of Cuba. As for *the roots of the Cold War*: ideologically it stemmed from the 1917 revolution in Russia, geopolitically from the Second World War, which left the USA and USSR in positions of dominance, and technologically from the atomic revolution of 1945.

This triad – Bolshevik revolution, the Second World War, and the nuclear era – was absolutely central for the genesis of the Cold War as the main structural phenomenon in international relations since 1945. Yet structure is not everything: history is about people. And no one was more important in the origins of the Cold War than Josef Vissarionovich Dzugashvili – known to history by his revolutionary pseudonym of 'Stalin', man of steel.

### The enigma of Stalin

Stalin's mind is a riddle. All men are divided by psychology into extroverts and introverts. Extroverts enjoy talking before the crowds; they are the darlings of newspapermen; they leave diaries; they write outspoken books like *Mein Kampf*; never afraid of revealing their real self, they insist on stenographers being present; they freely develop their ideas even before strangers. Introverts are different: they try to destroy every evidence of their earthly ways; their speeches, talks and books are carefully formulated; they always want to sound nice, always in accordance with the norms of morality of a certain group. When they reveal their real self they are like snails, ready any time to withdraw into the shell. They are simultaneously shy and fierce about their ego: shy to reveal it, fierce to protect.

That is why we should not expect too much from the Soviet sources concerning Stalin, the supreme introvert. Could there possibly be solid evidence on the state of Stalin's mind? So, when one comes to the task of analyzing Stalin's mentality, one has no other way but to collect the pieces of evidence from all sides, disbelieving most of them, some of Stalin's remarks included.

Some leaders devote their career to one major axis of ideas. However complicated their life pattern is, it develops around this particular axis. But other leaders are different; they move along several axes. To be more precise by changing the metaphor: some planets in the universe rotate around more than one sun. Stalin's planet was exactly of that kind. It had two suns: the sun of revolution and the sun of empire.

The two ideas – world revolution and empire – did not contradict each other at all. What, after all, was the ideal of communists? A universal state with total domination over the globe, a world without borders; in short, an unprecedented empire. Marxism was imperial by its nature. A true Marxist state must long for an imperial status, otherwise it does not have a *raison d'être*, it is doomed to be a satellite, and its government will be hated by the people. Only the idea of building the empire can arouse people's enthusiasm and provide revolutionaries with a decent task. Numerous apostles of world revolution would become lieutenants of the empire, its backbone. That is why Stalin was so successful in bringing the ideas of revolutionary eschatology (death of the old world and birth of the new one) and imperial glory together. Stalin viewed himself not only as a founder of a new – Soviet – empire, but also as an heir of the empire which had seemingly collapsed – the Russian empire.

Self-identification with the great heroes of the past was crucial for Stalin. The heroes he had subconsciously chosen were Lenin and Russian tsars. Self-identification with Lenin was first studied by Robert C. Tucker, who described it as a heroic self-image. Tucker was also the first to identify Stalin as a neurotic.[24] This Lenin fixation demanded acts of revolution, surpassing those of Lenin himself. Karen Horney in her fundamental book wrote: 'The neurotic's self-idealization is an attempt to remedy the damage done by lifting himself in his mind above the crude reality of himself and others.'[25] The deeds of self-heroization were enacted in the international arena, where Stalin at last put the theory of world revolution into practice, as well as inside the country.

There was one very important component in Stalin's mind: aversion to everything foreign. His brief stay in Vienna in 1913 (unlike other Bolshevik leaders he never spent much time abroad) became a trauma for him: lonely, isolated, surrounded by a hostile world. Of course Vienna was not the cause; the cause lay in Stalin's soul, because interaction with the outside world demanded a certain openness, a relaxed nature – qualities unknown to Stalin. The trauma of Vienna was very strong. Together with envy towards others (like Lenin, Trotsky and Bukharin), who felt themselves equally free in the tsar's gaol or in a Geneva café, it gave birth to a pronounced inferiority complex. That inferiority should have been displaced; the easiest way was clear – xenophobia. But the xenophobia of Stalin was not that of a prudent tyrant; it was the xenophobia of a neurotic. Stalin was therefore displacing a deep inferiority complex in a primitive and not very effective way. Such displacement only made the inferiority complex deeper and more painful. Only later, on becoming a member of a narrow circle of world leaders, did Stalin succeed in getting rid of it, and then only for a short period of time.

Every person has his own reference group, people whose opinion is important for him. A person usually does not care about everybody ('How can they understand me?'), but there are people whose respect he seeks. For Stalin petty apparatchiks like Molotov and Kaganovitch did not count; inferior in all senses, they were just puppets in his hands. He looked for his reference group abroad. Only important leaders like Hitler, Roosevelt and Churchill mattered. Of course, Hitler must have intrigued Stalin most of all; he must have felt that they shared a good deal. Who else but Hitler could understand a leader like Stalin? But interaction with Hitler was brief and never personal, notwithstanding the fact that in 1939–40 it had brought the best fruits of expansion one could ever wish for. That said, co-operation with the leaders of Britain and the United States proved to be very satisfactory in the psychological sense. The atmosphere was relatively relaxed; the Big Three behaved as a group with specific relations between the members, with common memories, even with jokes that only they could understand. At last Stalin had found the company of equals. It was an extremely important motive that pushed him towards post-war co-operation. In some sense this motive was the summing up of his 'human evolution', with all its complexes. As Karen Horney wrote of the neurotic personality: 'Nobody can function, or even live, under such conditions. The individual must make, and does make, automatic attempts at solving these problems, attempts at removing conflicts, allaying tensions, and preventing terrors.'[26]

The hypothesis that Stalin was displacing certain complexes, looking for a specific comradeship among the Big Three, does not mean that the relationship among them was ideal. Stalin had his doubts about his partners. In 1944 he told Milovan Djilas, pointing at the map of the Soviet Union: 'They will never accept the idea that so great a space should be red, never, never!'[27] Nevertheless Stalin enjoyed redistributing spheres of influence, with Churchill in particular in October 1944, when they were deciding the exact percentage of Moscow's and London's influence in post-war Eastern Europe.

So this psychological motive was pushing Stalin towards accommodation with the West. There were also more practical considerations. After all, the Big Three were engaged in a large-scale redistribution of spheres of influence during the War and afterwards. The process did not go all that smoothly, but in general one is struck by a spirit of mutual understanding in this imperialist circle: liberal Roosevelt, venerable anti-communist Churchill, communist Stalin. An imperialist fraternity was uniting them all, and the West was acknowledging Soviet predominance in Poland, the Baltics, Eastern Europe in general. Was it only the result of the Red Army's strength? No, because the allies had effectively recognized the Soviet conquests of 1940 long before Soviet victory in the War became a certainty.

Stalin knew it and he was prepared to co-operate with the West after the War. Taking into consideration Stalin's dependence upon archetypes, one can suggest that he was influenced by the archetype of the Vienna Congress of 1815, with himself as Alexander I (1801–25) and perhaps Churchill as Metternich? There is at least one piece of evidence that his self-identification with Alexander I as archetype was clear to Stalin himself. When he was asked by Harriman whether it felt good that he was dividing Berlin only several years after Germans had been standing at the walls of Moscow, Stalin replied that 'Tsar Alexander had reached Paris.'[28]

In the speech that is usually regarded in the West as the proclamation of the Cold War on 9 February 1946, Stalin actually proposed a specific model of peaceful coexistence. He said: 'It might be possible to avoid military catastrophes, if there were a way of periodically reapportioning raw materials and markets among the countries according to their economic weight – taking concerted and peaceful decisions.' He added: 'But this is impossible to fulfil in contemporary capitalist conditions of world economic development.'[29] This was an awkward reference to Western values, as he understood them. But the American embassy in Moscow overlooked this point. When he spoke about raw materials and markets, he must have meant reapportionment of spheres of influence; but many in Washington regarded his speech as a declaration of Cold War.

Stalin's rape of Eastern Europe preceded the Cold War and, as many argue, triggered it. Stalin did not understand the difference between the swallowing of eastern Poland, the Baltics, and eastern Prussia, on the one hand, and the construction of 'friendly' regimes in Poland and Czechoslovakia, on the other. And in terms of moral and international law there really was not any difference. What moral or legal argument underpinned the decision to give eastern Prussia to Stalin? Presumably, to punish Germany and to deprive it of a bridgehead in Eastern Europe. As a result, to Stalin, Western protests against changes in Eastern Europe and other regions seemed just a political game; by approving the earlier Stalin gains, the West lost the moral ground to protest against further expansion of the Soviet empire.

Today most historians speak about lost opportunities in the Cold War. But when one thinks about the real lost opportunities in 1945–8, the probable hypothesis is – the West was not firm enough, it did not check Stalin's imperial expansion.

In categories of 'good guys' and 'bad guys' Stalin was indisputably a bad guy in the Cold War. But he was also a bad guy during the Second World War and before it – and the good guys had actually encouraged him to go on being bad, for they needed his strength and also found themselves under the evil spell of totalitarianism. Stalin was allowed to feel that he was good when he was occupying eastern Prussia and preserving the lands conquered before the War. Then, suddenly, he became bad, without obvious reasons. He felt betrayed by former allies. But he was not prepared to wage the Cold War (that is, open confrontation without much diplomatic coverage) until 1948. Probably the coup d'état in Czechoslovakia in February of 1948 and the Berlin crisis that began four months later were the first battles of the real Cold War, when no compromise was hoped for, and when Stalin was waiting only for the contradictions in the Western camp to ripen and lead to another war in which, he hoped, imperialism would be buried. According to Molotov, Stalin had constructed a strict logical chain: 'The First World War had pulled one country out of the capitalist slavery. The Second World War has created a socialist system, and the Third will terminate imperialism once and for all.'[30]

His policies in the East displayed the same evolution – from cautious waiting to the promotion of expansion. In 1945–7 Stalin was not in a hurry to support Mao

Zedong, the leader of a relatively independent and undoubtedly strong revolutionary communist movement. As long as there was a possibility of coming to terms with the Americans, he was not going to ruin the fragile balance between the Nationalist Guomindang and the Chinese communists. He still preferred official relations with the Guomindang government of Chiang Kai-shek, though by revolutionary logic he should have denounced Chiang as a puppet of the imperialists. Even Chiang's pro-Western policies, of which Stalin was being constantly reminded by his agents in China, did not change his mind. After Stalin's death Mao complained to Pavel Yudin, Soviet Ambassador in Beijing:

In the last period . . . Stalin also made wrong estimates of the situation in China and of the possibilities of revolutionary development. He continued to believe more in the Guomindang's strength than in the Communist Party [of China]. In 1945 he insisted on peace with Chiang, on the common front with the Guomindang and the creation of a 'democratic republic' in China. . . . In 1947 . . . when our troops were winning victories, Stalin insisted on striking a peace with Chiang, because he doubted the strength of the Chinese revolution.[31]

Only in 1948, anticipating trouble in future, did Stalin reluctantly gave a firm handshake to Mao Zedong.[32]

Here we must ask ourselves a question: how was the Eastern front of the Cold War connected with the Western, in Stalin's eyes? Stalin, as well as most other Soviet leaders, was Eurocentric and, more precisely, German-oriented. His major ambitions and challenges lay westward. In part, this was because his psychological archetypes of glory and national interest were linked with Europe (the Middle East was one notable exception). Just like the Russian empire before, he had not regarded his vast provinces in Siberia and in the Far East as of extraordinary value. The geopolitical utility of the Far East seemed to Stalin of minor importance. Even if he was eager to take part in Japan's defeat and conquest, he readily relinquished his 'right' to occupation in exchange for Western acceptance of Soviet dominance in Romania and Hungary.

Stalin was developing expansion in Europe and adjoining regions with vigour and persistence, unlike in the Far East. Yet, ironically, he had a much more powerful natural ally in China than in Iran or even Greece. Had Stalin's imperialist aspirations been not much influenced by psychological archetypes, he would have used the opportunity to project his influence in the Far East, not in 1948–9 but at least three years earlier. Instead he was prepared to give China, Korea and Japan to the Americans as their share in the post-war division of the world, whereas in Europe he longed to take as much as he could.

It is not true, of course, that geopolitical considerations in the Far East were a matter of total indifference for Stalin in 1945–7. He was influenced by the same imperialist dreams that had pushed Russian tsars; he desired to re-establish spheres of influence lost by Russia under Nicholas II (1894–1917). There were other historical parallels. The Russian empire had turned its attention to the Far East only when the European powers made further expansion in Europe totally impossible. Similarly, Stalin switched his attention and his efforts to the Far East only when American power had stopped his expansion in Europe. Even when the Cold War developed into a global confrontation and then erupted into an open conflagration in Korea, its core, from Stalin's viewpoint, always remained in Europe, not in Asia.

The period from the fall of 1947 to the spring of 1948 was a kind of turning point for Stalin. The sun of world revolution seemed to rise again – as was reflected in the last works of Stalin. There he tried to present a concept of a post-war world. Churchill, wrote Stalin, became a warmonger. He and his friends exhibited 'a striking resemblance to Hitler and his friends'.[33] Billionaires and millionaires regarded war as a source of profits. 'They, these aggressive forces, hold in their hands reactionary governments and guide them.'[34]

Stalin expatiated again and again on the general crisis of capitalism. He insisted on the collapse of the world economy: 'One should regard the disinte-gration of the single integral world market as the most important economic result of the Second World War and its economic consequences.'[35] He admitted that after the War two prophecies had proved invalid: his own, on a 'relative stability of markets during the general crisis of capitalism', and Lenin's conclusion that, despite the crisis, 'capitalism in general is growing faster than before'.[36]

Stalin seemed not to understand the nature of the epoch in which he was living, especially its major characteristic – bipolarity. He still thought in routine categories of the pre-Cold-War history and was sure that the new war was inevitable. Stalin did not see a future war as a conflict between socialism and capitalism: a repetition of the scenario of 1937–9 seemed more probable in his eyes. He wrote:

Some comrades make a mistake when they say that 'contradictions between the socialist camp and capitalist camp are stronger than contradictions between capitalist countries, that the United States of America has subjugated other capitalist countries enough, stopping them waging wars with each other and weakening each other. . . .'[37] Wouldn't it be wiser to say that capitalist England, and then capitalist France will in the end have to break away from the USA, embrace and venture a conflict with it in order to secure independent policy and of course high profits? . . . To think that . . . [West Germany and Japan] would not try to become independent, to break away from the U.S. 'regime' and rush to the road of independent development – means believing in miracles.[38]

He believed Germany would be again a major European power, with Great Britain and France as a poor match.[39] Even earlier, in 1945, he warned Yugoslav commu-nists that the Germans were not 'finished':

No, they will recover, and very quickly. That is a highly developed industrial country with an extremely qualified and numerous working class and technical intelligensia. Give them twelve to fifteen years and they'll be on their feet again. And this is why the unity of the Slavs is important.[40]

He regarded the Cold War as something really emanating from the West, which had ignored his good will; one of a series of confrontations with imperialism which was to be resolved one day in conflict.

It would be a simplification to say that the Cold War was Stalin's choice or his child. He did not want it. He regarded it not as a logical consequence of his policies, but as a deliberate Western policy. He did not consider swallowing one country after another as something really capable of causing the crisis; he took it as his legal share. This process is known in psychology as externalization: 'I am not hostile to others; they are doing things to me.'[41]

For all its historical roots, then, Stalin's imperialism was not a simple continuation of the Russian imperial tradition. It represented an externalization of his power-hungry ego. Examining a post-war map, Stalin revelled in the new borders of the Soviet Union. 'Let's have a look at what has turned out. . . . In the North everything is all right. In the West everything is all right. . . . But here I don't like our borders!' – and Stalin pointed to the region to the south from the Caucasus.[42] In fact, the borders of the tsarist empire and its spheres of influence had been completely restored. The vassal states formed a huge Eurasian belt of which the tsars could not even have dreamt – Eastern Europe and Eastern Asia. It was too much even for Molotov. Although he said in 1975: 'It is good that the Russian tsars gained so much land for us. Now it is easier for us to fight capitalism,'[43] he regretted Stalin's claims to Turkey; his imperialism was of more down-to-earth, that of a bookkeeper, not a semi-deity. He admitted: 'In the last years Stalin began to get a swelled head.'[44]

Stalin's hyper-inflated ego might help explain why sometimes he tried to transgress all the traditional limits of Russian imperialism. Molotov recalled with a certain bewilderment:

Libya turned out to be necessary for us. Stalin says: 'Go ahead, push!' . . . At one of the meetings of the foreign ministers I declared that the national-liberation movement had appeared in Libya. But it is pretty weak, we want to support it and to build our military base there.[45]

Stalin even played with idea of regaining Alaska from the United States.[46]

In 1950 the Korean war broke out. Several sources today back up Khrushchev's version that Kim Il Sung came to Moscow at the end of 1949 and after long talks and consultations persuaded Stalin to support the war against the South. 'The North Koreans wanted to prod South Korea with the point of a bayonet,' Khrushchev recalled. He also remembered that Stalin had had doubts, afraid lest the Americans jump in.[47] According to Khrushchev, in the fall of 1950, when the American forces counter-attacked and marched to the Chinese border, Stalin was prepared to abandon North Korea rather than risk direct confrontation with the Americans.[48] That was a clear example of where American containment worked – after all, Stalin did not send Soviet troops en masse to fight for Kim Il Sung. Even the Chinese who sent their army to save the poor adventurist did not risk trying to liberate Taiwan.

Indirect participation in the Korean war was Stalin's last offensive in the Cold War. American intervention was like a cold shower. The hermit of the Kremlin retreated once again into his shell, a besieged tyrant in his lonely autumn.

To a far greater degree than in any other state discussed in this book, the foreign policy of the Soviet Union was the creation of its leader. Central though Stalin's mentality is to our understanding of the Cold War, however, we cannot stop there. In its external policy after 1945 the USSR was acting simultaneously as a 'normal' state playing international politics, as the centre of a revolutionary international party, and as an occupying power administering vast new territories. It is the interplay of Stalin's mind with these three sets of systemic imperatives which takes us to the heart of the Soviet Cold War.

### The Soviets and Cold War dynamics

There was a popular story among the veterans of the Second World War: when the Red Army met the American forces at the Elbe river, Marshal Zhukov insisted that the Soviets should continue the victorious march further to the West. But Stalin objected. Had he agreed, the Red Army allegedly would have reached the Channel in two weeks.

Stalin had a better chance of achieving predominance in Europe without war, using the multi-tiered foreign policy of a totalitarian great power. On the level of 'state' foreign policy, that is relations with the Allies, he made certain commitments at Yalta and Potsdam.[49] He came all the way to please the Americans on the United Nations: the UN Statute, written with direct Soviet participation, was a direct precursor of Gorbachev's new thinking in international relations. With an obvious Stalin nod, Maxim Litvinov, Molotov's rival and architect of 'collective security' in the 1930s, turned out many position papers aimed at the revival of his old designs of collective security.

The 'party' level became less prominent in Kremlin foreign policy with Stalin's dissolution of the Comintern in 1943. The Comintern's staff, however, stayed in the International Department of the Central Committee and its branches: the Sovinformburo, the Jewish Anti-Fascist Committee, and a number of secret institutes.[50] This department, together with the department of Agitation and Propaganda, continued to collect information form communist and 'progressive' network abroad. The network's low profile concealed high expectations Stalin had in 1945–6 about communist politics in Western Europe, especially in Italy and France. In a triumphant mood, Stalin told German communists that 'there would be two Germanies, despite all the unity of the Allies'. In a struggle for his Germany he planned to act through the unified KPD or Communist Party of Germany.[51]

There was a third level of Stalin's foreign policy, dealing with the countries and territories liberated, defeated and/or occupied by the Red Army. Some Politburo members were appointed by Stalin to supervise the countries of the Soviet sphere of influence in Eastern Europe – from Finland (Zhdanov) to Romania (Vyshinsky).[52] From the start a Soviet style of consolidation of new regimes in Eastern Europe implied a special role for native communists: most of them had lived in Moscow since the 1930s and returned in the rearguard of the Red Army under Soviet instructions. Among them were members of the Lublin Polish government, Walter Ulbricht in East Germany, Matyas Rakosi in Hungary, Anna Pauker and Georgiu Dej in Romania, Georgy Dimitrov in Bulgaria, and so on. Stalin, in conversation with Milovan Djilas, a Yugoslav communist, suggested that these countries must be up for socialization, with the help of the Soviet military administration. In fact, this approach was adopted by Soviet military administrators not only in Eastern Europe, but in northern Iran and North Korea. Yet in 1945 Moscow hoped to bring communists to power by parliamentary intrigues: either in alliance with agrarian parties against social democrats, or together with social democrats against the peasant parties. The directives to expel the non-communists and to eliminate the rudiments of parliamentary democracy came two years later.

The relationship between these three levels of Soviet foreign policy depended, largely, on how Stalin assessed the changing international situation. When his regular state diplomacy did not satisfy him, he turned to a party level, increasingly associated with his subordinate Andrei Zhdanov, Secretary and Politburo member. The underlying goals, though, were always unmistakably imperial. Molotov, a chief engineer of Stalin's foreign policy, put it in historical perspective:

Stalin used to say that [tsarist] Russia won wars, but could not enjoy the fruits of its victories. Russians are remarkable warriors, but they do not know how to make peace; they are duped, fobbed off. So I think, after this war, we scored a success, we built up the Soviet state. It was my major task . . . so that nobody would dupe us. Here we tried hard and, I believe, results were not bad.[53]

In 1945 and later all three levels were used to create the most favourable correlation of forces, which Stalin judged was crucial for the consolidation of his post-war empire. Initially the interstate, ally-to-ally relations were considered as important as the overtly imperial policies. Stalin agreed to sign the Yalta Declaration on Liberated Europe only because 'it was to our advantage to keep intact an alliance with America'.[54]

In early 1945 Stalin had a number of reasons to think that the correlation of forces was changing in his favour:

1. American foreign policy was determined by Franklin Roosevelt, who hated British imperialism. He was also prepared to withdraw American forces from Europe in two years and wanted to co-operate with Stalin as one of 'global policemen' under the aegis of the United Nations;

2. he believed that the United States could not defeat Japan without the Red Army;

3. Eastern Europe and East Germany were safely locked in the Soviet sphere;

4. in Italy and France communists had marvellous chances to come to power; in the rest of Western Europe the popularity of the Soviet Union was at its peak;

5. many believed that the world role of the United States would be crippled by a serious economic crisis and that America would seek an escape in isolationism;

6. Stalin had the world's best intelligence service and could look at opponents' cards while keeping his hidden.

By early 1947 Stalin was obliged to correct these assessments. The United States did not intend to resume its pre-war role in the world. Roosevelt was replaced by Truman. Imperialist contradictions between America and Britain were buried in an Anglo-Saxon alliance, increasingly dominated by the United States. Roosevelt's line was defeated in domestic politics by what one Soviet diplomat called the 'bloc of reactionary Southern Democrats and the old guard of the Republicans'.[55] Stalin helped the polarization a great deal by his insistence on bigger reparations from Germany and the dismantling of the Ruhr coal and steel industries, by his claim to have a role in Japan's occupation, by miscellaneous probes around the Soviet periphery (Turkey and the Straits, Iran, Manchuria) and even démarches outside the traditional Russian sphere of influence such as in Libya. Litvinov, frustrated and isolated, suggested that the West should be tougher with Stalin and Molotov. His complaints were overheard by the secret police, and must have triggered Stalin's anger and Litvinov's later assassination.[56]

In late 1945 and during 1946 Stalin clearly overplayed his hand. Military triumphs by the Red Army boosted his hubris to classical dimensions. It was at this stage, as Molotov admitted, years later, that Stalin toyed with plans to retrieve Alaska and get control over the Turkish straits – the dreams of Great Russian imperialists.[57] Most of those plans were clearly not feasible and were not pursued. But they characterized the state of mind and mood in the Kremlin at that time; and they scared many in the West.

Several factors contributed to Stalin's intransigence and arrogance. The atomic bomb placed in doubt the Soviet military role in the defeat of Japan and raised Truman's morale. In Stalin's eyes, it shattered the correlation of forces. This conclusion was borne out by the awkward attempts of Secretary of State James Byrnes to practise, momentarily, atomic diplomacy. Stalin instructed Molotov to undercut Byrnes's policy and personal credentials during the Allied negotiations. Consequently, the Soviets behaved as if the atomic bomb had not existed.

The striking contrast between the Soviet economy and the economic might of the United States also, ironically, made Stalin more, not less, arrogant. He refused to negotiate any American credits with strings attached. Participation of the Soviet Union in international economic cooperation and rehabilitation of Europe could reveal Soviet weakness or allow America to put its foot into the Soviet door. The Soviets waited for the world economic crisis to extract from the capitalists what they wanted, on their own terms.[58]

American pragmatic disengagement in Eastern Europe, manifested in the Harriman-Stalin deal in October 1945,[59] along with unexpected American pressure on the Soviets in Iran, must have confirmed Moscow's belief that American foreign policy was dictated by mercenary, traditionally imperialist interests such as Arab oil. This also contributed to Molotov's horse-trading and to the diplomatic impasse.

Finally, the Soviets initially had a clear edge over the Western powers in filling an enormous political vacuum inside the former Third Reich. The Soviet military administration in Germany (SVAG) launched a client party of Socialist Unity (SED), uniting communists with some social-democrats. In 1946, while the Social Democratic Party (SPD) and Christian Democratic Union (CDU) were still weak, SED and its trade unions attempted to win political control over the whole of Berlin and to make inroads into Western zones. The economic situation, especially food, in the Soviet zone was better than in the West. Efficient combination of party and occupation means seemed to guarantee an edge to the Soviets in Germany and could have encouraged Stalin to be self-confident in his conversation with U.S. Secretary of State George Marshall in Moscow in April 1947. 'When the partners exhaust each other,' he argued, 'a moment will come for possible compromises.'[60]

The Soviet boycott of the Marshall plan was a turning point towards the Cold War: state diplomacy was virtually buried; not only ideas of co-operation, but even a traditional diplomacy of balancing among powers were all abandoned in favor of bipolar confrontation ('two camps').[61] Party foreign policy triumphed for a while in

Soviet relations with both Western and Eastern Europe. With regard to the latter it dominated even over the common-sense needs of occupation policies. This led to the rise of Andrei Zhdanov and Nikolai Voznesensky and to the eclipse of Molotov, Lavrenti Beria, Georgi Malenkov and Anastas Mikoyan, who had run foreign affairs on a routine basis in 1945–6. Molotov, along with most state agencies that were interested in foreign credits, initially planned to join the European recovery program. Only after he sensed Stalin's mood did he make a U-turn and oppose the participation in the Marshall plan.[62]

Most historians now agree that Stalin miscalculated. Did he expect that both Western and Eastern Europe would knuckle under to his bull-like pressure? Zhdanov and later Molotov presented the Soviet reaction as a great counter-offensive and, in general, a great success. But Khrushchev recalled that after the war the leaders in Moscow had expected that economic chaos in Western Europe would reach 'the point of a revolutionary explosion'. Intervention by the powerful economy of the United States came as a great evil from two angles: it led to defeats for Western communists and it cushioned a future (and inevitable) economic crisis overseas. The next fear was a reunification of Germany under American hegemony.[63]

Using the Cominform (September 1947) as a tool, Stalin and Zhdanov sent foreign communists to snatch the chestnuts out of the fire for the Soviet Union. They egged on these collaborators ('you underestimate your strength') to frustrate the Marshall plan by fomenting strikes, nationalism and anti-Americanism. The party foreign policy helped the Soviet Union to gain time, amid the post-war demobilization, for the modernization of its armed forces. At the same time Stalin, in a year of hunger and want, widely used 'bread-and-butter diplomacy' to win the Polish, German, Czech and even Italian publics over to the communist side.

All the time the Soviet leadership was confident there was no immediate war threat from the United States, as long as Western Europe was in political turmoil. 'America may pull on our leg,' explained Malenkov to Italian communists, 'but war is out of the question now.' Zhdanov agreed that 'elements of blackmail prevail over the real war preparations'.[64] Even though some in the leadership talked about strangulation of the Soviet Union, the war scare came much later, in 1950–1.

The renaissance of Zhdanov was facilitated, in part, by growing crises in state and occupation policies, particularly in Germany. Throughout 1945–6 the negotiations on German government and Germany unity were deadlocked, and a struggle for the German soul was on. Before long the Soviet military administration and various state agencies ran rough-shod over traditional socio-economic structures in the Eastern zone; by February 1947 all military plants were transferred to the Soviet Union; various 'techno-science bureaux' pipelined German technology to the East.[65] In March, however, Stalin decided to step up a campaign for restoration of a unified German state: not only to be in better position to press for reparations without Allied interference, but also aiming at German nationalism.

One option was to transform SVAG (Soviet military administration in Germany), 'with its orders and peremptory commands, into a more flexible system, closer to civilian government'.[66] Another was to introduce a combination of party and occupation means to create a satellite East German regime. During 1947 the entrenched interests of the military and the East German communists coincided with Stalin's growing belief in the latter option. Gradually the military administration, with Stalin's approval, began to increase control over communications between the Eastern and Western zones – a process that eventually escalated into the Berlin blockade in June 1948.

From this time on Stalin over-reacted to Western hostile designs as he perceived them. He did not regard an Anglo-American bloc or American military expansion as immediate threats. But the addition of Western Germany to the bloc changed calculations drastically: it was seen as a force aimed at the re-acquisition of East Germany, in other words against Soviet imperial interests. Probably nothing could have shaken Stalin out of these convictions, especially since all intelligence after the fall of 1947 reported to him tailored conclusions in a single, centralized voice.[67] According to one authoritative source, Stalin received a pre-packaged cream of information, and precious little of it. Molotov, who was much more informed, often stood up against Stalin, but never on issues of strategic importance.[68]

Stalin did not unleash the Cold War to crush domestic dissent and impose his absolute control. Yet he had to deal with the fact that 'Ivan had seen Europe', first, when the Red Army captured European capitals, and second, when the thousands of Soviet military, managers, engineers and technicians who implemented the *Pax Sovietica* in Eastern Europe dismantled German industry. Also there were five million Soviet prisoners of war and forced labourers in the West, of whom two million were repatriated. The Soviet presence in countries far more advanced socially and technologically opened the dangerous possibility that some segments of the Soviet elite would be gradually Westernized. So there were plenty of reasons, even without the Cold War, for a crack-down on intellectual life in the Soviet Union, for the hardening of East European regimes and for an Iron Curtain keeping the West out of Soviet sphere of influence altogether.[69] But the Marshall plan and the economic division of Germany became a signal for weeding out *all* 'unreliable' elements; the West became an official enemy, and all foreigners in the Soviet sphere were to be isolated and closely watched. In 1947 Stalin passed a law that regarded marriage of a Soviet citizen with a foreigner as state treason.

Was the Cold War, then, the result of the spiral of misperceptions or was it a conflict of vital interests? On the Soviet side it was both. Stalin's misperceptions played a vastly greater role in world politics than anti-Soviet moods in London and Washington, because Stalin's control over Soviet foreign policy was total. His conclusion in 1947 that a global bipolar struggle now existed between Moscow and the Anglo-Saxon bloc made the Cold War inevitable. At the same time the Soviet system's vital interests were at stake in Germany and elsewhere: the system could not afford to reveal its weaknesses and could not modify its operational modes, even when this was dictated by common sense. In a way this systemic interest prevailed over the pragmatic side of Stalin's self – first in Germany, where the Soviets threw their support behind a rootless marionette government instead of building long-term Soviet-German friendship; second, in Korea, by supporting Kim Il Sung's *reconquista* of the South.

All missed opportunites, if they existed at all, had to be located in the period from late 1945 to early 1947. Conventional Soviet interpretations of the Cold War claim that the biggest misfortune, after Stalin's 'mistakes', was the death of Franklin Roosevelt. Under Truman no reliable state-to-state relations were possible, Stalin's suspicions were set in motion, and so on.[70] New evidence from the Soviet archives does not resolve this debate, but raises new questions. How did Stalin's absolute control relate to the plurality of foreign policies in Moscow and to the group interests that represented them? To what extent did the tail wag the dog, that is to say, how far did party and occupation policies, loaded intelligence, and other systemic factors, convert Stalin's misperceptions into disastrous policies? Could anybody, even Stalin, stem the rising tide of the Cold War? Some light on these questions can be obtained by comparing the 'Stalin phase' of the cold war with the period after Stalin's death.

### The Cold War after Stalin, 1953–5

Some Cold-War scholars look at the years after Stalin's death as a period of missed opportunities to reduce international tension and to check the arms race. A young American political scientist argued in 1987 that Soviet successors of Stalin pursued a strategy of Graduated Reduction of International Tensions (GRIT), which was unfortunately ignored by the United States.[71] But until now the evidence on the Soviet side did not support this argument. On the contrary, it indicated that the new Soviet leadership remained loyal to the basic guidelines of Stalin's foreign policy. As Khrushchev recalled: 'When Stalin died we went on as before, out of inertia. Our boat just continued to float down the stream, along the same course that had been set by Stalin. . . .'[72]

But some opportunities did exist, arising from the confusion in the Kremlin in the first months after Stalin's death. To hide this from the world, Moscow launched its biggest peace offensive of the Cold War. The new head of government, Georgi Malenkov, and especially secret police chief Lavrenti Beria expected to use this campaign to promote destalinization and their own political fortunes. This explains why, unlike all previous propaganda campaigns, this one included some deeds.[73] Its main elements were:

1. reduction of tensions on the immediate periphery of the Soviet Union, and diplomatic settlement in Korea;

2. redoubled efforts to prevent remilitarization of West Germany;

3. measures to alleviate the war scare at home and improve the image of the Soviet Union abroad (termination of the 'hate-America' campaign, of the 'Kremlin doctors' plot', and of the open hostility towards the diplomatic corps and foreign citizens in Moscow).

In retrospect this Soviet campaign marked a gradual, painful restoration of state foreign policy, relying on negotiations and other diplomatic means. With Stalin's death the party ideological component in Soviet behaviour was considerably weakened. Principal architects of Soviet policies – Beria and Malenkov, marginally Molotov – were mostly interested in consolidating the Stalinist state under conditions they regarded as less than favourable. They faced an immediate threat of vast American nuclear superiority; over-extension of the Soviet empire in the West and East; pressing domestic issues, from the struggle for power in the post-Stalin Presidium (Politburo) to the desperate situation in the agrarian and consumer sectors of the Soviet economy.

The collective leadership, however, was torn by the struggle for power among its members. Foreign policy often was used as one of arenas of conflict between the principal rivals. The German issue remained the cause célèbre, revealing substantial differences. Stalin left German policy in disarray. On 10 March 1952 he had suggested to Western powers the reunification of Germany. But it was not a return to the state diplomacy of 1945–6; too much in Stalin's actions compromised his proposal as a ploy. At the same time Stalin was giving full support to the construction of socialism in the GDR, to help Walter Ulbricht, an Eastern German communist leader, acquire full economic, as well as political, power. He might have hoped to reach a tactical alliance with West German Social-Democratic leader Kurt Schumacher against American influence in Germany (Schumacher died just a few months before Stalin). As a result nobody knew what was on Stalin's mind, but the Ulbricht regime became a burning issue in itself. Its domestic policies were disastrous, and the Soviets had to cover its financial and social losses.

In May 1953 the Presidium (a new name for the ruling party Politburo) saw a clash between two approaches to the German question. Molotov, as foreign minister, argued it was necessary to support the GDR as a socialist state. Beria and Malenkov suggested selling the Ulbricht regime down the river, in order to get a neutral 'democratic and peaceful' Germany. This spectacular proposal was perhaps the most radical detour from previous Soviet conduct in the cold war since 1947. If accepted, it would have meant a victory of *realpolitik* over ideology, and, perhaps, the dismantling of the Cold-War bipolar structures in Europe.

Molotov's approach won, for reasons that would dominate Soviet Cold-War behaviour for decades to come. He defended the same imperial platform as under Stalin: Soviet war gains had to be guaranteed and consolidated; the status quo in Eastern Europe was possible only under socialist regimes; negotiations with the West could be conducted only from the position of strength. The Beria-Malenkov proposal ran counter to all these postulates: it sacrificed a vital part of the Soviet empire and could have meant a spread of Western presence to the Polish border, with an unpredictable impact on all Eastern Europe.

Ironically, the only person capable of changing the doctrinal basis of Soviet foreign policy was the blood-stained security chief Lavrenti Beria. If he had come to power, that would have meant a final triumph of the secret police over the party. Beria's arrest in July 1953 and liquidation in December put an end to this dubious opportunity. Weak Malenkov was gradually losing power to Nikita Khrushchev, First Secretary of the CPSU, who, relying on the military, squashed the autonomy of the security forces.

A reunification of Germany, which was possible only with the revival of the state rationale in Soviet foreign policy, was a dead idea. Politics in the Kremlin brought about the ascendancy of the party and occupation interests in foreign policy. In addition, the uprising of workers in East Berlin in June 1953 pressed on the Soviets a conclusion, that, without the support of Soviet bayonets, the Ulbricht regime would fall. The Kremlin leadership was convinced that American intelligence was behind the revolt. Imperialism was clearly planning a major counterattack, and the reaction to it was precisely the same as the Stalin–Zhdanov ploy in 1947. The combination of party and occupation policies, meaning unequivocal support of the communist regime and the build-up of Soviet military power, determined Soviet attitudes towards the GDR until 1988.

Another opportunity stemmed from the rivalry between Khrushchev and Molotov for control over Soviet foreign policy. Molotov, despite his support for socialism in East Germany, was always wary of party solidarity with the Soviet satellites, often at the expense of Russia. Nationalist and Bolshevik at the same time,[74] he treated Kim Il Sung, Ulbricht, Rakosi and other communist leaders as clients, who owed everything to Stalin and Russian soldiers. In his mind, 'war was expected to break out at any moment'.[75] So he looked at the satellite countries first and foremost from the military-strategic viewpoint, as a possible front line. For that reason in 1953 he stood as an advocate of the diplomatic settlement in Korea. He believed that the Korean war was the result of Stalin's miscalculations and hubris, exploited by Kim Il Sung.[76] This threat of a second front against the Soviet Union in case of a global war had to be eliminated. For the same reason he was against the neutralization of Germany and Austria: the Soviet Army would have lost important footholds for its offensive, in response to the American atomic strike.

Khrushchev's foreign policy platform, less alarmist and much more activist, had twin tasks: to consolidate the socialist camp and to promote the cause of world communism. This dualism of communist/imperial commitments later left the Soviet leadership torn between its immediate concerns, domestic and foreign, and anxiety about its hegemony over the 'progressive forces', its 'internationalist duty' towards the tottering allies, and so on. Khrushchev, like Stalin before him in Korea, was heading into a dangerous trap for a superpower, by letting commitments produced by the Cold War determine the goals of Soviet conduct.[77] It harboured a danger of over-extension and adventurism.

This, however, did not develop until much later (though as early as 1953 the Soviets greatly increased aid to the People's Republic of China (PRC) and in 1955 they began seeking alliances with 'progressive' Arab regimes in the Middle East). At first this platform made Soviet foreign policy less rigid and militarist. The desire to promote the progressive cause and to present the Soviet Union as a bulwark of peace was behind a number of initiatives:

1. Moscow recognized a diversity of ways to socialism. Khrushchev and prime minister Nikolai Bulganin went to Yugoslavia bearing excuses to Tito for past Soviet behaviour. Across Eastern Europe the state's grip on economic and cultural life slackened.

2. Soviet forces abandoned several bases in Europe and Asia. In May 1955 Molotov had to sign a treaty with Austria, recognizing its neutrality. These steps were not unprecedented: in 1945–7 the Soviet leadership also expected to gain more in Europe by demilitarization and indirect control. Besides, by 1955 it had become clear that the Soviet occupation regime in Austria had failed to

bring communists to power and Soviet holding-companies there had become an economic embarrassment.[78]

3. The Soviets began unilateral reduction of their conventional forces in Europe and came forward with a package of proposals on disarmament (May 1955).

The demilitarization and disarmament measures were clearly designed to embarrass the Eisenhower administration, busy with building strategic bases and all kinds of politico-military alliances around the Soviet bloc. The primary logic behind Soviet retreat had been expressed in 1948 by Zhdanov to the Austrian communists: 'The Soviet Union withdrew its troops everywhere (in Iran, Manchuria, Bulgaria, Czechoslovakia, etc.), so as to deny to our enemies an opportunity to keep their troops in other countries.'[79] These steps reflected a more relaxed view of external threats – a gradual diminishing of the war scare of the early 1950s. But this relaxation did not entail any shift in politico-military doctrine, which, in essence, put a premium on territorial buffers and a pre-emptive offensive with superior conventional forces.

The development of thermonuclear weapons did not immediately revolutionize the mentality of the Soviet leadership. First, only a few people were aware of the Soviet nuclear program. After Stalin's death Beria kept it secret even from Presidium members.[80] Only after Beria had been arrested were Khrushchev and his colleagues briefed about the scope and terrible potential of the nuclear bomb. Second, in the Kremlin the nuclear arms race was still regarded as catch up or die issue. Vast American superiority and the proliferation of their strategic aviation within the reach of Soviet vital centres overshadowed everything else. Third, the leadership, particularly Malenkov, welcomed tests of the first hydrogen bomb in August 1953 as a desirable affirmation of the Soviet position of strength in the international arena.

Still, the testing did have a deep psychological impact on the management of the program. It found its expression in a response to the proposal of Eisenhower in December 1953 to build a 'peaceful atom'. The project's head, Veniamin Malyshev, and a group of nuclear scientists (I. Kurchatov, A. Alikhanov, I. Kikoin and A. Vinogradov) used this opportunity to make a statement about the insanity of nuclear war. A thermonuclear bomb, they wrote, can 'destroy all surface buildings in a city with multimillion population'. Even more dangerous was radioactive contamination and its biological consequences. 'Already in a few years the stockpiles of atomic explosive materials will be enough to create impossible conditions for life all over the globe. . . . So, one cannot deny that the threat of extinction of all life on the Earth has dawned upon mankind.'[81] On 12 March 1954 Malenkov, perhaps under the impact of this memo, publicly stated that a future world war would mean the destruction of world civilization. But at the next plenary meeting Molotov and Khrushchev denounced the speech and Malenkov had to return to traditional line, that a future war would end in destruction of imperialism.[82] In part, this was a result of Kremlin politics: Malenkov's days as a head of state were already numbered. Also, the Stalinist mentality of militarism and the inevitable victory of socialism heavily impregnated the hard core of the party and the armed forces. Several months after Malenkov's speech, Soviet military leaders attended a first military exercise in a radioactive area (a bomb of Hiroshima-type was detonated), and came to conclusions about a possibility of offensive warfare with atomic weapons in Europe.[83] Later, at the Twentieth Party Congress Khrushchev repudiated Stalin's thesis on the inevitability of world wars, but did not mention the nuclear revolution as a reason.

What role did assessments of Western plans and intentions play in the decision-making in the Kremlin? In these years, as well as under Stalin, the Soviet intelligence and information agencies reported to a large extent what the leadership expected to hear. The biggest blind spot in Soviet assessments was the lack of distinction between a threat of pre-emptive, premeditated war and a danger of accidental conflict. Related to this was confusion between operational planning in the West and actual Western plans for war.[84] The change of administration in Washington in January 1953 added to the uncertainty and fear in Moscow. This period became a moment of maximum danger for the Soviet leadership: the decision to launch a peaceful initiative immediately after Stalin's death was dictated in part by the war scare (although most tangible proofs of this are still classified in the archives).

Yearning to find somebody to deal with, Stalin's successors were looking for powers-that-be in Wall Street, in the Chamber of Commerce and even the Council on Foreign Relations.[85] There was little hope in the Kremlin about any accommodation with Dwight Eisenhower: the new president was considered a weak character, and his foreign policy was supposedly under the complete control of Secretary of State John Foster Dulles and other 'resolute enemies of a peaceful settlement of disputed issues'.[86]

The refusal of the United States to have a summit meeting with the new Soviet leaders in 1953 (as proposed by Churchill) was, perhaps, another missed opportunity. When the summit eventually took place in July 1955 in Geneva, Khrushchev had almost consolidated his power and was determined to negotiate with the West from a position of strength. An earlier meeting, at a time when the Soviets were really weak and locked in the crisis of succession, could not perhaps have yielded immediate results, but it might have led to long-term changes of the Soviet mentality – from Stalinist rigidity and militarism towards more advanced concepts of detente, stability and coexistence with the West.

### Conclusion

Today, when the Cold War has come to an end through and because of the global retreat and distingegration of the Soviet Union, the question remains – could it have been prevented, stopped at some early stage, or directed into less virulent forms? For those who believe that the biggest victors in the Cold War were Germany and Japan, American strategies in 1945–55 now look short-sighted – 'prudent, but not wise', to quote US historian Melvyn Leffler.[87] Hence the search for missed opportunities to make a post-war peace with Stalin and his regime. Our research, however, has left us in doubt that such opportunities were really present.

Some Western decisions and reactions might have been different, more balanced. But they mattered little to Soviet foreign policy, whose logic and politics (a political scientist would say 'micro-level') had their own dynamics. Of the three dimensions in Soviet foreign policy (the state, the party and the occupational), the latter two created a powerful momentum towards autarky and aggressive self-isolation.

Stalin's personal impact on Soviet foreign policy was great, his peculiarly dual mind-set as 'a synthesizer . . . of the revolutionary and the traditional'[88] pushed him inexorably up and up in the spiral of confrontation with the West. State relations with the West, despite his early hopes, ground to a halt. American economic might and nuclear monopoly did not make him cautious but, on the contrary, provoked his arrogance and animosity. The interplay between Stalin's personality and imperial politics often produced strange patterns in the Cold-War tapestry. While Stalin was in charge, he certainly could not monitor all dimensions of Soviet foreign policy. When temptations and momentum, generated by party and occupational policies would accumulate, or state policy would reach an obvious deadlock, Stalin would intervene – usually with disastrous consequences.

Typical was his reaction to the Marshall Plan. As the archives indicate, it was not a panicky backlash, spawned by weakness, but the triumph of the party over the state policy in expectation of a shift in the correlation of forces in favour of the Soviet Union. Stalin, who along with Zhdanov expected communist victories in France, Italy and Greece, cast his lot with the Cold War – and failed miserably. The same thing happened in the Far East in 1948–50 when Stalin first under-estimated the potential of the Chinese communists, and then attempted to outbid Mao in promoting the 'national liberation' of South Korea, using the proxy of Kim Il Sung.

Stalin's death and the ensuing political crisis in the Soviet Union often looks like a missed opportunity. It was indeed, in a limited sense, as the United States refused to cultivate bilateral relations with those Soviet leaders who, for different reasons, favoured de-Stalinization in domestic and foreign policies. Still, the scope and motives of Soviet foreign policy remained confrontational; the peaceful entreaties of Moscow were designed as only a temporary retreat. The previous years of the Cold War had already imposed on Stalin's successors a whole range of commit-ments, both imperial and ideological. This was demonstrated by the role of Ulbricht's puppet regime in East Germany. The protection of the socialist GDR, an increasingly dubious asset, became a standing commitment of the Soviet lead-ership, to an extent that later the tail began to wag the dog. In other words, Soviet geo-strategic concerns were distorted by their imperial/socialist obligations.

All these factors, except for the unique one, Stalin, have surprisingly many parallels in American behaviour during the same and subsequent stages of the Cold War. Although this remarkable parallelism bears only remotely on the causes, meaning and outcome of the Cold War, it might shed some light on its dynamics and exhausting durability.

### Bibliographical note

The bulk of Western literature on Soviet foreign policy, 1945–55, consists of American books, most of which share in the traditional interpretation of Cold War origins and dynamics. For a general survey of Soviet foreign policy and its domestic origins see Robert V. Daniels, *Russia: the Roots of Confrontation* (Cambridge, MA, 1985). A provocative but largely intuitive interpretation is Adam Ulam, *Expansion and Coexistence: Soviet Foreign Policy, 1917–73* (2nd ed., New York, 1974). On the evolution of Stalin's diplomacy see William Taubman, *Stalin's American Policy: from Entente to Detente to Cold War* (New York, 1982). For Stalin's personal impact on Soviet policymaking, read Walter Laqueur, *Stalin: The Glasnost Revelations* (New York, 1990). There is also the biography by Dmitri Volkogonov, *Stalin: Triumph and Tragedy*, ed. and transl. by Harold Shukman (London, 1991).

On the theoretical side one can consult Allen Lynch, *The Soviet Study of International Relations* (New York, 1987); Margot Light, *The Soviet Theory of International Relations* (Brighton, England, 1988); and Jack Snyder, *Myths of the Empire: Domestic Politics and International Ambition* (Ithaca NY, 1991). For general surveys see Walter LaFeber, *America, Russia and the Cold War, 1945–1989* (6th ed., New York, 1990); John L. Gaddis, *Russia, the Soviet Union and the United States: An Interpretive History* (2nd ed., New York, 1990); and two essays on the dynamics of the Cold War reprinted in Arthur M. Schlesinger, Jr., *The Cycles of American History* (Boston, 1986), ch. 8.

Some detailed studies look at the party and occupation dimensions in Soviet conduct, among them Vojtech Mastny, *Russia's Road to the Cold War: Diplomacy, Warfare, and the Politics of Communism, 1941–1945* (New York, 1979); William McCagg, *Stalin Embattled, 1943–1948* (Detroit, 1978); Gavriel Ra'anan, *International Policy Formation in the USSR: Factional 'Debates' during the Zhdanovschina* (Hamden CT, 1983); and James Richter, 'Reexamining Soviet policy towards Germany in 1953', *Europe – Asia Studies*, vol. 45, no. 4 (1993), 671–91. It should be noted, however, that such studies suffered until recently from the absence of substantial hard data and McCagg's arguments about Stalin are often misleading. On military matters David Holloway, *The Soviet Union and the Arms Race* (New Haven, 1983), is still the best source. His forthcoming book about Soviet nuclear developments promises to be a breakthrough in this murky area.

For recent Russian interpretations of the Soviet side of the Cold War, see Georgi Kornienko, 'U istokov kholodnoi voini' (At the Roots of the Cold War), *Novaya i Noveishaya Istoriya* (Moscow), 1990, no. 6, pp. 105–22; Vladislav Zubok, 'Esche raz o proiskhozhdenii kholodnoi voini' (The Origins of the Cold War revisited), in *USA: Economics, Politics, Ideology* (Moscow), 1991, no. 4; and Constantine Pleshakov, 'Joseph Stalin's World View' in Thomas G. Paterson & Robert J. McMahon, eds., *The Origins of the Cold War* (Lexington, MA, 1991), pp. 60–72. On the succession crisis after Stalin's death see L.A. Openkin, *Ottepel: kak eto bilo* (The Thaw: How It Happened), (Moscow, 1991).

Glasnost, as we noted earlier, did not precipitate an avalanche of revelations. For memoirs of interest see Jerrold Schechter & Vyacheslav Luchkov, eds., *Khrushchev Remembers: The Glasnost Tapes* (Boston, 1990); 'Vospominaniya Nikiti Sergeevicha Khrushcheva' (The Memoirs of N. S. Khrushchev), ongoing in *Voprosi Istorii*, 1991– ; *Sto sorok besed s Molotovym: Iz dnevnika F. Chuyeva* (140 conversations with Molotov) (Moscow, 1991); and Vladimir Yerofeev, 'Ten Years of Secretary-ship in the Foreign Commissariat', *International Affairs* (Moscow), 1991, nos. 8–9.

Collections of new archival revelations have not yet been published, although appearance of the so-called 'Novikov Telegram' in *Diplomatic History*, 15 (Fall 1991) produced a flurry of comment. Another interesting document is the party discussion in July 1953 of the German question and other diplomatic issues published in D. N. Stickle, ed., *The Beria Affair* (New York, 1992). For archival updates consult the *Cold War International History Project Bulletin*, from the Woodrow Wilson Center, Washington, D.C.

# PART TWO

# THE OTHER TWO

## 3  *Great Britain*

### DAVID REYNOLDS

'The Cold War has dominated American life since 1945', wrote historian Walter LaFeber in 1980.[1] As Anders Stephanson has shown (chapter 1), it also dominated the study of US foreign policy. In Britain, by contrast, it attracted much less attention from historians. D.C. Watt could write in 1978 that 'so far . . . there has been little or no serious writing on the Cold War in Britain'.[2] Instead, the story of post-war attitudes to the USSR and communism in general was usually treated as one facet of a larger problem, the dilemmas of Britain as a world power. Two distinguished overviews of post-war British foreign policy published in the mid-1970s illustrate this point well. For Joseph Frankel, 'Britain's postwar foreign policy is conceived of as the final phase of a long-drawn-out process of adjustment to a position of gradually decreasing power, which, in the main, consisted of the withdrawal from exposed positions in the world and of the acceptance of interdependence with Western Europe.'[3] Likewise, F.S. Northedge in 1974 considered that in the previous thirty years 'the most striking fact is, of course, the decline of British power continuously over that period', leaving Britain ready for 'a new start' within the European Community.[4] The Cold War was therefore seen as only one of the challenges to that crumbling global position, albeit of salient importance. In the words of diplomat Gladwyn Jebb in a lecture in February 1950: 'the phrase "cold war" so far as we are concerned, really involves the whole question of the maintenance of the United Kingdom's position in the world, and can therefore in the long run be equated with our general foreign policy.'[5]

There was, however, one main exception to this lack of attention. The attitude of the Labour party in the 1940s and 1950s towards the Cold War did attract some scholarly scrutiny. Following the election of July 1945, Clement Attlee formed Labour's first-ever majority government. Re-elected with reduced support in February 1950, it soldiered on until October 1951, when Winston Churchill and Conservatives were returned to power. In the inter-war years the two parties had exhibited significant differences in attitude towards the Soviet Union. Under Ramsay MacDonald, Labour extended diplomatic recognition in 1924 and resumed it again in 1929 after the Tories had broken off relations in 1927 over Soviet espionage activities. During the Second World War there had been considerable public sympathy for the Russian war effort and, on the left, suspicion of American capitalism. But the dominant figure in British diplomacy after the war was Ernest

Bevin, the burly former union leader who was Attlee's Foreign Secretary until March 1951. Bevin's distrust of communism was rooted in long battles to block their penetration of the labour movement. In 1937 he told the Soviet Ambassador in London: 'you have built up the Soviet Union and you have the right to defend it. I have built up the Transport Union and if you try to break it, I'll fight you – and fight to the death.'[6] The increasingly anti-communist and anti-Soviet stance taken by Bevin aroused vociferous dissent at times from the left wing of his party, who voiced aspirations for a 'third force' role between the United States and the Soviet Union. These battles were the subject of studies that appeared in the 1950s, although, significantly, they were the work of American rather than British scholars.[7]

It was not until the late 1970s that British work on the Cold War began in earnest. Two developments precipitated this. The first was the gradual opening of the archives for the post-war period from 1975 under the thirty-year rule. Over the following decade British policy for the years 1945 to 1955 became accessible to historians. The British were therefore lagging well behind American documents, both in time (some five years on average) and in availability, since a full selection of the relevant papers was published in the *Foreign Relations of the United States* series. This enabled US scholars more easily to examine their own diplomatic record, thus stimulating revisionist writing. And it was the wave of American revisionism which provided a second spur to British scholarship. Because the Cold War touched so much of American life, the debate about it was passionate and pervasive, akin to that over appeasement in Britain during and after the 1930s. As suggested by D.C. Watt – here, as on other aspects of research into British foreign policy, a stimulus to new lines of thought – British historians were in a position to offer a somewhat detached view on these matters, drawing upon the new British evidence.[8] More generally, the British materials offered a counterweight to an essentially American-centred view of the Cold War. They exposed its European dimension[9] and underlined the active role played by the Europeans, particularly Britain, in shaping Cold War Europe in the 1940s.

Perhaps the principal theme established by the new scholarship of the 1980s was the persistence of Britain's power. Preoccupations in the 1960s and 1970s with British decline – summed up in Dean Acheson's notorious epitaph that 'Great Britain has lost an empire and has not yet found a role'[10] – tended to obscure this fundamental point. In 1951, Britain, retaining conscription since the war, had over 827,000 men under arms. It was the leading economy of Europe, manufacturing as much as France and West Germany combined. It produced nearly a third of the manufacturing output of non-communist Europe as a whole and more weapons than all the other European NATO partners. In 1952 it became the world's third nuclear power, nearly eight years ahead of France.[11] Moreover, the abandonment of the Indian empire in 1947 and of Palestine in 1948 should not distract attention from the continuance of British imperialism in the Middle East. The British sought new treaty relations with important clients such as Iraq and Egypt, trying to preserve essential economic and defence interests without the formal burdens of empire. In countries such as Malaya and the Gold Coast they made unprecedented efforts to exploit neglected natural resources. And the wartime sterling area, formed by countries particularly reliant on London for their trade and financial services, was perpetuated into the post-war era as the main framework for British economic policy and for rebuilding Britain's position against the almighty dollar. Thus, globally, as in Europe, Britain remained a major force immediately after the war.[12] The fragility of that position in the longer term should not blind us to its reality in the 1940s if we wish to understand the British role in shaping the Cold War.

This representation of Britain as a residual world power helps throw new light on its relations with the United States. This has proved an especially fertile field for new scholarship, both British and American, in studies of wartime and post-war diplomacy. Penetrating beyond the mythology of the 'special relationship', they have exposed the ambivalence of the alliance. In Christopher Thorne's punning title, the two countries were 'allies of a kind' – in some ways remarkably similar in interests and values yet always partial in mutual allegiance and affinities.[13] In a positive sense, Britain, as the other leading non-communist power, mattered particularly to the United States. Aside from shared democratic principles, British power was valuable in the containment of communism, both in Europe and, through the bases and resources of the empire, around the world. In 1951 Paul Nitze of the Policy Planning Staff had no hesitation in using the term 'special relationship' in State Department discussions about US policy towards Britain.[14] Viewed negatively, however, Britain was in some respects a powerful obstacle to American policy. US opposition to the sterling area and British doubts about rapid trade liberalization in the face of American economic hegemony were issues of continuing controversy. More significant for the Cold War was the growing divergence from 1949 over the handling of communism in Asia, particularly policy towards Mao's China, the Korean War and, in 1954, Indo-China.

In this work, Britain is therefore depicted as still a world power in the 1940s and as an important but by no means compliant ally of the United States. These themes assume particular significance when one takes seriously the evidence about the incremental development of American Cold-War policy.[15] The equivocations of the Truman Administration in 1945 and its slowness in converting anxiety into action in 1946 all point to 1947 as the crucial period in which an American policy of containment emerged, with the Truman Doctrine in March and the Marshall Plan proposal in June. Here Washington's new sense of the limits of British economic power in the economic crisis of early 1947 was an important stimulus. Even so, the United States was making unprecedented commitments in an area where it had scant experience, against the background of continued domestic doubts about the abandonment of historic traditions of non-entanglement in Europe. The British could therefore make important contributions in firming up the Marshall Plan and in creating the Atlantic alliance.

This approach to the origins of Cold-War Europe was given its most prominent and widely-disseminated expression in the last volume of Lord Bullock's biography of Bevin, dealing with his foreign secretaryship.[16] This vast study, published in 1983, constituted the fullest archivally-based account to date of the evolution of British Cold-War policy. Inevitably, it focused on Bevin's role, both because it was biographical in scope and because it relied almost entirely on Bevin's own private office papers. Research of a more specific nature by younger scholars, using Foreign Office General Political Correspondence and the files of other government departments, has naturally made Bevin seem less olympian. The influence of his senior officials and their interplay with other interested Whitehall actors, especially the Chiefs of Staff and the Treasury, has attracted attention. Moreover, Clement Attlee, who mounted a remarkable challenge to Bevin and the military over Cold-War confrontation in the Mediterranean in 1946, has emerged from the shadows as a much less passive prime minister than conventionally thought.[17]

This detailed research is still in progress and our understanding of who made British foreign policy will surely become more complex. But, even if the cast list is gradually enlarged, the British presence on the Cold-War stage has now been firmly established. What follows is an indication of where recent historiography has suggested that Britain made a particular contribution to the drama of polarization.

### Forcing the pace, 1945–7

The thrust of this new work on the period 1945–7 is that it was Britain, as much as, if not more than, the United States which forced the pace towards confrontation with the Soviet Union. Churchill's objective since 1941 had been continued 'Big Three' co-operation in the interests of world peace. To that end he tried to agree spheres of influence with Stalin at Moscow in October 1944, over the Balkans (the famous 'percentages' deal), and at Yalta in February 1945, over Eastern Europe. The problem was to prevent a legitimate Soviet sphere of influence becoming a closed Stalinist bloc. Although Churchill left Yalta hopeful of success, the fears that haunted him at various times during the war returned with new force that spring as Stalin showed that his understanding of terms such as 'democratic' and 'anti-fascist' was very different from that of House of Commons. In May 1945 Churchill was warning Truman sombrely that an 'iron curtain is drawn down upon their front'.[18]

Churchill's volatility was a reflection of the oscillating weights of his ideological fears of communism, on the one hand, and faith in his powers of personal diplomacy, on the other. More consistent were the Chiefs of Staff and their military advisers, who, from 1943, had taken a gloomy view of Soviet policy. In July 1944 they warned the Foreign Office (FO) that although 'the immediate object . . . must be the keeping down of Germany . . . we feel that the more remote, but more dangerous, possibility of a hostile Russia making use of the resources of Germany must not be lost sight of'. The FO deprecated the military's tendency 'to regard the Soviet Union as a *potential* enemy', and the issue was not aired outside Whitehall.[19] But the Chiefs' attitudes were a reminder that, whatever the views of the Labour left, anti-Soviet feeling was a durable element in British military thought. It embodied two strains: historic fears about a Russian threat to the security of India, with Persia (Iran) a recurrent anxiety, coupled with a post-1917 anxiety about the Bolshevik menace. Whereas American relations with Russia before 1941 were characterized by aloofness and independence,[20] Britain's showed a history of persistent friction over more than a hundred and fifty years.

Churchill's successors, Attlee and particularly Bevin, shared his distaste for communism and his concern to perpetuate Britain's great-power role. In the second half of 1945, Bevin and his officials were unhappy about American acquiescence in the new communist governments in Poland, Bulgaria and Romania, but there was little that they could do. Truman's emissary, Harry Hopkins, settled the Polish issue on his visit to Moscow in June and Secretary of State James F. Byrnes finessed the composition of the Bulgarian and Romanian governments at the Moscow Foreign Ministers Conference in December. In both cases the British were largely bystanders. In two other areas, however – the Near East and Germany – British policy was more effectual.

The crescent from Egypt and the Suez Canal through Palestine to Iran was of no vital interest to the United States, even though America's oil stake in the region had increased in the war. For Britain, by contrast, this was the hinge of empire and the source of vital oil. Communist influence in key countries and the presence of the Red Navy in the Mediterranean would be alarming developments. This was the reason for the determined support given by both the Churchill and Attlee governments to anti-communist forces in the Greek civil war and for Whitehall's alarm at Soviet demands in 1945 for an international trusteeship in Tripolitania, part of Italy's former North African empire. After the London Foreign Ministers Conference in September 1945, Bevin's private secretary, Pierson Dixon, warned that 'the main objective of the Russians is access to and a base in the Mediterranean'. Although his seniors felt that this was too strong, they agreed that the Russians were playing a complex bargaining game around Europe which required a firm British line at every point. But at this stage, in the autumn of 1945, the uneasy consensus among Bevin and his staff was that 'the Russians still wish to collaborate with the Western Powers in the post-war problems'.[21]

Official FO thinking about the Soviet Union shifted substantially in 1946, towards the views long espoused by the Chiefs of Staff. Stimuli for this change in outlook were the cumulative effects of Soviet actions in Europe and the Near East and the new campaign of anti-capitalist propaganda emanating from Moscow in early 1946 which was directed particularly at Britain. The result was a new FO Russia Committee to monitor Soviet conduct and publicity, which henceforth became the focus for hardliners. The shapers of this new view were Frank Roberts, the British Minister in Moscow, who sent his own series of 'long telegrams' to London along lines similar to those conveyed by his American counterpart and friend, George Kennan, to Washington. On 17 March Roberts warned that 'Soviet security had become hard to distinguish from Soviet imperialism and it is becoming uncertain whether there is, in fact, any limit to Soviet expansion'.[22] Even more influential was the chairman of the new Russia Committee and head of the FO's Northern Department, Christopher Warner, whose memorandum of 2 April 1946, 'The Soviet Campaign against this Country and our Response to it', has been described as 'undoubtedly a key Cold War document which goes further than Kennan's memorandum of February [the "Long Telegram"]'.[23] Warner concluded that 'the Soviet Government, both in their recent pronouncements and in their actions, have made it clear that they have decided upon an aggressive policy, based upon militant Communism and Russian chauvinism. . . . The Soviet Government makes coordinated use of military, economic, propaganda and political weapons and also of the Communist "religion". It is submitted, therefore, that we must at once organise and coordinate our defences against all these and that we should not stop short of a defensive-offensive policy.'[24]

At this stage, FO officials were ahead of Bevin, who was still anxious to avoid a total rupture with the Soviet Union. They were also concerned about the apparent softness of American policy on the Near East, even though, in private, Pentagon planning papers were now emphasizing the importance of the British empire to the strategic interests of the United States.[25] It has been suggested that the failure of the Soviets to withdraw on time from Iran in early 1946, coupled with Churchill's Iron Curtain speech at Fulton in March, can be 'reasonably seen as the beginning of the cold War' because it resulted in new, collaborative policy of toughness by London and Washington.[26] But this is probably to exaggerate the significance of both Churchill's speech and the Iranian crisis in realigning American policy. The central Cold-War battleground was not the Near East but Germany. Here British policy was of particular importance.

At Potsdam in the summer of 1945, the Allies had agreed to a four-power occupation of Germany until a peace treaty could be determined. In principle, Germany was to be treated 'as a single economic unit', with decisions taken jointly in the Allied Control Commission. Soviet demands for reparations from the industrial zones of the west were to be offset by provision of food and raw materials by the Soviets from their largely agricultural zone. However, such an agreement depended for its operation on mutual trust, which from the first was lacking. Moreover, although formally stating the principles of German unity, the agreement was largely a spheres-of-influence arrangement, which left each power with a free hand in its zone.

The Soviets plundered their own zone and failed to provide primary products for the West. With the Soviet Union and France fearful of German resurgence, the Allies could not agree on appropriate production levels for German industry. Consequently, Germany was unable to pay for its own imports and Britain was left to feed its zone, the ravaged Ruhr, on grain bought with scarce dollars loaned by the United States for British reconstruction. In 1946 Britain provided 70 per cent of the food requirements of its zone of Germany. Such a situation clearly could not go on indefinitely. The new mood in the FO by the spring of 1946 prompted a reconsideration of the German stalemate. Primed by his advisers, Bevin presented a paper to the Cabinet on 3 May suggesting consideration of the 'Western' option, by which he meant consolidating the British or Western zones as a single economic unit to rebuild industry and counter incipient economic crisis. Although this ploy would confirm the Iron Curtain, it would at least ensure that communism stopped at the Elbe. This document has been called 'the primary source of Britain's containment policy'.[27]

The Cabinet did not formally adopt it in May. One reason was doubts about such an overt and irrevocable anti-Soviet démarche. But it was also acknowledged by the FO that the 'Americans are probably not ready for this' and that 'full American support would be essential'.[28] That support came on 11 July, during the Paris meeting of foreign ministers, when Byrnes offered to join the American zone with that of any other occupying power. This announcement, breaching Potsdam and presaging the Anglo–American 'Bizone' of January 1947, was of seminal importance in formalizing both the Cold War and the division of Germany. But it came in response to Bevin's own decision to bring matters to a head by announcing on the previous day, 10 July, that, in the absence of Allied reciprocity in implementing the Potsdam protocol, the British would 'be compelled to organize the British Zone of Occupation in Germany in such a manner that no further liability shall fall on the British taxpayer'.[29]

Recent work therefore presents British policy in 1945–6 as more assertive and more influential than previously understood. The British were not simply clinging to Uncle Sam's coat-tails. On the other hand, much of this work is an attempt to expose the riches of the British archives rather than a fusion of British and American sources. In due course, synthetic studies may portray Western démarches as symbioses of the two countries' policies rather than the result of one or other taking the lead. Furthermore, we should remember that, if the British were forcing the pace, it was out of growing desperation. In the Mediterranean and in Central Europe Britain's deepening economic problems meant that what the FO regarded as essential interests could no longer be preserved unaided.

### Dividing the continent, 1947

By 1947 Britain faced a grave balance of payments crisis. A post-war US loan of $3.75 billion was being consumed, the Treasury warned, 'at a reckless, and ever-accelerating speed'.[30] The root problem was the range of overseas commitments left over from the War. Failure to agree on post-war peace terms meant that the Government had to retain large occupation forces around Europe and Asia. At the same time it was struggling against anti-colonial insurgencies, especially in Palestine and India. This conjunction of Cold War and colonial crises meant that the armed forces could not be demobilized with the desired speed. Not only did foreign commitments absorb scarce foreign exchange directly, they also meant that manpower could not be redeployed in industry to increase exports and therefore help balance Britain's trade. The Treasury, under Chancellor Hugh Dalton, spoke out vigorously against 'paying reparations to Germany' and on subsidizing anti-communists in Greece. But what brought matters to a head was the appalling winter of early 1947, worse than any since 1881. Freezing cold and heavy blizzards brought transport, industry and the coal mines to a virtual halt for several weeks. Manufacturing output in February was 25 per cent down on January's figure, itself far worse than the previous autumn. In the middle of the month an exhausted Cabinet was forced to make a series of fateful decisions. In addition, to throwing in the towel over India and Palestine, it confirmed that Britain would terminate aid to Greece and Turkey by the end of March.

This was essentially a financial decision, taken amid crisis against the preferences of Bevin and the Chiefs of Staff. It would be wrong to see it as a calculated ploy to call in the New World to redress the balance of the Old. In fact the Pentagon and

State Department were already preparing for an enhanced American role in the Mediterranean in the winter of 1946–7.[31] Nevertheless, there is little doubt that the British notes, informing the State Department of this decision on Greece and Turkey, which were delivered on 21 February 1947, did force the Truman Administration to face the issue in public as an urgent political problem. And given the reluctance of Congress to assume foreign burdens and to pull Britain's chestnuts out of the fire, it seemed important to Truman to pose the issue in apocalyptic terms – not just the $400 million in aid to some faraway countries in the Near East but the future of a world teetering between two ways of life, 'freedom' and 'totalitarianism'. Thus the British abandonment of Greece and Turkey did not by itself force a change of policy, so much as accelerate an evolution already taking place. But it did help prompt an articulation of American policy in the starkest terms (the Truman Doctrine of 12 March), conjuring up images of global bipolarity not yet in accordance with events. And, in a more general sense, the British decision to pull out of Greece and Turkey was seen as symptomatic of Britain's inability to play its supposed historic role as the balancer of Europe. 'Was the U.S. ready to take its place?' asked *Time* magazine.[32] The economic crisis in Europe, exacerbated by the grim winter, together with the growing appeal of communism and the perceived limits of British power all conspired to precipitate the State Department policy review that led to Secretary George Marshall's offer on 5 June of a comprehensive aid package for Europe.

Thus, the Truman Doctrine and the Marshall Plan both grew out of a complex of events in which the American perception of British *weakness* was a salient factor. Nevertheless, the recent scholarship on British policy highlights the part played by Bevin and his advisers in making concrete the new American policy. At the end of July 1947 one State Department official likened the Marshall Plan to a 'flying saucer' in the sense that 'nobody knows what it looks like, how big it is, in what direction it is moving, or whether it really exists.'[33] Bevin helped bring it down to earth, although the story that he, virtually alone in London, appreciated the significance of Marshall's speech, thanks to a BBC radio report, is an exaggeration (the State Department had already prepared the British embassy in Washington).[34] But Bevin undoubtedly played a leading role, in Bullock's words, in 'conjuring up a European response of sufficient weight and urgency to give substance' to Marshall's offer.[35] Working closely with the French he created the forum in Paris for joint European discussions and also carefully ensured that Stalin did not, yet again, obstruct European recovery. His insistence that, as Marshall had requested, the Europeans propose a joint programme rather than send in separate national shopping lists was the stumbling bloc for the Soviets and they withdrew from further discussions. This outcome undoubtedly accorded with the predilections of most US policy-makers,[36] but they were not involved in the initial Paris discussions in late June and the parting of the ways was largely the upshot of Bevin's diplomacy.

As the Soviet Foreign Minister, Vyacheslav Molotov, rejected the Anglo–French proposals, Bevin whispered to his private secretary, 'this really is the birth of the Western bloc'.[37] This was true in part because Stalin ensured that none of the

Eastern European states within his sphere of influence participated in the discussions, despite the evident interest of the Poles, Hungarians and others. Marshall's offer and Bevin's packaging of it helped confirm the emerging division of Europe. But in the West, too, the process of consolidation now began to advance. An important line of research, developed particularly by John W. Young, has shown that in 1946–7 Bevin and his officials were genuinely keen to promote Western European co-operation, with Britain taking the lead. It was not simply a device to convince the Americans that Europe was worth supporting ('a sprat to catch the mackerel', in Bevin's notorious phrase).[38] In early 1947 Bevin and the FO negotiated the Anglo-French treaty of Dunkirk, signed in March, and were taking seriously the idea of a customs union with France. The precise import of the treaty is a matter of dispute,[39] and the customs union idea fell foul of intense opposition from the Treasury and the Board of Trade. Nevertheless, the vitality of this debate about European cooperation in Whitehall in 1946–7 reveals fundamental British uncertainty as to just how far the United States could be relied upon to support Britain as relations with the Soviet Union deteriorated. As Sir Orme Sargent, Permanent Under-Secretary at the FO, observed in October 1945, if America and Russia were going their own ways, 'it behoves us all the more to strengthen our own world position vis-à-vis of our two great allied rivals by building up ourselves as *the* great European power. This brings us back to the policy of collaboration with France.'[40]

Marshall's 1947 offer of aid, though welcome, did not by itself revolutionize the situation. British policy-makers were well used to the vagaries of American politics and had ingrained memories of the 'isolationism' of the 1930s. It should also be remembered that, although Marshall's speech was delivered in June 1947, it was not until April 1948 that the recovery program became law and appropriations were authorized. By this time, Bevin had finally come into the open about accepting the division of Europe and the creation of a Western bloc. Although pressed on this by the FO's Russia Committee for months, he had tried to maintain a framework of negotiation with Moscow and, even in the spring of 1947, he was trying to negotiate a new Anglo-Soviet treaty of alliance. As late as December 1947 he could still remark that 'he doubted whether Russia was as great a danger as a resurgent Germany might become'.[41] It was 'not until after the creation of Cominform in October, and more particularly the failure of the November Council of Foreign Ministers that Bevin, and with him the Cabinet, moved to the position long held by the Russia Committee'.[42] In the New Year, Bevin told the Cabinet that 'the conflict is between the Soviet desire to dominate Europe politically and economically and the desire of the three western powers to put Europe back on its feet again with American backing'. The aim of British policy should now be 'to reinforce the physical barriers which still guard our Western civilisation' and to 'organise and consolidate the ethical and spiritual forces inherent in this Western civilisation of which we are the chief protagonists. This in my view can only be done by creating some form of union in Western Europe, whether of a formal or informal character, backed by America and the Dominions.'[43] On 22 January 1948 Bevin went public on his plan for 'Western Union' to the Commons and thence to the world.

*Forging an alliance, 1947–9*

Bevin's initiative led eventually, in March 1948, to the creation of the Brussels Pact – an alliance between Britain, France and the Benelux countries. Over the next year this became subsumed in the North Atlantic alliance, concluded by treaty in Washington in April 1949, which linked Western Europe with the United States and Canada. More than anything else the Atlantic alliance represented 'a latter-day American revolution',[44] precipitated by fundamental changes in the American view of itself and its international responsibilities. Nevertheless, the new writing on British foreign policy in the period has again highlighted Britain's contribution to this reordering of Europe.

Of particular interest is the changing British attitude to European integration. FO ideas had always been couched in intergovernmental rather than supranational terms – co-operation between sovereign states rather than incorporation in a quasi-federal grouping – but, as we have seen, these ideas were advanced quite genuinely in 1946–7. Moreover, in the spring of 1948 Bevin envisaged the Brussels Pact as including economic, social and cultural co-operation, and not merely military support.[45] But by now the need to draw in the Americans was assuming ever-greater urgency as the European scene darkened. The Czech coup in February, alarm about Soviet pressure on Scandinavia in the spring, the Italian elections in April and, most of all, the onset of the Berlin blockade in June made it clear that the Europeans could not ensure their security unaided. The atmosphere in London that spring, as in other Western capitals, was apocalyptic. In a paper drafted by Gladwyn Jebb, Bevin warned the Cabinet: 'It has really become a matter of the defence of western civilisation, or everything will be swamped by this Soviet method of infiltration. . . . [P]hysical control of the Eurasian land mass and eventual control of the whole World Island is what the Politburo is aiming at – no less a thing than that.'[46]

As the sense of European weakness become more acute in London, so the evolution of policy in Washington gave hope of an unprecedented American commitment to European security – of a sort undreamt of by British diplomats brought up on inter-war cynicism about American isolationism. By January 1949 an inter-departmental committee, dominated by the FO and Treasury, set clear limits on Britain's future interest in European co-operation:

Since post-war planning began, our policy has been to secure close political, military and economic co-operation with the U.S.A. This has been necessary to get economic aid. It will always be decisive for our security. The means to this is now the Atlantic Pact. We hope to secure a special relationship with U.S.A. and Canada within this, for in the last resort we cannot rely upon the European countries. . . . Our policy should be to assist Europe to recover as far as we can. . . . But the concept must be one of limited liability. In no circumstances must we assist them beyond the point at which the assistance leaves us too weak to be a worth-while ally for U.S.A. if Europe collapsed – i.e. beyond the point at which our own viability was impaired.[47]

This was the criterion on which the British judged proposals for European co-operation for the next few years. Its implications for the future ordering of Western Europe were far-reaching.

In 1947 the Americans had taken the lead in the economic reconstruction of Europe, but the British had helped direct the new American initiative. The same happened in 1948 in the security sphere. A case in point was the shaping of policy in the early days of the Berlin blockade. Avi Shlaim has argued that at first, when US policy was indecisive, Bevin and the Cabinet took the initiative in announcing their determination to stay in Berlin. They also identified the airlift option as the best way to keep the city supplied. Not only was Britain not 'a mere appendage to the United States,' says Shlaim, 'it was consistently more "hawkish" about Berlin than its senior partner – more resolute in facing the Soviet challenge head-on, less open to bargaining and compromise, and more willing to accept risks, including the risk of nuclear war'.[48]

A similar pattern emerges from research on the origins of NATO. As a young diplomat, Sir Nicholas Henderson was a member of the international working party that drafted the treaty. His memoir of the negotiations, written in 1949 but not published until 1982, attacks the view that the Americans were 'the instigators of the North Atlantic Treaty' and argues that 'if one person was responsible at the time for canalizing the mood of Western Europe into the idea of the Treaty, this was Ernest Bevin'.[49] Once the archives had been opened, scholarly attention shifted from the US Senate debates about the treaty to the secret Anglo-American-Canadian discussions at the Pentagon at the end of March 1948, at which the essential shape of the treaty was defined. The British differed with the Americans at two important points. They wanted the treaty to embody an automatic commitment to offer military assistance if any member were attacked. At the insistence of the American delegation, however, subsequently confirmed by the Senate, article five of the treaty left it up to each signatory to define the form of aid it would offer. This preserved for the American Congress the right to declare war. Secondly, Bevin initially wanted the pact to cover only those states bordering on the Atlantic Ocean. He dropped that requirement quickly but remained particularly opposed to Italian membership, commenting: 'I am doubtful regarding the propriety of including this Mediterranean country in an "Atlantic" system.'[50] The British were primarily concerned about the Rhine and did not want the pact to be over-stretched. The Americans over-ruled this, deeming it politically essential to include Italy in view of the communist challenge there, but Bevin did successfully exclude Franco's Spain from the list of those invited to accede.

### Living with Germany, 1949–54

The North Atlantic Treaty of April 1949 represented a further stage in the evolution of America's containment policy. First by economic means (the Marshall Plan) and then by a mutual defence pact (the NAT), the United States was seeking to bolster Western European ability to resist communism and a possible Soviet military threat. The implication of this policy, however, was that the former enemy, Germany, was being built up as a potential ally. In 1947 its economic recovery was central to the philosophy of the Marshall Plan; in 1948–9 its political re-emergence was an integral part of American policy. And after the Korean War began, its revival as a military power became a basic American requirement in return for turning the Atlantic pact into a real military alliance. For the British, this trend was less alarming than for the French, but the issue of German resurgence did exercise the Labour Cabinet and party from 1948. And the French supranationalist response to the problem forced the British to clarify their attitude to European integration. Both these themes have attracted recent scholarly attention.

Bevin's concept of a 'Western bloc', to salvage as much of Europe as possible from Soviet influence, implied a reconstituted German state. His major Cabinet papers of January 1948 made that clear. The one on policy in Germany called (prophetically) for the establishment in the Western zones of 'a political and economic system to join which the Germans in the Eastern Zone will exert all their energy, and which will in the end prevail over the standards and system established in the Soviet Zone'.[51] British support for what became the Federal German Republic was clearly implied in this statement and over the next year Bevin worked with the Americans towards this end.

More problematic, however, for the Labour Government was the degree of sovereignty enjoyed by this new state. Some Ministers argued that Germany was now an essential bulwark against Soviet expansion and that it should be strengthened in every possible way, including rearmament. In the words of the left-winger Aneurin Bevan: 'we ought to build them up as much as we could. They were a better barrier against Communism than the French.' Similar views were expressed by Lord Pakenham and Sir Stafford Cripps. Hugh Dalton, however, was fearful of rebuilding Germany, and Attlee shared his doubts: 'The policy of using Satan to defeat Sin is very dangerous. This was just the illusion that the Tories had over Fascism and Nazism.' Bevin's own views were closer to the latter group. He believed in German economic recovery but was sympathetic to French fears and did not want to see a strong Germany in the heart of Europe.[52]

The new West German state that was founded in September 1949 was still under ultimate Allied control. Its rearmament, though now a goal of Pentagon policy, was not yet practical Alliance politics, given the fears of the French and British. The British Chiefs of Staff recognized that a serious Alliance defence strategy west of the Elbe would require a substantial German contribution, but they shared the FO's desire to avoid facing that issue for the moment. It could divide the Alliance and antagonize the Russians. A first step should be the formation of an armed police force, to match that in the Soviet zone. The Whitehall consensus, as expressed in the FO in December 1949, was to concentrate on rebuilding France while seeking so 'to entangle Germany economically and politically in Western Europe as to make it difficult for her to switch to an alliance with Russia'.[53] The Rapallo treaty of 1922 and the Nazi-Soviet pact of 1939 cast long shadows.

The outbreak of the Korean War in June 1950 changed the situation. Fearful that this presaged Soviet aggression in Europe, the Americans moved rapidly to 'put the "O" in NATO', in Averell Harriman's phrase – turning a loose defence pact into a co-ordinated military alliance, under American command and reinforced by American combat troops.[54] The quid pro quo demanded for this American action was increased European defence spending and acceptance of German rearmament.

Bevin had no choice but to acquiesce in New York in September. It was also clear that proposals for an armed police force would not satisfy the Americans. It was at this point that the form of German rearmament became the essential issue. And in the ensuing international debate British views towards European integration were crystallized.

Unable to keep Germany down, the French had been forced to modify their post-war strategy. 'If you can't beat them, join them', was in effect the philosophy behind both the Schuman and Pleven Plans, masterminded by Jean Monnet. Faced with a resurgent Germany and mindful of three ruinous Franco–German wars over the previous three-quarters of a century, Monnet argued that national sovereignty was no longer effectual. Better to sacrifice an element of French sovereignty if the Germans did the same, thereby reducing their ability to use national resources to make war. In addition, German industrial resources would be available for the French modernization plan. These were the ideas behind the proposal for a European Coal and Steel Community (ECSC), advanced in May 1950 by Schuman. They were also applied to German rearmament in October (the Pleven Plan) for a multinational European army, so that the new German armed forces would not be under direct German control.

Labour was deeply divided over German rearmament. Although acquiescing in principle, a significant part of the Cabinet shared Attlee's wish for 'this whole thing to be played very slow'.[55] They were helped by initial US uncertainty, but, by the summer of 1951, American support for the idea was clear and the Labour Government was obliged to clarify its own position. In September 1951, in the dying days of the Attlee Government, Foreign Secretary Herbert Morrison welcomed the EDC 'as a very important contribution to the effective Defence of Europe, including Germany', but made clear that Britain would not become a full member, although it sought 'the closest possible association with the European continental community at all stages of its development'.[56] This was much the same philosophy as had been adopted towards the embryonic ECSC.

In the ebb and flow of subsequent continental debate about the EDC, the British position remained essentially as Morrison had stated it. His policy was carried on by his Conservative successor, Anthony Eden.[57] Underlying it were the principles of a transatlantic special relationship and of 'limited liability' on the Continent which had been articulated in January 1949 and reaffirmed frequently thereafter. When the French Assembly finally rejected the EDC in August 1954, in part because of lack of British support, it was Eden who crafted an alternative framework for German rearmament, using the Brussels Pact of 1948. This should not be regarded as a sudden bright idea dreamt up by Eden in the bath, as he claimed in his memoirs.[58] Rather it stands in clear continuity with the trend of British Cold-War policy since Bevin came out with his 'Western' option in 1948. Britain wanted closer European co-operation in the face of the threats of communism and Soviet power. But it believed that this would have to be linked to US support. And it wanted the European pillar of the Alliance to be formed by inter-governmental co-operation rather than quasi-federalist structures. Hence the agreement in Paris in October 1954 to admit Germany into NATO via the 1948 Brussels Treaty Organization (renamed Western European Union), with restrictions on its armaments. The parallel commitment of four British divisions and a tactical air force ensured French consent.

On the form of European security co-operation, Britain therefore carried the day, not least because of its importance as Europe's leading military power. Germany was rearmed on an inter-governmental basis, within an Atlanticist structure. But on the economic front, the supranationalist approach proved more effectual. The Schuman Plan foreshadowed the Messina proposals of 1955 which led in 1958 to the European Economic Community (EEC). Here a French compact with Germany, re-emerging as the strongest European economy, set the pattern. Thus, British policy played an important but complicating part in determining the institutions of Cold-War Europe. It helped to ensure that the European Economic Community was not complemented by a European Defence Community.

### Restraining American globalism, 1949–55

Throughout this period British policy in Europe was always seen in a global context. That has been emphasized repeatedly by recent scholars, using the newly-opened archives. Thus, the British did not regard the symbolic events of 1947 as signalling the end of Britain as a great power. In Washington at the time it seemed that 'world power was at that moment changing hands'. Likewise, to later American historians, post-1945 Britain, 'nearly bankrupt, dependent, and unable to police its empire, was reduced to a resentful, second-rate power'.[59] For the British Government, however, the Atlantic alliance relieved them of primary responsibility for the prosperity and security of Europe and enabled them, after the shocks of 1945–7, to concentrate on maintaining their global interests. The special relationship was envisaged not as a form of dependence but, to quote a FO memo of 1944, as a way of 'making use of American power for purposes which we regard as good'.[60]

British global policy is not the focus of this essay, but a few points should be made briefly. Economically, one should not judge Britain's position simply by the crisis of 1947.[61] That reflected continued wartime commitments exacerbated by the appalling winter. The worst financial burdens were relieved by withdrawal from India and Palestine and the late 1940s saw a sustained and successful export drive, complemented by the exploitiation of the dollar-earning potential of the sterling area. By 1948, Britain's current account was again in balance and by 1952–3 UK trade with the dollar area was also in rough equilibrium.[62] This is not to deny the underlying, structural problems of Britain's industrial uncompetitiveness, which re-emerged in the mid-1950s with the German recovery. The point is that around 1950 Britain's economy seemed to have overcome its immediate post-war crisis and this was the context in which British Cold-War policy evolved.

It was on the global stage that Anglo-American tension became apparent. The old friction over colonialism, which had bedevilled relations during the war, was now overlaid by British concern that Americans were developing an undiscriminating phobia about communism which was dragging them into global commitments that distracted them from holding the line in Europe.

These fears had been expressed in a muted way within the FO at the time of the Truman Doctrine.[63] They became vocal and intense after the so-called 'fall of China' in October 1949 and the onset of the Korean War in June 1950. British policy-makers feared that the USA would give the Asian Cold War priority over European security and would turn the former into a hot war, maybe using nuclear weapons. Thus, Britain and the United States parted company over recognition of Communist China in January 1950. Bevin, conscious of the position of Hong Kong, recognised the new government, while the Truman Administration waited on events.[64] In the Korean War, the British provided token support but, when the Chinese entered the conflict and Truman made noises about using nuclear weapons, Attlee rushed to Washington in December 1950 in an attempt to restrain him. This issue, and the question of 'branding' Chinese aggression in the UN, led to acrimonious exchanges between London and Washington.[65] And in 1954, British policy over Indo-China irritated Eisenhower's Secretary of State, John Foster Dulles. First the British refused to support a US air strike to aid the beleaguered French at Dienbienphu and then, in the ensuing peace negotiations, they worked with the Russians to secure a settlement for Indochina against American wishes. Unlike Dulles, Eden did not consider the region an area of notable importance.[66]

In retrospect, one might find the situation somewhat ironical. The British had encouraged the Americans to take the Soviet and communist threats seriously in the mid-1940s. By the early 1950s they were concerned lest the Americans were carried away by Cold-War enthusiasms. America's containment policy had 'provided an answer to Britain's security problem but only at a cost of hardening the East-West conflict into the cold war'.[67] It was not merely US globalism, particularly the view of 'Red China', which alarmed them, but also the rigid posture of confrontation adopted by Washington towards Moscow.

The latter became an obsession of the ageing Churchill in his premiership of 1951–5. Again one might find a certain irony in the Cold Warrior of Fulton becoming a leading apostle of détente, but Churchill was convinced that the vastly enhanced power of the hydrogen bomb, tested by both superpowers in 1952–3, had transformed everything. He told his private secretary, John Colville, that 'we're now as far from the atomic bomb as the atomic bomb was from the bow and arrow'.[68] Recent scholarship has highlighted his efforts, after Stalin's death in March 1953, to thaw the Cold War. On 11 May 1953 he called publicly for a summit conference, arguing that 'the immense problem of reconciling the security of Russia with the freedom and safety of Western Europe' was not 'insoluble'.[69] This harked back to his wartime faith in the efficacy of personal diplomacy and in the idea of agreed spheres of influence. His stroke that summer precluded further action but he returned to the charge in mid-1954 and cabled Moscow unilaterally in July, proposing a personal visit. This *démarche* prompted threats of resignation from several Cabinet members. It was opposed also by the Eisenhower Administration and by Eden and the FO, all of whom believed that such a move would only unsettle the absorption of West Germany into the Atlantic Alliance.[70] Nevertheless, when Eden became premier in April 1955, he was as keen as Churchill for East-West summitry. 'How much more attractive a top-level meeting seems when one has reached the top', observed Churchill wickedly.[71] Eden's efforts at the Geneva conference in July 1955 were emulated in turn by his successor Harold Macmillan, with his flight to Moscow in February 1959 and assiduous backstage diplomacy to prepare the way for the Paris summit of 1960. In other words, all British premiers of the 1950s saw themselves as loyal but not uncritical US allies, who had a particular role to play in moving the world from Cold War towards détente.

### Conclusion

The new scholarship examined in this essay has drawn particular attention to the British role in shaping the institutions of Cold-War Europe. In 1945–6 Britain was more at odds with Russia than was the United States. In 1947 the British pullout from Greece and Turkey helped forced America into decisive and public action. Bevin helped to give substance to the Marshall Plan and, in 1948, built the European pillar of the Atlantic alliance. Thereafter, the British became increasingly a brake on American globalism, contesting their view of China and its implications for Asian policy and seeking to promote a thaw in relations with Moscow.

It is important to reiterate that this work has concentrated mainly on throwing open the British record. In reaction to an excessively American-centred view of Western Cold-War policy, it has placed the focus on British actions. In consequence, as with any revisionism, it probably exaggerates its case. In particular, it was often British weakness rather than British power which drew in the Americans – as over Greece in 1947. Similarly, the stimulus was often American reaction *against* British policy rather than belated espousal of it – as has been suggested in the case of Iran in 1946.[72] This new material must therefore be gradually synthesized with the American work, and that in other countries, to provide a more rounded picture.[73]

It is equally important to consider the larger implications of this work for our understanding of how and why and Cold War began. American revisionism, though a spur to research, had only a limited influence on British scholarship about the origins of the Cold War.[74] And post-glasnost revelations about the nature of the Stalinist regime provide much more evidence for the view that the Cold War was largely the responsibility of Soviet policy. Some of the recent British scholarship is firmly of this opinion. Alan Bullock argues that 'if Stalin miscalculated in throwing away the goodwill which Russia had accumulated in the West, there is nothing to show that anything Bevin or any other Englishman could have said would have persuaded him to act differently.' Subsequent history did not suggest that 'an accommodation could have been reached between two such different views of the future of Europe'.[75]

That said, it is nonetheless worth noting that some of the new scholarship does indicate that British policy, like America's, was not simply reacting to Soviet actions. Anne Deighton's work on Germany has important implications since it suggests that the British, for good domestic and economic reasons, forced the pace in making division a reality. Of course, Soviet and Anglo-American views of Germany did conflict at this time. Nevertheless, by cutting through the impasse and promoting Bizone and then the Marshall Plan, the British and Americans did make the rift explicit and unbridgeable.[76] John Kent has painted a similar picture for the Near East. In 1944 Churchill accepted the idea of Russian naval penetration of the Mediterranean, provided British interests in Greece were secured. But in 1945–6 Bevin and the FO, backed by the military planners, redefined British interests in the region much more toughly as part of a drift away from Churchill's spheres-of-influence policy and of a new interest in retaining and developing the resources of the British empire for British use.[77]

In this context, the changed perspective on Clement Attlee is especially instructive. According to conventional wisdom, the terse, pipe-smoking premier was a capable chairman of the board, but did little more than back up Bevin over foreign policy. 'There is less there than meets the eye', Churchill told Truman in 1946. When the President defended Attlee – 'he seems a modest sort of fellow' – Churchill responded: 'he's got a lot to be modest about'.[78] It is now clear, however, that in 1946 Attlee mounted perhaps the most sustained attack from any twentieth-century British premier on the fundamental strategic wisdom of his advisers. Attlee was more sceptical than Bevin or the Chiefs or Staff about the inevitability of confrontation with Russia and the irrelevance of the UN. More particularly, he contested their insistence on the importance to Britain of the eastern Mediterranean, arguing that air power and Indian independence both made naval control of the sea routes via Suez and the Red Sea less important than hitherto. 'We must not, for sentimental reasons based on the past, give hostages to fortune.'[79] This opened up an extended debate with the FO and the military, in which the growing significance of oil and the utility of air bases in the region for striking at Russia were among arguments advanced against Attlee. Also invoked were the lessons of appeasement. Bevin told Attlee in January 1947 that to hope for agreement with Russia 'would be Munich all over again, only on a world scale, with Greece, Turkey and Persia as the first victims in place of Czechoslovakia'.[80] This controversy over the Near East was only ended in January 1947 when the Chiefs of Staff threatened to resign unless Attlee desisted – an indication of just how intense the struggle had been.

No mature verdict on Attlee's proposals can be given until we have a clearer idea of what motivated Soviet policy and whether alternative Western actions would have had any effect. What can be said here is that this debate would not have taken place in 1946 but for the fact that Britain was and remained a global power. It was the British presence in the eastern Mediterranean which made the possibility of the Red Navy moving through the Dardanelles or establishing bases in North Africa such a concern. At the London Foreign Ministers Conference in September 1945 Molotov made precisely this point. After the war, he said, Britain was left with 'a monopoly in the Mediterranean'. Could it not 'find a corner' for the Russians?[81] In other words, it was because Britain was an extended global power that its leaders found Soviet post-war expansion so disturbing. This feeling was accentuated by two sets of historical memories. One was the recollection of the German hyperinflation of the 1920s and Depression of the 1930s, generally thought to have been the soil in which Nazism flourished. This made it appear essential to promote German and European economic recovery urgently, regardless of Soviet sensitivities. The other 'lesson' of the past was that derived from the costly failure of appeasement in the 1930s. Talking with totalitarians only left them stronger, it seemed clear, whereas firmness was the best form of deterrence.

Ultimately, only knowledge of the Soviet archives will indicate whether it might have been possible to deal with post-war Russia on any other basis than that of Cold War. What is evident is that Britain's heritage as a global power and its recent historical memories left its leaders with little inclination to give Stalin the benefit of the doubt. In most of the great disputes of the first half of the twentieth century, Britain was able, with some justice, to cast itself as the peace-loving status quo power, trying to prevent the aggression of others from overturning the existing order. That was its stance in 1914, 1939 and again after 1945. Yet the status quo, conveniently, had been formed around British power. As Churchill admitted before the First World War, 'our claim to be left in the unmolested enjoyment of vast and splendid possessions, *mainly acquired by violence, largely maintained by force*, often seems less reasonable to others than to us'.[82] That observation was equally valid after the Second World War. As Gladwyn Jebb, quoted near the beginning of this essay, observed in 1950, for the British the Cold War was about the maintenance of Britain's global power. Given the suspicions and animosity aroused by the British Empire in (friendly) Washington, more extreme reactions in (paranoid) Moscow would not be surprising.

In other words, the recent work on British Cold-War policy is in danger of becoming misdirected. That is partly because it may exaggerate the British influence on US policy. But some of it also fails to take with full seriousness the reason why the British enjoyed potential influence in Washington – namely the persistence, albeit shaky, of British *power*. Attlee's remarkable campaign for imperial retrenchment highlights that point. It also opens the question of whether concessions, for instance on a Soviet role in the Mediterranean, might have induced Stalin's co-operation or simply whetted his appetite. Although after 1989–90 it is hard to avoid the conclusion that Soviet expansion and Stalinist conceptions of security were the primary cause of the Cold War, the continued assertion of British power was surely a contributory factor. Taking *Great* Britain seriously might offer scope for a truly revisionist view of British foreign policy and the Cold War.

### Bibliographical note

Useful introductory essays are Victor Rothwell, 'Britain and the First Cold War', in Richard Crockatt & Steve Smith, eds., *The Cold War Past and Present* (London, 1987), pp. 58–76, and, on the literature, Peter Weiler, 'British Labour and the Cold War: the Foreign Policy of the Labour Governments, 1945–1951', *Journal of British Studies*, 26 (1987), 54–82.

A compressed narrative can be found in the British section of Lawrence Aronsen & Martin Kitchen, *The Origins of the Cold War in Comparative Perspective: American, British and Canadian Relations with the Soviet Union, 1941–1948* (New York, 1988), and, more fully, in Elisabeth Barker, *The British between the Superpowers, 1945–1950* (London, 1983), which is based on documents in the Public Record Office. Alan Bullock, *Ernest Bevin: Foreign Secretary, 1945–1951* (London, 1983), offers a detailed and sympathetic account of Bevin's diplomacy. As a counterbalance see the summaries of work by younger scholars in two collections of essays: Michael Dockrill & John W. Young, eds., *British Foreign Policy, 1945–56* (London, 1989), and Anne Deighton, ed., *Britain and the First Cold War* (London, 1990). The view from the Foreign Office is documented in Victor Rothwell, *Britain and the Cold War, 1941–1947* (London, 1982), which is strong on Germany, and in John Zametica, ed., *British Officials and British Foreign Policy, 1945–1950* (Leicester, 1990), which includes pertinent pieces on Roberts and Hankey. There are useful collections of essays in Ritchie Ovendale, ed., *The Foreign Policy of the British Labour Governments, 1945–1951*, (Leicester, 1984) and in the successor volume edited by John W. Young, *The Foreign Policy of Churchill's Peacetime Administration, 1951–1955* (Leicester, 1988). For a geopolitical interpretation see Peter J. Taylor, *Britain and the Cold War: 1945 as Geopolitical Transition* (London, 1990).

Relevant published documents may be found in the collection, *Documents on British Policy Overseas* (London, 1984–), edited variously by Rohan Butler, Roger Bullen, M.E. Pelly, H.J. Yasamee et al. Two series are so far in progress, one starting in 1945, the other in 1950. The volumes are excellently edited but to date only a few have been published. Also useful is Peter G. Boyle, ed., *The Churchill-Eisenhower Correspondence, 1953–1955* (Chapel Hill, N.C., 1990). Interactions between defence and intelligence are explored in Richard Aldrich, ed., *British Intelligence, Strategy and the Cold War, 1945–51* (London, 1992).

# 4    *France*

## GEORGES–HENRI   SOUTOU

France's role in the Cold War has been complicated by three factors, which did not exist, or at least not to the same extent, in America or Great Britain. First, there was a disagreement about the real threat: was it Germany or the Soviet Union? Through the period there was a gradual shift from the former to the latter, but even in 1955 French people remained divided on this issue. The second factor was the weight of the French Communist Party (PCF), which had played a prominent role in the wartime Resistance and which was supported by about 25 per cent of the electorate during the post-war decade. Friendships and solidarities stemming from the Resistance resulted in the desire of many non-communists to avoid breaking completely with the PCF or for that matter with the Soviet Union.

The third factor, very different from the American situation for instance, was that the Cold War did not absorb anything like the whole scope of French foreign policy: national interests of a more traditional nature remained very much in evidence. Successive French governments did take part in the Cold War, but their relationship to the East-West conflict was complex. Wholly supportive of the Western alliance against the Soviet threat, they believed that the Cold War was carried too far when it entailed the rearmament of Germany. At the same time they did not miss the chance to further old French interests under the mantle of the defence of the West, as in the case of the Indo-China War. In other words the French, or at least a majority of them, experienced the Cold War simultaneously as a necessity, a bother and an opportunity.[1]

### The Cold War as French history

There has not been nearly as much academic discussion in France about the origins of the Cold War as in the USA. It is not that the political discussion at the time was not heated and sometimes violent: to convince oneself of the contrary it is enough to read Raymond Aron's *Memoirs* or his collected foreign-policy articles in *Le Figaro – Les articles du Figaro, tome I, La Guerre froide 1947–1955*, ed. Georges-Henri Soutou (Paris, 1990). Aron's articles, by the way, give some of the best insights into French foreign policy during the Cold-War period. But French archives for that period were opened to researchers only from 1979, that is well after the high point of ideological polarization during the 1960s and early 1970s.

Important works are only now beginning to come out, while the general spirit of the French academic world is in any case much more serene today than formerly. And even during its heyday, the French equivalent of the New Left did not really use the origins of the Cold War as a central argument.

One should add that French internal politics have attracted more attention than foreign policy; this has to do with current historical fashion, but also with the fact that France's international role was perforce much more limited than that of America or Great Britain. Above all, for the French the Cold War was not so much an outside event as an internal problem: the question of whether France itself would not become a kind of popular democracy was often more urgent than the overall East-West balance. It is therefore not surprising that, for instance, the role of the Communist PCF and its place in the body politic have been the object of several important studies (particularly by Philippe Robrieux, Phillipe Buton and Stéphane Courtois). It should be noted that these studies, while of course dwelling mostly on domestic politics, are very relevant to an understanding of French foreign policy.

Another topic that has drawn much attention, in a way recalling the controversy about the origins of the Cold War in the United States, has been the colonial wars, and particularly the one in Indo-China, which was *also* an East-West conflict. Philippe Devillers, in several books, argues that it would have been possible in 1946 to make a deal with Ho Chi Minh and to prevent the Indo-China War. François Joyaux holds a much less sanguine view in his several books, among them his seminal *La Chine et le règlement de la première guerre d'Indochine, Genève 1954* (Paris, 1979), the first French book on the Cold War based on archives. But the most recent contribution is in the very good chapters about Indo-China by Jacques de Folin in a recent book on French policy in that period: Pierre Gerbet, *Le Relèvement 1944–1949* (Paris, 1991).

For some years there have been three more pointed debates about the American influence in France at the time: about the Blum-Byrnes financial and trade agreements of May 1946, about the ousting of communist cabinet ministers in May 1947, and about the Marshall Plan. In each instance it had been argued that Washington made full use of its opportunities to conduct an imperialistic policy toward France. It is now generally recognized that the Truman administration had nothing to do with the departure of the communist ministers, even if it was quite happy with the outcome, and that the Blum-Byrnes agreements and the Marshall Plan were mainly beneficial to France.

The orthodox view among French historians nowadays (which I do not wholly share, as the reader will see) is that the French government did not enter the Cold War before the Moscow Conference of March–April 1947. Because Stalin refused to grant any support to Paris on the German problem, France was obliged at that point to align itself with the Anglo-Saxons and to abandon its bridge policy between East and West. There are, of course, various opinions about the ulterior motives of French ruling circles – more nationalistic and fearful of Germany for Raymond Poidevin, more sincerely European for Pierre Guillen, more Atlanticist for Pierre Mélandri. The current hot debate in France, much more than the Cold War, is the degree of continuity in foreign policy from the Fourth to the Fifth

Republic in 1958 (the issue number 58 of *Relations Internationales*, Summer 1989, being a good sample of that debate).

There is one dissenter: Annie Lacroix-Riz, in numerous articles and in her distinctly revisionist book *Le choix de Marianne* (Paris, 1985). She argues that very early, as soon as the end of the War, French ruling circles chose to align themselves with the United States (which was embarking as early as 1945 on a course toward the Cold War) in order to escape the social and political consequences of the foreseeable swing left by the French people after the War, and that Washington quite soon imposed on the French its plans about the reconstruction and rearmament of Germany. This argument is certainly excessive, so excessive that there has not even been a real debate. But it remains true that things began to move long before 1947: as early as 1945, some perceptive French leaders, including de Gaulle, became very suspicious of the Soviet Union and began to look for alternative policies. They could not say as much publicly, for obvious political reasons, as we shall see, but it is clear that France's entry into the Cold War was not a sudden decision in 1947, but a two-year-long process. Thus, the years 1945–7 merit close attention in what follows.

### 1944–6: From the Franco-Soviet alliance to official neutrality between East and West

France was one of the Big Four occupying powers in Germany and its policies played an important part in the evolution of the Cold War. Yet its experience of the Second World War was fundamentally different from that of the other two Western powers, America and Britain, and this needs to be emphasized in order to understand France's foreign-policy priorities after 1945.

Britain had been bombed but not invaded by Germany during the war. The mainland of the United States remained totally untouched by Nazi attack. France, by contrast, had been defeated in June 1940 after a battle lasting less than six weeks. The Germans then occupied northern France, leaving the southern part under the compliant Vichy regime until they took full control after the Allied invasion of French North Africa in November 1942. Because of the experience of defeat and occupation, coming after two other major wars with Germany in 1870 and 1914, the French view of Germany was necessarily more suspicious than that of America or Britain. Recriminations about collaboration with the German occupation polarised French politics around *collabos* and *résistants* for years after. For France the Second World War was, in part, a civil war.

The leader of the Free French forces in exile in London after June 1940 was General Charles de Gaulle. He had to accept British and American assistance in the struggle but bitterly resented the humiliations that this entailed, such as exclusion from the major conferences with Stalin, at Teheran and Yalta. On 25 August 1944 de Gaulle entered liberated Paris and established a new government. Whereas for America and Britain the sense of victory was unalloyed, for France it had a bitter-sweet taste. De Gaulle was determined to rebuild France as a great and independent power. Although that policy centred on France's position in Europe, no French government could see European politics in isolation. Like Britain, France remained an imperial power, albeit in truncated form. Indeed, until 1962, French politics were rarely free of colonial crisis, first the bloody battle to recover French Indo-China from the Vietminh communists under Ho Chi Minh (1946–54) and then the bitter civil war in Algeria (1954–62) which eventually destroyed the Fourth Republic itself.

The first major event of French foreign policy after the Liberation was de Gaulle's trip to Moscow and the signature of the Franco-Soviet treaty of 10 December 1944, which amounted to an alliance against Germany.[2] The main object of his Moscow trip for de Gaulle was to secure Stalin's support for his German policy (separation of the Ruhr, Rhineland and Saar from the Reich, international control of the Ruhr, French control over the Saar and Rhineland) and also to use Russia as a counterweight to the dreaded Anglo-Saxon hegemony. As is well known, Stalin refused to support French aims towards Germany; from the French standpoint the treaty was actually a failure from the start and that became evident in Paris as soon as the spring of 1945.

Moreover the treaty included disquieting features (the very sparse archives on the negotiation of the treaty do not explain how those features came about). The pact did not only apply in the case of German aggression (as was the case with the Anglo-Soviet treaty of 26 May 1942) but also covered a situation in which one of the two signatories had launched a preventive war against Germany! A very heavy obligation indeed for the partner, especially for the less powerful one – that is France. It is worth noting that a similar clause could be found in the Czech-Soviet treaty of 12 December 1943 and in the treaties signed by Moscow with Yugoslavia and Poland in April 1945. Evidently in 1943–5 Stalin was trying to build a European security system in the expectation of a prompt American exodus from Europe. This system would have been dominated by Moscow and would have included France, in the name of necessary vigilance against the ever-present German danger.

Furthermore de Gaulle had to pay a price for the treaty, a price which was highly significant in symbolic and political terms on the eve of Soviet domination of Eastern Europe. Of course de Gaulle did not agree to recognize formally the new Polish government, as Stalin initially wanted as a condition of the pact, but he had to agree to exchange informal representatives with Warsaw, thus being the first Western Power to establish a link with the new Polish regime.

The fact that the French communist leader Maurice Thorez, who had deserted from the Army in 1939 and had escaped to the Soviet Union, was pardoned by de Gaulle and authorized to come back on 6 November 1944, only two days before the General officially asked to meet Stalin, has led to much speculation. Was there a link between the two events? Did de Gaulle let Thorez come back to facilitate his own trip? Did he go to Moscow partly to outflank the French Communists, aside from his foreign policy motives? Or was the decision about Thorez (which had been in preparation for three weeks) above all linked with internal considerations and specifically with the necessity to placate the Communists in order to have them agree to disarm their militias, the *Milices*? This last explanation would appear to be the right one but the strong relationship between foreign and domestic policy is in this case (as generally for the French side of the Cold War) inescapable. To underscore the complexity of the situation at that time let it be said that it appears from recent research that the French Communist Party itself considered the political opportunities in France to be basically similar to those in Eastern Europe and hoped to come to power through a large antifascist coalition, after an initial transitory participation on a minority basis in de Gaulle's provisional government.[3]

De Gaulle certainly did not harbour any illusions about the ulterior motives of the Communist Party or of Stalin, even if he looked at him more as the chief of a powerful Russian Empire than as the head of a world revolutionary movement.[4] His Moscow trip, although ultimately unsuccessful and potentially risky, must be placed in the context of his overall policies: the General wanted to group a powerful Western Europe around France – including Belgium, the Netherlands, Luxemburg and the Ruhr. His public repudiation of the West European Bloc concept, in a press conference on 25 October 1944, in order to placate Stalin, was certainly less than candid: this concept had evolved in French government circles in Algiers since 1943 and remained very much present, for both economic and strategic reasons. De Gaulle counted on the Soviet Union to help him separate the Ruhr from Germany against American and British opposition; thus, in return, the material foundation of the West European Bloc under French control would be laid, and France, vastly reinforced through the potential of the Ruhr and also through the ambitious industrial plans already envisioned at that time in Paris, would have been able in de Gaulle's view to prevent Soviet influence from spreading toward Western Europe. De Gaulle was quite willing to strike an agreement with Stalin to further his aims but he did not, in my view, forget the necessity of a balance of power in post-war Europe, even if his conception would appear to overtax French possibilities.[5] It must be added that French public opinion at that time certainly did not follow de Gaulle so far: punitive treatment of Germany and friendship with the popular Russia was all that really interested a country still at war, where the Communists were seen as major contributors to the *Résistance*, and where rightist or even moderate parties were for the time discredited.

In 1945 de Gaulle maintained the same course for his German policy: he rejected the setting up of central German administrations and demanded that the Reich east of the Rhine be divided into several states, which might be allowed at the most to form a loose confederation.[6] But the General began to harbour second thoughts about Soviet policy. Although publicly he refused to take sides in the emerging East-West rift, he nonetheless insisted in an internal note of April 1945 that a continued presence of the United States in European affairs was necessary: one should 'link in the future the United States with the security of the European continent and establish through their presence the conditions of a necessary balance of power in Europe'.[7]

During his visit to Washington in August 1945 de Gaulle was glad to note that Truman was more alert than Roosevelt to the emergence of a Soviet threat.[8] Apparently de Gaulle's shift away from Moscow was provoked by developments in Eastern Europe, which he considered to be a traditional zone of French influence. At the end of 1945, noticing that the Soviet Army was not being truly demobilized, de Gaulle began to take seriously the possibility of a Soviet military challenge. As early as October 1945 the General Staff, which was closely supervised by de Gaulle, developed the concept of a strong Western European defence organization, with an American and even a German contribution.[9] Those studies were of course not yet politically relevant but they were revealing of a changing climate in official circles.

After de Gaulle's departure in January 1946 a Tripartite government, made up of communists, socialists and Christian democrats, came to power. The new government refused to take sides in the now widening rift between America and Russia; it promoted instead the idea of France as a bridge between East and West. It is true that the presence of communists in the government precluded any other diplomatic orientation. But at the time, although there were already other currents at work which we shall mention later, this neutralistic orientation was not just a formal lip service to the wartime alliance against Hitler: it was deeply rooted in the political, administrative and military organs of the country. The main reasons were certainly the heavy communist presence in many departments of state, which in the difficult climate of the time could only lead people who were not enthusiastic about the alliance with Moscow to be very cautious, and also the fact that in 1946 France had not yet renounced the tough German policy we have described. But this policy needed the support of the three Allies and France could not afford to antagonize the Soviet Union.

This foreign-policy line of neutrality was compounded by the Third Force approach of the socialists, who were at that time still seeking an organic union with the communists and believed in a French mode of socialism, midway between Western capitalism and Soviet communism. For many socialists, but not for all of them, as we shall see, this domestic policy orientation entailed a foreign-policy course equidistant from Moscow and Washington.[10] But we believe that the Third Force was a concept limited to the socialists (and once again not to all of them) and that French neutralism in 1946 had more to do with a quite traditional view of French national interests (especially in the German question) than with any real ideological stand.[11]

But, behind the scenes and in utmost secrecy, some factions were already promoting a different policy. At the London conference of September 1945 Foreign Minister Georges Bidault refused, to the fury of de Gaulle, to insist on the French scheme to internationalize the Ruhr. As soon as it became evident that the Anglo-Saxons feared that such a scheme would help the Soviets to extend their influence in that part of Germany, Bidault recognized that it would not be in the French interest to persist.[12] In February 1946 some Christian Democrat members of the Cabinet wanted to send the deputy Chief of Staff, General Pierre Billotte, an important Gaullist officer, to Washington, in order to study the possibility of a common defence against the Soviets. The socialist head of the Government, Félix Gouin, killed the mission, but the episode is revealing of the true leanings of the Christian Democrat leaders, even if they could not express them publicly at that time.[13]

Even the Socialists began, during the spring of 1946, to initiate actions that may be seen in retrospect as the beginning of a Franco–American rapprochement. In March Félix Gouin publicly announced an important shift in Paris's German policy: the Ruhr and the Rhineland would no longer have to be separated from Germany. Gouin had to recant quickly, in the face of public uproar and the staunch opposition of both communists and Christian democrats, but it would appear that his move had been secretly prepared with the Americans.[14] From March to May, Léon Blum, the Socialist leader, was sent to Washington to negotiate financial help. The Blum-Byrnes Agreements at the end of May 1946 provided France with much-needed dollars, but in exchange Paris accepted the American position on international trade as expressed through the Open Door principle. Blum and the French negotiators – at their head, Jean Monnet – understood perfectly well that those agreements meant France's inclusion in the capitalist West. This inclusion was in no way forced on them by Washington, but met their conception of the necessary modernization of the French economy in a liberal international framework. Blum assured the Assembly upon his return that the Americans had not attached political conditions to their financial help, and the American documents confirm that such was the case. But both Blum and his American partners were fully and explicitly aware of the political advantages of a financial agreement helping to stabilize the French economy and French society, and thus reducing communist influence, especially close to the very important elections scheduled for 2 June 1946.[15] In that instance Blum was certainly one step ahead of his party.

Officially French policy toward Germany remained in 1946 as tough as in 1945. But in fact it began to evolve prudently, the notion of a control over the Rhineland and the Ruhr becoming now more important than the actual separation of those two provinces from Germany. At a high level meeting on 6 November 1946, Bidault upheld the harsh 1944–5 programme, but less out of conviction than because he believed public opinion would not tolerate any mitigation of that programme. Confidential talks with the Americans and the British showed that an agreement might have been possible on the basis of international control of the Ruhr and the Rhineland, if France in return accepted the creation of central German administrations, which many people in Paris thought advisable. Most important was that Bidault fully agreed with London and Washington on a crucial point: no solution of the German question, even on terms favourable to France, should allow the extension of Soviet influence over Western Germany.[16]

The change in French policy had thus begun, at least for parts of the political leadership, even if it was too soon to admit as much publicly because of the political context of tripartism and of a public opinion still favourable to the Soviet Union. Blum, head of the provisional government in December 1946 and January 1947, went one step further by discarding clearly the separation of Ruhr and Rhineland from Germany, thus disposing of a major obstacle in the way of a rapprochement between Paris, London and Washington.[17]

### 1947: the shift to the West

In February–March 1947, French foreign policy, rather stagnant in 1946, exhibited a sudden flurry of activity: on 13 and 14 February Paris suggested to the Poles and the Czechs the renewal of their pre-war alliances with France, on 4 March the Dunkirk Treaty was signed with Great Britain, and two days later Bidault raised with the new Italian ambassador the possibility of a Franco-Italian alliance. This return to the traditional pre-war policy, based on a net of bilateral arrangements, was explicitly directed against Germany, which was the only possible adversary mentioned in the Dunkirk Treaty and in the projected alliances with Poland and Czechoslovakia. It was not directly concerned with the East-West rift. But it would seem that there was at least an indirect link: Paris had by now abandoned any hope of getting Soviet support for its German policy and, in the face of raising East-West tensions, probably felt the urge to reactivate traditional friendships. And quite possibly Paris, following the advice of its ambassador to Prague, did not wish to leave Poland and Czechoslovakia depending only on the Soviet Union.[18]

It was at the Moscow Conference of March-April 1947 that the big change in French foreign policy, which, as we have seen, had been contemplated in certain quarters for months, became evident. Paris was now ready to align itself with London and Washington against Moscow. It has been generally assumed that this change happened because Stalin refused to support French claims on Germany, especially on the Saar. But in fact the change had been in the offing even before the Conference and was caused not only by the Saar but by a far-reaching realignment of French policies. Consistent with his suspicions about Moscow's German policy, which were evident by September 1945, as we have seen, Bidault told the American ambassador, Jefferson Caffery, in February 1947, that the main danger was not so much Germany itself as a Germany which would have fallen completely under Soviet influence.[19] This view, which was quite widespread in informed French circles, was a very important intellectual link between the perception of the old German menace and the perception of the new Soviet one, thus easing the plunge into the East-West divide.

An immediate cause, but no less important, of France's change of mind, her abandonment of former aims in Germany and her alignment with the British and Americans was the European fuel crisis of winter 1947. In order to get enough coal, France was obliged to co-operate in the Ruhr with the British and the Americans, and this entailed acceptance of their German policies. In particular, this crisis led the Christian Democrats to revise their German policy;[20] this change was obfuscated in public speeches and in Parliament because of the still-strong Gaullist influence and because of the state of public opinion, but it was quite real.

The deeper cause, however, was the Truman Doctrine speech of 12 March: America was now willing to take a stand against the Soviet Union. Those policy-makers who had tried to establish a security link with Washington in 1946 and who had become apprehensive of Soviet aims felt now encouraged to take sides and abandon the Third-Force rhetoric. There is conclusive evidence that the firmer attitude of Bidault in Moscow was caused mainly by the Truman Doctrine.[21]

As a result the new line was now set: in an important talk with Marshall on 20 April Bidault announced that Paris was ready to accept the Anglo-American position on Germany, that France would link up with the Western powers, and that the communist ministers would eventually have to leave. Bidault also asked for American economic help. Marshall outlined what was to be in effect his plan of 5 June, and both men agreed that Germany would be included in it. Thus the foundation for the Western reconstruction of 1947-9 was laid.[22] Of course things were not yet as clear as they might appear to be in retrospect: when Marshall announced the European recovery programme in June, Bidault tried hard to persuade the Soviets to join it; he was not yet reconciled to the division of Europe. But Moscow's adamant refusal to consider the multilateral European economic scheme and its veto of Polish and Czech participation enlightened Bidault about Soviet aims in Europe. Final reckoning came when, during the summer of 1947, Stalin insisted that the Franco–Polish and Franco–Czech treaties being negotiated at that time should include a provision covering any third country helping Germany even in an indirect manner. His target of course was the United States. Bidault realized that Stalin wanted to build a European security system against America and in November he abruptly stopped the negotiations with Warsaw and Prague.[23]

The shift in foreign policy corresponded with a tidal change in domestic politics: in May 1947 the communist ministers were expelled from the government. The break took place over a social problem, not on foreign policy, and it was not the result of American pressures, contrary to what has been frequently asserted, but it had of course foreign policy consequences of the first magnitude.[24] At the time the break did not appear to be final: both Communists and Socialists hoped to restore the Tripartite system. The definitive rupture came with the international communist conference in Szklarska Poreba in September and the founding of the Cominform, followed by the new hard communist line and the big French strikes of November–December 1947. Then the socialists finally abandoned hope of bringing the communists back and accepted (although with difficulty) the new foreign and domestic policy line, which exhibited more of a Christian Democratic ethos.[25]

The big and violent communist-led strikes of late 1947 were the last straw in the now frayed Franco–Soviet relationship. At a time of strict Stalinist discipline in the world communist movement, nobody doubted that Stalin was ultimately responsible for those strikes, whose aim was to thwart the Marshall Plan. The French government reacted with a police raid on Beauregard Camp near Paris, which belonged to the Soviet embassy, on 14 November. More important than the actual reason for the raid was the fact that Paris wanted in that way to signal its new resolve to resist Soviet pressure.[26]

In April 1947 de Gaulle had founded the Rassemblement du Peuple Français (RPF), with a pronounced anti-Soviet and anti-communist posture. French political life became now polarized not so much along the Vichy versus Resistance line inherited from the war, but on the communists versus anti-communist axis. The united workers movement splintered at the beginning of 1948 into communist and socialist unions. Anti-communism had become once again legitimate, and this also had consequences for foreign policy.

But in most parties there were people who, even though anti-communist, did not want to break completely with the Soviet Union, which they viewed as a useful counterweight against Germany. Those people were a complicating factor in the ensuing years. Though a minority, they could wield enough influence (mostly because of popular fears of Germany), to ensure that French policy was constantly more prudent – although firm – toward the Soviet Union than that of other Western countries.

### 1948–9: militant but cautious France

As early as July 1947 the General Staff had stated the new strategic constellation for Prime Minister Ramadier: neutrality was no longer possible, both for political and strategic reasons. In the face of the Soviet threat, France needed American support. France should take the lead in Western Europe to negotiate a military alliance with the United States. Thus France would play the leading role on the European side in this alliance and would prevent Germany from playing that role in the future. Moreover, the alliance would strengthen French security against Germany; this last interesting consideration was to have a discreet but important impact in the next years.[27] Bidault followed the General Staff's advice and in October told Marshall that America should contribute to European security.[28] On 17 December, after the failure of the London foreign ministers' conference, Bidault, Bevin and Marshall held important talks: Bidault was now ready to reach an agreement over Germany with America and Great Britain, and agreed with Bevin that they should hold Franco–British staff talks which would later include the Americans.[29]

Back in Paris on 19 December, Bidault outlined to the Cabinet a grim situation. There were Soviet threats against Austria and Czechoslovakia and civil disorders in France and Italy. In fact there was a danger of war. A neutralist course would not diminish the Soviet menace, but would convince the Americans to leave Europe. Bidault asked from the Cabinet and obtained, despite misgivings from the socialist President of the Republic, Vincent Auriol, the authorization to enter into talks with the United States, Great Britain and the Benelux countries to achieve a military organization.[30] Immediately afterwards, Bidault asked General Billotte, then a member of the French delegation at the UN, to begin talks with the Americans in order to reach a secret military agreement. This ultimately led to clandestine conversations between Generals Billotte, Ridgway (United States) and Morgan (Britain) near New York in January 1948.[31] The principle of a common security policy was affirmed.

These talks with Washington and London were deemed in Paris to be more important than the European perspective opened by Bevin's famous 'Western Union' speech on 22 January. When London, on 13 February, suggested a collective security pact between Great Britain, France and the Benelux, Paris reacted negatively: the most Bidault was ready to accept in that respect at the time was a system of bilateral treaties with the Benelux countries on the Dunkirk model, that is directed only against Germany. A collective pact not limited to the German threat would, in his view, aggravate the division of Europe and might drive the Americans to believe that their commitment to European security was no longer really necessary. Not to antagonize the Soviets while welding America to European security were Bidault's two priorities. But things changed in Paris because the Benelux countries insisted on a collective pact not solely directed against Germany, because of the Prague Coup in late February and because on 3 March Washington let it be known that Dunkirk-style bilateral treaties would not be enough to justify American involvement in Europe. A collective pact was therefore necessary and the French Cabinet accepted it on the same day, in order to achieve American support.[32]

One should emphasise the importance for France of the Prague coup. The Soviet threat had previously remained a rather abstract possibility; it then became urgently real. The French wish not to antagonize the Soviet Union in any way, which was still evident before the coup, gave way to a more militant attitude. The events in Prague had more resonance in France than other similar events elsewhere in Eastern Europe. Czechoslovakia was seen as a western-type democracy, which could not be said of other East-European countries before the war. It must be added that less blatant communist tactics in Poland and Hungary had somehow blurred the appreciation of what had actually happened in those countries since 1945.[33] The events in Prague developed the fear of a similar coup in western Europe, especially in Italy or even in France, the Soviet threat at the time being seen in Paris mostly as a combination of external pressures and internal upheaval.

It should also be pointed out here that the French reacted much more forcefully to the Prague coup in February than to the Berlin blockade starting in June 1948. This was quite a different reaction from that of the Americans or the British. Generally speaking, France kept a low profile during the Berlin crisis.[34] This corresponds probably to what was instinctively perceived in Paris as the real nature of the threat – more an internal communist coup supported by the Soviets than an outright Russian onslaught against Western Europe. The magnitude of the Berlin crisis and the role of Germany as the real Soviet objective in this crisis were not yet fully understood. Furthermore, the linkage of the Berlin crisis with plans for the formation of a West German state, to which Paris had difficulties in reconciling itself, certainly also worked as a brake on any vigorous French reactions.

Of course, with the Korean war in June 1950 the perception of the threat became more pointed: it was now and for a time seen as the possibility of an outright Soviet military attack in Europe. More research in this area is needed, but it would seem that, even then, the different French governments saw the threat more in a general political sense than in a strictly military one. The first aim of the Western military alliance, in French eyes, was always to build a framework of cohesion and political stability. That, they judged, would be enough to deter the Soviets from any imprudent action, up to a point independently of the actual military balance. And anyway they were anxious that the necessary military build-up should not be seen as provocative, and should not upset public opinion.

The Prague coup removed French opposition to the British concept of a European security pact and the Brussels Treaty was signed on 17 March 1948. But, for Paris, the most effective security guarantee remained American involvement in Europe. The only real use of the Brussels Treaty would be, in Bidault's view, to provide the modicum of European self-help which was necessary to convince Congress that Europe was worth helping. On 4 March (one day after the French cabinet had accepted the principle of the Brussels Pact) Bidault wrote Marshall a most secret letter asking for immediate political and military talks between Washington, London and Paris. Washington did not grant the French their wish immediately. Marshall's answer on 13 March was tepid, and very secret Anglo-Canado-American talks took place from 21 March to 1 April without the French, although Bevin informed them on 16 March of the impending conversations. These were to lay the foundation for the North Atlantic Pact.[35] Washington's prudence was due to strong opposition in Congress to any European entanglement.

On 13 April Bidault wrote Marshall a second letter advancing a new consideration. The conference in London which had begun in February and which was preparing the creation of a West German state had already caused a strong Soviet reaction. In Bidault's view there was a military risk which made an American commitment in Europe urgent. In other words, Bidault was telling Marshall that French acceptance of a West German state (which was very much opposed in France) would depend on America's willingness to ally itself with Western Europe. This ploy was very effective: on 23 April Bevin told the Americans that only an Atlantic security system would persuade the French to accept a West German state. And the Vandenberg resolution of 11 June was also devised to ease the vote on the London conference recommendations in the French Assembly.[36] Although the North Atlantic Treaty was not to be signed until April 1949, by the summer of 1948 Bidault's main objective was achieved: the Vandenberg resolution had cleared the way for the American involvement in Europe and in July an American military mission joined the military committee of the Brussels Pact in London. Despite the fact that France did not participate in the secret talks between London, Washington and Ottawa in March 1948, its role in the inception of the Atlantic Alliance would seem to have been instrumental.[37]

France was also very active in insuring that the Alliance would be as effective as possible in military, but above all in political, terms. She fought, for instance, for the inclusion of Italy. A strongly organized Alliance was of course also seen as a way to promote French national aims, the best instance being the Standing Group which formally at least gave France the same status as the United States and Great Britain.[38] It should also be pointed out that for Paris the Atlantic Alliance, although mainly directed against the Soviet Union, did also provide an Anglo-American guarantee against Germany.[39] Even if the real fear, at least in informed circles, was no longer so much Germany itself, as a Germany that would align itself with Russia, the German question still mattered. Thus the Atlantic Alliance became an all-encompassing tool of French foreign policy: it was to provide for security against both Russia and Germany, and ensure France an exalted status in Western Europe.

In French eyes there was another major dimension of the communist threat and hence another role for the Atlantic Alliance: the Empire, and especially in those years, Indo-China. The French tended to see themselves as soldiers of the Free World in Asia; this rationalized a conflict which had also of course other, more complex causes. There were certainly ulterior motives in this view of things (if only the wish to get American aid for the war in Indo-China), but it was also sincere and it belonged to the complex ideological and political framework of those years, where differences in foreign policy and internal politics criss-crossed at every point.[40]

But, despite its militancy in 1948–49, France was careful not to miss any opportunity for a dialogue with Moscow. On 19 April 1949, Vincent Auriol and Robert Schuman, who had succeeded Bidault as Foreign Minister in July 1948, agreed in principle that the West should be ready to accept a conference with the Soviet Union to promote better relations, even if Schuman was convinced that the main problem arose from the expansionist tendencies of the Soviet regime.[41]

### The evolving Franco-German relationship

At the occasion of the London conference on Germany from February to June 1948, Bidault realized that it was necessary to accept the formation of a West German state in order to get American participation in the defence of Europe. That meant abandoning the previous French aims against Germany, and France risked finding itself without a viable German policy. The only way to retain some control over the new Federal Republic was to embed the Franco-German relationship in a larger European setting. Europe would provide a politically and psychologically acceptable cover for French leadership.[42] When Robert Schuman succeeded Bidault as foreign minister in July 1948, he adopted the same policy and strove for an amelioration of Franco-German relations in a European framework. In Schuman's vision, Germany would be integrated in a mesh of European economic and political ties, and its security would be guaranteed by the three Western allies. Thus Germany would be under control and prevented from drifting eastward, which was for Schuman the main danger.[43]

The blueprint for this vision was the French proposal for a supranational European authority to control the coal and steel industries. Its underlying intent was to fuse French and German industrial power, developing ideas canvassed between the wars. (The main coal and steel areas of these two countries, Alsace-Lorraine and the Ruhr, had been controlled first by Germany and then by France in the period 1870–1925, and a Franco-German steel cartel had been created in 1926.) The proposal was drawn up in great secrecy by Jean Monnet, architect of France's postwar national plan for economic recovery, and Schuman announced it on 9 May 1950. Monnet insisted that there must be supranational control and, to avoid British procrastination, Schuman demanded that all interested parties must declare themselves by 2 June. The British Labour government refused to make an a priori commitment to supranationalism, but 'the Six' – France, Germany, Italy and the three Benelux countries – agreed to start discussions. Although the European Coal and Steel Community would not come into existence until August 1952, the essential, pathbreaking decisions had been taken in May 1950; and they set a course towards the European Economic Community of 1958.

This solution of the years 1949–50 was the one best suited to French interests: there was now only one adversary, the Soviet Union, which resolved the previous contradiction of French policy, and the German potential would not drift to the East. But France would retain a much more important status than the Federal Republic in the Western system, and of course Germany would remain disarmed and would not become a member of the Atlantic Alliance. This convenient arrangement, which for the French should have been a long-term one, was to be promptly shattered by the Korean war and the American decision to rearm Germany.

### 1950–2: the problem of German rearmament and the European solution

Since 1948 the French military, as well as their American and British counterparts, knew that it would be necessary to rearm Germany.[44] For the politicians, however, this was still anathema; Schuman, for instance, repeated several times from the autumn of 1948 to the spring of 1950, and most forcefully, that rearming Germany was out of the question.[45] But the war in Korea in June 1950 convinced the Truman Administration of the need to rearm Germany. In July Washington decided to grant the Europeans their wish and to step up American military commitments in Europe, but on the condition that twelve German divisions would be armed and put under NATO command. At the conference in New York in mid-September, the French were isolated and under heavy pressure to accept German rearmament. On 16 September Schuman made a speech about Germany which was full of distrust. He had been encouraged to remain firm by Jean Monnet, who feared that a rearmed Germany would once again do her traditional balancing act between East and West.

The French attitude was the cause of a severe crisis between Paris and Washington. Schuman knew that American military assistance to France and Europe could be put in jeopardy. Alternatively the Americans could decide to over-ride French opposition and integrate German elements in their forces in Germany. Now was the time of reckoning: German rearmament was the price to be paid for Western solidarity, for a bigger American involvement in Europe, for an American supreme commander for NATO forces (all things for which the French had been clamouring since 1948). The pretence that the Western alliance was useful as much against Germany than against the Soviet Union (a pretence that had been helpful to get French public support for the 1947–9 shift) had outlived its usefulness and had now to be discarded.

Jean Monnet found the way out of the crisis: he suggested to Schuman the concept of a European army organized along the lines of the European Coal and Steel Community which France had proposed to her European partners on 9 May. Thus security against the Soviet Union would be achieved without recreating a German national army. Minister President Pleven introduced the European army plan before the National Assembly on 24 October. In this army German units would be integrated at the lowest possible level, that of the battalion. A Council of Ministers from the participating countries, a European minister of defence and a European Assembly would control this Army, which would be integrated into NATO and placed under NATO, that is American, command – the main objective being to implicate as fully as possible the United States in the defence of Europe. The scheme was very complex, all the more so because France would retain unintegrated units for overseas duty. The French Assembly adopted the plan, but in fact it voted less *for* a European Army than *against* German rearmament.

This European solution would allow Paris both to please the Americans and to control Germany. There was also a sincere European spirit at work, which was born during the War and had been nurtured in the belief in common values shared yesterday against Hitler, today against Stalin. But this European conviction was of course intermingled with more specifically national motives: everyone in Paris agreed that Europe should be under French leadership.

But the European solution – the French concept of a European army, which had been devised both to control German rearmament and to make it acceptable for the French public (only five years after the war!) – actually made things worse. We shall not dwell here on the intricacies and contradictions of the European army plan, although two well-known quips express the situation better than anything: 'the European Army should be stronger than the Red Army but smaller than Luxembourg's'; 'after having tied Germany to us to control her we strive hard to untie ourselves'. But the main problem was French public opinion, as we know it from the polls: it was willing to support the Western alliance; it was, by a very thin majority, ready to accept the necessity of Germany rearmament; but it was certainly not ready to accept the dissolution of the French Army into an integrated European army. In fact, ironically, the solution that best suited French public opinion was the American proposal of 1950: German divisions under NATO command without European integration.[46] It came to that eventually in 1954 under the Paris Agreements.

The European army concept had first of course to be accepted by the Americans and the Germans, both initially very reluctant. Schuman managed to convince Chancellor Adenauer that the French concept better protected Germany's equality of rights than the American one, and on 8 November 1950 Adenauer adhered to the idea of a European army. In June 1951 Jean Monnet persuaded Eisenhower, then NATO commander-in-chief, that the French concept was workable. Thereafter the Americans became the staunchest supporters of the European army. Meanwhile talks had begun in Paris on 15 February 1951 between France, Italy, Luxembourg, Belgium and Germany. On 24 July 1951, the conference finished a report suggesting the creation of a European Defence Community and the formation of German divisions integrated into European corps.

On 23 August the Cabinet adopted the EDC: it would be the best guarantee against German militarism and it would weld Germany to Western Europe and prevent her either aligning herself with the Soviet Union or practising a balancing act between East and West. Furthermore the EDC and the European Coal and Steel Community would lead to a European political union under French leadership. But it was also understood that Germany should not be admitted into NATO and that France should retain forces under national control for use overseas.[47] The conclusions of the cabinet meeting on 23 August are thus quite revealing of the intermingling of Cold-War problems and traditional national interests which characterized French policies at that time. Particularly telling in that respect was the refusal of Paris to see Germany join NATO: thus France would keep a margin of superiority in normal times and even a guarantee of security in case Germany changed her foreign policy orientation.

Finally two treaties were signed in May 1952: the Bonn treaty on the 26th, ending the occupation statute for Germany, and the Paris treaty the following day creating the EDC. Those two treaties were linked and could not become valid before having been both ratified by all partners. This *Junktim* was the result of very difficult Franco-German negotiations, Paris not wanting to give sovereignty back to Germany before the EDC became effective. The most difficult point in the Bonn treaty touched the 'reserved rights' of the Allies on German reunification and on Berlin: Paris, against Bonn and with only tepid supports from London and Washington, maintained that only a final peace treaty with Soviet participation could replace the Yalta and Potsdam agreements and that those should not be voided by the May 1952 treaties. France did not want to affront Moscow on this point and wished also to keep a lever on the German question and not to leave Germany alone to discuss her reunification with Russia. Furthermore Paris insisted that in case of Germany being reunified it should remain in the EDC: a major fear in Paris was to see German reunification jeopardizing the European system which was meant to control Germany, particularly if, as Schuman and Monnet were convinced, this reunification eventually should come about. And finally Schuman achieved a declaration by the British and the Americans that they would consider a break-up of the EDC as a threat to themselves.[48]

It should be pointed out here that one of the motives of French European policy was also to alleviate the East-West rift and to prevent the Cold War from getting out of hand. The idea was that a united Europe would be more independent from the United States and could prevent them from following too aggressive a policy towards the Soviet Union. On the other side, it was thought in many quarters (wrongly but no doubt sincerely) that Moscow would come to look upon the European unification movement as a security guarantee against an eventual rebirth of German nationalism. Jean Monnet most explicitly shared those views, as early as May 1950, as he devised the Coal and Steel Community scheme, and even more so with his European army concept in September of that year. The outbreak of the Korean war made it all the more urgent that Europe should be in a position to exert a moderating influence on America; the war should by no means be escalated (if only to prevent a diversion of American resources away from Europe) and China should be treated very gingerly, not least because it was understood in Paris by 1950 that no solution of the Indo-China war would be possible without Chinese participation.

Not all leaders shared Monnet's views to the extent of seeing united Europe not only as a member of the Atlantic community but also as a kind of third force between America and the Soviet Union. But many leaders felt that the 1952 treaties, which both constricted Germany in a European framework and made sure that reunification could not take place without the agreement of the four occupying countries, including the Soviet Union, could be the basis of an unspoken Franco-Soviet agreement to control the development of the German question and prevent the forming of a close link between both 1952 treaties, as we have seen. Few leaders believed that there would be no Franco-Soviet agreement on Germany, even unspoken, and that the best solution would be the ultimate reunification of a Germany firmly embedded in a European union. This was Robert Schuman's view, but he was fairly isolated, most leaders agreeing in 1952 to German rearmament for a mixture of the avowed reasons and ulterior motives listed above.

A last-minute complicating factor had been Stalin's note of 10 March 1952 proposing the neutralization of Germany and, at least outwardly, its reunification.

While understanding quite well that Stalin's major objective was to block the EDC, the French government took the Soviet note quite seriously. In particular, the prospect of a neutralized and rearmed Germany seemed for Paris the most disquieting. Schuman was convinced that it was therefore necessary to accelerate the Western integration of the FRG but at the same time that one should negotiate seriously with the Soviets, in order not to relinquish to them the principle of German reunification: in Schuman's eyes, nothing would have been more dangerous than to let the Germans believe that only Moscow cared about their reunification.[49]

The 1952 treaties and the French reaction to Stalin's note encompassed the kind of programme which was developed between 1948 and 1952 by a group of diplomats with the full support of Robert Schuman (Foreign Minister from July 1948 to December 1952). (The same programme would be to some extent also valid under Prime Minister Pierre Mendès-France in 1954 and under Foreign Minister Pinay in 1955.[50]) The main points of this programme were:

– the inevitability of the Cold War because of the ideological preconceptions of the Soviet Union;
– the absolute necessity of western unity;
– but also the need to avoid giving the Western alliance a militaristic, provocative turn and to keep the door open for negotiations;
– the need to bind Germany to the West in a European framework;
– but also the advisability of taking into account the problem of German reunification.

### *1953–4: the ordeal of German rearmament and the national-neutralist temptation*

Stalin's note of March 1952 convinced part of public opinion and Parliament that one should at all costs try a final negotiation with Moscow before rearming Germany. French diplomats at the time believed that the Soviet notes of 1952 had made the ratification of the EDC very difficult, if not impossible. In any case it is clear that the opposition to EDC grew strongly in the second part of 1952. On 6 June de Gaulle publicly condemned the EDC: although he believed German rearmament was necessary, he rejected the concept of European integration. In October the old and influential Radical leader Edouard Herriot also rejected the EDC. In December the Pinay government fell, partly because Schuman was being heavily criticized on account of the EDC. In the René Mayer cabinet in January 1953 the new Foreign Minister was Bidault: both men tried to strike a deal with the Gaullists; the EDC treaty would be modified by 'additional protocols' largely depriving it of its supranational character. Although Mayer went a long way towards successfully negotiating such protocols with France's partners, he fell in May. In the meantime the EDC had become the centre of deep political crisis, reminiscent of the Dreyfus Affair at the beginning of the century. In March Marshal Juin, speaking in fact in the name of the Army, had publicly condemned the EDC.[51] On the other side the Christian Democrats tried to save the EDC by a bold move to form immediately a supranational European political union. But this rush forward augmented the opposition to the EDC, as people now felt France would disappear as a country.[52]

The fight for or against the EDC had become very bitter; old dividing political lines tended to disappear, giving way to surprising combinations, for instance between Gaullists and communists.[53] A new factor was Stalin's death in March 1953 and the general expectation that détente would become possible. Influential people on the left, in the small but important 'Union progressiste', comprising so-called neutralists and fellow-travellers, in a complex net of small groups, in publications such as the weekly *Observateur* which had been founded in 1950 explicitly to promote neutralist ideas, campaigned now for a complete foreign-policy change. They demanded that France should renounce German rearmament, dissolve or at least tone down NATO, and negotiate with the Soviet Union a new European security system. For instance Claude Bourdet from the *Observateur* suggested in its 18 February 1954 issue the constitution of a 'European Entente' including all European countries – Western, Eastern or neutral – and guaranteed both by the United States and the Soviet Union.

But in fact a close study of the arguments coming from this group shows that they were often less neutralist than nationalist. Anti-Americanism and a deeply traditional anti-Germanism were very much in evidence: NATO and the EDC were going to make France dependent on both Germany and America. The way out was said to be a deal with Russia, in a most traditional sense recalling the 'Alliance franco-russe' of 1891 or the Pact of 1944. This explains the otherwise astonishing links between this group and the Gaullists (from time to time both used the services of the same publicists!) or with elements of the rightist parties, not to mention the Radicals and many socialists. There were of course also ideological factors at work in this fight for or against EDC: it tended to be for many also a fight for and against communism.[54] But it is important to point out that the national standpoint was for many more important than the *ideological* one. Not only does this explain a great deal about the otherwise difficult-to-follow French vagaries on the EDC, but it also explains much about the succeeding years, particularly the foreign policy of the Fifth Republic and the support it got from otherwise astonishing quarters.

Nevertheless, the Christian Democrats, who made up the core of the Laniel Cabinet which succeeded Mayer's, and also Georges Bidault remained steadfast in their support of the EDC and of the Atlantic foreign policy developed since 1948. They could count on the majority of the socialists, about a half of the Radicals and a good proportion of the Moderates. Bidault in particular remained quite firm, despite the legend of the 'global Deal'. In 1952 the German magazine *Der Spiegel* had ventilated the idea that France would be willing to trade Soviet help for a negotiated settlement in Indo-China against the European army. Bidault was suspected in 1953–4 of harbouring such ideas, but the record proves that he did not contemplate such a scheme and indeed explicitly rejected it.[55] For instance, at the Berlin Four Powers conference in February 1954 Bidault was the first to reject the Soviet proposals, amounting in fact to the neutralization of West Germany without a real reunification and to the establishment of a European security system without the United States.

Nevertheless Bidault's German policy and his conception of the East-West conflict were not exactly the same as those of Schuman. Whereas Schuman believed that the partition of Germany was neither durable nor desirable, Bidault was perfectly happy with it; for him this partition allowed the perfect solution – French security against Germany was guaranteed by the division of the country; French security against the Soviet Union was guaranteed by binding West Germany to the West.

One can detect two different attitudes toward the Cold War in French governing circles: Schuman's school, and Bidault's. Both schools agreed on the extent of the threat, on its ideological nature, on the need for strong western unity. For Schuman, however, the Cold War was first of all a competition for Germany and Europe, whereas for Bidault it was a global competition, which affected the French empire as much or even more than Germany. For the first school a European framework inside the western alliance was all-important. For Bidault and his ilk the European union was less vital than the direct link to Washington to guarantee the security of France and of its empire against the Soviet Union. He believed that, thanks to her empire and to her direct links with America, France would retain a world role similar to that of Great Britain – the German problem being well cared for by the partition of Germany.[56]

### *1954: Pierre Mendès-France and the disillusion of the national-neutralists*

By the spring of 1954 France was in deep crisis: the EDC dispute was more acute than ever and on 7 May the Indo-China crisis boiled over when the camp at Dien Bien Phu fell. On 14 June Pierre Mendès-France was called upon to form a new government. His mandate was to extricate France from the war in Indo-China and also to solve in one way or the other the EDC question.[57] Mendès-France's advent aroused hope and many expectations in national-neutralist circles: he was on the record as an opponent of the war in Indo-China, he was not a supporter of EDC and generally speaking it was felt that he would follow a line more independent of Washington and seek détente with Moscow. Furthermore, his government included Gaullist ministers and some of his nearest aides were very close to the neutralists.

But in fact Mendès-France's policies, by and large, would dismay those circles, who in fact turned against him as soon as the autumn of 1954. First of all, and contrary to hostile rumours coming from Bonn and Washington, Mendès-France did not contemplate a 'Global Deal' any more than Bidault. He saw Molotov in Geneva on 10 and 21 July but there was no question of exchanging a settlement in Indo-China against an abandonment of EDC. In fact Molotov not only did not give a hint that such a deal would be possible, but went out of his way to make it very clear, although in a roundabout way, that a global deal was out of the question. As for Indo-China the agreement at the Geneva Conference on 21 July was more favourable to Western interests than many, including John Foster Dulles, had thought possible: Vietnam was partitioned as far north as the 17th parallel, instead of the 13th demanded by the Vietminh; Laos and Cambodia were free from

Vietminh interference and could enter international security arrangements.[58] After Geneva, instead of a rapprochement with North Vietnam, as was wished for by many in left-oriented circles, Mendès-France agreed that France would be a members of the South-East Asia Treaty Organization (SEATO), sponsored by Washington. Generally speaking, Mendès-France felt it was now up to the United States to prevent south-east Asia from falling under communist influence.[59]

As for the EDC, Mendès-France's closest councils were deeply divided. Some felt that France should not endanger her relations with Moscow by being party to German rearmament or at least should do everything to promote a deal with the Soviet Union that would, through a combination of general disarmament and a solution to the German question more or less on the neutralist line defended by Moscow, suppress the need for EDC. But others believed that although EDC certainly was not the last expression of wisdom, if there were no Western security organization including the FRG, the latter might be tempted to make a deal with the Soviet Union. Mendès-France was to follow the advice of the second group. After having tried vainly in August with the European partners to modify the EDC in a way acceptable to France, and after the final failure of the European army in the French Parliament on 30 August, Mendès-France quickly retrieved the situation with the very effective help of the British. The Paris Agreements of 23 October finally solved the problem: Germany would get her full sovereignty (apart from questions concerning Berlin and reunification); she would be rearmed and would be admitted to NATO and to the Brussels Treaty of 1948, which became the Western European Union (WEU). This solution, which amounted to the rearmament of Germany in an Atlantic framework without the absorption of French forces in an integrated European system, had been in fact all along what French public opinion preferred or at any rate disliked least. It had the further big advantage of binding Great Britain to the defence of Europe through the Western European Union, which had not been the case with EDC. Thus Mendès-France had contributed mightily to the ultimate success of the Western effort to organize a security system including Western Germany, one of the biggest achievements of the post-war period. No wonder the national-neutralist circles were deeply disillusioned!

Through all those negotiations Mendès-France showed that he understood the need to maintain good relations with the United States, although the Eisenhower Administration at first remained very suspicious of him. Mendès-France feared that, if Paris did nothing to replace the defunct EDC, Washington would either establish a special relationship with Germany or disengage itself from Europe. As for Germany, Mendès-France expressed publicly on several occasions the need to 'chain her to the West', which had been the basic philosophy of his Christian Democratic predecessors. Furthermore, after a difficult beginning, he established a good working relationship with Adenauer, solving with him the vexing Saar problem.[60] He also agreed not to discuss Germany with Moscow without prior consultation with Bonn, encouraged French industrialists to deal with their German counterparts, and discussed with the Germans an economic rapprochement underpinned by the fact that both countries were now respectively their best trading partners. It is not going too far to say (because economics, politics and geography have their own compelling reasons) that the Common Market and the Franco-

German co-operation under de Gaulle after 1958 were in some way prepared under Mendès-France.

At the same time Mendès-France was very careful to guard specific French interests. When NATO prepared itself to adopt the 'New Look' nuclear strategy of massive retaliation announced in January 1954 by Dulles, Mendès-France insisted that the very quick decisions that would have to be taken in a nuclear war should be discussed in an inner circle of the Atlantic Alliance, between the American President and the British and French Prime Ministers. Thus France would retain a margin of superiority over Germany, even after her accession to NATO. This consideration also played a role in the secret decision of 26 December 1954 to launch a military nuclear effort.[61]

Finally Mendès-France was convinced that it would be necessary to talk with the Soviets after the Paris agreements had been ratified. He wanted to be able to announce those talks quickly to ease ratification in the French assemblies. In fact the ratification in the National Assembly in December was very difficult and prompted fears for the outcome in the Senate later. And probably Mendès-France felt he owed such talks to that part of his political base which had been clamouring for them since 1952. But, and this was a big difference with his leftist supporters, he was ready to contemplate a conference with the Soviet Union only *after* the rearmament of Germany had been secured, and not *before*. He probably believed that détente could be achieved with Moscow once the West had reached the position of strength underscored by the ratification of the Paris Agreements. It appears that Mendès-France had a concept for managing East-West relations and overcoming the Cold War: the West should of course achieve the necessary level of military security, but the real confrontation with communism was not on the military but on the economic and social level. Excessive insistence on military preparations would divert the resources of the West, and leave open the field of peaceful competition to the Soviets, with catastrophic effects on Western public opinion. On the other hand, the right policy could force Moscow to devote more resources to peaceful ends, leading to a lessening of tensions and even to a transformation of the Soviet system.

On 22 November 1954, in his speech before the UN – a speech which was for him evidently very important, Mendès-France offered a package to promote an East-West Détente: a Big Four Conference in May 1955 (that is after ratification of the Paris Agreements), an initiative to unstick the negotiations over the Austrian State Treaty, a system of arms control for Eastern Europe similar to the one included in the Paris Agreements for the WEU, later a European security arrangement based on an agreement between WEU and the East-European arms-control system.

Those proposals went a long way to accommodate Soviet views: the Austrian Treaty was meant to prevent an *Anschluss* with Germany (a fear in both Paris and Moscow). Paris was now ready to discuss a European security arrangement *before* German reunification, which was anathema to Washington and Bonn. Paris was also willing to contemplate arms control *without* verification, which ran contrary to stated Western doctrine but which coincided with Soviet views, as also in the case of the priority given to European security before German reunification.

Mendès-France was undoubtedly loyal to the Western alliance; but he felt compelled to put forward those proposals in order to secure ratification of the Paris Agreements. There were other reasons, too – such as his views on the Cold War and sensitivity to the more leftish part of his constituency. He also wished to avoid pushing German rearmament too far and to achieve a minimum of indirect understanding with Moscow about Germany, or at least to reassure Moscow that the West would not abuse its position of strength after rearming Germany. But the Soviet government, in the throes of unresolved leadership problems at the time, did not appear to pay the slightest attention to Mendès-France's views: they were probably seen as too destabilizing for Eastern Europe. And on 5 January 1955 Mendès-France tried in vain to convince London and Washington to hold a Big Four conference, if not in May at least during the summer. In his attitude toward the United States or the German problem, and in his prudence with respect to the Soviet Union, Mendès-France was much nearer to his predecessors than is usually assumed.

### 1955: Détente?

On 5 February 1955 the government of Mendès-France fell. He was succeeded on 23 February by Edgar Faure, who had always been interested in Russia and who thought détente was now possible. Furthermore Faure wanted to put up a show of independence toward the United States. This was, however, more appearance than substance, and anyway the very Atlanticist Foreign Minister Antoine Pinay and the professional diplomats at the Quai d'Orsay did not really modify the previous line.

Paris was convinced a period of détente was now possible, because Stalin's successors wanted to lessen international tensions – owing to the vexed settlement of Stalin's legacy, to economic and doctrinal difficulties, and to the fact that the West had pushed through the rearmament of Germany, thereby achieving a position of strength.[62] But the French diplomats and Foreign Minister Pinay remained convinced that the long-term objectives of Moscow remained unchanged, despite its current tactical agility: the dogmatic certainty about the final victory of communism over capitalism was still evident and the Soviet Union would bide its time, trying to break up the Western block through subtle tactics.[63]

The first indication that Moscow was ready for détente came with Molotov's speech on 8 February, which for the first time alluded to a possible settlement of the Austrian question.[64] This turn in a negotation which had remained blocked since 1949 promptly led to the signature of the Austrian State Treaty on 15 May. The Quai d'Orsay believed that Moscow intended that the Austrian treaty should be the model for a German settlement and that this was the reason for its speedy conclusion. Moscow apparently no longer strove for an internationally guaranteed neutral status for Germany, but would be content with a Germany free of any international attachment: that would be enough to jeopardise the western system.[65]

The Austrian question had elicited much interest in Paris since the autumn of 1954; as we have seen, Mendès-France in November at the UN had suggested solving this question as a first step toward détente. Many in Paris believed France and Russia had a common interest in solving quickly the Austrian problem now that the FRG was going to get her full sovereignty and be rearmed, in order to prevent an eventual *Anschluss*: this is another instance of an enduring French national interest despite the European and Atlanticist rhetoric.[66]

But the major concern in Paris was the ratification of the Paris Agreements by the Senate, which was set for March 1955 and promised to be difficult. Edgar Faure, who believed in détente, decided to exploit this apparently difficult situation to further his aims. He saw the Soviet ambassador, Vinogradov, on 22 March and said that the Paris Agreements would certainly be ratified but that France would insist in London and Washington on a summit conference of the Big Four at the beginning of the summer. On the same day, Faure wrote to Eisenhower and to Churchill that he had to be able to promise the Senate such a summit in order to secure ratification of the Agreements.[67] This piece of diplomatic blackmail was successful: the British and the Americans, until then very cautious, agreed to begin the preparations among experts for the summit respectively on 29 March and 11 April.[68] The Soviets formally accepted the conference on 11 May, Faure and Pinay could assure the Senate there would be a summit, and the Paris Agreements were ratified by a comfortable majority on 28 March.

It was understood in Paris that, whatever the results of the conference, a divided or reunified Germany should remain firmly bound to the West. But at the same time it was necessary to be ready to exploit any opportunity to solve some of Europe's problems, taking into account legitimate Soviet security interests.[69] The French felt that the Americans and British took a much too stereotyped view of possible Soviet moves. The Eden Plan of February 1954, which still had the support of London and Washington, and which foresaw all-German elections and reunification before the conclusion of a peace treaty, seemed too rigid and could be easily circumvented by Russian proposals that would be difficult to resist. It was therefore, in the French view, important to be prepared to set conditions for the status of the future German government and for the eventual peace treaty as necessary precautions against Soviet manoeuvres or even German claims.[70] Those conditions amounted in fact to one: that the future German government should be wholly free of Soviet interference and really free to join the Western security system.[71]

Although Paris recognized the need to offer the Soviets security guarantees in exchange for German reunification and agreed with London that security in Europe and reunification should be discussed in tandem in Geneva, it does not seem that the Quai d'Orsay developed such elaborate proposals as Eden's plan of a demilitarized zone between East and West. German ideas along these lines, according to which the Eastern part of the country should remain demilitarized after reunification as a security guarantee to the Soviets, met with much scepticism in Paris.[72] The French were very cautious, believing that under the pretext of European security the Soviets would in fact try to single out Germany and erode her links with NATO.[73] The most Paris was willing to contemplate was a general reduction of forces, which should not be limited to Germany or even to Europe, but should also include the United States and the Soviet Union. For Paris refused to see Germany singled out in any force reduction, and a disarmament limited to

Western and Eastern Europe – because of the military importance of the respective countries concerned – would be too advantageous for the Soviets.[74]

Because of Edgar Faure's personal attitude it has usually been thought that France was readier than her partners to make concessions to the Soviets in Geneva. This impression has been reinforced by the fact that Pinay, who was much more cautious, was a less flamboyant personality. But the record shows that France was in fact very uncompromising in Geneva, much more so at any rate than Great Britain, although she had been instrumental since 1954 in bringing about this conference. This conference was in fact felt to be necessary above all to placate public opinion and Parliament; in substance Paris was not ready to sacrifice Germany's links with NATO, which were deemed essential for French security with respect to the Soviet Union but also to Germany. The worst possible outcome would have been that of a reunified, rearmed Germany free of binding commitments.

Thus it is not surprising that the French did not share the general feeling of elation after the July summit.[75] For them it was clear Moscow was not ready to reunify Germany. And if the Soviets were willing to sign a Security Pact, their real objective was thus to emasculate NATO and WEU.[76] The reaction in Paris was the same after the conference of the Foreign Ministers in Geneva in October–November. There the three Western Allies had proposed a comprehensive European security plan with controlled force limitations to be put into effect at the time of German reunification, but the Soviets had shown no interest. Paris's conclusion was now that a neutralized reunified Germany would not be enough for Moscow: a reunified Germany should be politically dependent on the Russians. The Western aims in Geneva had been, first, to bring the Soviet Union to negotiate, although the prospects were dim; second, to show Western public opinion that the Allies were ready to concede to Moscow a security compact in exchange for German reunification, and that they did not seek simply to push the military boundary with the East to the German-Polish border; third, to show the Germans that Moscow and not the West was the real obstacle to German reunification. The last two aims had both been achieved.[77] It would thus seem that the French leaders, despite some illusions harboured by Edgar Faure, were now free from the national-neutralist ideas which had seemed so strong in 1953–4. They had not entertained unwarranted hopes in Geneva, which was for them first of all an exercise in managing public opinion.

### Conclusion

France did play an important role in the Cold War and helped to shape some of its features, particularly the Western security build-up. The French role was complicated, however, by several factors. First, France did not for a moment renounce opportunities to further her own national interests. She took care as much as possible, through the Standing Group and through the secret preparatory decision in 1954 to build an atomic bomb, to preserve her world role on the same standing as Great Britain. The concern for national interests was very much in evidence with respect to Germany, which was both the hereditary enemy and the ally in the new struggle against the Soviet Union. And the national interest underpinned, of course, the French wish to see the defence of the Empire recognized as a legitimate part of the general East-West conflict.

Internal politics played a very important part in the French contribution to the Cold War. In particular the Communist Party was both an incentive to do something to prevent an internal disaster and thus to build up a European and Atlantic security system as a guarantee of French stability, and at the same time a brake that prevented France from waging the Cold War as wholeheartedly as the British or the Americans. But up to a point the same could be said of the Gaullists, who were simultaneously anti-communist and also careful not to waste the chance, one day, of using the Soviet Union, as in 1944, as a counterweight to the United States, in order to follow a very independent line. And national-neutralist ideas, which were in content very different, did often pull in the same direction. The curious cocktail of communist, Gaullist and national-neutralist influences could be extremely potent, as was evident through the EDC crisis.

Nevertheless the heart of the Fourth Republic's body politic, comprising the Christian Democrats, most socialists and a majority of the moderate parties, maintained all in all a constant line of firmness toward the Soviet Union, even though it was more careful than the Americans to make sure that the responsibility for the different Cold War crises should rest clearly, in the eyes of Western and particularly German public opinion, in Moscow. But of course Paris could afford to remain more prudent than Washington because it did not bear the brunt of East-West confrontation.

### Bibliographical note

For a broad introduction see Alfred Grosser, *The Western Alliance: European-American Relations since 1945*, trans. Michael Shaw (London, 1980), which is particularly strong on France, and the early chapters of Michael M. Harrison, *The Reluctant Ally: France and Atlantic Security* (Baltimore, 1981). The only major study in English to exploit the French archives on the 1940s is John W. Young, *France, the Cold War and the Western Alliance, 1944–1949* (Leicester, 1990). On American influence see Irwin M. Wall, *The United States and the Making of Postwar France, 1945–1954* (New York, 1991), originally published in French in 1989.

As for the literature in French, there is as yet no comprehensive book about France and the Cold War (we intend to write one). The best synthesis remains Alfred Grosser, *La Quatrième République et sa politique extérieure* (Paris, 1961). Three major studies, published more recently, help to understand the French position: Pierre Mélandri, *Les Etats-Unis face à l'unification de l'Europe, 1945–1954* (Paris, 1980), Raymond Poidevin, *Robert Schuman, Homme d'Etat, 1886–1963* (Paris, 1986) and Pierre Gerbet, *Le relèvement 1944–1949* (Paris, 1991). On the start of the Cold War there is the archivally-based study by Annie Lacroix-Riz, *Le choix de Marianne: les rélations franco-américaines, 1944–1948* (Paris, 1985). On the availability of archives see note one.

# PART THREE

# THE VANQUISHED

## 5 *Italy*

### ILARIA POGGIOLINI

In discussing Italy and the Cold War, what deserves to be emphasized right at the start is the peculiarity of the country's role in the post-war ideological confrontation. A founder of NATO, Italy was simultaneously trying to transcend her status as a defeated nation of the Second World War. A Cold War ally of the United States, she was, internally, a prime European battleground in the struggle against the 'communist danger'. These ambiguities are central to what follows. Therefore, my purpose is fourfold: first, to analyze how Italy worked her passage from enemy to co-belligerent in the wake of the armistice signed in September 1943; second, what made her a test-case in East-West relations in the course of Allied occupation and the elaboration of the peace treaty eventually concluded in 1947; third, to explore the internal dimension of Italy's post-war stabilization and pro-western foreign policy presided over by the Christian Democrat leader Alcide de Gasperi between 1945 and 1953; fourth, to show how Italy tried to overcome her marginality in NATO during the 1950s and secure revision of the punitive clauses of the peace treaty. I shall focus also on the most debated issues in historiography, and offer some remarks on Italy's post-war experience.

Two sets of preliminary considerations will help to put into context the political and academic environment in which the historiographical debate on Italy's post-war choices took place. Firstly, it has to be pointed out that both domestic and foreign policies were perceived at the time as equally affected by the Cold War. As a result, the political and ideological struggle between the right, the centre and the left of the political spectrum had a major impact on the analysis of events elaborated in Italy during the early post-war years. This explains why one can observe during those years a marked prevalence of an ideological approach over a scientific and academic one. Secondly, before the archives were opened, the study of diplomatic history was in a very early stage in Italy. Considerable difficulty was experienced in reconciling traditionalism, Marxism and the recent impact of the political sciences on the field of diplomatic history.

Thus, Italian foreign policy towards the Cold War was first discussed within the context of the debate between two basic options described as 'restauration' and 'innovation' (see bibliographical note). Restauration meant the continuity of the state represented by the ruling Christian Democrat Party and the alliance with the United States in foreign policy. Innovation referred to the failed attempt of the political forces emerging from the Resistance against the Germans to achieve a complete renewal both of structure of the state and also of Italian foreign policy. Within this context the Cold War was perceived as the turning point which contributed to the success of the conservative option against the radical project of innovation.

More recently, during the late 1970s and 1980s, this schematic view of a supposedly forced choice between these two contrasting options was reconsidered by diplomatic historians. They could finally base their interpretations on primary sources. Moreover, time had elapsed and the ideological passions were less intense than before. However, the numerous interpretative approaches and methodologies within Italian diplomatic history were not easily reconciled. What had a large share in prompting a reassessment of Italy's role in international relations in the post-war years was the intensity of the historiographical debate on the origins of the Cold War at the *international* level.

As a result, scholarly attention shifted from the post-war internal political struggle to the process of normalizing Italy's foreign relations with the victorious powers. This shift in the focus of historical analysis resulted, firstly, in enlarging previous knowledge of the interaction between internal stabilization and diplomatic normalization during the years from the signing of the armistice agreements in 1943 to the revision of the Italian peace treaty during the early 1950s and, secondly, it contributed to a better understanding of Italy's role as a test-case in East-West diplomacy during the passage from co-operation to competition.

## An ambiguous co-belligerency (1943–6)

On 10 July 1943 Allied forces invaded Sicily. Two weeks later, on 25 July, the Fascist Grand Council overthrew Mussolini and the King seized the opportunity to appoint Marshal Pietro Badoglio as head of a new government. Badoglio opened negotiations with the Allies. From 3 August, at Lisbon, Tangier, Madrid and again Lisbon, Italian and allied representatives met to discuss the conditions of Italy's surrender. Meanwhile, the Germans increased their forces in the north of Italy and were moving south in order to counteract the Anglo-American offensive. The war on Italian territory way going to last until the spring of 1945.

Furthermore, negotiations for the armistice were soon to make clear that Italian expectations of changing sides at once and of receiving mild armistice terms could not be easily reconciled with the formula of unconditional surrender elaborated by the Allies at Casablanca on 24 January 1943. The terms that Giuseppe Castellano, the Italian representative, and General Eisenhower, Supreme Commander of the Mediterranean Theatre, signed at Cassibile in Sicily on 3 September 1943, were mainly concerned with the war situation and took the form of a military capitulation. A longer document (the 'long armistice'), establishing political, economic and financial conditions, followed.[1]

On the whole the armistice agreements were unpalatable but they did not coincide with a total collapse of the state. An Italian government did not cease to exist even if, following the announcement of the armistice, the Italian army dissolved and Italian institutions were seriously threatened. Hopes faded that a large allied force would land by air in the neighbourhood of Rome before the announcement of the armistice, which took place on 8 September. The next day the Germans reached Rome (which had been deserted by the king) and the government was now under the protection of the Allies in the south. The capital had been left defenceless against German retaliation.

With the armistice agreements, Italy's external relations were to be controlled by the occupying powers. The Allies committed themselves to return the administration of all liberated areas to the Italian government, but only after the end of military operations. What Italy achieved under the armistice was the ambiguous status of co-belligerent. This meant that her contribution to the war on the side of the allied powers would supposedly provide an opportunity to work her passage out of military and political turmoil.

However, making that transition was to prove a long and arduous task because the occupation of Italy and the Italian *resistenza* gave rise to serious disputes between the three major Allies. Washington and London disagreed about the future of the peninsula and consequently about the ultimate aim of their occupation policies. Furthermore, their approach to the definition and implementation of the armistice agreements was dissimilar. On the basis of her traditional interests in the Mediterranean, Great Britain aimed at playing the role of senior partner in Italy. This was denied by Washington, which could also not ignore the pressure of the Italo-American community for a more lenient approach than the British towards Italy.

Moreover, even before negotiating the armistice, in early 1943, the problem of relations between the wartime Allies had affected the future of Italy. British ambitions and the fact that the occupation of the country was developing into a test case of post-war collaboration within the Grand Alliance inevitably led to the establishment of rules of behaviour in dealing with liberated countries. The British request to be acknowledged officially as the senior partner in the occupation of Italy was rejected by the Americans throughout long diplomatic discussions finally concluded at the Trident Conference in Washington in May 1943. Of course, this did not put an end to the dispute but it avoided establishing a ranking between the Allies.[2]

As for Soviet participation in discussing and implementing the Italian armistice, the British Foreign Office was in favour of offering Moscow a *droit de regard*, not excluding her from the Western policy of occupation in Italy. By doing so they hoped to prevent the Soviets from dealing with the countries liberated by them in Eastern Europe without consulting the western Allies. However, as soon as it was clear that the signing of the Italian armistice would not be followed by the end of the War, the idea of allowing Moscow to join the Allies in the administration and control of the peninsula faded. The Soviet government was forced to accept being represented by the western Allies at the signing of the Italian armistice and it was left unclear how the Commission which Moscow was expecting to supervise allied armistice policies could be reconciled with London's and Washington's obsession not to weaken Eisenhower's military power in the Mediterranean theatre.[3]

At the Moscow meeting of the Foreign Ministers in October 1943 a compromise was reached. An Advisory Council for Italy, with representatives from the Soviet

Union, was created in order to satisfy Moscow's demands without actually giving it any operative role in Italy. During military operations in the peninsula, this body would have only consultative functions. It would not have any executive powers over the Italian government, as this responsibility remained in the hands of the Commander-in-Chief controlling the actual executive body – the Allied Control Commission – under the orders of the British and American governments. The Allied Control Commission was a *quasi* government, parallel to the Italian one, with the power of authorizing or prohibiting those initiatives which might be in conflict with military operations.[4]

The exclusion of the Soviet Union from the Allied decision-making process in Italy was presented as a matter of necessity. Soviet interests were only partially covered by the existence of the advisory body on which Moscow was represented, and Soviet dissatisfaction over Italy grew. It was not surprising, then, that so unbalanced a situation would be the source of Soviet retaliation in Eastern Europe and in the peninsula itself. The latter took the form of Soviet diplomatic recognition of the Italian government in March 1944. The initiative came after negotiations between Renato Prunas, Secretary General of the Italian Foreign Office, and Andrei Vishinsky, Soviet representative at the Advisory Council. Between 7 and 8 March 1944, Alexander E. Bogomolov, replacing Vishinsky as Soviet representative at the Allied Advisory Council, told Marshal Badoglio that the Soviet government was ready to exchange diplomatic representatives with the rank of ambassador. Badoglio accepted the offer while communicating it to the occupation powers.[5]

The Western reaction was one of disappointment and fear because the re-establishment of direct relations between Italy and the Soviet Union seemed to reopen the question of Moscow's role in the peninsula. Furthermore, the recognition came at a time in which it was likely to exploit the lack of agreement characterizing British-American policy towards Italy. With London still favouring a monarchical restoration controlled by the military, and Washington supporting the appointment of a regent in place of the King and the formation of an Italian government in which all the anti-fascist parties would be represented, the Soviet initiative introduced a third hypothesis that was far from satisfactory for the occupation powers. Such a hypothesis was also the result of the communist leader Palmiro Togliatti's political mediation.[6] Togliatti, back in Italy from Moscow thanks to Soviet-Italian agreements, made possible the formation of a new Badoglio government representing all the major anti-fascist political parties from the Resistance. He made clear to the Italian left that a communist uprising would not be supported by Moscow and that the *Comitato di Liberazione Nazionale* (CLN) – the collective expression of the Resistance representing all the anti-fascist parties – had to come to terms with Badoglio for the sake of Italy's liberation. Furthermore, the king remained in place but he promised to delegate his son Umberto to represent him as *Luogotenente Generale del Regno* after the liberation of Rome.

This so-called *svolta di Salerno* could not have been more of a turn-around. In internal policy it led to a coalition government in which both continuity and change were equally represented. In international relations it prompted London and Washington to rethink their Italian policy and it showed that the breaking-up of the

Grand Alliance was now coming closer. Prunas, who had been negotiating Soviet recognition, told the British and Americans very clearly that the Italian government could not refuse an offer which was meant to improve Italy's status. He also remarked that it was incumbent upon the Western Allies to counteract the Soviet initiative with the revision of their oppressive occupation policy.[7]

As a result of the March 1944 events and of Italian pressure, first the British and then the Americans supported the idea of a preliminary peace treaty. But they could not reconcile themselves to the formation of a new coalition government by Ivanoe Bonomi, a pre-fascist politician and President of the *Comitato centrale di liberazione nazionale*. Before his appointment, London had planned to put an end to the armistice phase by elaborating a new agreement. However, in June, after the liberation of Rome, the nomination of the *Luogotenente* and the formation of the Bonomi government, the British opposed the idea – which was now supported by the Americans – and vetoed the appointment of Carlo Sforza (a prominent anti-fascist *émigré* in the United States during the fascist regime) as foreign minister of the new government.

The preliminary peace plan project faded when Sforza was not appointed (because of the British perception of him as a threat to the monarchy), yet the urgency of improving Italy's status was still on the agenda. Roosevelt and Churchill met at the end of the year at the President's home of Hyde Park and committed themselves to support a 'New Deal for Italy'. The new formula brought into line British and American policies towards Italy and pledged the Western Allies to the amelioration but not the general revision of the armistice clauses. The Allied Control Commission changed its name to Allied Commission and London and Washington recognized diplomatically the Italian government.[8]

In the meantime the political and juridical relations between the CLN in Rome and the CLN in the north of Italy (CLNAI) were undergoing serious difficulties. Tensions arising between groups still active in the north against the Germans and the anti-fascist central government were only resolved when a prominent group of representatives from the north reached an agreement with Rome. This was achieved on 26 November 1944 and was immediately followed by a government crisis which resulted in the formation of a second Bonomi government without the Action Party and the socialists. The new cabinet recognized the CLNAI as the legitimate representative in the north but also aimed at controlling what became known as the 'wind from the North'.

Before the agreements, on 13 November, General Sir Harold Alexander, the Supreme Commander of the Mediterranean theatre, had officially proclaimed that the Allies were not going to be in the position to offer military support to the Resistance in the course of the coming winter. He requested therefore that the partisans would refrain from their activities until the following spring. This move has been interpreted as an attempt to crush the Italian resistance which, in particular in the North, was characterized by a strong leftist component.[9] However, even if competition and hostility did characterize relations between the northern Resistance and the Allies, General Alexander seemed to be perfectly aware of the risks, and even the impossibility, of carrying out his own request. In reality, the lack of support he could offer reflected military necessity.[10]

With the spring offensive of 1945 the liberation of the peninsula came closer. In April, the cities of the north rose up against Nazi occupation and the reunification of Italy was finally achieved. However, the general relief and joy at the end of the anti-fascist struggle and the liberation of the country from the Germans were somehow poisoned by the numerous acts of violence against actual or alleged fascists. Mussolini, captured by a group of partisans, was executed without trial at the end of April.

The wind blowing from the north had also a significant impact on internal political life. A few days after 25 April 1945, a CLNAI delegation went to Rome. On 11 June, Bonomi resigned and on 20 June, Ferruccio Parri, a hero of the Resistance under the name of Maurizio and the leader of the Action Party, succeeded in putting together a new coalition government. The wind from the North had been so powerful that it swept Parri (a rigorous anti-fascist, head of a minority party and an uncompromising intellectual) into the office of Prime Minister. The leader of the Christian Democratic Party, Alcide De Gasperi, was appointed Foreign Minister and the communist Palmiro Togliatti Minister of Justice.

Unfortunately, this was going to be the last attempt to shore up anti-fascist political unity. It failed because Parri's pragmatic and innovative approach did not develop into a coherent project and seemed not to address effectively the growing popular need for security and normalization. In late November 1945, first the liberals, than the Christian Democrats and finally the communists seceded from the government, forcing Parri to resign. The 'great illusion' of putting in motion a radical but democratic change in Italy had faded.[11]

In December 1945 the Christian Democratic leader, Alcide De Gasperi, became Prime Minister. This was a time of great anxiety in Italy. The liberation of the north had only deepened the gulf between a section of the country which had been quickly liberated by the Allies and the other half which had played a substantial as well as prolonged contribution to the war against Germany. Furthermore, the economic situation was deteriorating daily with a shortage of essential goods and rising inflation.

In this context conservative political forces regained influence. Moreover, in Sardinia and Sicily, separatist movements won a remarkable degree of popular support. De Gasperi's government was still a coalition of the parties represented in the CLN, but the Action Party had not entered it and pressures coming from the right and the Church were now stronger than ever before. As far as the occupation powers were concerned, they openly supported De Gasperi and in doing so they handed back to his government the administration of northern Italy. The government, with Togliatti still at the Ministry of Justice, carried on a program of political pacification with the result that, even in public administration, continuity seemed to prevail over a long-desired change.

De Gasperi's government also addressed the major question of how a choice between the monarchy and the republic should be made. The head of the Christian Democratic party favoured the thesis of holding a popular referendum instead of letting the Constituent Assembly choose. There was an intense debate which involved the internal political forces as well as the Allies and saw the King abdicating in favour of his son in a move which might have jeopardized the chances of a republican victory. Finally, it was decided to hold both a referendum and general elections on 2 June 1946. The victory of the republic was not overwhelming but it finally put an end to an ambiguous division of power which had characterized the early post-war period and it marked the success of the republican regime over the past. At the general elections, the Christian Democratic Party won 35.2% of the electoral vote, the socialists 20.7% and the communists 19%. All the other parties failed to bridge the gap already existing between them and the mass parties and they were each left with less than the 10% of the vote.

In the course of two years, the Christian Democratic Party had won the confidence of a large section of the electorate and continued to expand it through the party's links with the Church. The Christian Democratic leadership had also increased its credibility as a potential partner of the United States in carrying on the stabilization of the country. However, De Gasperi's post-election government, due to the presence within it of socialist and communists, together with Christian Democrats and republicans, was not yet in a position to reassure entirely those groups in Italy which kept fearing a communist uprising.

Furthermore, even in Washington, where hopes of good East-West relations were undergoing a dramatic decline, the government was considered quite unbalanced. Local elections in Italy at the end of 1946 strengthened the right, thereby showing that a coalition government with the left would soon be superseded by a radical polarization of the internal and international scene. Increasing ideological confrontation reduced communist manoeuvring capacity within the coalition government and eventually spoiled the innovative role of the left.[12]

In historiography, the debate over the first three years of post-fascist Italy has largely focused on the international dimension of the country's transition from the fascist regime to the republican one. The overthrow of Mussolini and the subsequent negotiation and implementation of the armistice have been analyzed as problems connected with Allied strategy in the Mediterranean. Particular attention has been paid to how London and Washington addressed the question of political change in Italy. This was particularly relevant because British support of the monarchy and the military and American early contacts with the Vatican, through Myron Taylor, Roosevelt's special envoy, had long-term repercussions on post-war internal political life in Italy. The struggle of the Italian *Resistenza* to liberate the country has also been discussed in connection with the question of British, American and Soviet influence in Italy.

Indeed, the emergence of new political forces from anti-fascism and the war of liberation was perceived as a potential threat to the Western policy of granting the continuity of Italian institutions. The question of how the anti-fascist democratic forces became part of the process of reshaping Italian political life is therefore strictly linked with the debate on the exclusion of the Soviet Union from the occupation of Italy and on the role actually played by the Communist Party within the country. The *svolta di Salerno* and Soviet recognition of the Italian government were both test cases of how internal and international issues came to be intermingled in Italy. The historiography of the subject has therefore aimed at achieving a deeper understanding of the immediate and long-term effects of Togliatti's turnaround in 1944. Finally, the debate on the passage from anti-fascist collaboration to

Christian Democratic hegemony has been of great intensity. In the 1970s and 1980s, it developed into a less ideological and more scientific discussion in which analysis of the major international variables played a significant role.[13]

## Between War and Cold War (1946–7)

It is conventionally accepted that Italy's pro-Western choice (*la scelta occidentale*) came about between 1947 and 1949, namely with the 18 April 1948 elections, the Marshall Plan and the Atlantic Pact. However, there is a tendency in recent historiography to trace the origins of Italy's ties with the West back to the end of 1945.[14] This was the time when De Gasperi became Prime Minister and the Council of Foreign Ministers (CFM) met in London to open diplomatic negotiations for the peace treaties with Italy and the countries of Eastern Europe. As result of military priorities, strategic ambitions and fears of the communist danger, the occupation forces had exerted various degrees of pressure on Italian post-fascist governments. Moreover, collaboration between the parties from the Resistance had been wrecked by their unsuccessful attempts to elaborate a common post-war policy, whereas De Gasperi and the Christian Democratic Party had gained internal and foreign support in the course of 1945 and 1946.

As far as Italy's international status was concerned, a peace treaty was needed in order to put an end to the state of war still existing between her and the Allies and to free the country from the occupation. According to the mechanism of peace negotiations set up at Potsdam, the Italian case was supposed to be given priority over the ex-satellites of Germany in the course of diplomatic negotiations. Speeding up the procedure of treaty negotiations would have quickly provided Italy with a new post-war status.[15] But this was not to be. At the CFM in London at the end of 1945 and during subsequent sessions in the spring and summer 1946, competition between former Allies had turned into overt confrontation. This major change in East-West relations caused a deadlock in peace diplomacy, and the collapse of Italian expectations as well as of American hopes of achieving a quick and 'just' settlement.[16]

Thus, in Italy the process of internal stabilization and the search for a new international status actually progressed jointly until 1947. The course taken by the negotiation of the Italian peace treaty, with the failure of the London meetings of the CFM to reach an agreement over the most relevant issues – borders, reparations, colonies and disarmament – made East/West confrontation unavoidable. At this stage of peace negotiations, the Italian government was well aware of the risk of not being able to obtain a satisfactory treaty. Rome therefore decided to step back and requested the postponement of any final decision.

The deadlock in Allied peace negotiations was overcome at the Moscow Conference in December 1945, but at the price of depriving Italy of the priority in peace-making accorded to her at Potsdam. The agreement at Moscow, to negotiate the Italian and Eastern European treaties simultaneously, was going to increase East/West tension and the tendency to play one country against another. Rome felt betrayed and even more inclined than before not to accept a disappointing treaty. Moreover, in a climate of hostility between the superpowers, even London and Washington could not reconcile their views about the future of Italy. Instead of favouring the relaxation of the armistice, like the Americans, the British insisted on proceeding with peace negotiations even if confronted by Soviet obstructionism.[17]

Notwithstanding the fact that the settlement of the Yugoslav-Italian border required Soviet consent, the appeal of a separate peace between the Western Allies and Italy had gained a substantial amount of support among State Department analysts in Washington. When finally the CFM resumed in Paris, the Western representatives shared a new containment attitude towards the Soviet Union, but they were also becaming aware of the fact that firmness had to be coupled with patience in order to avoid a final break-down of peace talks.

The Italians, on the eve of their first post-war national elections in June 1946, feared that this combination would lead to a policy of Western sell-out and kept requesting the revision of the armistice agreement and the postponement of peace negotiations. On the former, they achieved their aim because the victorious powers agreed to abolish the Allied Control Commission and a number of military restrictions. However, after an interruption, the CFM met again in the second half of June 1946 and the ultimate result was the creation of the Free Territory of Trieste, roughly midway between Soviet and American positions but highly disappointing for the Italians. They felt betrayed, and refused to accept a treaty that would deprive them of Trieste and impose reparations as well as military restrictions. But the Peace Conference, held in the course of the summer of 1946 in a climate of East/West tension and suspicion, confirmed the majority of provisions agreed by the CFM. The recommendations of the Conference were subsequently forwarded to the CFM, which began meeting in New York on 4 November 1946. By 12 December, following the last Soviet-American confrontation at the peace table, the great majority of the recommendations were adopted.[18]

Among the major issues addressed by the negotiators, the Yugoslav-Italian border caused endless diplomatic conflicts and was a source of particularly profound disappointment for the Italians. The question can be traced back to the First World War, to the London treaty of April 1915 – which promised Trieste to Italy – and then to the following peace negotiations at Paris where Italian requests were resisted. The problem was subsequently settled with the Rapallo treaty of 1920 and finally, in January 1924, with the treaty of Rome which granted Italy not only Trieste but also Dalmatia (along the eastern coast of the Adriatic Sea) with the city of Fiume.

In 1945, confronted by the actual danger of Yugoslav expansionism, the Italian government was more willing than after the First World War to limit its request to the city of Trieste and the surrounding area. However, at the CFM, notwithstanding the attempt of a commission of experts to draw an equitable line taking into account ethnic factors, the support given by the United States to Italy and by the Soviet Union to Yugoslavia turned the problem into a flashpoint of East-West confrontation. It was only through subsequent compromises that the Free Territory of Trieste came to be recognized as an acceptable solution by all the parties concerned, with the exception of the Italians. Indeed, the loss of Trieste could only be rejected by the great majority of Italian people because this was the very issue on which no party or faction within the country was willing to compromise. However, after the failure of the Security Council of the UN to appoint a Governor, the Free Territory was left divided into two zones, the one controlled by the Anglo-Americans and the other one under Yugoslav occupation. Rome continued to claim the city of Trieste until 1954, when it was finally handed back to Italy.

The Italian peace treaty also settled the question of border adjustments with France, allowing the French to retain a limited but strategically and economically crucial border area on the Alps, previously belonging to Italy. The settlement of the border dispute between Italy and Austria was the only positive achievement of Italian diplomacy. The De Gasperi-Gruber agreements of September 1946, incorporated into the peace treaty, left unchanged the 1919 borders.

Further diplomatic negotiations following the signature of the peace treaty in 1947 resulted in Italy's complete loss of all her colonies, with the exception of Somalia (in East Africa) which was left under Italian trusteeship for a period of ten years. Regarding reparations, the British, American and French governments renounced any claim against the Italians in 1945 but the Soviet Union, Yugoslavia, Greece, Albania and Ethiopia kept requesting their share of reparations, which were to be accepted as part of the economic provisions of the treaty. Finally, the military clauses imposed on Italy the demilitarization of her borders with France and Yugoslavia and of the majority of her coasts and islands. The Italian navy was dismantled and the reconstruction of the army and the air force was strictly limited.[19]

Between doubts, resentments and the first signs of an emerging Italian revisionism, the peace treaty was signed on 10 February 1947. The Italian government and people experienced a strong feeling of disillusion, but they became progressively more aware of the polarization of Europe, a trend from which Italy could not remain aloof. The American State Department was now determined to promote German and European recovery regardless of Soviet wishes, and feared that depression would only play into the hands of the communists. Its planning resulted in Marshall's Harvard speech on 5 June, the discussion in Paris for a joint European recovery programme and the refusal of the Soviets and their satellites to participate. In Italy the spring was equally momentous. In May the left was excluded from De Gasperi's latest attempt to form a durable coalition government, and the following month the Italians joined the Paris discussions about American aid for European Recovery. In both its domestic and international orientation, therefore, these months proved definitive in Italy's post-war history.

### The 'pro-Western choice'

Traditionally, Italian historiography about the first crucial months of 1947 has regarded the visit paid by De Gasperi to the United States as a turning point in American-Italian relations. It is true that the major achievement of the meetings was the fostering of a feeling of mutual understanding. But the interpretation of the visit as the occasion when the exclusion of the left from the coalition government was planned tends to overestimate the significance of the talks. At that time the Christian Democratic leadership had not yet won the confidence of the Truman administration. It was the coincidence of the journey with the concluding stage of the American debate on European stabilization that enabled the Italian leader to put forward his demands for economic assistance and to emphasize his commitment to prevent political unrest. In return, the Truman administration assured De Gasperi that Italy was going to be part of the new plan for European recovery.[20]

What cannot be denied is the fact that, from early 1947, the decline of the wartime Grand Alliance shaped internal political life in Italy. Two years of fears and hopes were about to end with the tightening of the two blocs. As the East/West conflict deepened, Italy became one of the main theatres of the Cold War and tension grew in internal political life accordingly. In the early months of 1947, with the formation of the third De Gasperi government, the Christian Democratic Party and the minor moderate parties moved towards a definitive pro-European and pro-American commitment.[21] The next step was going to be the exclusion of the left from the coalition.

This process had been put into motion by the need of the moderate political forces to prevent the paralysis of any relevant decision on economic issues caused by the lack of common aims within the government. The American position was that unequivocal economic choices could be made only by homogeneous coalitions. Therefore, not only in Italy but also in France, Belgium, Norway and Denmark, the presence of the communist party was seen as the major obstacle preventing those decision being taken. If a policy of productivity and modernization was the aim, the moderate Western European parties were left by the Americans confronting the dilemma of how to achieve that aim. Strong pressures from Washington were not needed because the paralysis which the coalition governments were experiencing suggested that the solution could only be found in a new political and economic environment. In Italy this meant that De Gasperi started planning the 'unloading' of the communists and socialists from the government in order to move on towards an effective strategy which was supposed to lead the country out of the tunnel of economic crisis.

This had not been on the agenda at the time of De Gasperi's visit to the United Sates in January, but it became an issue in April when the government asked Alberto Tarchiani, the Italian ambassador in Washington, to return to Rome for consultations. Tarchiani made it clear that there was a urgent need to form a homogeneous government in Italy in order to achieve Washington's full support. On his return to Washington he obtained from the State Department further assurances that the move would be approved and supported.[22]

The subsequent government crisis of May–June 1947 broke up the anti-fascist coalition and led to the dismissal of the communist and socialist parties. Only six days later the Marshall Plan was announced and immediately received Rome's unconditional support. The new climate of confidence in Italy's stabilization was not spoiled either by a violent reaction of the left or by a realistic perception of the limited short-term benefits involved in Italy's participation in the Marshall Plan. Actually the Plan only came into being one year later and the emergency assistance (Interim Aid) did not become available until the beginning of 1948.[23]

As for the immediate reaction of the leftist parties to their dismissal, Togliatti strongly advocated moderation, arguing that an open confrontation would only play into the hands of the moderate parties. Until the Marshall Plan was rejected and denounced by Moscow in July 1947, and the Cominform, co-ordinating all the European communist parties under Soviet supervision, was created in September, the left attempted not to undermine its chances of re-entering a coalition government in the future. By the end of 1947 this hope had faded and the difficult dialogue between the government and the left shifted to open confrontation.[24]

As the historiographical debate shows very clearly, the impact of the Marshall Plan on the realignment of internal political forces and on the decline of East–West relations has therefore been of major consequence. Scholars have also discussed how the American message of 'productivity' was perceived in Italy and what this meant for the Italian society.[25] As far as the government was concerned, the Marshall plan was to promote economic reconstruction and the reassessment of Italy's international relations. The original, moderately reform-minded Christian Democratic program had been overcome by a laissez-faire policy which had the effect only of aggravating inflation and exacerbating the political debate on economic choices. The Catholic leadership was able to reassess its approach – according to contrasting historiographical interpretations abandoning, or strengthening, the original programme. Finally, by the first half of 1947, a systematic attempt to control credit in order to achieve financial stability was put into motion. This was going to become known as the *linea Einaudi* (named after the economist Luigi Einaudi, Minister of the Budget, who was responsible for it). The announcement of the Marshall Plan provided an environment favourable to financial stability and to the success of the alliance between the government, the Vatican, and the United States.[26]

Notwithstanding Rome's successful attempt to keep afloat while increasing international turbulence upset internal political life, the ambiguity of Italy's status persisted. Only at the end of July 1947, amidst complaints and frustrations, did the Constituent Assembly adopt a bill authorizing the government to ratify the peace treaty as soon as the Big Four had done so. In September, as the expiry date for registering ratification approached, Yugoslavia attempted to violate the treaty by sending her troops back to Trieste. This threat was all the more appalling to Italians because of Western plans for demobilisation from the Trieste area, supposedly after the appointment of a Governor for the newly-established Free Territory.[27] Agreement between the superpowers over the appointment of the Governor was never to be reached and the demobilization was accordingly postponed. This could not however be foreseen by the Italian government, which endeavoured to convince Washington of the gravity of the communist danger and of alleged threats to Italy's security and internal stabilization.

The uncertainty regarding the ultimate destiny of Trieste, of the Italian colonies and of the economic and military provisions imposed on Italy by the peace treaty were all related issues. The United States was anxious that the peace clauses, which had barely come into force, should be revised in order to strengthen Italy internally and to exploit her potential role as a bastion of democracy in the Mediterranean.[28] However, a bilateral arrangement on the basis of agreements between Italy, the United States and Britain seemed the only realistic possibility, even more because, towards the end of 1947, the failure of the attempt to keep alive four-power diplomacy at the CFM in London presaged a future in which East-West joint diplomatic negotiations were going to be suspended or abandoned.

In internal political life the battle lines were drawn for the electoral confrontation of April 1948 between the government and the left. The state of the controversy between the Christian Democratic Party, leading a centre coalition with the social democrats, the liberals and the republicans, on the one hand, and the left, communists and socialists, running on a joint ticket labelled 'People's Bloc', on the other, had shifted from substantive economic and political issues to an emotional and irrational level. During 1948, East/West confrontation seemed inescapable and ideological hostility grew in Italy accordingly.

The two main factors in the campaign for the 18 April 1948 national election were the *grand peur* of a communist take-over and the myth of the American way of life – the most popular slogan of the moderate parties. But the latter's cause was also aided more concretely by the expectations connected with the European Recovery Program and with the announcement of the Tripartite Proposal for the return of the Free Territory of Trieste to Italian sovereignty on 20 March 1948.[29]

Fears and hopes were also fostered by developments in Eastern Europe, such as the communist take-over of Czechoslovakia, and by the influence on the Italian electorate from the Vatican and the Italo-American lobbies in the United States – all exerting various degrees of pressure on the Italian vote. As a consequence, De Gasperi's party came to be recognized by the moderate electorate as the only effective bulwark against communism; so it is not surprising that historiographical debate about the 18 April elections has been particularly intense.

In fact, the overwhelming victory of the centrist coalition was chiefly determined by the Cold War, the articulation of the Marshall Plan and, in general, the climate of intense political and ideological confrontation at home and abroad. In internal political life, the victory of the Christian Democratic Party put an end to the attempt to keep alive the experience of the Resistance and to pursue a radical renovation of Italian institutions.[30] Instead, a substantive restoration of the old economic and social structures was likely to take place.[31] The overwhelming success of the Christian Democratic Party also led to an over-estimate of Italy's future role in American planning, a misconception based on the assumption that the normalization of Italy's foreign relations would inevitably follow the victory of the moderate forces. But this was not to be the case, as the debate on Western security revealed in the course of 1948 and 1949.

The negotiations for the Atlantic Pact did not merge easily with the process of Italy's internal stabilization. During the months preceding the election, the Italian government had subordinated its membership of a new Western security system to the goal of internal stabilization. However, soon after the electoral victory of the moderate forces, Rome approached London in order to negotiate the price of the country's adherence to the Brussels Pact – the security treaty between Britain, France and Benelux concluded in March 1948.[32] This overture was bluntly rebuffed, but rejection by London did not undermine the belief cherished by the Italian government that the United States would reward Italy by her involvement in defence planning as soon as America became the main actor involved in building up a military alliance. This proved too optimistic. In fact, severe obstacles to Italy's adherence to the Atlantic Pact were posed both by her geographical position and by the limitations on her rearmament established in the peace treaty.[33]

Italy's official approach to the negotiations for the Atlantic Pact was directed to achieving treaty revision and to completing the official West-oriented internal and international political option: the so called pro-Western choice debated at length in historiography.[34] However, the internal opposition of the extreme right and left to military alliances was extremely strong and doubts and uncertainties also spread within the government. Anglophobia and anti-Americanism characterized the opposition from the right, while the communists opposed the military and anti-Soviet character of the alliance, and the socialists based their objections to the Pact on their tradition of neutralism and anti-imperialism. Despite this opposition, the government could count on a vast majority in Parliament. Therefore, the real obstacle to Italy's adherence to a military alliance was more likely to originate within the governmental majority or outside the country, in negotiations between the Brussels Pact, the United States and Canada.

At the very beginning of international negotiations, both Carlo Sforza, the Italian Minister of Foreign Affairs, and De Gasperi had not yet rejected the arguments of the neutralists. But, as they were chiefly concerned with political and diplomatic goals, both Sforza's neutralism and De Gasperi's reluctance to ask the support of the Church in order to win over the opposition of the Catholics were overcome by Tarchiani's insistent pressures. The Italian ambassador in Washington was the crucial figure in reshaping Rome's misperceptions regarding Italy's alleged freedom to either join a military alliance or stay neutral. Tarchiani pointed out that there was no choice if the country aimed at stabilizing its position in international relations, achieving a new status and at gaining security.

De Gasperi and Sforza gradually became involved in the issue of Italy's adherence to the Atlantic Pact by the end of 1948. This was a process which required a rethinking of foreign policy strategies, in particular of the idea that status and security would have been for the most part achieved through Italy's deep involvement in European economic and political unification. When the Italian government started focusing on the problem of joining a Western military alliance, the Brussels Pact had been formed and was going to be expanded into an Atlantic alliance with the participation of the United States and Canada. Even if the Italian government had been ready to take part in these negotiations, only France seemed likely to support Italy's candidature.

Therefore, the role of the Italian ambassador in Washington was again central in explaining to Sforza and De Gasperi that, militarily, the actual weight of the country in defence planning was regarded as almost non-existent by the negotiators of the alliance. Furthermore, including Italy in the Atlantic Pact meant stretching the original Atlantic idea on which the alliance was supposedly based. It was French determination to include north Africa in the Pact which helped make possible the invitation for Italy to join the alliance.[35]

In the meantime the Italian government had to face British opposition. The decline of the role played by Great Britain in the peninsula, a role essentially taken over by the United States from late 1946 onwards, had been followed by a period of further tension in Anglo-Italian relations. This tension was due also to the conflict of interests between the two countries regarding the final destiny of the former Italian colonies, then under debate at the United Nations. London objected that Italy's entry into a Western alliance would impose a military and financial burden upon the new organization. In addition to this, Great Britain (now the champion of European defence planning, and the strongest advocate of permanent American involvement in Europe) feared the dispersion of future military aid as a consequence of stretching south the original Atlantic framework.

Domestic anxieties reinforced external opposition. The Italian government could move only gradually towards military involvement, which potentially could upset public opinion if such a policy shift were perceived as a reversal of the early post-war tendencies towards neutralism and Europeanism. As for the American attitude towards Italy's adherence to the Pact, Truman's approval and the support of the Congress were obtained only in March 1949, after a formal request by the Italian government. This was also the result of lobbying activities by the Italian embassy and of the advice of some sympathetic members of the State Department. London maintained its opposition, but declared that it would accept extending an invitation to Italy after an explicit American consensus and on the condition of not allowing the country to take part in negotiation at any stage.

Finally, after having reached an agreement along these lines, the Italian government received a formal invitation on 8 March, and was then confronted by the need to achieve internal consensus. On 11 March De Gasperi argued in front of the Parliament that the Atlantic Pact was a defensive alliance, a step towards European integration and a necessary choice if Italy wanted to transcend the isolation caused by her defeat. The parliamentary debate which saw moments of strident confrontation between the government and the opposition, and also a remarkable degree of resistance to abandoning neutrality within the coalition itself, ended with the approval of Italy's adherence to the Atlantic Pact.[36]

But, on joining the Atlantic alliance, Italy found herself once again in a very ambiguous and insecure position. The Atlantic Pact had no effect on the military or other provisions of the Italian peace treaty and did not mean the immediate extension of NATO military guarantees to the whole Italian territory. Italy, therefore, did not solve the problem of security or improve her international status dramatically. The destiny of the Italian colonies was still undecided and the return of Trieste to Italy had been frozen by the Tito-Stalin schism, which prompted a more conciliatory Western policy towards Yugoslavia. One year after the signing of the Atlantic Pact the military limitations of the Italian peace treaty had not been revised and, furthermore, even the idea that they should be acknowledged had not faded in Washington. If attacked, Italy could still rely on the limited forces authorized by the peace treaty, but not on help under the Atlantic Pact. And the Soviet Union continued to veto Italy's admission to the United Nations until 1955.

Thus the internal political confrontation over Italy's adherence to the Atlantic Pact had a lasting effect on the process of political stabilization because it sanctioned an explicit pro-Western choice. In international relations, however, the country remained a second-class member, still marked by the stigma of fascism and defeat.

### *From national self-assertion to neo-Atlanticism (1950–4)*

The debate over Italy's participation in European rearmament arose as a result of the tension caused by the Korean war. But no answers were found to the dilemma of reconciling the revision of the military clauses of the Italian peace treaty and her marginal role within the Atlantic alliance with the attempt to keep East/West peace negotiations on Austria and Germany open. The Soviet Union had made a point of obstructing the discussion on the Austrian settlement because of alleged Western violations of the Italian peace treaty with regard to Trieste and to the military clauses. Further steps in rearmament or actions in favour of the return of Trieste to Italy were very likely to put additional strain on relations with the Eastern bloc.[37]

From the Italian perspective, the lack of progress towards the goal of treaty revision was unacceptable. So too for Washington. By April 1950 the National Security Council (NSC) had reached the conclusion (NSC 67/1) that a 'liberal' interpretation of the military terms of the peace treaty was needed in order to allow Italy to take advantage of the Mutual Defense Assistance Program (MDAP) which Congress had passed only after the announcement that the Soviet Union had developed an atomic bomb. MDAP was intended to improve the rearmament of the NATO countries with the assistance of the United States.

In January 1951, the NSC 67/3 recommended that action should be taken in order to remove the obstacles posed to Italian rearmament by the military limitations of the peace treaty. This was particularly important at a time when Italy seemed hesitant to approve an increase of military expenditure which only could entitle her to a share of American aid. Rome's attitude was a sign of the conflict existing between the ambition to achieve an international status of equality and the unwillingness to accept the related costs and responsibilities of this new condition.[38] However, the formal revision of the treaty remained a crucial issue for the Italian government's attempts at a complete post-war rehabilitation. At the end of 1951 Rome requested that Great Britain, France and the United States amend the obsolete Italian treaty. As a result of this request British, French and American representatives worked out a five-step process of revision which was approved and completed at the end of 1951.[39]

The revision abolished the political and moral provisions of the treaty and declared the military clauses inconsistent. As far as Great Britain, France and the United States were concerned, Italy was no longer under legal or moral obligations from the treaty of 1947. However, these developments had little impact on those countries which were not parties to the declaration, namely the Soviet Union and Yugoslavia. In 1952 Rome replied to Moscow's fifth veto of Italy's UN membership by declaring null and void her treaty obligation to the Soviet Union.[40]

The problem of Trieste was still unsettled. In mid-1951, Rome and Belgrade had opened direct negotiations over Trieste, but these ended a year later without reaching an agreement. The Pleven Plan for a European Defence Community

(EDC) had been welcomed in Italy but it had also increased fears of a 'northern' European strategy of defence in Europe. Lacking strength and geographical advantages, and being unable to commit herself to increasing military expenditure, Italy regarded herself as a very vulnerable and marginal ally.[41] At a time when Japan had received a 'peace of reconciliation' and West Germany was going to be included in the security plans of the West, the inconsistency of leaving Italy lagging behind the major enemies of the Second World War had become glaringly apparent.

Moreover, defence collaboration in the Adriatic was affected by the lack of agreement between Italy and Yugoslavia about Trieste. Great Britain and the United States did not cease promoting plans for the partition of the disputed area, but they had no success. Fears of repercussions on Italy's parliamentary ratification of the European Defence Community treaty prevented the Western allies from putting pressure on Italy about Trieste. Instead, Rome endeavoured to extract from the United States a substantive commitment regarding the return of Trieste to Italy, in exchange for her ratification of the EDC treaty. But the attempt failed because the Italian government stuck to the Tripartite Declaration of March 1948, which granted the return of the entire Free Territory of Trieste to Italy and this inflexibility allowed no room for negotiations.[42]

Actually, as the historiography on the subject shows very clearly, in Italy the abortive creation of the Free Territory of Trieste had remained the most unpopular of all the provisions agreed by the victorious powers at the CFM. Post-war Italian governments never dared to underestimate the internal repercussions of a settlement depriving Italy of Trieste and the area surrounding the city. The issue was closely linked with the creation of an Atlantic/Adriatic security system. After the Tito/Stalin schism in 1948, the Western hope that the Yugoslav heresy would spread, to the advantage of the Western scheme of security, had undercut Italy's favourable position in the dispute. But even Stalin's death, followed by the Malenkov peace offensive and Soviet-Yugoslav realignment, did not divert the Western intention to push Italy and Yugoslavia towards a direct agreement. Rome blamed London, even more than Washington, for the lack of progress in the Trieste dispute and for Britain's positive response to Soviet openings.[43]

Indeed, during the period preceding the Italian national election of July 1953 and immediately afterwards, the new international atmosphere played a major role in internal political life. De Gasperi's unfortunate attempt to change the electoral law introducing a seat bonus (which would have given two-thirds of the seats in Parliament to the coalition parties achieving fifty percent plus one of the electoral vote) was strongly opposed. The communists named it the swindle law because it aimed at turning a nominal majority into an effective one. Furthermore, De Gasperi's foreign policy based on Europeanism, revisionism and Atlanticism appeared less persuasive in the eyes of Italian public opinion at a time when peaceful co-existence with the Soviet Union seemed possible.[44]

At the elections the government coalition failed to qualify for the seat bonus. All the coalition parties lost and the opposition, from the communists to the neo-fascists, gained. The parliamentary rejection of De Gasperi's eighth and last cabinet one month after the election was the prelude to a shift towards the right in

Italian political life. Right-wing nationalistic political tendencies, aroused by Italy's marginality and lack of success in achieving a new status, could not be underestimated by De Gasperi's successors, who had to rely on less moderate and less secure parliamentary support. Under Giuseppe Pella, who succeeded in forming a caretaker government in August 1953, a military confrontation between Italy and Yugoslavia was barely avoided. A new Western proposal to hand Trieste back to Italy proved abortive and severe unrest in the area ensued.[45]

It was only at the end of 1954 that Italy and Yugoslavia gave their assent to the Memorandum of Understanding sponsored by the United States and Great Britain. Under this agreement the Free Territory of Trieste was to be partitioned between Italy and Yugoslavia.[46] 1954 was also the year of the defeat of the EDC treaty. Thus the end of De Gasperi's leadership, the trend towards a relaxation of the Cold War, the solution of the Italo–Yugoslav dispute, and the failure of the European Defence Community together marked the passing of an era in Italian foreign policy.

In the course of the previous eight years, De Gasperi had been the outstanding figure in Italy advocating post-war Western collaboration and European unification. He favoured the Organization for European Economic Co-operation (OEEC), the Atlantic Pact, the Council of Europe and the ECSC, and he personally sponsored the creation of a European Political Community with the aim of overseeing the EDC. As De Gasperi simultaneously practised Europeanism, Atlanticism and revisionism, the question of whether his support of European unification was largely tactical has to be addressed.[47]

It is self-evident that Italy, a defeated country in search of a new identity and dependent on foreign assistance, needed a new ideological framework. De Gasperi had been personally committed to the idea of European unification; but he had also endeavoured to let Europeanism play a significant role in smoothing the opposition to Italy's choices of necessity, namely the ratification of the peace treaty and adherence to the Western military alliance. This brings up another question: whether Europeanism, after having replaced nationalism at a time of strong internal and international political confrontation, coexisted with the resurgence of nationalistic feelings in the 1950s.

At the end of De Gasperi's era, in 1953, Europeanism seemed in decline and nationalism resurgent. Italy's emergence from the ruins of the War at a time of relaxation in East/West tension encouraged rising expectations and gave impetus to a new wave of national self-assertion. In this context the newly-appointed American ambassador, Clare Boothe Luce, feared a decline of Washington's influence on Italian affairs and repeatedly put pressure on the Italian leaders to adopt a stronger anti-communist commitment. But the real problem in Italy seemed no longer to be communism. De Gasperi's successors – Pella, Fanfani and Scelba in 1953–4 – could have hardly been regarded as soft on communism, but their behaviour was perceived in the United States as more self-reliant. The appointment of Giovanni Gronchi (from the left wing of the Christian Democratic Party) to the Presidency of the Republic in 1955 reinforced American concerns about Italy's independent inclinations.[48]

Even De Gasperi in 1954, before Gronchi's appointment, had criticized his successors for belittling Italian Europeanism and shaking American belief in Italy's loyalty to the Western bloc. De Gasperi's perceptions and those of Ambassador Luce came from what can be called a Cold-War approach to foreign policy. This was exactly the attitude that Gronchi did not seem likely to share. He questioned the NATO oligarchy for not allowing Italy to take part in the actual decision-making process of the Alliance and advocated more equal treatment and standing within NATO.[49]

However, although Italy's attitude towards her allies had changed, her aspiration to be recognized as an equal partner in the Atlantic Alliance was consistent with her previous efforts to achieve a new status. It should also be noted that despite the impact of nationalist feelings on Italy's attempt to improve her role in international relations, Rome had no intention of straining relations with Washington. As the cases of the EDC treaty and, more strikingly, the Suez crisis showed very clearly, a conflict between the Western powers seriously disconcerted Rome, which was not at ease with any international situation in which European and American interests conflicted.

In the 1950s Italy's Western choice had ceased to be an issue of internal political confrontation. Socialists and communists did not run a joint ticket for the election of 1951/52 or 1953. In July 1955 the Soviet-American summit served to moderate the anti-Atlanticism of the Socialist Party. If the military alliance could promote international collaboration and economic development, the Socialists argued, the alliance would cease to be regarded as an instrument of military confrontation by them. A flexible approach also characterized the Socialist attitude towards the European Economic Community. At the Parliamentary debate in the fall of 1957 the socialists, unlike the communists, did not vote against the EEC.

Their abstention was meant to be a criticism of the economic interests which lay behind the new institution and not of the process of European unification itself. The idea of a centre-left alliance was making progress in Italian political life.

As far as foreign policy was concerned, to achieve a balance of European and Atlantic vocations was once again the main issue, particularly at a time when tendencies towards integration merged with a need to achieve an independent role in international relations. Furthermore, the crisis of the colonial empires opened new aspirations for an Italian 'Mediterranean vocation'. This goal could be attained only by not interfering – at least openly – with colonialist policies or nationalistic movements in Africa, and by maintaining good relations with France and with the United States. It was therefore only after the independence of Tunisia and Morocco and the signing of the treaties of Rome that Italy could attempt to fill her new role of European 'bridge' across the Mediterranean.[50]

Thus, in Italy, the relaxation of the Cold-War approach to foreign and internal policy was the result of economic reconstruction and of an increase in national confidence. Even the so-called neo-Atlanticism, the attempt to pursue an independent role within the existing NATO system, did not prevent Italy from contributing actively to the elaboration of the treaties of Rome in 1957. Indeed, in the mid-1950s, relaunching European economic co-operation and pursuing a new regional role were regarded in Rome as two sides of the same coin.

*Conclusions*

What conclusions can be drawn from this survey? Was Italy's road into the Cold War and out of it a peculiar one? Does Italy's experience suggest that an ideological framework is needed in order to achieve stabilization? Is there any evidence that a decline of bipolarism can revive national self-assertion or even nationalism?

Between 1943 and 1947, Italy was a theatre of British, American and Soviet competition. During this time the country was drawn into the Western camp as a result of the military occupation. It was co-belligerency that gave her a peculiar status. Neither enemy nor ally, Italy was kept in limbo until the signing of the peace treaty in 1947. In the course of the following years up to 1949, the internal political struggle between the left on one side and the Christian Democrats on the other was resolved, thereby accomplishing Italy's pro-Western choice. One decisive factor was the Cold War, but the other can be described as peculiar to Italy: the role of the Roman Catholic Church in providing the basis of a mass political following for the Christian Democratic party and in supporting the strengthening of Italo-American relations.

Even before the fall of Mussolini, Roosevelt had attempted to open a channel of negotiations with the monarchy through Myron Taylor, his personal envoy to the Vatican. The link was established and in the following years the presence of Myron Taylor in Rome become a permanent source of intelligence for the American government. As a result of the early practice of collecting the soundings of Rome's intentions via the Vatican, and of the traditional Italo-American lobby's Catholic heritage, the role of the Church remained central in relations between Italy and the United States in the Cold-War period.

Actually, this role was strictly linked with the increasing post-war capacity of the Church to affect deeply the formation of political consensus within the Italian society. This was due to the fact that the war and the slow process of liberation, with the monarchy and the government under the protection of the Allies far away from the capital, contributed to relaunching the image of the Vatican as a symbol of continuity and order. After the liberation, when the 'wind from the north' seemed so strong as to blow out any resistance to radical political changes, the Italian moderate electorate, traditionally lay and liberal, saw in the Catholic Church and the Christian Democratic Party the best guarantee against the success of the left.

Therefore, the role played by the Church during a period when uncertainty regarding the future of all major institutions and the fear of the communist danger were very strong, had the effect of aggregating a large but heterogeneous consensus around the Christian Democratic party. To shape this consensus, based on a large popular base but also on both a lay and clerical conservative components, required a party's apparatus which the Christian Democrats, early after the war, did not have. Here, again, the capillary organization of the Church was the vehicle through which the consensus was achieved.

However, the united front of the Catholic forces, which was a factor in the election of 1948, was not to be a permanent feature of the collaboration between the Vatican, the Catholic organizations and the different factions within the Christian

Democratic party. The answer to the threat posed by the left in 1948 was unity, which certainly did not characterize the state of future relations between the various Catholic groups. In 1948 the objections to the involvement of the Catholic Church apparatus in political issues had come essentially from the opposition. In the early 1950s, though, the aggressive conservatism of the Church and the *Azione Cattolica*, her lay counterpart, was criticized within the Christian Democratic party itself.

The Vatican and the Catholic Church did not cease to have a role in Italian political life, then, but this role was reshaped at a time of détente. In the new international scene which coincided with the end of De Gasperi's era, the growth of the Christian Democratic party's apparatus and the emergence of distinct factions within the Catholic political forces contributed to reducing the influence of the clerical power on the decision-making process.

Unfortunately, it was too late to revive the early post-war expectations of radically reshaping political and economic life in Italy. Not only had the Christian Democratic Party and the clerical forces succeeded in carrying on internal stabilization, but the more innovative forces emerging from the Resistance had failed to elaborate a common approach to the huge task of reconstruction. Furthermore, the lay parties which emerged after the fall of fascism had been progressively marginalized by the polarization of the political struggle between the Christian Democratic Party and the left. The Marshall Plan provided a model of economic growth and social stabilization which had long-lasting effects on Italy's economic and political life, but the Italian government resisted American suggestions of implementing a substantial policy of social and economic reform. The problem of the modernization of the south of Italy was addressed in the early 1950s with the intention that public investment – still under the Marshall Plan – would attract private capital. However changing a tradition of protectionism and the lack of initiative took time and effort, as the opposition of Italian industry to Rome's plans for European economic integration soon revealed.

But from the perspective of the Italian government, the meaning of Europeanism went far beyond the economic sphere. Rome's policy ranged from promoting collaboration to pursuing the goal of full membership of the country in the post-war Western strategic and economic system. Indeed, Italy's experience suggests that an idealistic goal, such as that of European integration, could help in smoothing internal opposition to fundamental issues in foreign policy, namely the ratification of the peace treaty and the adherence to the Atlantic Pact. Italian Europeanism can therefore be regarded as neither purely economic nor directly related to federalism.

The *illusion lyrique* of a federal Europe had faded in the late 1940s with the creation of a powerless institution, the Council of Europe, and with the detachment of Great Britain from continental economic and political collaboration. Once reconstruction was achieved, the process of European unification promoted by the governments shifted towards new goals: the creation of a defensive alliance and the promotion of a functionalist, sector-by-sector approach, to progressive integration. Rome joined in, but this policy shift made more difficult the integrating of Italy's peculiar needs with those of the other continental countries.

The rejection of the EDC treaty in France and the end of De Gasperi's leadership almost coincided. These were events which contributed to the decline of the role of Europeanism in shaping public opinion's consensus on foreign-policy issues.

In the mid-1950s, after the solution of the Trieste dispute, Italy regained confidence in her national identity. She explored new paths for internal policy, namely 'the opening to the left', and balanced her traditional Mediterranean interests with her new Atlantic ties and Europeanist policies. In April 1955 these tendencies were given concrete embodiment in the election of Giovanni Gronchi to the Presidency of the Republic.

Although the Italian case can be seen as peculiar, one can argue that at a time of détente the resurgence of national confidence did not preclude international collaboration and regional solidarity. Furthermore, a relaxation in East/West tension made possible the emergence of a minor country like Italy, too weak to acquire an independent role in a strictly bipolar system. Gronchi addressed the problem of how to reduce the burdens of participation in NATO but not at the price of renouncing American assistance. The answer was a policy of neo-Atlanticism which aimed at de-emphasizing the military side of the Atlantic alliance and emphasizing instead the political, economic and cultural sides. Modifying NATO's basic character at a time in which the danger of war and aggression appeared to be declining was intended to create an opportunity for Italy to become an independent ally within the alliance. The more the military character of NATO was replaced by a reorientation towards political and economic collaboration, the more Rome would be able to reconcile neo-Atlanticism with both Europeanism and her Mediterranean focus. Therefore, in the mid-1950s, détente posed a new basic frame of reference for Italian international life and contributed to bringing about a non-communist opening to the left in internal policy.

### Bibliographical note

General introductions to the problems posed by Italy's defeat and post-war political and economic stabilization are Stuart J. Woolf, ed., *Italia 1943–1950, La ricostruzione* (Bari, 1975), Norman Kogan, *A Political History of Post-War Italy* (New York, 1956) and Paul Ginsborg, *A History of Contemporary Italy: Society and Politics, 1943–1988* (New York, 1990). Basic for an understanding of Italian expectations and fears as well as of the intellectual currents at the end of the War and in the early post-war period is Ennio Di Nolfo, *Le paure e le speranze degli Italiani 1943–1953* (Milan, 1986).

On the 'restauration' - 'innovation' debate in Italian internal post-war policy, see Leo Valiani, *L'avvento di De Gasperi* (Florence, 1949); Vittorio Foa, *La ricostruzione capitalistica e le origini della repubblica in Italia 1945–'48* (Turin, 1974); Antonio Gambino, *Storia del dopoguerra dalla liberazione al potere DC* (Bari, 1975); and Pietro Scoppola, *La proposta politica di De Gasperi* (Bologna, 1978).

Bruno Arcidiacono's *'Le précédent italien' et les origines de la guerre froide: les Alliés et l'occupation de l'Italie 1943–1944* (Brussels, 1984) is an outstanding study of British policy towards Italy at the time of the armistice and a solid contribution to the historiographical discussion of the impact of Allied policies of occupation on the origins of the cold war. David Ellwood, *Italy 1943–1945* (Leicester, 1985), has also addressed the internal and international implications of the Anglo-American occupation of Italy. On Allied diplomacy for the elaboration of the Italian peace treaty at a time of transition from East-West collaboration to post-war competition, see Ilaria Poggiolini, *Diplomazia della transizione: gli alleati e il problema del trattato italiano* (Florence, 1990).

James Miller's *The United States and Italy 1940–1950: the Politics and Diplomacy of Stabilization* (Chapel Hill, N.C., 1986) is a compact survey of American-Italian post-war relations. It discusses the role of the United States in reshaping internal and foreign policy in Italy. On Soviet-Italian relations see Mario Toscano, 'Resumption of Diplomatic Relations between Italy and the Soviet Union', in his *Design in Diplomacy* (Baltimore, MD, 1970). The volume edited by Elena Aga Rossi, *Il Piano Marshall e l'Europa* (Rome, 1983), furnishes a substantial introduction to the major economic, social and political factors posed by the Marshall Plan in Italy as well as in the major European countries.

The following studies debate the internal and international process which eventually ended in the invitation to the Italian government to join the founding members of the Atlantic Alliance: Mario Toscano, *Pagine di Storia contemporanea, 11, Origini e vicende della seconda guerra mondiale* (Milan, 1963); Ennio Di Nolfo, ed., *Trent'anni di alleanza atlantica* (Rome, 1979); Pietro Pastorelli, *La politica estera italiana del dopoguerra* (Bologna, 1987); Antonio Varsori, *Il Patto di Bruxelles tra integrazione europea e alleanza atlantica* (Rome, 1988) and Timothy Smith, 'The Fear of Subversion: the United States and the inclusion of Italy in the Northern Atlantic Treaty', *Diplomatic History*, VII (1983), 139–55. See also the pertinent essays in Josef Becker & Franz Knipping, eds., *Power in Europe? Great Britain, France, Italy and Germany in a post-war world 1945–1950* (Berlin, 1986) and Ennio Di Nolfo, Romain Rainero & Brunello Vigezzi, eds., *L'Italia e la politica di potenza in Europa 1945–1950* (Milan, 1988). By the same editors, but focusing on the 1950s, is *L'Italia e la politica di potenza*, vol. 1, 1950–1960 (Milan, 1993). The Italian diplomatic documents collection *Documenti diplomatici Italiani* (Rome, 1954– ) has reached the early 1940s with the 9th series (1939–43). The first volume of the 10th series was published in 1993.

# 6    *Germany*

## WOLFGANG  KRIEGER

On 9 November 1989, the day the Berlin Wall was opened, the two German states embarked on a dizzying race toward unification. Anyone with a sense of history knew that it meant the end of the Cold War in Germany. The history books would have to be rewritten. But how? What historical perspectives would emerge?

For two main reasons we still cannot assess Germany's place in the Cold War with complete confidence. First of all, new documents and surprising facts keep emerging from the archives, particularly former Soviet-bloc archives, which directly challenge what had previously been assumed. Secondly, our frameworks for interpretation keep being shaken by the ongoing difficulties with German unification in political, economic, social and cultural terms. Here, too, past assumptions are at odds with East German realities as we see them now. For example, the fundamental misjudgements of the qualitative level and competitiveness of East German industry are not simply due to statistical errors but reflect much wider misperceptions of reality. Looking beyond economic data, it obviously makes a great difference to our historical analysis whether we consider East Germany to have been an advanced industrial economy or whether we assume that it had been frozen in a relatively primitive state of economic development. Each assumption leads to a different interpretation of the character and the downfall of European communism.[1]

This essay will examine some of the major 'established' interpretations which have been offered on Germany since the Second World War. At the same time it will provide information on and tentative assessments of current historical debates, particularly those relating to the issues of German unity and to the history of East Germany, the former German Democratic Republic (GDR). Readers are warned that the word 'tentative' is to be taken literally. With masses of new documents in the offing we must expect the unexpected. By the same token, however, the enormous opportunities for research in this field urge one to provide at least some orientation and thus to assist researchers who may wish to become involved in those historical debates or simply want to know where things stand at the moment.

Two problems, one specific and the other more general, arise in evaluating German Cold-War historiography today. The specific problem has to do with the usual difficulties of getting access to contemporary records. As a rule historical sources are more easily and more completely available if the subject under study dates back three decades or more. It also becomes easier if the persons and issues involved are no longer of operational political concern.

But this rule has more exceptions than meets the eye. In the case of the former GDR, the document-generating bureaucracies are obviously dead, at least at the central level, and the *nomenklatura* has been either forcibly retired or charged with crimes of various kinds. Thus one would assume that all files could be thrown open immediately. Yet this is not the case. In part there are valid reasons of privacy for not doing so, though government officials the world over tend to use that venerable liberal notion to protect themselves and their peers from public scrutiny. In part one suspects that certain East German files are held closed by their new masters because they would obviously reveal a good deal about bilateral relations which are still heavily protected on the West German side. Incidentally the ex-GDR files are also bound to reveal a great deal about what is still buried in West European and north American archives.

This comes as no surprise to anyone familiar with the ways in which other nations handle and have handled unpleasant aspects of their respective pasts. In comparison, Germany was unusually frank in addressing its unpleasant pre-1945 history, more so than Japan and Austria for example, and after 1989 Germany is again much more open-minded in this respect than are the other states of the former Soviet empire. Both those for and those against a rapid, even ruthless, opening of records claim that sinister political purposes are on the minds of their opponents. In other words, archival access is a highly political matter.

The second, more general problem arises from the very nature of historical interpretation. Knowing the end of a historical structure or of a person's life fundamentally affects our judgement of what was important or beneficial and what was not. Historical assessment is largely based on comparison. Therefore our conclusions change along with our database of experience.

The present revolutions east of the former Iron Curtain provide some stark illustrations of this point. Before Mikhail Gorbachev took power in 1985, the historical meaning of the Bolshevik revolution seemed much clearer than it is now. Then came *perestroika*, which made seven decades of communism look like a long and tragic detour on the road to political and socio-economic modernity. Now, after the dissolution of the Russian empire, it is even less clear how far one needs to go back in history to establish a basis for comparison and continuity.

Or take the Hapsburg empire. Until recently a matter of largely academic interest, its place in history looks very different today than in, say, 1918 or 1968. Compared to four decades of Soviet domination, a Hungarian and even a Czech may now think of the Hapsburg monarchy as a sadly failed effort in European integration.

Of course things did not change as drastically in Germany. But the history of Eastern Germany and of German relations with its eastern neighbours is nevertheless being placed in a very different historical context. For example, a wholly novel relationship between the new united Germany and post-communist Poland is emerging which changes the face of Europe in a manner similar to the Franco-German rapprochement since the 1950s.[2]

### Germany's place in the world

Any reflection on Germany during the Cold War must begin with a reminder of the centrality of Germany in the East-West confrontation. Thus we have to begin our survey with Germany's failed Second World War attempt to become a world power. Better still, we should look back to the days of the Boshevik revolution of 1917 when Germany was a key factor in the rearranging of Europe's balance of powers.

We can divide the period from 1917 to 1945 into four phases. The end of the first phase is marked by the Versailles peace treaty of 1919 which, despite its punitive elements, sought to secure political stability in Germany. The victors feared that anything less might bring communism to central Europe and even to parts of western Europe. As it turned out, Lenin's revolution failed to spread much beyond Russia's borders. The Bolsheviks remained preoccupied with their civil war and with ideological fratricide. Germany used this weakness to get the Soviets to assist in certain breaches of the Versailles treaty, particularly with respect to military restrictions. Increasingly Berlin confronted the victors with forceful demands for an equality of status.

When Hitler openly defied the peace order during phase three, from 1935 onward, the great powers thought they could tame and thereby limit or at least channel his expansionist strategy. In this way a gradually more powerful Soviet Union would be balanced by a stronger Germany; but Stalin set out to counter this strategy by initiating his own version of appeasement in the Hitler-Stalin pact of August 1939. Now the West would either have to offer Hitler yet more concessions or to confront him squarely – the latter with a Soviet Union growing steadily stronger and likely to support Hitler even more substantially.

Phase four was then opened by Germany's attack on the Soviet Union in June 1941, after it had defeated all other European powers except Britain, which found itself in mortal danger. With the Americans unlikely to send forces soon, Churchill saw no alternative to an alliance with Stalin. Soon this odd couple of allies obtained rather unexpected help from Hitler, who brought about yet another radical international change by declaring war on the United States. Without Hitler's declaration of war it is far from certain that the Americans would have sent land forces to Europe so soon (or at all?), even after the Japanese attack on Pearl Harbor.

The resulting war alliance against Hitler had only one purpose: to defeat Germany. On most issues the deep rift between the Soviets and the West persisted. The long list of disagreements included coalition strategy, post-war planning and relations toward other European and Asian states. This was evident everywhere beneath the surface of alliance harmony. Unlike at least some of his Western partners, Stalin never saw the wartime alliance as a permanent constellation which would end the East-West confrontation for good.

It would, however, be wrong to think of the Cold War since 1946–7 as having been inevitable. While we have every indication that Stalin did not strive toward a cordial relationship on a give-and-take basis, we can assume that he may have hoped to get along with the capitalists tolerably well for an extended period. In this way he could have avoided such spectacular clashes as the Berlin crisis of 1948–9 and the Korean war of 1950–3. The Soviets could have concentrated on building up their country's power resources to the level of a true superpower – and perhaps even further.

As we conclude phase four of our scheme, it ought to be abundantly clear that the East-West confrontation over Germany neither originated at the Yalta or Potsdam conferences of 1945 nor could have been averted there. No settlement in 1945 could have put to rest for good the fears of the great powers with respect to Germany. Inevitably they would keep asking themselves what kind of Germany they wanted and how it would affect the overall correlation of forces (a favourite Soviet term). In other words, one needed to know the global East-West relationship before one could define Germany's place in it.

Only on two points did both sides agree: neither was willing to see Germany incorporated by the other camp. And under no circumstances would the Germans themselves be allowed to decide independently which side they wished to strengthen. For these reasons even small German events were nervously observed and checked against two questions. Did they reveal anything about the world-wide intentions of the other side? And did they amount to a shift in the overall power game?

Put differently, the Cold War was a period of extreme uncertainty about the real motives of the key players. Each side assumed that even minor changes might have enormous consequences. For these very reasons the great powers eventually stopped gambling over Germany and went for a safer option. An economic demarcation line was drawn in July 1947 when the Soviets refused to join the Marshall Plan. In the military and political spheres the Berlin crisis of 1948–9 played a similar role. Further defining elements were added from the Korean war to the second Berlin crisis in conjunction with the Cuban missile confrontation, a dual conflict which lasted from 1958 to 1962. In other words, the founding of two German states in September/October of 1949 was only the most visible confirmation of this demarcation process.

In hindsight one could ask why the Soviets ended their gamble from July 1947 onwards, even though they probably could have frustrated the Marshall Plan at least for a while by staying in the game to spoil it. Was it due to the growing hostility in Europe toward Soviet influence and to the unexpected willingness of the Americans to pour financial aid into Europe? Surely the West Europeans, particularly the British and the French, were also eager to draw a line somewhere in central Europe, because the near complete withdrawal of American military forces left Europe unable to mount a credible defence against the Soviet Union. American nuclear weapons were an uncomfortable, perhaps even unreliable, stopgap at best.[3] Against this background, it may be helpful to summarize what happened inside Germany during this crucial 1945–9 phase of global reorientation.[4]

The Potsdam agreement of August 1945 provided the master plan for the restructuring of Germany. All vestiges of Nazism were to be removed. Gradually new German political and administrative institutions would be set up, starting at the municipal level. In Berlin, the Allied Control Commission (ACC), staffed by the four occupying powers, was to run all aspects of public life. No permanent division was intended, at least for the time being. Even the territories east of the Oder–Neisse line (absorbed partly into the new Poland and partly by the Soviet Union) were not severed from the rest of Germany by international treaty, although for practical purposes they were outside joint Allied control. For reasons of administrative convenience Germany west of the Oder–Neisse line was divided into four zones under the United States, the Soviet Union, Britain and France. Each occupying power was charged with implementing joint policies in their respective zones. To counteract any trends toward political fragmentation, Germany would be treated as a single economy.

As the Allies argued about the treatment of Germany and failed to implement substantial portions of this master plan, the Americans were increasingly concerned that the need for food imports would rise endlessly as long as the German economy was held back by disputes among the victors. Since the requisite funds for these imports were available only in Washington, the British and French zones became dependent on dollar subsidies. Thus, in late 1946 the American–British Bizone for economic co-operation was formed, with France joining formally in 1948.

Soon after the Deutschmark was introduced in June of 1948, the economic borders of the Trizone became political ones. A new federal constitution, the Grundgesetz, was approved in May 1949. The political parties and the major interest groups, including the trade unions, split along the new Elbe border. The Cold War became an omnipresent fact of German life. The leader of the Christian Democratic party (CDU), Konrad Adenauer, became the first West German chancellor, holding the post until 1963.

In 1948–9 the Soviets tried to stop this move toward a separate Western Germany by using Berlin as a hostage.[5] At stake were the economic viability of West Berlin and the safety of the Germans and the Allied personnel. The Soviets blocked off all road, rail and water access but the Western powers managed to supply by air over two million people for nine months, and no shooting war resulted. In fact, the unarmed transport planes of the airlift received their flight clearances from a four-power air control centre in Berlin which included Soviet officials.

### The Cold War: a blank spot in German historiography?

With German developments so closely interwoven with the early development of the Cold War, it comes as no surprise that there were lively public *political* debates on the never-ending German question, that is the origins and implications of the division of Germany, and on the prospects for reunification. Yet the major controversies among German historians seemed to have very little to do with the Cold War in its world-wide ramifications. While there was a certain amount of interest in German domestic developments of the early post-war years, the great debates dealt with earlier periods and problems of German history.

Why this discrepancy? Part of the answer is that German historians fought the Cold War on other battlefields. For example, numerous writings appeared on the famous debate on German war guilt in 1914. Indeed, from the early 1960s key historians' careers became linked with it. Far from being a narrow quarrel over evidence and interpretation, its implications went well beyond the crisis of July

1914. Deep down Fritz Fischer and his chief opponent, Gerhard Ritter, sharply disagreed over the extent to which Nazi foreign policy had derived from pre-1918 German expansionist designs.[6] In various ways this issue became linked with the equally protracted debate on the domestic impact of Bismarck's imperialism and the extent to which Wilhelmine Germany was a repressive political system which foreshadowed the Nazi dictatorship.

Both debates were highly politicized and focused on post-1945. The arguments emphasizing continuity were expressions of deep-seated fears about the ease and speed with which the Federal Republic had managed the transition from Hitler to being a Western front-line state against Soviet expansion.

The most recent example of such large-scale historians' debates was the so-called *Historikerstreit* (historians' quarrel), in which some scholars claimed that others were seeking to diminish the uniqueness of the Holocaust.[7] Those in the dock were charged with striving toward a more harmonious German national history which could be used to support a feeling of German national identity. Allegedly they wished to rescue the German people from never-ending charges of collective guilt and to prepare them as well as the rest of the world for a more assertive German role on the international stage.

Without going into the finer points, it seems appropriate to report that none of these radical propositions fared well. Few historians today would support Fischer's claim of a near-singular German war guilt in 1914; and much evidence has been brought to light showing that Wilhelmine authoritarianism has been vilified out of all proportion. Most quasi-'inevitable' causal links and comparisons with the Nazi regime tend to belittle the terrors of post-1933 rather than offer any real insight. This is even true with efforts to draw a straight line between pre-1918 German antisemitism and Auschwitz.[8]

The *Historikerstreit* produced more heat than light. The fact remains that no senior academic historian in Germany denies the Nazis' war guilt and the atrocities committed by them. No reasonable comparison can therefore be made with the post-1919 debates on Wilhelmine Germany's war guilt, which were directed against the so-called Versailles system. In the 1920s and 1930s such debates did much to make Nazi foreign policy acceptable both within and outside Germany. In the 1980s, when opportunities for a more assertive West German role offered themselves, the Bonn government and the German people proved to be less than eager to step forward.[9] Indeed, when Polish and Soviet reformers made sweeping offers for German eastward economic expansion, West German political leaders remained cautious. The subsequent collapse of the Honecker regime found Bonn not in an imperial mood but rather puzzled and pulled along by events. Not surprisingly, the *Historikerstreit* vanished along with the Iron Curtain.[10]

A brief aside might be added on Ernst Nolte, whose hefty *Deutschland und der Kalte Krieg* (Germany and the Cold War) came under heavy fire for being a fundamentally flawed, ideological work and whose controversial views on the Holocaust sparked off the *Historikerstreit* later on.[11] In his view the Nazi holocaust was not only comparable to the mass murder of 'class enemies' under Lenin and Stalin, but in important ways he considers these to be directly connected with the concept and reality of the 'final solution'.[12] By contrast Nolte's opponents insist that

Auschwitz is historically unique and therefore not immediately comparable to what happened in the Soviet Union or to other examples of genocide. But their arguments are often more political than scholarly. We still await a full analysis of the Soviet Gulag, which seems to have more than matched the Nazi crimes in scale.[13]

If academic discussions of Germany's 'unmasterable past' (Charles S. Maier) often took the place of studies of the Cold-War period proper, a similar pattern existed among politicians and the press, both in Germany and abroad. Just how much and in what contexts history was used as a political tool is strikingly demonstrated in Michael Wolffsohn's *Ewige Schuld?* (Eternal Guilt?), which places the issue in the wider framework of German-Israeli relations.[14]

Two main arguments were used to associate Germany's earlier quest for hegemony with its place in post-war Europe. In terms of power politics it was claimed that the division of Germany had to continue because history had demonstrated that German efforts in democracy did not run deep enough to give any comfort to the world. The security of her neighbours could not be based on blind trust in German democracy. Although the evidence supporting this argument was weak and is becoming weaker, variations of this notion were evident in foreign reporting on various neo-Nazi activities and, somewhat surprisingly, on the ecologist and peace movements in the 1970s and early 1980s. The latter were often portrayed as feeding on anti-Western and thereby anti-democratic popular sentiments.

The second argument claimed that the Nazi crimes made it a matter of historical justice to veto the German claim to national unity. A divided Germany would be a living monument to the Holocaust.

Usually the two arguments were made in combination and rarely in such blunt terms. But they can be identified in major newspapers throughout the post-war era, particularly in the United States, in Britain and in Israel, and they surfaced again when the Berlin Wall was opened and made a united Germany a realistic prospect.[15] (In parenthesis it must be added that German critics of the rush toward reunification, particularly among the Greens and the left, made the very same points.) Although more conciliatory pronouncements were subsequently issued by the Israeli government, the World Jewish Congress and by others, it was clear that such reminders of Germany's historical legacy would not disappear from practical politics soon.

A further reason for the historiographical neglect of the Cold War lay in the rapid expansion since the 1960s of social history at the expense of diplomatic and international history and even political history.[16] Until the late 1970s it was hard to find a major academic historian whose career was based on work relating to such topics as post-1945 power politics, the Cold War, the relations between the Soviet Union, Western Europe and the United States, the history of the nuclear arms competition or Stalinism. This was due more to ideological preferences than to the dearth of archival sources. Indeed a small band of scholars such as Ernst Deuerlein, Richard Löwenthal, Wilhelm Cornides, Hans-Peter Schwarz, Gerhard Wettig and Jens Hacker, to name only a few, masterfully demonstrated what could be written on the basis of published materials.[17] While the emphasis on social history was also evident in France, Italy, Britain, the United States and elsewhere, the

German case more than any other reflected a feeling of dismay with international power politics.[18]

In resenting power politics, German historians (and German political scientists) fed directly into the Marxist revival of the 1960s. Garnished with scientific jargon they argued the death of political history. It became fashionable to dismiss any scholarly analysis of the communist world as a blatantly reactionary effort designed to deflect attention away from the inevitable decline of late capitalism, as it was then called. Specifically any focus on totalitarian practices in the communist world was denounced as a sinister attempt to detract from the Nazi legacy and particularly from the guilt of the German business leaders and administrative elites who, it was alleged, had stayed in power unreformed in the 'bourgeois capitalist system' of the Federal Republic.

If various sorts of Marxism were fashionable throughout the Western world, German intellectual debates were sufficiently different to reflect both specific German intellectual traditions and the historical circumstances after 1945. This became obvious during the 1970s when Alexander Solzhenitsyn's eye-opening *Gulag Archipelago* and an outpouring of similar publications failed to bring forth in Germany anything comparable to the French *nouveaux philosophes*, to neo-conservatism in the United States and in Britain and to the vigorous identification with Soviet dissidents and human rights issues there and elsewhere. The German left found it difficult to reject communism from a liberal, let alone a libertarian, standpoint. While the Federal Republic as a country gave a great deal of support and practical help to Soviet and other dissidents and refugees, the intellectuals' response to post-Vietnam human rights issues was muted.[19]

### Bonn Republic: old system or new?

Against this political and intellectual background the main trends in German Cold-War historiography come into focus more sharply. What issues have been of interest to German historians? What specifically German characteristics are found in their writings? And finally, where have they made a particularly valuable contribution?

Three major concerns can be identified around which historical debates have centred. The first is about the Federal Republic's legitimacy in terms of its constitution, its socio-economic order and its ideological orientation. The second addresses its foreign and security policy. The third deals with its elites.

On the first issue, did the West German political system represent the will of the German people or was it imposed by the Western Allies?

In appraising the nature of the debate one has to recall that immediately after the War the Germans were mere objects of Allied policies. They became political players only later on. Theoretically speaking, if the victors had remained completely united, there would have been little opportunity for the Germans to take an active part in their own destiny. For an unspecified period they would have largely carried out Allied orders. It was Allied dissent and, from the Berlin crisis onward,

Allied conflict which gave the Germans a real say in their own affairs. West Germany's sovereignty evolved incrementally in parallel with the East-West confrontation.

The first Berlin crisis of 1948–9 gave the new German leadership a certain amount of leverage vis-à-vis their Allied masters, simply because the superpower tug of war in central Europe could not be waged without German participation. When the Soviets blocked the land access to Berlin they sought to win the hearts of the German population while blaming the international crisis on the Western Allied powers. But the Berliners refused and sided with the West, although it was far from certain that the Western airlift operations would provide even the bare essentials needed for survival.

Paradoxically, the new German leaders could take advantage of this situation only because Allied policy as embodied in the Potsdam agreement gave non-Nazi politicians a head start over the old Nazi elites. Without Potsdam the Berlin crisis might easily have benefited the enemies of democracy. In other words the 'new Germans' gained domestic popular support both from Allied consensus and from Allied discord.

At that stage the Western powers were still quite reluctant to grant 'their' Germans sovereign rights to determine their own policies. When a West German state was established in the fall of 1949 it came under an Occupation Statute, which reserved as Allied prerogatives such areas as foreign policy, foreign trade and exchanges, all defence matters, and the responsibility for domestic security. It also placed certain restrictions on German research and development (for instance on nuclear energy) and on industrial production of such goods as aircraft and large ships.

Soon thereafter the Korean war convinced Western Allied governments that an effective defence along the Iron Curtain required a German contribution. The United States offered to bring massive reinforcements to Europe, provided the Europeans accepted German soldiers into the Western alliance. It was easy to predict that France in particular would find it hard to agree. But the Bonn government, too, was thrown into a dilemma. On the one hand, German military forces would improve West Germany's security; on the other hand, the German public was strongly opposed, particularly if German soldiers were to be used as quasi-mercenaries under Allied command.

Eventually a consensus emerged. Germany would provide some 500,000 soldiers, but these forces would be national contingents placed under NATO command. West Germany would become a nearly sovereign state and be accepted into NATO under the Paris agreements of October 1954. The remaining limitations on West German sovereignty were to be balanced by a promise from the three Allied powers to support the German quest for national reunification. In a sense this package deal found its final confirmation in 1990, when German unification was supported by them, albeit somewhat reluctantly, and when Allied rights were abandoned in return for a number of voluntary restrictions which the united Germany accepted.[20]

While the new political leaders in Western Germany were more and more seen as the effective and legitimate representatives of German interests, the East German communist leaders failed to acquire any such democratic legitimacy, because they invariably supported Soviet policies no matter how repressive or exploitative. Their position was made even more uncomfortable by a Kremlin which, for a long time, could not quite decide between supporting its communist brethren in East Germany and seeking a deal with the other victor powers. This ambivalence was most blatantly evident in Stalin's March 1952 proposal for a unified, neutral Germany which would almost certainly have spelt doom to the East German communist party. Soviet wavering finally ended in August 1961 when the wall went up in Berlin. This drastic measure was to make sure that the GDR would not lose even more than the two million people who had already fled westward.

Finally in 1989 the East German communists made a last ditch-effort to win democratic support by introducing sweeping Gorbachev-style reforms, but by then it was too late to win public confidence. To most people the unification of Germany now seemed the only definitive way to end communism and Soviet domination.

The relationship between the East German communists and their Soviet masters was full of ironies and never free from tensions. At least some of the time the Germans sought to assert their own national and economic interests. Curiously the most outspoken dissent was their refusal to adopt Gorbachev's reform programme, while the East German public whole-heartedly supported Moscow, for the first time willing 'to learn from the Soviet Union', as one of the stale communist slogans read. But Erich Honecker and his collaborators would have none of it and lost all control when Moscow refused to tolerate any violent measures against the growing reform movements. Finally the Soviets were prepared to cut the umbilical cord.

What resulted was not only the fall of the communist regime but also the disappearance of East Germany's statehood. The distinct identity which had developed during forty years of separation could not be employed to support a separate nationhood. This came as a surprise to many people, among them many Western observers, who had assumed that some sort of tacit separate national identity and thereby legitimacy had developed in the GDR since the 1960s.

Let us come back to the question whether post-1945 Germany developed a legitimate, that is democratically supported, new political order or whether it was one largely imposed by the Allies.

As mentioned earlier, the four victor powers were united on one fundamental point: Germany should never again be an independently-acting great power. Somewhat to their surprise, and in contrast with the fateful post-1918 era, the German people did not oppose this position this time round. What the majority of Germans strongly objected to were only the Allied *methods* of rendering Germany less dangerous. Even people who had been anti-Nazi resented the denazification boards, the tight economic controls, the dismantling of industrial equipment, and the frequently awkward attempts at re-education. Worse still, in the wake of the Potsdam agreement millions of ethnic Germans from the east were forcibly re-settled and a quarter of pre-war German territory was transferred to Poland and to the Soviet Union. In the eyes of the 'good Germans' such Allied policies would fatally undercut internal German efforts to build a peaceful, democratic Germany.

As we now know, that did not turn out to be the case, but it illustrates the uphill struggle that the new democratic German politicians were facing. Their non- or anti-Nazi background set them apart from most other Germans who had more or less openly agreed with Hitler, at least some of the time. Their credentials from the Weimar days did not make them popular either, because most Germans considered Weimar a politicians' mess. And they had no way around the occupation authorities since Germany's new political institutions, parties and media were at the Allies' mercy in so many ways – not least financially! Their popularity with their German electorates rested on their ability to postpone, modify or even thwart Allied programs for the internal restructuring of Germany.[21]

In this context one question in particular has been the subject of extensive controversy among German historians: did the Allies, especially the Americans, force capitalism on a German people who would have preferred extensive socialization and nationalization of natural resources and of large corporations?

In support of this proposition it was argued that not only the opposition Social Democratic Party (SPD) and the trade unions but also large sections of the ruling Christian parties were in favour of a mixed economy (to use the contemporary British term), that is of a capitalist economy with a large public sector. Yet detailed historical analysis brought to light much evidence which speaks against this hypothesis of capitalism-by-American-fiat.

Beyond any doubt there was a strong populist sentiment against reinstating German big industrialists who had done well out of the War while the little people had lost their families' bread-winners and seen their homes and modest possessions destroyed. Indeed these sentiments left their mark on party political statements and in several state constitutions which originated in 1946–7. But these were gut feelings of economic justice rather than abstract blueprints for socialism. And after the currency reform the majority of Germans eagerly took advantage of the rapidly increasing consumer production and market opportunities. As a consequence the urge for large-scale economic restructuring eventually petered out.[22]

The issue came to a head during the first federal election campaign of 1949 when the major political parties focused on the ideological choice between a free-market system and a state-managed economy. The latter, it must be remembered, smacked of Nazi-style war economy, complete with ration cards and big government bullying both employers and workers.

The 1949 election can be regarded as a referendum on the economic system of the Federal Republic. If socialism or another alternative to Economics Minister Ludwig Erhard's liberal credo of a social market economy had been widely popular, why was it that the SPD did so poorly not only in 1949 but in successive postwar elections? Why did they do worse in 1949 than even at the end of the Weimar Republic although, in contrast with 1932, the communists were but a tiny minority?

Discussions on the failure of democratic socialism in post-war Germany focused on the leadership of the SPD and the trade unions.[23] From a far-left position it was argued that they were too modest in their demands, too accommodating to the bourgeoisie and too anti-communist. In reply moderates asked for proof that more leftist policies would have led to greater electoral success. They emphasized that a strong working class identity as expressed in what used to be a social-democratic subculture was largely destroyed during the Nazi period. Therefore working-class voters had become much less distinct from the rest of the population. After all, the fundamental impact of the Nazi era on traditional political structures also affected the Catholic subculture, particularly its working-class strongholds in the industrial Rhineland.[24]

At the level of a broader historical analysis the charges brought against the moderate SPD leadership are based on the more or less tacit assumption that the German working classes – unlike all other parts of German society – had somehow been left psychologically and politically unspoilt by the Nazis. Nothing, however, justifies such optimism. Certainly workers, like the vast majority of post-war Germans, were glad to see the Nazi regime abolished after it failed to deliver material comforts and to win the War. But neither the socialist nor the Catholic working class had been unanimously opposed to Hitler, even though their support for the Nazis stayed noticeably below the German average.

Thus any notion of a broad, deep-seated anti-fascist consensus after the end of the War proved highly unrealistic. When free elections were held in the Western zones, distinctly left-wing parties faced an uphill struggle from the start. In the Soviet zone no amount of encouragement on the part of the communists made any difference either. The German communists lost the early free elections by such wide margins that the anti-facist façade of the Sozialistische Einheitspartei (socialist unity party or SED) could be upheld only by doing away with free political expression. Clearly the early post-war elections went against left-wing positions, not because of any 'false policies' on the part of the SPD or of the communists but because of a social revolution in German society which had occurred during the Nazi regime.[25]

In fact the SPD leadership was fully aware of the extent to which the collapse of the Weimar Republic and the subsequent Nazi policies had eroded their traditional political base. In response they sought to reorient their party away from being a distinctly working-class movement toward a socially much broader based national party. That reorientation was enshrined later on in the Bad Godesberg party program of 1959.

Kurt Schumacher, the towering SPD leader in 1945–52, was driven not by class ideology but by a fervent conviction that his party was morally entitled to win the first national election because the SPD alone had consistently opposed the Nazis. But principled moralism was obviously not what the German voters wanted. They preferred personal advancement instead.

In the wake of 1968 a voluminous literature, more *marxisante* than Marxist, romanticised what little anti-fascist consensus had existed in the immediate post-war days. It was suggested that local anti-fascist groups (Antifas) based on a wide left-wing consensus would have produced a new kind of society, while in reality those groups had been merely spontaneous expressions of local democracy encompassing a fraction of the German people and engaging only in narrow local activities. There was simply no comparison with the momentum and mass support of the Räte (council) movement of 1918–19 which had prepared the way for Weimar democracy. As the victors of 1945 began to license political parties and to set up a parliamentary system, the Antifas disappeared quietly.[26]

If Germany was unlikely to become socialist, for reasons quite independent of what the American capitalist occupiers did or didn't do, what is the evidence to show that the Yankees even made an effort to enforce capitalism? Much of the discussion on that issue centred on the American decision to postpone the nationalization of large industries until a central German government could be formed.[27] This move, however, was much more a political than a socio-economic one. First, the Americans were not prepared to see the German state apparatus strengthened by putting it in charge of large parts of the economy. Such control or even ownership would have undermined the Allied concept of decentralization and federalism. Second, the Americans did not wish to see too much power in the hands of works councils and trade unions because they were afraid of communist interference. Particularly in the highly industrialized Ruhr area, such political and industrial forces might easily have extended their influence to the political institutions and thereby undercut their authority. Further down the road such a power shift might have provided the Soviet Union with critical leverage in West German politics.

All of this is not to deny that leading American officials were genuinely convinced that private initiative and a free-market economy would create wealth faster than would government regulations. General Lucius D. Clay, the American military governor, who was a strong believer in Jeffersonian democracy, argued that German capitalism had been badly warped by an unhealthy concentration of ownership, cartels and other restrictive practices and finally by massive government controls under the Nazis. In his view the Germans had yet to experience the blessings of a free-market economy.[28]

### Integration versus non-alignment

The second major area of historical debate was the issue of West Germany's foreign-policy orientation. Apart from massive structural changes prescribed at Potsdam in 1945, European integration was the key concept used by the Western Allies to tame German power in the long run.

As a first important step the Americans explicitly connected the Marshall Plan with the reconstruction of the German economy because they thought it would be impossible to rebuild Europe's economic viability without a German economic recovery. While the Marshall Plan was supported by all political forces in Germany (except only the communists), further steps toward integration, particularly the Schuman Plan of 1950, met with considerable opposition. Much of this opposition came from the SPD and was a reflection of its profound disagreement with the economic as well as the foreign policies of Chancellor Konrad Adenauer's first cabinet.

The SPD, however, was not against European integration as such. Its hostility to the Schuman Plan rested on the assumption that the French really sought to prevent Germany from becoming an equal partner in Europe. In Adenauer's opinion, European integration would eventually lead to a status of equality for Germany with the other Western countries.

The key difference between Adenauer and Schumacher was not one of ideology or of national aspiration. It was one of political judgement as to whether the prospects for German unity would improve or diminish as the Federal Republic was progressively being drawn into the Western camp. Neither leader could of course imagine that the German people would ever acquiesce in a permanent division of their fatherland. Before the rise of the Green movement in the 1970s no established politician dared to argue in favour of a permanently divided Germany. It was simply unthinkable, at least in public.

The allegation of selling out to the Allied powers was a favourite SPD charge which Kurt Schumacher used forcefully against the policies of Adenauer. At one point, after Adenauer had concluded the Petersberg agreement[29] with the three Western High Commissioners in late 1949, Schumacher made his famous pronouncement that Adenauer was not serving the German people but was really the 'chancellor of the Allies'. This was the ultimate insult: it illustrates the aforementioned dilemma of having to seek simultaneously Allied consent and German electoral support.

These and other contemporary charges are widely echoed in the historical literature. Some historians claim that realistic opportunities for national reunification were wasted by focusing West German foreign policy exclusively on integration with the West. In their view the Federal Republic should have pursued a policy of non-alignment. It should have acted as a bridge between East and West, making it possible for the Soviet Union to let their occupation zone be reunited with the three Western zones by disentangling Germany from the superpower confrontation. But Adenauer and his circle firmly believed that Germany could not survive in a no-man's-land between the two blocs. It would be exposed to Soviet blackmail and it might not remain a liberal democracy. For them unification on acceptable terms, that is coupled with free self-determination, could be achieved only from a Western position of strength.[30]

That concept, however, had neither a time horizon nor a practical definition. In fact it withered away from the mid-1950s with the rapid build-up of nuclear forces and the eventual nuclear stalemate between the two superpowers. As the Berlin Wall crisis of 1961 showed, the United States were not prepared to enter into a nuclear crisis for the sake of German unification. Neither was anyone else in Europe, the Germans included. The only practical alternative seemed to be what came to be called *Ostpolitik*, that is to find common ground with the communist-bloc countries rather than to search for elusive Western positions of strength.

Dissent with Adenauer's position came not only from the SPD but also from influential intellectual circles and even from the military. One of the first Bundeswehr officers, Colonel Bogislaw von Bonin, suggested in the 1950s that the Federal Republic should adopt a purely defensive strategy rather than NATO's concept of forward defence coupled with nuclear deterrence.[31] This argument was widely echoed by people who more or less opposed German rearmament, a movement which incidentally included many former Wehrmacht officers from the Nazi era.

Such suggestions, too, lost much of their appeal when the world from the 1950s to the 1970s was faced with massive Soviet arms build-ups, virtually uninterrupted by various phases of détente.[32] The SPD made its 1960 foreign-policy turn-about in support of the Bundeswehr and NATO, which it now regarded as a reality without any practical alternatives. It even produced a few of its own defence intellectuals, most prominently Helmut Schmidt who became Minister of Defence in 1969 and who was Chancellor in 1974–82.

Two historiographical propositions flowed from these debates about West Germany's foreign-policy orientation. One sought to argue that the Marshall Plan was not central to Germany's economic revival, thus implying that Germany could have become prosperous again without becoming part of the Pax Americana. The other focuses on the aforementioned Stalin notes of 1952 in which the Soviet Union offered a reunification of Germany in return for a policy of non-alignment.

While much of the Federal Republic's economic history still remains to be written, it seems quite clear that the first of these propositions overlooks some important facts. To begin with, the Marshall Plan was significant very far beyond the actual financial aid to West Germany.[33] Quite likely West Germany would have seen an economic recovery of one sort or another in the long term. But would the speed and orientation of the West German recovery have been the same? Would it have provided political stability at home and confidence abroad to a comparable extent?

What needs to be understood here is the fact that the Marshall Plan was really a political programme garnished with financial incentives to make its tough medicine more palatable to national European politicians and to their interest groups. Once admitted to the ranks of the participating nations, each of them had to submit its reconstruction and investment policies to a supra-national body. This was an attempt to avoid national economic strategies hostile to the rebuilding of international trade. Most importantly, the recipients of Marshall aid had to open their markets to each other. In this manner, West Germany gained access to European markets, which in turn was essential if her export industries were to flourish again for the benefit both of the Germans and their Western neighbours alike. In other words, to discuss the significance of the Marshall plan only in terms of American funds sent to Europe is to miss its overall role for post-war Germany and indeed for the Western world.

On the second proposition, which was connected to the Soviet diplomatic notes of March 1952, the established view deems Stalin's surprising offers for quick reunification-cum-neutrality a political ploy. Stalin simply wished to lure the Federal Republic away from military integration under the proposed EDC treaty which had just been signed. This view held up rather well after a good deal of the Western diplomatic sources became available. Efforts to revive the old myth of golden opportunities lost delivered precious little documentary evidence.[34] Such notions of a tragically misunderstood Kremlin make even less sense since Soviet archives began to open up.

*West German elites: old or new?*

The third major area of German historical debate on the Cold War deals with the Nazi legacy in terms of continuity of elites. Its starting point is the question of successes and failures of denazification during the occupation period and after.

When the Western Allies first entered Germany in September 1944 they carried 'white lists' with names of individual Germans who were known to have been free from Nazi involvement and who could be appointed to administrative and key private sector positions. These lists had been assembled chiefly from Allied intelligence and German émigré sources.

But what was to be done with the millions of Germans who did not have a clean record? Initially the Allies themselves took the initiative. They enforced various measures of denazification. A select group of prominent war criminals were tried by the International Military Tribunal at Nuremberg in 1945–6 and by subsequent Allied trials on a zonal basis. Eventually a vast amount of denazification work was turned over to the rather reluctant German authorities.

The white-list leaders were less than eager to carry out this particular task which only served to isolate them further from the average Germans and to make them look like lackeys of the Allies. Clearly, the majority of Germans considered those trials and screening boards to be a form of retribution at the hands of the victors, even though few people were sympathetic to the plight of Hitler's lieutenants. As the Cold War came to dominate Allied policies on Germany, the Western powers and their Germans sought to wind up quickly at least the bulk of the lighter cases.

When the first demands for rearmament were made, opposition to denazification was considered a bargaining chip at the hands of the Germans. Former Wehrmacht officers plainly stated that they were not prepared to engage in the defence of the West without the release of former comrades who had been sentenced for war crimes.[35] In the end both the new Bundeswehr and the Bonn government wished to avoid further embarrassment. A special vetting commission was established to weed out any potentially compromising people. As a result the military went through a much more thorough cleansing than most other professions. Elsewhere, even in the higher civil service, numerous people with a highly questionable record, in some cases even with an outright criminal one, were reinstated or at any rate sent into early retirement with comfortable government pensions.

That legacy came to haunt Germany in 1968. The failure to purge that state apparatus more openly and more effectively went on to poison German public life for many years. In a number of highly publicized cases it took massive public protest or even court proceedings to get rid of certain compromised public figures. Despite some major trials in the 1960s and 1970s, a sizeable number of war criminals remained unscathed and free to roam around post-war Germany. Sadly the legal profession itself set a bad example: it failed to bring to trial even a single Nazi judge for the appalling ways in which many courts had operated under Hitler.

This 'cold amnesty' (Jörg Friedrich) or swift reintegration of most Nazis into German post-war society occurred largely under the impact of the Cold War.[36] It only became a subject of historical debate in the late 1960s, that is in the era of superpower détente and in the wake of the American débâcle over Vietnam. Anger with this foul legacy was then largely directed against America for having made the Federal Republic a pillar of the West so swiftly and for having made it so easy for former Nazis to pledge allegiance to democracy behind the smokescreen of a crusade against communism.

Closer historical investigation revealed, however, that British, French and particularly Soviet military government officials with their vague notions of collective guilt – either ethnic or class-based – had little faith in any *épuration* (cleansing) of the German people. It was the more idealistic American occupation authorities, philosophically opposed to the notion of national collective guilt, who fiercely believed in punishing all Nazis. After all, millions of Americans had German ancestors, and the Germans were one of the largest ethnic groups in American society.

The Americans were also the ones who sought to introduce many more liberal reform measures than most Germans, including the new white-list leaders, found desirable. Ironically, this was discovered in the records of the American occupation administration at the very time when the Vietnam debates were swaying emotions in the direction of anti-Americanism. Historians with leftist sympathies sought to explain this apparent contradiction by attributing such reform policies to 'good Americans', many of whom had been left-wing New Dealers with little affection for American big business and for red-baiting at a time when Washington allegedly came to be more and more dominated by the 'bad Americans' who propagated the Cold War in the 1940s and who became guilty of starting the Vietnam war later on.[37]

From this perspective, bitter charges were also directed against the West German political, social and business elites. The notion was propagated that the Bonn Republic was a product of the way in which the Americans had rebuilt Germany in the late 1940s and early 1950s to fit their own Cold-War interests. Prominent examples were at hand, such as Chancellor Kurt Georg Kiesinger (1966–9) who even in the 1960s claimed he had not known about the Holocaust while serving as a middle-rank official in the Nazi propaganda machinery. As late as 1978 the head of the government of Baden-Württemberg, Hans Filbinger, had to resign for having been a Nazi judge. (In the last months of the War he had passed several death sentences on German sailors who had refused to follow politically and militarily insane orders.[38])

Speaking superficially, one might say that American McCarthyism had hounded people because of their leftist sympathies, while German society integrated people despite their questionable or even criminal Nazi record. But this would be a cheap shot. It would overlook the special character of the Cold-War legacy in Germany.

To some extent it is of course true that the fight against communism was instrumentalized for class as well as for ideological purposes. But the initial steps were taken rather innocently during the Berlin blockade when the Germans were permitted to identify with the West. It was tempting for them to feel that somehow the Nazi legacies no longer mattered in the face of a massive Soviet threat to central and Western Europe. By loading the planes for the airlift and by resisting Soviet pressures in Berlin, the Germans were all of a sudden seen to be serving the cause of freedom. Two years later, when war broke out in Korea, Western strategists believed that Europe rather than some isolated Asian peninsula was the real battle-field of the Cold War.[39] Now the Federal Republic would be tied into the Western defence alliance without too many further questions asked about denazification. Indeed, re-education turned from an instrument to combat the Nazi legacy into a political gospel of anti-communism. One hardly needs to add how eager many former Nazis were to jump on that particular bandwagon.

A careful distinction must be made, however, between public and intellec-tual perceptions of German society on the one hand and the social changes which actually occurred on the other. After 'Hitler's social revolution' (David Schoenbaum), German society saw another wave of fundamental changes which was caused among other things by the influx of some ten million eastern refugees to the territory of West Germany. In addition there was a massive restructuring of the West German economy. The resulting social and cultural changes became evident only gradually, and they have not been fully studied by historians.[40]

What studies we have not only provide a more subtle understanding of post-war Germany but also reflect the mood of the 1980s when the Federal Republic had demonstrated its political stability during the upheavals of the international oil crisis and had stood up to German terrorism and to the crisis over Soviet SS-20 missile deployment. Their guiding question was: 'How did stability become pos-sible?' That mood is significantly different from two decades earlier, when critics tried to explain the upheavals of the 1960s by asking 'Why did old structures persist for so long?'

In the wake of the failures of Weimar and of the Nazi crimes, a mature West German democracy only seemed plausible if one could identify fundamental changes which provided the basis for a totally different social, political and psy-chological reality. After all, in 1945 few observers dared to hope that authori-tarian structures and mentalities would disappear as completely as they have and that democracy would become a way of life down to the villages and kindergartens.

After unification West Germany's history came to look even more of a success story when compared to the utter failure, corruption and viciousness of the old GDR regime. Racist and chauvinist incidents in Eastern Germany began to expose some worrying attitudes toward foreigners and alternative lifestyles. To a certain extent traditional German authoritarianism seems to have been preserved among the former GDR population and it must be hoped that this cultural lag will vanish in due course as economic modernization succeeds east of the Elbe. But historians are not in the business of being either optimistic or pessimistic about such issues. Rather they need to look for factual evidence and for usable interpretative frame-works. Both have become harder to find in recent years.

### Trends in historical research

Finally, it is time to review some major achievements and recent trends in German Cold-War historiography.

Until the 1960s little original research could be done because few archival sources were available. From then on archives slowly began to open up, but for a long time access was very uneven, which in turn accounts for the peculiar development of historiography at that time.

On most political issues the sources crucial in the early period were held in Washington, London, Paris and Moscow, because the occupying powers rather than the Germans were the ones who made all the important decisions. Among them the Americans were the first to grant access to their files on a wide scale. As a consequence many of the earlier studies were not only about American policy but were in fact written from the perspective of American sources. By the time British and French archives opened up, their impact on historiography was bound to be much smaller, and it will remain to be seen if Soviet archives will change that picture in the future.

Writing the history of a country with the help of foreign archives is at the same time unusual and yet typical of Germany's situation. Only when the Germans began to have more influence on their own destiny did their government records become more valuable to historians. By the same token, however, those sources also became more sensitive, even potentially embarrassing, to the Germans. This explains why American and British records became accessible way ahead of the German ones. Archival policies in Washington and London are still the main driving force. Without them the closely-knit higher civil service in Germany would probably delay archival access to an even greater and more annoying degree than at present.

While the published memoirs of key Allied officials provided much information prior to the opening of archives, the German autobiographical literature for the same period is relatively poor. This was of course another disincentive to research. Only Adenauer's memoirs stand out by the extent to which they draw heavily on source materials (which were not available to researchers for a very long time). But in terms of literary elegance and wealth of information nothing really compares to the published recollections of Charles Bohlen, George Kennan and Dean Acheson, to name only a few American examples. Things get somewhat better for the period since the mid-fifties, when Germans became international players in their own right.[41]

In the political heat of the 1960s young German historians wrote essentially ahead of the opening of the records. Not surprisingly, their work tended to re-fight the battles of the American revisionists, who themselves had access only to some of the American archival sources.[42] This trend was enhanced by several 'local' factors. As mentioned earlier, Soviet foreign policy after 1945 had not been a popular subject.[43] When peace research emerged as a discipline its protagonists largely used the assumptions of the American revisionists and their German disciples. Soviet policies were pictured as having been mostly reactive and pitiful. Arms races were analysed without much reference to their historical or global or ideological contexts. The blossoming social sciences of the 1960s were largely ahistorical anyhow, at least from the perspective of professional historians of a more traditional stripe.

While the American revisionists and their German epigones had eager audiences, the same cannot be said about the American, British and French realist school of historians who carried the debates back again to the archives and returned with fundamentally different results. Eventually, post-revisionism came along, but again it is significant that only Daniel Yergin's book was published in German – indeed it inspired a popular German text by Wilfried Loth – yet none of John L. Gaddis's work found (or sought?) a German publisher.[44] Perhaps the most valuable German study on Germany and the Cold War is still a book-length essay by Richard Löwenthal dating from 1974. But then Löwenthal's outlook on foreign affairs was largely shaped in exile in Britain during the War, by his study of communism undertaken at American research centres and by his biographical background as an ex-communist and left-wing socialist. It hardly needs to be added that such views were far from what the Zeitgeist held to be politically correct in the 1970s.[45]

From the mid-1970s onward a number of major publications of German sources began to appear which opened the field for much new research, particularly on domestic aspects of Cold-War Germany.[46] They were prepared mostly by the Bundesarchiv (German Federal Archive) and the Institut für Zeitgeschichte in Munich who also publish a considerable number of highly illuminating diaries and memoirs from their archival holdings. Beginning with Adenauer's negotiations with the Allied High Commissioners, a German series of diplomatic papers was started under the auspices of the Bonn foreign ministry.[47] Other key documents dealing with rearmament, diplomacy and economic questions have been published piecemeal in such scholarly journals as *Militärgeschichtliche Mitteilungen*, *Vierteljahrshefte für Zeitgeschichte*, *Europa-Archiv*, *Deutschland-Archiv*, and *Osteuropa*. On German security issues after 1945, a massive history of German defence issues prior to the founding of the Bundeswehr in 1956 was begun by the Militärgeschichtliche Forschungsamt.[48] Given its full access to German official records, it is particularly strong on internal German debates and early planning efforts.

By far the most flourishing part of the business has been the examination of Konrad Adenauer and his policies. Among a great many biographical and topical studies, Hans-Peter Schwarz's new biography and his two Adenauer volumes in the semi-official history of the Federal Republic are now yardsticks for everyone.[49] Today Adenauer is regarded as some sort of demi-god to whom all German foreign policy debates defer. It seems hard to believe that in 1963 he was deserted and practically sacked by his own party half-way into his fourth term in office. More ironically still, it was Willy Brandt who helped to elevate him to these heights by claiming that his own Ostpolitik was in complete harmony and continuity with Adenauer's foreign policy and that it was merely complementing integration with the West.

In the last few years, we have seen a revived interest in Ludwig Erhard, the powerful economics minister from 1949 to 1963 who stamped his own model of a social market economy on the Federal Republic and who was largely credited with master-minding the German economic miracle.[50] In part this revival is aimed critically at the Adenauer cottage industry which took hold of the debates to such a large extent. But there are also powerful business interests involved which like to see the principles of free enterprise promoted in the face of calls for state intervention. Obviously the enthusiasm for market principles in the (former) communist world gave additional encouragement. This background is an important element in the historical arguments about the significance of the Marshall Plan mentioned above. Highlighting the achievements of entrepreneurs, of American capital investment and free trade carries an obvious message in the face of leftist views of how the Federal Republic emerged.

What can be said at this point about historical writings on East Germany?

A short answer must begin by pointing to the peculiarities of research in the former GDR.[51] Throughout the 1950s all publications stood under the Stalinist diktat of a prescribed and instrumentalized view of history. This hardline approach began to soften somewhat in the 1960s. From then on dedicated Western observers went over the texts with a toothcomb to look for any deviations or hints of liberalization, in much the same way as one pored over *Pravda* and *Neues Deutschland*.

Then during the 1970s the GDR began to modify its approach to German history by restoring to national significance such prominent historical figures as Martin Luther and Prussia's King Frederick the Great, who had earlier been denounced as bloodhounds of the oppressive classes. Such revisions obviously sought to accommodate certain pre-socialist patriotic sentiments which, in theory, were not meant to exist any longer.[52] The earlier gross misrepresentations and even forgeries of history lost all credibility when the great majority of East Germans found ready access to Western information. In a sense the Germans were progressively becoming united by common, that is Western, television.

While the regime became somewhat less blatantly ideological with respect to Germany's earlier historical heritage, such openness was notably absent from historical publications dealing with the post-war period. Yet even here many of the blatant forgeries of historical photographs and documents were more or less tacitly put right. Anything further was feared to imply an acceptance of Gorbachev-style reforms which the leadership under Erich Honecker went out of its way to avoid. Thus gradual de-Stalinization did not produce historical works on the Cold War which one can use in an ordinary scholarly fashion. Needless to say, after the collapse of the GDR the authors of such discreetly revisionist writings found themselves in a highly compromised situation.[53]

For more reliable works in and around East Germany we have to turn to Western research. Though much of it was supported by the Bonn government, the results were by no means always pleasing to officials and to interest groups such as the arch-conservative refugee associations. The co-option of many left-wing historians and of a sizeable number of refugee scholars from East Germany made sure of that.[54] By carefully analyzing published materials they could assemble a surprisingly detailed picture of what happened on the other side of the demarcation line. Judging from spotty recent revelation, however, it seems likely that some major areas have remained terrae incognitae.[55] For example the number of full-time employees of the omnipresent State Security Service (Stasi) was more than three times higher than had been estimated.[56] It goes without saying that this agency had made the greatest of efforts to hide the extent of its control of the state apparatus and of the entire population. Another reason for the blanks in our knowledge of the GDR is the dearth of such first-class insider reports as Wolfgang Leonhard's autobiography as a young hopeful in Walter Ulbricht's early entourage or Erich Gniffke's report on his time among the SED leadership.[57]

It is hoped of course that many more original sources will come to light in the next few years. In all probability they will give us unprecedented insights not only into politics, ideology and society in East Germany but also into Soviet policies vis-à-vis that peculiar and important ally of Moscow's. If in the past the history of East Germany was a field in which German historians made a vital contribution to our understanding of the early Cold War, that contribution is likely to become even more important in future. For the dissolution of East German sovereignty and central institutions resulted in archival access of a kind which may not be achieved in most former communist countries simply because all except the GDR (and recently Yugoslavia and Czechoslovakia) remain intact as nation states. The complete disbanding of the GDR armed forces and of the intelligence organizations alone has yielded materials which offer unique insight into national as well as international communist politics.

In conclusion we can state that Germany is not only a special case in the history of the Cold War. It is an even more unique beneficiary of its ending. To make this ending intellectually and politically fruitful for the Germans and for their eastern neighbours, we need to understand better the burden of the Cold-War legacies. And that goal requires us to do much more historical research, which should be undertaken with a profound understanding of how crucial it is for nations and for civilizations to face historical truths. It is hoped that this will be appreciated by historians as well as by those who control access to historical records, to research funds, to the mass media, and, not least, to school textbooks.

### Bibliographical note

For English-speaking readers the best history of the Federal Republic is Dennis L. Bark & David R. Gress, *The History of West Germany* (2 vols., Oxford, 1989). The larger historical background can be found in David Calleo, *The German Problem Reconsidered: Germany and the World Order, 1870 to the Present* (New York, 1978) and Harold James, *A German Identity, 1770–1990* (London, 1990).

Various specific issues are covered in Bruce Kuklick, *American Policy and the Division of Germany: the Clash over Reparations* (Ithaca, N.Y., 1972); James F. Tent, *Mission on the Rhine: Re-education and De-Nazification in American-Occupied Germany* (Chicago, 1983); John H. Backer, *The Decision to Divide Germany: American Foreign Policy in Transition* (Durham, N.C., 1978); and in two books by John Gimbel, *The American Occupation of Germany: Politics and the Military, 1945–1949* (Stanford, CA, 1968) and *The Origins of the Marshall Plan* (Stanford, CA, 1976). For the Berlin crisis see Hannes Adomeit, *Soviet-Risk-Taking and Crisis Behaviour* (London, 1982). Lucius D. Clay, *Decision in Germany* (Garden City, N.Y., 1950) is still valuable, as are the *Memoirs* of Konrad Adenauer, of which unfortunately only the first volume has been translated (London, 1966).

English-language histories of East Germany include Henry A. Turner, *The Two Germanies since 1945: East and West* (New Haven, 1989 reprint) and David Childs, et al., *East Germany in Comparative Perspective* (London, 1989). Charles S. Maier is preparing a history of German unification.

# PART FOUR

# SMALL STATES AMONG BIG POWERS

## 7    *Benelux*

### CEES  WIEBES  &  BERT  ZEEMAN

On 5 September 1944, shortly before the liberation of Belgium and Luxembourg and with the Netherlands still firmly in the grip of Nazi Germany, the governments-in-exile of these three nations concluded in London a customs union treaty, to become effective after their total liberation. Historic ties, geographic proximity, economic interests and the wartime boost for international, especially European, co-operation all contributed to the conclusion of the agreement. Because of the continued occupation of the Netherlands (until 5 May 1945) and the economic disequilibria caused by the Second World War, the agreement became effective only in 1948. In the meantime, Benelux (as the new combination was to be known) attracted world-wide public attention as the prime example of co-operation between neighbouring countries with common interests and common goals. They had even more in common, these small, densely populated, highly industrialized and urbanized constitutional monarchies located at the north-western corner of the European Continent.

Belgium's surface area of nearly 12,000 square miles is somewhat larger than that of Maryland (which ranks among the ten smallest American states). Its northern border is with the Netherlands, its southern with France and its eastern with Germany and Luxembourg. In the west the nation faces the Channel and North Sea. At present Belgium has a population of about 10 million (8.5 million in 1945), the country being divided into three linguistic segments: the Walloons (speaking French), the Flemings (speaking Flemish/Dutch) and a small German-speaking community.

In 1830 a provisional national government proclaimed independence from Holland. At the London Conference nine years later, its independence and its neutrality were both formally recognized by the then Great Powers. In the scramble for Africa in the 1880s King Leopold II secured as foremost possession the Congo; a colony (now called Zaire) which after a colonial war became independent in 1960. The Congo State and the other Belgian overseas dependencies in Africa were an important source of raw materials and brought the nation much prosperity.

At the beginning of the First World War Belgium's neutrality was brutally violated by the German invasion in August 1914. The government fled to France and continued the war on the side of the Allies. After the War Belgium sought an alliance with both France and Britain, but only the French were prepared to negotiate one in 1920. Four years later the government joined France, Britain, Germany and Italy in the Locarno Treaty, only to return to a policy of strict neutrality in 1936 after the German reoccupation of the Rhineland. In May 1940 another German incursion made evident that this policy was also unsuccessful. More than 70,000 Belgians were killed during the German military occupation. After the Second World War Belgium became an important platform for international organizations, housing both the (civilian) headquarters of NATO and the Commission of the European Communities in Brussels.

Belgium has always been a constitutional monarchy, the king serving as a symbol of unity for the nation. Real executive authority is exercised by the prime minister and the cabinet. In direct contrast with the Netherlands, cabinet ministers may keep their parliamentary seats. Parliament consists of a Chamber of Representatives (212 members) and a Senate (182 members) and terms last four years unless a cabinet crisis takes place necessitating new elections. None of the political parties has ever been able to muster a lasting majority in parliament. Governments therefore are most of the time coalitions of two or more of these parties.

The Netherlands at present have more than 15 million inhabitants (in 1945 nearly 10 million) living in an area of almost 16,000 square miles (which is two-thirds the size of West Virginia). Its population density of over 900 inhabitants per square mile is one of the highest in the world. The country once had an impressive empire with colonies spanning the globe in Asia, Africa and North and South America. After independence for Indonesia (1949) and Surinam (1975), the Kingdom of the Netherlands at present embodies only the European mainland proper and several small islands in the Caribbean, the Netherlands Antilles. Its southern frontier is with Belgium and its eastern with Germany. The western and northern borders are formed by the North Sea.

In foreign policy successive Dutch governments also pursued a policy of neutrality, which was one of the reasons why the country stayed out of the First World War. This policy was resolutely adhered to again in the period leading up to the Second World War but this time it did not prevent a German invasion in May 1940. German aircraft destroyed the city centre of Rotterdam and tens of thousands of Dutch Jews (among them Anne Frank) were deported and killed. In Asia the Netherlands East Indies (Indonesia) were conquered by Japanese forces in 1941–2 and, despite the reoccupation in 1945, the Dutch government was forced, after a lengthy armed struggle with Indonesian nationalists, to grant this former colony independence in late 1949.

As in Belgium, the constitutional monarchy functions as a symbol of unity. Genuine executive authority is exercised by the prime minister and the cabinet, controlled by a Parliament consisting of a Second Chamber (150 members; 4 year-terms) and a First Chamber or Senate (75 members; 4 year-terms). Since no single political party has ever been able to command a majority of the popular vote, there have always been coalition governments that remain in power (if there are no crises) for a period of four years.

The Grand Duchy of Luxembourg covers an area of only 1000 square miles and has at present 378,000 inhabitants (300,000 in 1945). It is a land-locked country, nestling between Belgium, France and Germany, even smaller than America's tiniest state, Rhode Island. For this reason one commentator once joked that this ministate is so small that every time a person rolls over in bed, he has to show his passport. Luxembourg joined Belgium in 1830 in splitting away from the Netherlands but only in 1867 was its existence as a neutral state guaranteed by the major powers. Like Belgium, Luxembourg suffered from German invasions in both World Wars in spite of a policy of strict neutrality. In 1921 it joined Belgium in a customs union, the Belgian-Luxembourg Economic Union (BLEU), leading to close economic and political relations between the two countries. After the Second World War Luxembourg joined its Benelux partners in breaking away from neutrality and adhering to NATO.

The structure and inner workings of the constitutional monarchy and governmental process are identical to that of Belgium and the Netherlands, although Luxembourg has only a unicameral legislature. The Chamber of Deputies has 60 members elected for a term of 5 years. As in the other two countries, coalition governments are the rule since no single political party has ever been able to command a majority in the Chamber.

In traditional accounts about the role of Belgium, Luxembourg and the Netherlands (i.e. the Benelux countries)[1] in the early Cold-War years, there appears to be an almost complete consensus among Benelux and foreign scholars. These three nations, it is said, were small, could not influence major political events in Europe (let alone the world), were not able to take care of their own national security and defence, and were extremely worried about Soviet intentions and capabilities. All these factors resulted in their seeking an alliance with the larger powers of Western Europe, the United States and Canada, culminating in their adherence to the North Atlantic Treaty in April 1949. This step is considered by many scholars as the definite break with their pre-war policy of neutrality. Later, in the beginning of the 1950s, the Benelux countries were depicted as being staunch supporters of European co-operation in different fields and were often portrayed as extremely loyal allies of the United States. Lumped together with the other smaller European countries, there appear to be no independent characteristics for each of the three Benelux nations.

However, in 1981 the Danish political scientist Nikolaj Petersen showed that despite their common background of smallness, neutrality and the failure thereof, the roads of Belgium, Denmark, the Netherlands and Norway toward alignment differed fundamentally in some respects. Whereas for the Benelux countries alliance membership symbolized a continuity of wartime and post-war policies, for Norway and Denmark alignment represented a sharp discontinuity primarily motivated by an acute sense of military insecurity.[2] New research, mainly based on contemporary archival records, slowly brings to the fore the fact that even Petersen's characterization of Belgium and the Netherlands as two of a kind involves serious elements of distortion. What emerges is that these minor powers have quite often displayed an independent foreign and national security policy which was unanticipated and sometimes in stark contrast with the general scholarly opinion described above. The more we study their role in and contribution to the shaping of post-war Europe in detail, the less reasons there are to lump them together.[3]

### Belgian and Dutch historiography

Belgian and Dutch historical research on the first post-war decade has not kept in step. Foreign-policy issues clearly take a more prominent place in Dutch than in Belgian historiography.[4] The difference in accessibility between Belgian and Dutch records is a major cause of this state of affairs. According to the Belgian Archives Law, government documents are declassified and become open to the public only after a 50-year lapse. In practice, researchers can get permission to consult papers of, for instance, the foreign ministry after 30 years, but permission is not easily granted. Access to the minutes and papers of the Belgian Cabinet is strictly governed by the 50-year rule. In contrast, in the Netherlands all government papers are declassified, and thus opened to the public, after a 30-year interval; and even this rather generous rule is not strictly applied. For instance, the minutes and papers of the Dutch Cabinet are opened to qualified researchers after 20 years and in some cases the archives of the foreign and other ministries can be consulted after a still shorter period.[5]

The discrepancy caused by the differences in accessibility is reinforced by several other circumstances. Post-war Belgian politics (certainly from 1944 until 1951) was dominated by the so-called Royal Question, the public debate about the role of King Leopold III during the Second World War and his return to the throne after Belgium's liberation (Leopold did not follow the Belgian government into exile; he even met Hitler in November 1940). For a long period the country was divided along linguistic and religious lines about this – the Catholic Flemish supporting and the socialist/communist Walloons opposing Leopold. Although after Leopold's abdication in 1951 Belgian internal affairs returned to a state of normalcy, one of the side-effects of the Royal Question to this day is its negative influence on the accessibility of public and private archives.

Moreover, so-called private cabinets are an important element in the Belgian political system. Each time a new government is sworn in, all ministers also appoint their own *chef de cabinet*, head of their private office in the ministry acting as a buffer between the minister and the departmental bureaucracy. Each time a government is brought down in parliament or breaks up of its own accord, as they leave, ministers and their *chefs de cabinet* are able to collect a multitude of government papers and take them home as their private archives. Consequently, the archives of the ministries themselves seldom possess the complete files on subjects of political relevance.

With regard to the post-war era, the decolonization issue is also of special significance. Whereas Belgian politics in the first post-war years was dominated by the Royal Question, Dutch politics centred on the decolonization of the Netherlands East Indies. The conflict dominated Dutch political life until 1949 and has become the object of a major historiographical debate. Given the international, global repercussions of the two conflicts with the Indonesian republicans (the first from 1945 until 1949 about Indonesian independence and the second from 1949 until 1962 about the fate of the Dutch island of New Guinea, close to Australia), colonial and foreign policy take a rather prominent position in Dutch historiography. Although Belgium has a rich tradition in nineteenth-century colonial historiography, attention to the post-war decolonization process as regards the Congo and the other African colonies seriously lags behind that of the Netherlands.

Finally, the study of foreign policy (as an element of *national* policy) does not seem to be as firmly embedded in Belgian academia as it is in the Netherlands. Compared to the Netherlands, in Belgium the number of historians and political scientists specialising in the study of post-war Belgian foreign policy is relatively small. The possibility of studying Belgian foreign policy using primary sources in, for instance, American, French or British archives has not yet found much following. There is no tradition in publishing a 'FRUS'-like historical-documentary record of Belgian foreign policy,[6] whereas in the Netherlands the series *Documents on the Foreign Policy of the Netherlands* started in 1957 with the year 1848 and publication has now progressed well into the 1940s.[7]

As a consequence publications of studies on Dutch post-war foreign policy clearly outnumber those on Belgian post-war foreign policy. Belgian publications about the role and planning of the government-in-exile in London during 1940–4 hardly exist. If we take a look at the post-war period, most accounts of the Belgian road towards alignment and European unification are almost exclusively based on scarce memoirs and printed sources. Most studies analyze policy only as it is documented in white papers, official memoranda and parliamentary debates, and consequently often produce rather traditional studies. Belgium remained largely unaffected by the renewed interest in the origins of the Cold War sparked by the opening of American and British archives. Only Jean Stengers's paper on Paul-Henri Spaak and the Brussels Treaty, published in 1986, is of paramount importance, in more than one sense.[8] His was the first contribution based on contemporary Belgian archival records, which until then had been considered almost impenetrable. Unfortunately his study did not have a successor on, for instance, the North Atlantic Treaty, and analyses of the Belgian role in the process of European integration are still relatively scarce. Considering the socialist Spaak's dominant position in post-war foreign and domestic policy, either as Prime or as Foreign Minister, it is most unfortunate that we lack serious studies of his role (although, given the inaccessibility of his personal papers, this may not come as a complete surprise).[9]

In contrast, in the Netherlands the wartime ideas about regional alliances in the post-war world and the overall behaviour of the government-in-exile have received wide attention. Detailed studies have been written about topics ranging from the recognition of the Soviet Union (1942) to the future role of the colonial empire. National security policy in the early-Cold-War years and the post-1950 period has also produced a number of studies. Some, based on declassified Dutch records, were the first to document security policy during the War and in the late 1940s in detail.[10] The Brussels and Atlantic Treaty talks, though, have received limited attention until now. What has been written does not add much to our knowledge either, and renders only superficial observations on the Dutch role in the alliance-making process.[11] On the other hand, the armed conflict in the Netherlands East Indies in 1945–9 and the controversy with Indonesia until 1962 about Dutch New Guinea has inspired a number of scholars to study their nation's foreign and defence policy in a global context.[12] Finally, a number of studies have been published recently which deal with the Dutch role in the European unification process.

Belgium and the Netherlands nevertheless have in common the fact that research in the past ten–fifteen years has led primarily to specialized studies published as articles or contributions to collective volumes. Comprehensive accounts dealing with either Belgian or Dutch post-war foreign policy that transcend the issue-focused narrowness of these specialized studies are almost non-existent. The appearance in the Netherlands in 1991 of a volume of articles published chiefly in the past decade that document Dutch foreign policy in the nineteenth and twentieth centuries is a suitable illustration of this state of affairs.[13] Paradoxically, given the situation described above, the only attempt to present such a comprehensive account deals with Belgium: Jules Gérard-Libois' & Rosine Lewin's *La Belgique entre dans la Guerre Froide et l'Europe (1947–1953)*, published in 1992.[14] As much as possible this study and the other new work published in the past fifteen years will form the basis for our own analysis of the role of the Benelux countries in the shaping of post-war Europe; an analysis that starts in London, with post-war planning.

### Post-war planning, 1942–5

Most studies about Allied post-war planning have thus far concentrated almost exclusively on the thinking of the major powers, leading to the creation of the United Nations Organization (UN). Of course this is not surprising, but it discriminates against the original ideas generated by the Benelux countries. All three of them were among the founding members of the UN, but without much enthusiasm and without much faith in its usefulness in enforcing post-war peace at a regional level. All three foreign secretaries (Spaak, Eelco N. van Kleffens in the Netherlands and Joseph Bech for Luxembourg)[15] evinced this lack of enthusiasm in the parliamentary debates on the ratification of the UN Charter in the final months of 1945. They abhorred especially the veto powers of the five great powers and the secondary role allocated to the lesser powers, and they questioned the suitability of a *global* organization to deal with the issue of peace, and enforcing peace, at a *regional* level. Specifically with this aim in mind, the Belgian and Dutch governments developed during their exile in London concrete plans suited to their national interests.

Belgian planning began early and quite energetically after the government arrived in London in 1940. It was more limited and more comprehensive than Dutch planning at the same time. More limited in the sense that Belgium's future was sought in a Western European entente under British guidance; more comprehensive in the sense that one should aim for military, political *and* economic co-operation at the same time. Spaak envisaged close co-operation at all these levels between the three Benelux countries, France and Britain. He therefore tried persistently to lure the British into a bilateral Anglo-Belgian agreement as a first step towards the more encompassing Western European entente, only to be rebuffed by his British hosts. British concurrence was a *sine qua non* for a successful implementation of the scheme, but Soviet participation was for Spaak also of paramount importance; he even assessed the 1942 Anglo-Soviet treaty of alliance as 'the cornerstone of world peace'.[16]

Dutch planning, ably guided by Van Kleffens,[17] was much more global in orientation. In 1941-3 he developed a scheme for post-war security which must be evaluated as a creative and novel contribution to the thinking about the maintenance of post-war peace.[18] According to Van Kleffens 'no universal or quasi-universal organization (could) be the corner-stone of international order and its preservation'. He therefore proposed the creation of six regional security organizations, grouped around the world's oceans and seas,[19] to be based on sea-power and with active American participation. In addition, he envisaged similar organizations based on land-power in Eastern Europe and the Balkans with a prominent role for the Soviet Union. Significantly, his ideas were studied and to some extent embraced by some larger powers, only to be shelved because of the plans for a future United Nations.

Apart from security against Germany and Japan, the only real threats in his view, Van Kleffens was clearly also thinking about the ideal way to safeguard Dutch world-wide interests. In this respect the government claimed a middle-power status in the post-war world and wanted to remain involved in regions other than Europe. By becoming a member of several regional security organizations, because of her colonial possessions in Asia and the Caribbean, the government expected to occupy a middle position between the big haves and the small have-nots and accordingly to hold their own vis-à-vis the outside world. It is in particular the originality of both the middle-power concept and the idea of regional security pacts on a global basis (as opposed to Norwegian Foreign Minister Trygve Lie's idea for a regional security organization just for the Atlantic) which stand out and which have been unjustly neglected thus far in the literature of post-war planning and alliance formation.

United as Spaak and Van Kleffens may have been in their rejection of the United Nations, in their choice of the preferred alternative they opposed each other almost diametrically. Spaak aimed for a Western European association under British leadership that should deal with economic, political and security issues at the same time. Van Kleffens, a regionalist and Atlanticist par excellence, opted for various regional arrangements covering the globe in which the United Stated had to participate. He stressed a solution from a military point of view, whereas for Spaak, apart from security, the prime desideratum was to lay a sound economic foundation. In their choice of primary allies they also differed: Spaak pinned all his hopes on Britain, so much so that the press at the time commented that 'Belgium is Britain's Baby'. Van Kleffens, on the other hand, expected salvation from the other side of the Atlantic. He preferred to play the American 'ace' instead of the British 'king'.[20]

Their primary motivation to seek alignment must be found in the need to prevent another German invasion (and also in the Dutch case another Japanese attack). Their specific choices for a (British-led) European-regionalist solution versus an (American-led) Atlantic-regionalist solution must to some extent be explained by their perception of their own role in world affairs. The self-image of the Belgians was that of a small country with limited security interests (although wider economic interests). These could best be furthered in a regional European framework in which Britain appeared to be the leading friendly power. On the continent she was the ideal power broker, having no aggressive designs, and economically her Empire and Commonwealth offered unprecedented opportunities for Belgian exports.

Van Kleffens on the other hand wanted involvement in regions outside Europe. By joining various security arrangements the Netherlands would accordingly participate in four pacts and would be able to avert the disgrace of being relegated to the 'rank of Denmark'. Van Kleffens started from the assumption that Dutch post-war standing would be one of a 'middle power' with dependencies in Asia, Latin America and the Caribbean as part of a world increasingly dominated by the United States. The latter was considered the only power able to replace Britain, after the collapse of the Pax Britannica, as the world's political and economic guardian. He was therefore extremely annoyed when the final UN blueprint did not grant an explicit role for the middle powers or a permanent seat for these powers collectively in the Security Council.

These Dutch world-wide interests contrast with the Belgian preoccupation with its regional-European future. Spaak feared that his country, with only limited security interests, would risk becoming involved in extra-regional conflicts. This fear of 'entrapment', which stemmed primarily from their inter-war experiences, meant that the Belgian view of collective security was not as wide during the war as that of the Dutch. Moreover, in economic respects Belgium was much more dependent on intra-European trade than the Netherlands. Before and immediately after the War Belgium's trade with France, for instance, tripled that of Dutch-French trade.

These contrasting approaches can easily be illustrated by taking a closer look at the creation of the Benelux customs union. Discussions about such a union were initiated in January 1943. Until then Van Kleffens had aborted all attempts to open bilateral Belgian-Dutch discussions on post-war issues, but the new initiative, focused specifically on economics, proved something like the breakthrough that Spaak had been seeking for a long time.[21] Within a few months financial experts negotiated a monetary agreement, signed on 21 October 1943, but the two governments (the Belgians also negotiating on behalf of Luxembourg) did not leave it at that. Simultaneously negotiations were conducted about a customs union. Success proved to be much harder in this field, especially with regard to common tariffs. Months of long negotiation between financial experts in London resulted in the signature of the customs union agreement on 5 September 1944.

It is important to stress the absence of Van Kleffens in the process leading up to the Benelux agreement. He was clearly not as interested as Spaak in the improvement of bilateral relations and closer intra-European co-operation. He was willing to give his economic and financial colleagues the freedom to negotiate an agreement with their Belgian counterparts, but when rapprochement seemed to be available his reaction was immediate and negative. All attempts to extend Dutch-Belgian co-operation to the military and security plane were cut short by his personal intervention. Spaak's insistence on closer co-operation with the French led only to the creation of the powerless Tripartite Economic Commission in March 1945, a committee created to foster economic co-operation among the three countries.[22]

### Before the rupture, 1945–7

The ascendancy of the universalist concept over regionalism and the continuation of the wartime Grand Alliance as the basis for post-war international cooperation were both short lived. In the course of 1945–7 wartime unity slowly crumbled away and within thirty months the break-up of the Grand Alliance was gradually effected. The Cold War was the inevitable outcome of the Second World War, in the sense that the three protagonists pursued conflicting goals that in the end did not satisfy the minimum requirements of (one of) the other side(s). Stalin's search for a security glacis along his western border and a permanent stake in the economic and political future of Germany ultimately foundered on Britain's European designs, on the one hand, and the American refusal, on the other hand, to accept anything smacking of pre-war spheres of influences, together with its attempt to rebuild (Western) European democratic capitalism in its own image on the other. The year 1947 witnessed the decisive turning points in the gradual demise of the Grand Alliance; the Cold War took hold and East-West relations steadily deteriorated. But as Reynolds has observed correctly, 'the shape of cold war Europe was still not fully defined'.[23]

What effect did this transitional period have on the Benelux countries? As far as internal affairs are concerned, all three conformed to the general swing to the left experienced all over Europe.[24] Support for the communist parties rose spectacularly in comparison with their pre-war following. Immediately after the liberation the Dutch communists were invited to take part in a government of national unity; they declined the invitation. In Belgium communists joined socialists, Catholics and liberals in a broadly-based coalition government. In the first post-war general elections (in Luxembourg in October 1945, in Belgium in February 1946 and in the Netherlands in May 1946) the communist parties polled the best results in their history. They continued their participation in government in Belgium and joined a government of national unity in Luxembourg, but in the Netherlands social democrats and Catholics negotiated a coalition to the exclusion of others.

In Belgium there was continuity in foreign-policy matters under the direction of Spaak. Co-operating loyally in the build-up of the UN and at the same time clinging desperately to his wartime projects, Spaak experienced a long period of aborted hopes, frustration and failed overtures. Each time he invited the British government, effectively Ernest Bevin, to accept the leadership of Western Europe (and to start with a simple Anglo-Belgian agreement), the British reacted in a civil but non-committal way. British reticence placed the Belgian government in a difficult position vis-à-vis the French, since the latter constantly pressed Brussels into accepting closer relations with them. Spaak, however, was prepared to face French wrath, as was evidenced by the Belgian military contribution to the British occupation of Germany in a sector claimed by the French government.[25]

Spaak's activities in favour of a Western European regional association were heavily criticized by Moscow. To counter Soviet criticism Spaak offered in January 1946 to negotiate a Belgian-Soviet treaty of alliance on the lines of the 1942 Anglo-Soviet and 1944 Franco-Soviet treaties. Although the offer was received favourably at first, nothing came of it. It must be evaluated as a token of Spaak's willingness, addressed to his communist partners in the coalition and to the outside world, to co-operate with all the larger powers including the Soviet Union. However, in the gradual deterioration of the East-West relationship, the Soviet Union slowly came close to replacing Germany as the most likely threat to Belgian security; Stalin's rejection of the Marshall-Plan offer must be considered a watershed in this respect. The attacks of and on the left intensified, resulting in the departure of the communists from the coalition government in March 1947. They refused to accept an increase in the price of coal and tendered their resignation. Two months later, both in France and Italy communist governmental participation also came to an end. However, there is no 'Belgian example' in the sense that Belgium was the first 'victim' of a concerted American move to eliminate the communist presence from Western European governments. In all the countries concerned specific national circumstances made themselves felt. In Belgium the communists took the initiative, hoping to strengthen their position in a reconstituted coalition. In France they were dismissed after having refused to support a continuation of the government's wage freeze. In Italy communists and socialists were eliminated from the coalition in an attempt to create a homogeneous right-wing government. In all three countries, it should be noted, the return of the communists was initially considered a viable option.[26]

After the general election in May 1946 the career diplomat C.G.W.H. Baron van Boetzelaer van Oosterhout became Foreign Minister in the Catholic-social democrat coalition government. Under his direction Dutch acquiescence in the UN even acquired a positive connotation. All attempts to create bi-, tri- or multilateral treaties of alliance were pushed aside as premature, unnecessarily provocative and counter-productive. H.A. Schaper has justly characterized Van Boetzelaer's policies as 'wait-and-see' manoeuvring, intended not to antagonize any of the great powers.[27] Their continued co-operation was considered essential to realize the prime Dutch objective: to become involved in the discussions about Germany and thus to be able to influence the economic future of the former enemy.

Apart from the colonial struggle in Indonesia, Germany posed the most pressing problem for the Dutch government. At all costs the government wanted to prevent a repetition of German aggression, but, on the other hand, to survive economically the Netherlands needed a thriving German economy. They therefore welcomed the creation of the Bizone in January 1947 and, when the occupation powers invited them (and the other smaller European states) in the same month to present their views about the future of Germany, the government opted for security based on the UN and James Byrnes' demilitarization treaty, and the economic reintegration of Germany in Western Europe.[28] Given the absence of agreement among the four occupation powers, the Benelux ideas carried hardly any weight, and consequently Van Boetzelaer persevered in his 'wait-and-see' policies.

The divergence in Belgian and Dutch policies in this transitional period manifested itself pointedly when France and Britain negotiated the Treaty of Dunkirk in the beginning of 1947. While they were still completing the text, Spaak had already proposed to integrate Belgium in this alliance 'since an alliance solely with either would be unacceptable to Belgian public opinion'.[29] He even repeated his offer of a treaty of alliance with the Soviet Union and suggested that the Dutch take the same initiatives. Van Boetzelaer, however, reacted with annoyance, considering Spaak's unilateral initiative ill-timed when the American attitude towards the security of Western Europe was still unclear. Spaak was told that the Dutch were not prepared to copy Belgian 'pactomania'. The Dutch minister even suspected more sinister motives, as he professed to detect behind Spaak's initiative the direction of the French government to whose siren calls the Belgians were never impervious. (Jan-Willem Brouwer has pointed out, however, that these suspicions were unfounded.[30])

The Belgian initiative floundered: both the British and French advised Spaak to wait for the outcome of the Moscow Council of Foreign Ministers (CFM). The failure of that conference brought him back into play again, only to be rebuffed by Bevin. Aiming then at the Dutch, he tried to convince them that Washington would not turn its back on a united Europe but, on the contrary, would help those who were ready to help themselves.[31] Spaak's next initiative in the summer of 1947 was somewhat more successfully tuned to Dutch thinking,[32] but concerted Anglo-French action killed it off. In their opinion talks about an alliance were inappropriate in view of Marshall's proposals for European economic rehabilitation. In Bevin's words: 'I have great doubts about pressing political issues when I am trying to keep everything on the economic plane.'[33] Spaak was again sent back to the waiting-room.

In this immediate post-war period Belgian and Dutch objectives were clearly not identical. Spaak, paying lip service to the UN and even chairing the first session of the General Assembly, still tried to lure Britain into leading a Western European association. Van Boetzelaer, on the other hand, endorsed the primacy of the UN, the wartime Atlantic-regionalist preference for the time being an undercurrent or second-best solution.

To explain this difference we have to take a closer look especially at the internal, economic, situation of the two countries. Belgium's rather favourable economic position contrasted sharply with that of other European nations and there was no acute need for outside financial assistance. Until the summer of 1947, Belgium was an island of economic success surrounded by a European sea of distress. The Marshall Plan offer was of course welcomed, especially as a solution to intra-European trade and balance-of-payments obstacles. The Belgians in particular sought to loosen the quantitative import restrictions that governed the trade between the participating nations and they intended to use American dollars to speed up economic recovery by making intra-European trade more flexible. But economic recovery in a European framework under British direction was considered the prime solution to both economic and security issues.

In the Netherlands the economic situation was completely different. Dutch war damage was estimated at 33 per cent of their pre-war Gross National Product (as opposed to 15 per cent for Belgium). Official post-war studies estimated that 70 per cent of all the German plunder in the Netherlands happened in the period after September 1944, when Belgium was already liberated.[34] Economic recovery had to start from scratch. It had been given the highest priority by the government, but there was a need for massive financial and economic aid. The involvement in a colonial conflict, resulting in almost the entire Dutch army being deployed in Indonesia, constituted an enormous drain on their financial resources. In the spring of 1947 the Minister of Finance Piet Lieftinck predicted a financial collapse similar to the one the British were facing with regard to their obligations in Greece and Turkey. Solutions for these pressing problems could be found only in Washington. The Dutch were (compared to the Belgians) in greater need of an alliance with the United States since such a permanent tie would take care of financial and economic aid for their war-battered economy and arrange for the military assistance needed to rebuild their armed forces. Also the possibility to free-ride on American military expenditure was attractive.

As in the Belgian case, events in the summer of 1947 were instrumental in bringing about a reorientation. Acquiescence and rejection of alliances both gave way; Dutch foreign policy was in for a fresh start. Although Benelux itself still did not function as originally intended (under a convention signed in March 1947 the customs agreement was to become effective on 1 January 1948), Spaak, Van Boetzelaer and Bech decided to negotiate with one joint delegation during the conference on Marshall's aid offer. Thus the three countries were able to counter British-French dominance and to secure important concessions. At their insistence the multilateralization of intra-European trade and the convertibility of the European currencies were accepted as the basis of the European recovery program. Defying French obstinacy, they championed the cause of (Western) Germany's economic reintegration as a *sine qua non* of Western European reconstruction.[35]

Although all involved realized that to take Marshall aid on American conditions signified a choice for the West, neither Spaak nor Van Boetzelaer yet accepted the division of Europe into two opposing camps. With unusual caution Spaak reacted negatively to a suggestion by Van Boetzelaer in the autumn of 1947 to discuss the alliance issue. In this respect the failure of the London CFM session on Germany had been of paramount importance. Both in Brussels and The Hague policy-makers anticipated in the weeks following the collapse the fundamental choices to be made in the early weeks of 1948.

## The Brussels Treaty: united front, 1948

The fundamental idea guiding traditional research in the field of Benelux post-war alignment in the past has been that their adherence to the Brussels Treaty and the North Atlantic Treaty was a response to an actual military threat. For instance, the Belgian political scientist Frans Govaerts claims that 'security was the overriding consideration for small nations after the war, and alliance an expedient means to attain it'.[36] Likewise, Paul van Campen, author of the long-time classic on Dutch post-war foreign policy *The Quest for Security* (1958), claims with regard to the Netherlands: 'There can be little doubt that it was the security factor which dominated all other considerations in the evolution of Netherlands foreign policy from neutrality, via universal and collective cooperation, to membership of a regional defensive organization.'[37]

A careful analysis of the Benelux role in the creation of the post-war alliances shows, however, that fear of an external threat cannot be assumed as the sole or even primary motive for alignment. Admittedly, Germany was no longer considered the principal threat to their security and this role was now performed by the Soviet Union, which was seen not as an immediate military danger, capable and on the verge of mounting a surprise military attack against Western Europe, but simply as a potential future aggressor and a possible instigator of internal trouble. Even so, it would be a gross exaggeration to attribute the Benelux stand vis-à-vis Bevin's initiative for a Western Union merely or even primarily to fear of immediate Soviet aggression or a fifth-column threat. Fear does not explain satisfactorily the specific choices and negotiation strategies of the Benelux countries in the alliance-making process. Other political and economic factors have to be taken into account for a full discussion of why these countries aligned and why they opted for specific, and different, solutions. In assessing these different incentives of the Benelux countries to take part in the Brussels Treaty talks, we must balance the concern about Soviet motives against other factors such as the direction of European (economic) cooperation, possible American involvement in European security matters, the chance of creating a colonial entente, and power political factors (such as 'containing' France, utilizing Britain as balancer on the Continent, or creating an independent third force).

The invitation to start negotiations arrived on the eve of Bevin's celebrated Western Union speech on 22 January 1948 in the House of Commons. The Benelux countries were informed about its contents and Bevin's ideas on closer Western European co-operation.[38] Spaak warmly welcomed the move and immediately broached consultations with Van Boetzelaer and Bech. Britain finally seemed willing to take the lead he had been requesting for over five years, and the fulfillment of his war-time dream seemed imminent.[39] Van Boetzelaer, on the other hand, did not instantly accept Bevin's plans with open arms. He still did not want to rush things, but he did agree with Spaak that a prompt reaction was needed. The Benelux countries therefore decided to use an already scheduled meeting of prime and foreign ministers to discuss Bevin's proposals. They agreed to act together and to present the British and French with a united front.[40] Given the fact that they were not the inviters but the invitees, the Benelux countries considered themselves in a stronger position to realize their special demands.

Negotiations started in earnest after the exchange of separate, but identical, British and French memoranda and a joint Benelux memorandum in mid-February 1948.[41] The Anglo-French offer consisted of the expansion of the Dunkirk Treaty by a series of bilateral treaties linking Britain and France with each of the Benelux nations. In their opinion there was no need to depart from the Dunkirk model. However, the Benelux counter-proposal proposed from the outset a multilateral, five-power, treaty covering not only military assistance but political and economic co-operation as well. They considered the Dunkirk Treaty 'an insufficient basis' since that Treaty did not correspond any longer to the changed international situation. Their preference was to a large extent motivated by Spaak's vision of Western European co-operation. After all those years of waiting and the changes in the East-West relationship, he did not want to end up in the dead-end alley of bilateral treaties.

The Benelux countries were successful. First Bevin and subsequently Bidault gave up resistance to the multilateral approach. In traditional accounts the scare created by the so-called 'Prague Coup' in February and by sinister Soviet moves towards Norway a few weeks later were deemed instrumental in bringing the British and French into line. A careful examination of the weeks preceding the conclusion of the Treaty of Brussels shows, however, that Benelux tenacity and American pressure were as important, or even more important, in this process as the events in Czechoslovakia or Norway. The threat of the Benelux countries in the early days of March not to negotiate at all if the British and French were to persist in proposing bilateral treaties, is a telling example of the matter-of-fact, no-nonsense atmosphere in the Benelux capitals in these weeks.

More Benelux successes followed during the actual negotiations in Brussels from 4 until 15 March.[42] Unknown to their British and French counterparts, the Benelux negotiators prepared for all five-power conferences in secret Benelux meetings with a view to harmonizing their policies and formulating common Benelux attitudes towards specific issues. During the actual negotiations they acted as a single Benelux delegation. With regard to closer economic co-operation they were thus able to overcome British resistance. Likewise, with regard to the creation of permanent organs, the Benelux team was also successful in convincing the British, thus creating a new forum in which it would be able to influence British and French policy. With regard to the mutual-assistance pledge, Benelux demands also prevailed and their opposition to a clause without geographical limits proved effective. In order not to become involved in conflicts in the Sudan or (with foresight!) the Falklands, they advocated automatic military assistance only in the case of aggression against the metropolitan territories in Europe. The British and French ultimately agreed.

Although it would be unfair and unbalanced to present the final outcome of the Brussels Treaty negotiations as a catalogue of Benelux successes (for instance, in the case of deleting references to Germany in the treaty they did not have it their way), the final result definitely bore their stamp. The prime reason for their success was undoubtedly their concerted action. Faced by a united front, the British and French were all too ready to give in. The Benelux position was of course strengthened by the fact that in the background the American government supported almost all the issues the Benelux countries hoped to include in the treaty, but they were certainly not manipulated by the Americans as some have claimed.[43] One can not deny that Spaak (and Van Kleffens as Dutch ambassador in Washington) were in close contact with American diplomats and officials, but this only strengthened their conviction that their proposals with regard to the future treaty were the right ones.

If we have to summarize the motives for Benelux alignment it is clear that the prospect of a European entente and a permanent link with Britain dominated

Spaak's mind. Thus a viable community in Western Europe could be created which, in the military and economic spheres, might also count on American support. It is important, however, to stress that Spaak's brand of Atlanticism embodied a dumb-bell-like relationship of, preferably, equal partners on both sides of the Atlantic and not a Western Europe led or dominated by the United States. Such enthusiasm did he display for Bevin's plans that Western Union, like Benelux in the past, began to be known as 'Spaakistan'.

On the other hand, the main Dutch incentives for supporting Western Union were the chances of future American military involvement; the stimulation of the economic co-operation; the economic reintegration of Germany into Europe; and the prospects of an Atlantic alliance. The creation of a European alliance was considered a viable option primarily from the angle of accomplishing other, more important goals. The Netherlands' world-wide interests still prevented an exclusively European orientation. The main Dutch objectives were therefore to mould the treaty in a way that would please the Americans, not to direct the pact against Germany, and also the inclusion of the colonies in the economic paragraphs. In the end, the new pact offered the Dutch a number of benefits. Most important was a say in Germany's future. As Paul van Campen has observed, there is 'no need to explain the absolutely fundamental importance of Germany for the Netherlands in military, political and, above all, economic terms'.[44] Finally, the multilateral set-up ensured the containment of France, a British continental commitment and, last but not least, defence on the cheap.

Traditional and even new accounts about the creation of Western Union are therefore one-sided and incomplete if they disregard the important role of the Benelux countries in the shaping of the Brussels Treaty which formed the basis for the Brussels Treaty Organization or Western Union.[45] Bevin undoubtedly gave the main impetus, but the filling-in of the treaty was to a large extent done on Benelux conditions. Before and during the actual negotiations there was a balance, to say the least, in their concessions and those of the other delegations and, from the Benelux point of view, this was a very positive result. Bearing in mind Anglo-French acceptance of the multilateral nature of the treaty, the scale even clearly dips in their favour.

After the official signature of the Brussels Treaty the process of alliance formation continued. The Benelux countries immediately formulated joint proposals to give substance to the newly-created Western Union, advocating a permanent organization, a secretary-general with meaningful powers and a council of foreign ministers. The British especially dismissed these proposals and the negotiations over the Western Union set-up became inextricably tangled up with those over the Marshall Plan organization, the Organization for European Economic Co-operation (OEEC). In the process of give-and-take the Benelux countries secured the secretary-generalship (the Dutch diplomat Eduard Star Busmann became the first secretary-general of the Western Union), the creation of the Western Union Consultative Council and Spaak's chairmanship of the OEEC Ministerial Council. London became the seat of the Western Union secretariat and Permanent Commission, whereas Paris became the seat of the OEEC secretariat and Robert Marjolin its first secretary-general. The Benelux countries, especially Belgium, were genuinely disillusioned about the lack of British leadership and initiative only a month after the Brussels Treaty had been signed.

Bevin, however, had other priorities. Since January 1948 his strategy had been twofold: organizing Western Europe but also bringing in the United States to restore the balance of power in Europe. Days after signing the Brussels Treaty, the British began hammering out the contours of a future North Atlantic Treaty with the Americans and Canadians.[46] These Pentagon talks at the end of March 1948 were kept secret from Britain's new allies, although Ambassador Van Kleffens in Washington was soon aware that discussions were taking place.

Given Truman's caution in an election year, Bevin focussed all his attention on convincing the Americans to proceed in the direction agreed during the Pentagon negotiations. Only when Truman secured, with the Vandenberg Resolution in June 1948, an *ex post facto* legitimation of the negotiations, was the green light switched on. Within a fortnight invitations were sent to the Brussels Treaty powers and Canada to start talks about an Atlantic alliance.

### The North Atlantic Treaty: separate strategies, 1948–9

The invitation exposed cracks in the Benelux co-operation that had seemed so firm in the first four months of 1948. The first rifts could already be discerned during the Congress of Europe in The Hague in May 1948, the meeting of all the unofficial bodies advocating European unity. On the topic of European integration Spaak displayed much more enthusiasm than Van Boetzelaer. Joining other European leaders like Winston Churchill, he advocated the establishment of a European parliament and the economic union of (Western) Europe. In contrast, the Dutch government, although being host to the conference, kept an extremely low profile during the actual proceedings.

The second crack in Benelux unity occurred on the eve of the start of the North Atlantic Treaty talks. The Benelux countries were invited to participate on an equal footing with their larger allies. Earlier on the Americans and British had expressed their preference for a single Benelux representative (favouring Van Kleffens), but Spaak insisted on separate representation. Being aware of Van Kleffens's Atlanticist bent, Spaak preferred not to be represented by him and wanted to have a say of his own. When he visited Washington and Ottawa in early April, in all his conversations with leading politicians and policy-makers he placed all his hopes on closer Western European co-operation with some American backing. He did not aim for, and he certainly did not expect, an Atlantic alliance to come to fruition within a short period of time. He therefore wanted to have his own representative at the conference table in Washington.[47]

During the actual negotiations, taking place from 6 July until 10 September 1948, from 10 until 24 December 1948, and from 14 January until 15 March 1949, the Belgian and Dutch representatives did not play as prominent a role as their American, British or French colleagues. In his contemporary account of the negotiations, Nicholas Henderson concludes with regard to Belgian ambassador Baron Robert Silvercruys that he, while serving as an excellent lubricant, 'rarely contributed much in the way of ideas'. Henderson is more positive with regard to Van

Kleffens, who was invariably sensitive and sensible. He always 'sought to contribute by clear analysis and timely suggestion to the success of the negotiations'.[48]

The Benelux countries were clearly the minor powers at the conference table,
hardly able to dominate the negotiations or to propose controversial issues. Mostly,
at least during the first phase in the summer of 1948, they occupied a middle
position between the British and the French; the Dutch leaning more to the British
in their insistence on an Atlantic security arrangement and the Belgians leaning
more to the French point of view that priority should be given to American military
aid and emergency planning.

The Belgian attitude is especially notable. After a month of negotiations, one of
the Canadian representatives reported full of exasperation to Ottawa that the
Belgian contribution, like the French, had so far been 'exactly zero'.[49] Spaak, in the
summer of 1948, still seriously doubted the wisdom and urgency of concluding an
alliance that would tie the United States to Western Europe. The confusion created
by Spaak during his visit to Washington and Ottawa in April, the instructions to his
representatives in Washington,[50] and his attitude during the meeting of the Brussels Treaty members at the end of July in The Hague,[51] all point to the fact that
Spaak was not one of the most outspoken supporters of an Atlantic alliance in the
preliminary stages of the talks.[52] He advised Silvercruys to take a low profile during
the discussions, showing as little as possible of the Belgian cards. During the
Western Union foreign ministers' meeting he sided with his French colleague
Georges Bidault in disclaiming the necessity of an alliance with the United States.
Instead he advocated the cementing of Western Union ties, at the same time also
supporting Bidault's proposal for a Council of Europe.

In the autumn the Belgian attitude changed. The diplomatic situation was now
very different: the American administration increasingly showed itself prepared to
tie the United States on a permanent basis to the European continent; the Berlin
blockade heightened tension between East and West; and even the French government accepted the urgency of an Atlantic alliance. Consequently, the Belgians fell
in line, for fear of being abandoned. They supported the conclusions of the joint
report prepared in Washington during the summer, and from this moment onwards Belgian doubts about the necessity of transatlantic ties in the form of a
written, treaty-like arrangement were no longer voiced.

The Belgian attitude in this period contrasts sharply with the constructive role
of the Dutch representatives in the negotiations; a contrast that has to be explained
by a closer look at the situation both governments were facing. In mid-1948 Spaak
was dissatisfied with the lack of progress towards closer European co-operation.
After the creation of the Western Union under British leadership, Bevin had failed
to live up to his expectations. On the contrary, he blocked an early build-up of the
Western Union organization. Unmistakably, in the summer of 1948, the Belgians
had moved closer to the French. The French were as reluctant as the Belgians
about a treaty arrangement, and for a surprisingly long time Spaak sincerely and
tenaciously doubted (like the French) the necessity and advisability of concluding
an Atlantic pact. Although, in the autumn of 1948, Spaak was forced to accept the
notion of an Atlantic pact, he continued to advocate a dumb-bell-like relationship
of equal partners with a European anchor and a north American one. Belgium's

future was European, if need be in an Atlantic setting. Her problems were of a European nature and colonial considerations exercised hardly any influence since there were then no doubts about her continued sovereignty over the Congo. In the months to come the Belgians therefore tried to restrict the geographical scope of the projected treaty as much as possible, opposing the inclusion of countries such as Italy and favouring a simple business-like arrangement between the Western Union countries, the United States and Canada. Here an apparent fear of entrapment, of being dragged into a great-power conflict, manifested itself as a left-over from the inter-war years. This apprehension was to some extent neutralized in the North Atlantic Treaty via a limited geographical scope and the consultation mechanisms.

The role of the perception of the Soviet and/or communist threat in the evolution of Spaak's policies must be considered of secondary importance. Belgian assessments of Soviet intentions did not change profoundly in the course of 1948. Much has been made in the past of Spaak's public display of Belgian (European) fears of Moscow's intentions in his famous 'Nous avons peur . . .' speech ('We are afraid . . .') to the UN General Assembly in September in Paris,[53] but at the official level a different picture emerges. Here the minister was rather detached as to the likelihood of an immediate Soviet assault. Spaak's hesitations until late September 1948 about the wisdom of concluding an Atlantic pact support the conclusion of a certain indifference towards Soviet intentions. The Dutch government held similar views, which were repeatedly expressed in Cabinet meetings. It is a reminder that the threat factor was not the dominant motive; other political and economic factors guided the Benelux countries on the road towards alignment.

In contrast to the Belgians, the Dutch government did not consider the Western Union an end in itself, but the first step on the road towards Atlantic alignment. Their financial exhaustion as a consequence of deploying almost the entire Dutch army in Indonesia made the Dutch extremely dependent on outside financial assistance. The government was stretched to the limit, no longer able to count on any American or British background support. In particular the American administration was vehemently opposed to its colonial policy in Indonesia. Many Dutch decision-makers were on the verge of collapse, and instability crept into the coalition government where conflicts among ministers themselves and between ministers and party officials became more and more frequent. In order to improve their bargaining leverage in general, but in particular vis-à-vis Washington, the Dutch government decided to tie Dutch colonial difficulties in Indonesia to the North Atlantic Treaty talks. To save as much as possible of her jeopardized global (middle-power) status, Van Boetzelaer's successor Dirk U. Stikker entered into several secret deals to this effect.

In January 1949 a secret agreement was made with French foreign minister Robert Schuman in which Stikker undertook to support the French demand for inclusion in the North Atlantic Treaty of Italy and French north Africa. In return Stikker ensured that the French delegation in the UN Security Council lobbied vigorously on behalf of the Netherlands. A second deal was made with the Canadians and arose from the latter's desire to include an article in the treaty dealing with economic and social co-operation. Thus far this had attracted virtually no support;

in particular the Americans were not enthusiastic. So a deal was made. Suddenly Stikker himself declared to be in favour of what would become Article 2 of the North Atlantic Treaty. He was even able to win over Belgian and Luxembourger support for the Canadian proposal; in exchange, Stikker obtained the full backing at the UN of the Canadian representative in the Security Council, Andrew McNaughton, who conferred secretly with the Dutch in order to reach the best possible solution.[54]

However, these secret deals improved the Dutch stance only slightly, because the State Department's attitude did not change. Stikker decided to use what he considered his ultimate weapon. A policy of blackmail was followed by threatening the Americans that the Dutch would not join the North Atlantic Treaty. In early March, only a month before the signature of the treaty, Stikker for a short period of time seriously contemplated this option. Despite the advice of his senior advisors, he instructed the embassy in Washington to inform the State Department of the Dutch state of mind. The Americans, however, were not that impressed by Stikker's threat. Whereas the inclusion of the so-called 'stepping stone' countries (Iceland, Denmark, Norway and Portugal) was considered essential from the American point of view, the Netherlands was regarded as *une quantité négligeable*. As the British and Canadians were thinking the same way, the Dutch threat only backfired.[55]

To summarize: in a general sense, both the Belgian and Dutch governments wanted to tie the United States to the European continent and obtain protection against an external threat, be it Germany or the Soviet Union. But the Dutch welcomed the alliance as a way of shoring up their global empire, and thus their status as a middle power, whereas the Belgians accepted it, more reluctantly, as a necessary buttress for western European co-operation. In economic terms, the Dutch regarded American assistance as a necessity, while the less destitute Belgians hoped mainly for some free-riding on American military spending.

Given these different motives in seeking an alliance with the United States, a Benelux coalition strategy, such as executed during the Brussels Treaty talks, did not come about during the Atlantic Treaty negotiations. Spaak's interpretation of the transatlantic relationship differed fundamentally from that of the Dutch, as to both the nature of the bond and the relative weight of the Western European group. Belgium therefore wanted to act alone and the Benelux countries were forced to operate in a different manner during the North Atlantic Treaty talks.[56] Consequently they were less able than in the Brussels Treaty negotiations to influence the proceedings. Nevertheless, the origins and character of the North Atlantic Treaty cannot be fully explained without reference to their views and actions.

In the Belgian case, Spaak's doubts until late September 1948 about the wisdom of concluding an Atlantic pact clearly enhanced similar hesitations in the American administration. Thus important sections in the State Department, almost convinced of the wisdom of such a treaty, started to vacillate again in the summer of 1948. The qualms of Spaak intensified these doubts and tempered American resolve to continue the negotiations. Some officials successfully used Spaak's doubts to improve their leverage in their own administration.[57] When Spaak became fully converted to the idea of an Atlantic Treaty in October 1948, the Belgian delegation changed from a passive to a more active stance. They particularly lobbied for a limited geographical scope, but substantial contributions in other domains cannot be recorded. In the end Spaak served as an intermediary between the Americans and the Dutch over Indonesia.

Moreover, a full history of the establishment of NATO can also not be written if one neglects the unique Dutch contribution. Taking into account Stikker's blackmail strategy, the Dutch clearly influenced the negotiations by bringing in their colonial problems in Indonesia. By making secret deals and coalitions with other delegations they were able, to some extent, to influence the talks, for instance with regard to Article 2 on economic and social cooperation and to the inclusion of Algeria. Also the debate about the division of military aid among the future allies was for some time inspired by Dutch vacillation about whether or not to join the Atlantic pact. In the final days before the signature their attitude led to serious disagreements between the United States on the one hand and the Western Union nations on the other. Whereas the Europeans suggested a military aid package to the Western Union as a whole (to be distributed by themselves), the American administration insisted on bilateral arrangements, thereby enabling them to discriminate against the Dutch in case of their continued rejection of Indonesian independence. The American view (naturally) prevailed.

A final word about the role of the Dutch delegation. Van Kleffens and his team were far more dynamic than the Belgians. For this they were valued by the others. Although the principal Dutch contribution did not lie in the sphere of steering the talks in a certain direction (they simply had not enough leverage), all the same they kept the negotiations flowing and took care that European obstacles did not become major stumbling blocks, thus definitely killing the treaty. The Dutch took part in timely coalitions to prevent a weakening of the mutual-assistance pledge. Nor should we forget that Van Kleffens had already set out the course towards an Atlantic solution to the Dutch security problem during the war. His political views are certainly an additional explanation for his dynamic stance. The North Atlantic Treaty signified to Van Kleffens what the Western Union signified to Spaak. They each had their own pet project.

Moreover, this comparative perspective underscores the importance of individual characteristics and motivations in assessing the questions of why and how nations join alliances. Discussing the different roads towards alignment taken by small(er) states, Belgium and the Netherlands have often (not to say always) been lumped together with all other smaller countries or characterized as two of a kind, different from, for instance, the Scandinavian NATO members.[58] A careful analysis for the years 1945–9 shows that even an attempt to lump Belgium and the Netherlands together leads to serious distortions; and the differences in their national interests thereby revealed also help to explain contrasts in their approaches to European integration in the years that followed.

### Building Europe, 1950–5

In the period of the creation of NATO the Belgian government was much more interested than the Dutch in European co-operation in the political, economic and military spheres. This did not mean that the latter fully rejected such collaboration. On the contrary, they were willing to draw together in Europe through intergovernmental co-operation in an Atlantic framework. In order to exploit the American support they were even ready to play the role of 'exemplary model' in this particular field. However, this caused a clear dilemma. If they wanted to stimulate the process of European co-operation and unification, much closer Benelux integration in the economic sphere was required – exactly what was rejected at the highest official level in view of the drastic consequences for the autonomy of each national economy.[59]

The Dutch government was especially afraid of closer economic collaboration and feared that the Netherlands would be locked up in a continental European combination dominated by France. The French were the most important advocate of supranational European co-operation because it would grant them access to larger markets and raw materials, make French industry more efficient, and boost their leading role on the European continent. In August 1947 France had begun negotiations with Italy about a customs union. These failed in early 1949 and, shortly after the signature of the North Atlantic Treaty, the French government broached new negotiations not just with Italy but also with Belgium. The first talks were held in August.

On Belgian insistence the Dutch were invited to take part the next month. This invitation sealed the fate of the attempts to create a customs union of France, Italy and the Benelux countries ('Fritalux'). The Dutch government insisted on the participation of both Britain and Germany, although prepared to abandon British participation given the attitude of the Attlee government towards customs unions. Belgium and Luxembourg by now considered Dutch participation a *sine qua non* and, since France considered German participation unacceptable, the negotiations foundered in November/December 1949.[60] Attempts to rejuvenate the discussions in the OEEC framework, now termed 'Finebel', also failed on the issue of German participation.

Although the Benelux countries had joined forces again during the Fritalux/ Finebel negotiations with regard to German participation, their differing attitudes towards closer European co-operation were still evident. For those who failed to see the obvious, the reactions of the Benelux countries to the proposals forwarded in May 1950 by Robert Schuman proved another case in point.

The Belgian and Luxembourger governments were both wholeheartedly willing to start talks about the projected coal and steel community, since they were more dependent on the Western European market for their steel exports than any of the other future members.[61] Spaak's successor as foreign minister, Paul Van Zeeland, largely continued the policies of his predecessor. Contrary to their Benelux partners, the Dutch reacted reluctantly. They were unwilling to join a continental body without British participation and this was again the key issue since the Attlee government still refused to accept a supranational framework. However, the Dutch were confronted with the awkward situation that the plan could succeed whether or not Britain joined.

What really worried the Dutch government at this moment was the stagnation in the process of trade liberalization. Therefore they launched in June 1950 the

Stikker Plan, pleading for liberalization of intra-European trade by the removal of tariff barriers in certain sectors on the one hand and for reinforcement of the European economy through sector-by-sector modernization on the other. However, in view of the Schuman Plan the Dutch proposals were welcomed half-heartedly, the drafters of the Stikker Plan soon lost faith in the viability of their ideas, and the plan faded out towards the end of 1950.[62]

After Italy and West Germany's Konrad Adenauer also gave the Schuman Plan proposal their blessing, negotiations started. The Dutch were willing to participate only with the reservation that they could bail out if they did not like the final outcome. However, the Benelux delegations soon found out that by acting together and joining forces they could have a greater impact on the proceedings. So they tried again to work closely together, although each held a different interest in the final outcome.[63] They especially objected to the vast and undefined supranational powers to be invested in the High Authority and they insisted on detailed and absolute provisions for the powers of this body. The debate ended with the establishment of a Council of Ministers which would review the decisions made by the High Authority.

The treaty establishing the European Coal and Steel Community (ECSC) was signed in April 1951, and it came into force on 25 July 1952. In August 1952 the High Authority of the ECSC started its work in Luxembourg. The Belgian government signed because they would receive extra American financial assistance to cover the price differential between Belgian and German coal. In the high-cost and inefficient Belgian mining industry they would be able thus to avert mine closings and widespread unemployment.[64] The Dutch signed the treaty because the Schuman Plan offered the participation of Western Germany in European reconstruction on an equal footing and could be seen as an example of a sector-by-sector approach towards economic integration as embodied in the Stikker Plan. Apart from that, they were guaranteed that the prices for coal and steel were kept as low as possible and there would be no interference by the High Authority with wages, as this could harm the Dutch government's economic policy.[65] The opening of the German and French steel markets to the Luxembourger steel industry and the choice of Luxembourg as the seat of the ECSC convinced the Luxembourger government of the advantages presented by the treaty.[66]

The debates about the Pleven Plan launched in October 1950 offer a repetition of the positions taken during the Schuman Plan negotiations. In September 1950, after the outbreak of the Korean War,[67] the American administration's proposal for German rearmament came to many as a great shock. In particular the French were terrified by the idea, and accordingly French Prime Minister René Pleven announced on 24 October the so-called Pleven Plan. The French government proposed the creation of an integrated European army, wherein France, Germany and other European nations would participate, under the auspices of a European Defence Community (EDC). In this manner they hoped to control any future revival of German militarism. It was a supranational solution to the problem of a West German defence contribution to Europe.

Chancellor Adenauer (initially reluctant) was ready to begin talks and so were Italy, Belgium and Luxembourg. The Belgian government was enthusiastic because they considered the projected EDC another important step towards a united Europe. Again the Dutch government showed itself reluctant to join, and anew the chosen supranational structure was the main obstacle. The possibility that the simultaneous creation of ECSC and EDC would lead to a European political union under French leadership was totally unacceptable to the Dutch. Stikker therefore advocated German rearmament in a NATO framework, but the French government was very hostile to this idea. Although it was clear from the start that any future EDC would be tied to NATO, the Dutch government was very suspicious of the French designs. Why would Washington remain interested in Europe after the establishment of a European army? Stikker developed a compromise between rearmament of Germany in a NATO framework and an integrated European army, but due to lack of any interest he was forced to drop this scheme.[68]

Initially the conference on Pleven's proposals, opened in Paris in February 1951, was attended by the Dutch only as observers, just like Britain and the Scandinavian members of NATO. Belgium and Luxembourg, on the other hand, participated on a full-member status. Only when the American administration became convinced in the summer of 1951 that the creation of the EDC would pave the way towards German rearmament and started to support the negotiations in Paris, did the Dutch government fall in line. Stikker had to abandon his resistance and the Dutch started to participate (although reluctantly) in October 1951 as a full partner at the conference table. Having been forced to adopt this change, the Dutch government immediately tried to restore the common Benelux front, especially with a view to promoting Dutch ideas. Despite the fact that political relations between the three nations had somewhat deteriorated since 1950, Van Zeeland was not opposed to closer co-operation. He had become slightly worried about the prospect of being absorbed into an EDC which the three largest nations (France, Germany and Italy) would dominate. He feared that Belgium would later occupy a position of permanent inferiority in view of her relatively minor military contribution to the projected European army.[69] A united Benelux front again commended itself.

The negotiations in Paris became a fight between the 'Big Three' (France, Germany and Italy) versus the 'Small Three' (the Benelux countries). The latter especially feared that they would be dominated by the three larger partners and that 'the EDC plans would be expanded into the political field far beyond the original concept'.[70] At the end of 1951 the EDC conference almost collapsed over the Benelux countries' refusal to cede any ground despite American pressure to take a more positive attitude. Dutch attempts to forge a Benelux front during a conference of Stikker, Van Zeeland and Bech were only partly successful, but the French government was clearly worried over the prospect of a united Benelux stand, and therefore immediately accepted a Belgian demand for a conference of the foreign ministers in order to discuss the political problems with respect to the EDC. During this high-level meeting the Benelux countries managed to secure the internal machinery necessary to grant them representation in an adequate manner.[71] This common Benelux front further prevailed during the final stages of the EDC negotiations, and on more issues they were thus able to secure some victories, such as the creation of the Atlantic Council providing for a close link between NATO and the EDC.

On 27 May 1952 the EDC treaty and protocols were signed by the six nations concerned. Two years later, in April 1954, Belgium, Luxembourg and the Netherlands had ratified the treaty. In all three countries objections to the surrender of national sovereignty were overcome.[72] The greatest opponents were thus the first ratifiers. However, for various political and military reasons the French (despite Belgian mediation attempts[73]) started to retract and in August 1954 the French National Assembly buried the EDC treaty for once and for all. The Belgian and, particularly, Dutch governments were not unhappy about this decision, since German rearmament could now be realized in the Atlantic framework advocated by the Dutch all along. The Benelux countries therefore welcomed the British plan for incorporating Germany in a new inter-governmental organization (the Western European Union, an enlargement of the Western Union) and for German admission to NATO.

After the rejection of the EDC by the French parliament and the subsequent downfall of the European unification process, the combination of Spaak (in 1954 back as foreign minister) and Stikker's successor Johan-Willem Beyen inaugurated a new phase in Benelux co-operation.[74] Beyen was more Europe-minded than Stikker. The latter favoured European co-operation only in an Atlantic framework, including Britain and preferably also the United States. Beyen, on the other hand, considered European economic co-operation a precondition for successful Atlantic co-operation and he therefore advocated the creation of a viable internal market.[75] Thus the Netherlands would be able to achieve several goals at the same time: take the initiative with regard to the future direction of the European integration process; forestall a Belgian 'defection to the south'; and prevent a resurgence of economic bilateralism as evidenced by the Franco-German discussions following the EDC failure.

However, the winter of 1954–5 was considered an inopportune time to launch a new initiative. During a Benelux summit conference on 25 November 1954 Spaak, Beyen and Bech agreed that the time was not yet ripe. An initiative at this moment would have been difficult indeed, since Spaak was thinking along different lines to revive the momentum of European integration. In conversations with Jean Monnet he was convinced by the latter of the necessity of extending the powers of the ECSC to other sectors of the economy, such as nuclear energy and transport. This idea of sector integration clearly clashed with Beyen's more general approach.[76]

During a new Benelux summit in March 1955 Spaak, Bech and Beyen decided that the time had come for a fundamental discussion among the ECSC countries about the future of European economic co-operation. In preparation for that meeting Beyen convinced the Dutch cabinet of the necessity of a combined Benelux initiative, otherwise they would be able merely to react to proposals by others. He proposed the creation of a customs union on a supranational basis, an initiative not incompatible with the possible extension of the ECSC to transport and energy. On 4 April 1955 Beyen informed Spaak of his ideas.

Spaak's response was positive but pessimistic. He suggested a combination of Beyen's general approach and Monnet's sectoral ideas. This combination became the basis of the Benelux memorandum of 20 May 1955 presented to the governments of the ECSC countries. The essentials of the memorandum were accepted by all six during the Messina conference in June. Spaak was to head the experts conference that was to prepare new plans for the economic integration of Western Europe. This initiative laid the basis for the European Economic Community.

## Conclusion

Compared to fifteen years ago, the role of the Benelux countries in the restructuring of post-war Europe has taken a definite shape. Neither instigators of Cold-War developments nor simple pawns in the emerging conflict between East and West, the Benelux countries were also 'present at the creation', trying to defend their national interests in an uncertain world. A careful study of their policies in the years 1945–55 will not lead to a fundamental redirection of the study of the origins of the Cold War, but any attempt to present a balanced history of early post-war Europe can no longer simply bypass the influence of these three small countries. The Cold War was not a bi- or even tri-lateral affair.

The Benelux countries made their mark when vital national interests were considered at stake. In 1947 during the Marshall Plan negotiations they successfully countered British-French dominance during the Paris conference, paving the way for Germany's economic reintegration in Western Europe. In early 1948 they successfully moulded the Brussels Treaty to their (and American) liking, forcing Britain and France to abandon their bilateralism. During the North Atlantic Treaty negotiations in 1948–9 they were accepted as equal partners at the conference table, although in the end the United States considered their participation of less importance than that of the so-called stepping-stone countries, Iceland, Norway, Denmark and Portugal. In the early 1950s they joined Germany, France and Italy in laying the foundations of the present European Communities, providing an essential initiative in 1955 after the failure of the EDC in August 1954. Given their central position, geographically, on the Continent – bordered by Germany, France and Britain – their role in the shaping of post-war Europe was much more important than that of other lesser powers in Europe, such as the Scandinavian countries.

Equally important, in view of conventional stereotypes, is the fact that Benelux was no monolith. A remarkable feature of the 1945–55 period is the ebb and flow in Benelux co-operation. Founded in 1944, only very slowly becoming an economic reality towards the end of the 1940s, Benelux as a political entity made its mark in 1947–8. It was a post-war novelty for these three states to act as they did with joint delegations at the Marshall Plan and Brussels Treaty negotiations, and at the 1948 London conference with the United States, Britain and France on the future of western Germany. Despite these successes, however, Benelux co-operation faltered from the summer of 1948. Differences of opinion over the future course of European economic co-operation and the nature of the relationship with the United States prevented a fruitful continuation. Faced by the French initiatives in the field of European integration, co-operation reasserted itself in the early 1950s to counter the tendency of the larger powers to neglect the interests of the smaller ones. However, despite the creation in March 1952 of the Benelux Consultative

Committee for Foreign Policy, co-operation in 1952–4 was piecemeal, uncoordinated and issue-centred. Only the presentation of the Benelux memorandum in May 1955 signified a return to joint policies.

However, as Kersten correctly notes, the dimension of co-operation in comparison with 1947–8 had drastically changed. The idea of a joint stance by means of a single Benelux delegation (pressure group) no longer dominated official thinking. It was replaced by informal co-operation on different levels with regard to specific issues considered of vital importance to the national interests of the Benelux countries. Economic self-interest, European idealism, pleasing the American administration, and fear of British and/or French dominance had brought the three countries together. Belgian fear that the Dutch would try to dominate their national security policy and Dutch fear of French influences on Belgian foreign policy defined the margins within which co-operation could flourish.[77]

The recent work on Belgian and Dutch foreign policy in the first post-war decade has done much to facilitate a more balanced assessment of their role in the shaping of post-war Europe. But there are no grounds for complacency. As to Belgian foreign policy, given the archival situation, research is still in the early stages, and the study of the role of Paul-Henri Spaak especially needs to be taken up seriously. The unqualified opening to researchers of his personal papers is in this respect a *sine qua non*.[78] As far as Dutch post-war foreign policy is concerned, the plethora of detailed studies clamours for syntheses, weaving together the results of these specialised studies. Certainly, a fine start has been made, but what is needed now is consolidation, deeper understanding, and the integration of Benelux historiography into Cold-War historiography in general.

### Bibliographical note

A useful introduction to the pre-1940 history and political developments of Belgium and the Netherlands is E.H. Kossmann, *The Low Countries 1780–1940* (Oxford, 1978). For the post-war period, John Fitzmaurice, *The Politics of Belgium: Crisis and Compromise in a Plural Society* (London, 1983), and Ken Gladdish, *Governing from the Centre: Politics and Policy-Making in the Netherlands* (London, 1991) offer a good start. For Luxembourg Christian Calmès, *The Making of a Nation: from 1815 to the Present Day* (Luxembourg, 1989), and James Newcomer, *The Grand Duchy of Luxembourg: the Evolution of Nationhood 963 A.D. to 1983* (Lanham, MD, 1984) present general introductions.

Belgian post-war foreign policy is analysed in Jonathan E. Helmreich, *Belgium and Europe: a Study in Small Power Diplomacy* (The Hague & Paris, 1976). Interesting but perhaps hard to find is Howard Bliss, *A process of Federalism: Belgium's Participation in the European Community* (Ann Arbor, MI, 1967). Frans Govaerts, 'Belgium, Holland and Luxembourg', in Omer de Raeymaeker et al., *Small Powers in Alignment* (Leuven, 1974) is still a useful overview. For the Netherlands a bit dated but still very informative are S.I.P. van Campen, *The Quest for Security: some Aspects of Dutch Foreign Policy, 1945–1950* (The Hague, 1958), and Amry Vandenbosch, *Dutch Foreign Policy since 1815: a Study in Small Power Politics* (The Hague, 1959). J.J.C. Voorhoeve's *Peace, Profits and Principles: a Study of Dutch*

*Foreign Policy* (The Hague, 1979) offers a broad, politically rather biased, overview of different aspects of Dutch post-war foreign policy. For the 1950s an attractive little book is R.T. Griffiths, ed, *The Netherlands and the Integration of Europe 1945–1957* (Amsterdam, 1990). J.H. Leurdijk, ed., *The Security Policy of the Netherlands* (Alphen aan den Rijn, 1978) brings together interesting contributions. Finally, for an introduction to the Dutch conflicts with Indonesia one should use Robert J. McMahon, *Colonialism and Cold War: the United States and the Struggle for Indonesian Independence 1945–49* (Ithaca, N.Y., 1986), and Arend Lijphart, *The Trauma of Decolonization: The Dutch and West New Guinea* (New Haven & London, 1966).

In the field of memoirs, two should be mentioned: Paul-Henri Spaak, *The Continuing Battle: Memoirs of a European 1936–1966* (London, 1971), and Dirk U. Stikker, *Men of Responsibility: a Memoir* (London, 1966). J.H. Huizinga, *Mr. Europe: a Political Biography of Paul-Henri Spaak* (London, 1961), offers a biography of the leading Belgian politician. Ample attention to the role of the Benelux is given in Alan S. Milward, *The Reconstruction of Western Europe 1945–1951* (London, 1984). James E. Meade, *Negotiations for Benelux: an Annotated Chronicle 1943–56* (Princeton, 1957) offers useful data.

# 8   *Scandinavia*

## HELGE Ø. PHARO

In the years from 1945 to 1950, as today, the three Scandinavian countries, Denmark, Norway and Sweden, projected an image of similarity, if not of actual unity. Such perceptions were not restricted to the ordinary interested observer of world affairs, but at the time appear to have been shared in broad terms by the foreign-affairs bureaucracies of the three great powers of the wartime Grand Alliance.

There were good reasons to view Scandinavia in such a manner. All three states were constitutional monarchies that had been dominated politically by social democratic parties since the early or mid 1930s. Social democrats formed post-war cabinets in Sweden and Norway in 1945 and in Denmark in late 1947, all bent on modernizing their economies and expanding their more or less rudimentary welfare service systems. The Scandinavian social democratic parties maintained close co-operation and consultation from the inter-war period, advocating and developing still closer means of co-operation between their respective nations in the early post-war years. The foreign ministers met on a regular basis to co-ordinate policies within the many new post-war organizations, particularly the United Nations.

Yet, with the onset of the Cold War and particularly with international tensions increasing dramatically during early 1948, the three Scandinavians divided over the questions of their military security and the maintenance of their national sovereignty. As the continental Western European nations and Great Britain first joined in the Brussels Pact and then started negotiating for a north Atlantic security system with the United States and Canada, the Scandinavians were faced with the choice between continuing their non-aligned policies separately, joining together in a non-aligned Scandinavian defence union, or seeking protection against the perceived Soviet threat through alliance membership or other less formalized arrangements with the West on a separate or collective basis.

After a year of agonizing negotiations and at times bitter if subdued and secret recrimination, Norway led the way into NATO. Denmark followed suit very reluctantly, and Sweden decided to stay on its non-aligned course. To many, and particularly to social democrats in Denmark and Norway, this division represented a traumatic experience. From the moment of joining NATO the Norwegian government started hatching plans for bridging the gap that had been created. For such purposes the non-military organizations of the early Cold War could be employed – the Organization for European Economic Cooperation (OEEC), the Anglo-

Scandinavian co-operation organization (UNISCAN), the projected OEEC-wide free trade association and the proposed Nordic economic organization of the late 1940s and 1950s as well as the Nordic Council of 1952.

Neither the assumed closeness and cohesiveness of the Scandinavian states nor the reasons for their choosing different paths in early 1949 have as yet been intensively researched by Scandinavian historians. In fact, as far as Sweden and Denmark are concerned, the historical study of post-war foreign policy and foreign economic policy is still at an early stage. The domestic dimensions of foreign policy have likewise been relatively neglected in these countries.

There appear to be two sets of reasons for this state of affairs. In the first place, both in Denmark and Sweden foreign-ministry archives have only very recently been opened for the period up to 1949. Some studies have, however, been produced on the basis either of privileged access to archives or of British and United States archives. Until recently the Public Record Office in London and the National Archives in Washington, DC, have offered the best primary sources for the study of Danish and Swedish foreign policy during this period. This holds true for aspects of domestic policies as well because of the very informative embassy reports and official correspondence. In addition to normal diplomatic reporting from the American embassies, the missions of the Economic Co-operation Administration (ECA), and for Denmark and Norway also the Military Assistance Advisory Groups (MAAG) provided excellent analysis of economic and political develop- ments and decisions during the Marshall–Plan period and beyond.

Clearly this lack of archival access failed to stimulate historical studies of post- war foreign relations. In addition, it seems fair to assume that the preoccupation of Scandinavian historians with recent and theoretically more interesting historiographical trends – such as social history, the use of quantitative methods and methodological issues in general – did not leave much room for the historical study of foreign relations. In fact, in Denmark and Sweden political scientists have by and large shown more interest in the topic than have historians. To some extent interest in the international environment has in all three countries been channelled into third-world studies.[1]

We may note two exceptions to this relative lack of interest in the main aspects of recent Scandinavian foreign relations. The first is national historical research on the Second World War. All three nations organized major projects for the study of their respective countries during the War. Paradoxically, Sweden, which in a narrow sense was the least affected by the War, ran the best-endowed effort.

Secondly, as to Cold-War historiography, Norway represents the exception, even though there were strong reasons for members of the Norwegian historical profession to adhere to the norm. Generally Norwegian historians have been ori- ented towards the study of domestic history. Furthermore, Norway has a very short history as a modern and independent nation-state. A part of Denmark from late medieval times until 1814, Norway was transferred to Sweden early that year as a consequence of the Napoleonic wars. Norwegian elites, with popular support, used the interregnum between the Peace of Kiel and the final defeat of Napoleon to give Norway a constitution and secure the basis for self-government. The foreign policy of the dual Scandinavian kingdom was, however, to be the preserve of the joint king and his predominantly Swedish advisers. Only with the separation from Sweden in 1905 did Norway gain full independence.

Norway thus has a very short foreign-policy tradition, and the major historiographical debates on Norwegian history have as a rule not turned on issues of foreign policy. Historians have, on the other hand, played a major role in Norwegian political life, establishing a separate past for the new state. The profession has also supplied two outstanding foreign ministers: the doyen of the profession, Halvdan Koht, from 1935 to 1940, and Halvard Lange from 1946 to 1965. Another eminent historian, Arne Ording, professor at Oslo University, served as main adviser to foreign ministers Trygve Lie and Halvard Lange from 1940 to 1958.

Ording inspired an interest in foreign relations and international history. Norwegian Second World War studies were clearly more oriented towards international history than those in the neighbouring countries. When some of Ording's former students came to occupy central positions within the Norwegian historical profession from the early 1960s, they in turn created the basis for a remarkable growth in the study of contemporary international history and Norwegian foreign relations from the early 1970s. The study of foreign relations and international history naturally is secondary to that of domestic history in Norway, but, as concerns the post-war period, it had by the late 1980s achieved a position of prominence.[2]

The interests of prominent historians and the milieu that grew around them provides part of the explanation for this state of affairs. We find another contributory element in Norway's brief history of independence. The decision to join NATO has been considered by many a major turning-point in Norwegian history. As such it is intimately linked with the German invasion of April 1940, and these two dramatic events in the history of modern Norway constitute part of the same historiographical issue. Finally, and not least important in explaining Norwegian dominance of the historiography, while Norway had no formal declassification rules until 1988, the Foreign Ministry in practice has been very liberal in granting archival access to researchers at all levels. In many instances materials less than twenty years old have been made available also to graduate students. This provides one reason for concentrating on Norwegian history in this survey.

A second reason is that within Scandinavia Norway was the prime mover of Cold-War realignment. The first significant public deviation from the bridge-building and non-aligned policies of the Scandinavians is represented by the Oslo Labour-Party resolution of 3 February 1948 in support of British Foreign Secretary Ernest Bevin's parliamentary speech of 22 January calling for Western European co-operation. As the international situation deteriorated during the subsequent months, Minister of Defence Jens Christian Hauge in February and Foreign Minister Halvard Lange in an 8 March démarche communicated Norwegian worry and need for support to the British and American embassies and foreign ministers. By April the Danes and the Swedes realized that the Norwegian change of course required action on their part. In early May Swedish Foreign Minister Östen Undén launched his proposal for a Scandinavian Defence Union, which ultimately failed some nine months later.[3]

For historical and historiographical reasons, Norwegian policies will therefore serve as the point of departure for the subsequent analysis. With the partial exception of the Svalbard issue the themes are, however, common to the history and historiography of all three nations. (Svalbard is made up of the Spitsbergen archipelago and a number of smaller islands between 74 and 81 degrees north and 10 and 35 degrees east, the southernmost being Bear Island: see map 2.) While defence and foreign policy questions will be of primary importance, issues of domestic and foreign economic policy will be touched upon as well.

### Varieties of foreign policy: Norwegian bridge-building

By European standards Sweden and Norway are large countries, covering an area of 450,000 and 324,000 square kilometres respectively. By comparison France covers some 544,000, Germany (east and west) some 357,000 and Great Britain some 244,000. Thinly populated, Sweden and Norway in 1950 counted respectively some 7.0 and 3.3 million inhabitants. Small and heavily populated Denmark maintained 4.3 million people within roughly 43,000 square kilometres. In comparison Britain had 48 million, France just less than 42 million and Germany, east and west, some 68 million inhabitants in 1950.

Denmark in 1945 was a strategically exposed nation, the northern extension of continental Europe guarding the entrance to the Baltic. Soviet forces were positioned in close proximity. Denmark's fate in any conflict would be decided by the balance of forces on the continent, as had demonstrably been the case since the Dano–German war of 1864. In the traditional European power configurations Sweden and Norway had been less at risk. However, as the Second World War had shown, the large and sparsely populated northern Scandinavian countries were not easily defended against great-power intervention. None of the three nations could be expected to uphold its independence and territorial integrity in the face of a great-power attack without support from another great power. This fundamental fact of life for Scandinavian cabinets after the Second World War was most succinctly expressed by the Norwegian Ministry of Defence in its 1946 Three Years' Plan for the reconstruction of the armed forces. The Ministry stated that the United Nations could not be considered able to guarantee the peace. A strategically exposed country thus had to prepare its own defences. Norway would not be able to defend itself against superior military power. 'But Norway's armed forces must be able to hold on alone until we get effective assistance from those who might become our allies.' Clearly the cabinet had Britain in mind.[4] While the Swedes and the Danes shared that initial small-power premise, in public they drew different conclusions from those of the Norwegians.

Norway's foreign policy since the Second World War was dubbed 'bridge-building'. The term carries connotations of active mediation between opposing forces. As such it is clearly misleading: no bridges were ever constructed. Nevertheless the term is important as a many-faceted symbol and for its foreign-policy implications. Bridge-building was aimed at domestic as well as foreign audiences. Neutrality, or rather non-alignment in peace aimed at neutrality in war, had been discredited by Norway's Second-World-War experience. Bridge-building thus became the catch-all for a variety of foreign-policy preferences. Within its fold could be accommodated pro-westerners as well as pro-Soviets, pro-Scandinavians as well as unreconstructed neutralists. Its vagueness was conducive to creating a superficial foreign-policy consensus.

Yet bridge-building was not non-alignment in a different garb. Non-alignment aimed at neutrality in war. Norwegian bridge-building took as its fundamental premise that Norway was not likely to remain outside another war between the great powers. Thus Norway ought in the first place to strive to prevent conflict between them, or at least pursue policies that did not aggravate tension. As far as Norwegian foreign-policy makers were concerned, bridge-building also required a fall-back position. In the event of great-power conflict Norway belonged in the West. Norwegian bridge-building and Swedish non-alignment thus represented fundamentally different strategies for the maintenance of national security and sovereignty. In terms of domestic politics, however, the fall-back implication of bridge-building was not generally recognized either by those who soon came to favour a Western alignment or by those who were to oppose it. While the vagueness of the term contributed to creating a foreign-policy consensus in the short run, in the longer run it gave rise to both domestic struggle and foreign misconceptions.

In the actual pursuit of Norwegian foreign policy the foreign ministers of the labour government (Trygve Lie until early 1946, when he was elected Secretary-General of the UN, and from then on Halvard Lange) maintained a consistently low profile. Above all they tried to keep Norway from being embroiled in any of the post-war disagreements over the settlement of the peace. A low profile also implied a reluctance to take on international responsibility. Neither the cabinet nor Trygve Lie's closest advisers were in favour of his accepting the position of UN Secretary General. His presumed role of peace-maker might cause trouble for his native land. The Norwegians declined when asked to join the first Security Council. In such a position Norway could not avoid taking a stand in conflicts involving the great powers. At best bridge-building could be conceived of as a way of helping to maintain an acceptably civil great-power relationship by keeping a strategically sensitive area out of the fray. As such it could remain a workable policy as long as individual great-power conflicts were of a temporary nature and confrontational alliances were not frozen firm. At worst, of course, bridge-building could be seen as merely a way of hiding your head in the snow while hoping not to be hit by the passing storm.[5]

In order to gain the fullest possible understanding of bridge-building, we shall have to extend our picture to the entire period of Norwegian independence. While to all appearances pursuing a non-aligned or neutralist policy from 1905 until the German strategic attack of 9 April 1940, Norwegian governments in reality assumed that the nation was safely situated underneath a British defence umbrella. It was axiomatic that Britain could not accept another great power controlling the Norwegian coastline, and that the Royal Navy sufficed to prevent such an eventuality. April 1940 shattered that illusion. The subsequent campaign in Norway furthermore gave proof that military assistance to be effective in wartime had to be prepared in peacetime. Aid from potential protectors could not be improvised.

As Olav Riste has pointed out in a number of works, the government in exile in London from 1940 to 1942 carried out a major shift in the formal posture of Norwegian foreign policy. The implicit guarantee from the West, which had been considered an adequate insurance for Norwegian security and sovereignty, had failed. It had to be replaced by an explicit one. Norway sought safety by proposing and soliciting support for a north Atlantic security system including both the British and the Americans, allowing if necessary allied bases on Norwegian territory. This security system, it should be noted, was directed against a renewed German threat, not against a Soviet one.[6]

Even while this formalization of an Atlantic orientation was taking place in 1940–2, support was not unanimous either among exiled Norwegians in Britain, the United States and Sweden, nor among resistance leaders at home. There were apprehensions about the attitude of the Soviet Union, and about the detrimental effects of Norway's Atlanticism on inter-Nordic relations. After Stalingrad the Soviet Union loomed ever higher on the Norwegian horizon. There were even fears that it would try to gain north Norwegian territory. By 1944, and particularly after Foreign Minister Molotov raised the issue of joint militarization of Spitsbergen and the transfer of Bear Island to the Soviet Union, the need to avoid antagonizing Russia was a major determinant of Norwegian foreign policy.

However, the reappearance of the Soviet Union was not the only reason for the Norwegian shift towards bridge-building. During the period from 1942 to 1944 the Norwegians had gained only insignificant Western support for their regional north Atlantic approach. The Americans very clearly preferred a universal security organization, and Churchill and the British government in that situation did not attempt to promote an alternative. The international context itself made wartime alliance plans obsolete and paved the way for bridge-building. The new foreign-policy concept incorporated the lessons of the spring of 1940. Western great-power protection had to be explicit and prepared in peacetime, as stated in the 1946 defence plan. As emphasized above, bridge-building was intended as a two-stage concept. Norway's Western orientation was in fact implied while the political cost of having it formally stated was postponed.

International development tallied nicely with that of domestic political forces. Within Labour as well as the bourgeois parties isolationist or small-power sentiments still ran strong. Until 1940 Norwegian political parties were in the pleasant position of being able to have their cake and eat it too. Being protected by the British at low cost to themselves, they could at the same time indulge in small-power neutralism and moralistic lecturing on great-power politics. While neutrality of pre-war vintage held no appeal for post-war Norwegian political parties, the underlying sentiments remained quite strong in many circles during and after the War. The Home Front leadership in 1942 notified the government in exile of their objections to Western alignment, the comments being penned by Halvard Lange, later to be Foreign Minister. The exiles in Stockholm were in a milieu of both a more Nordic and a more European orientation. A north Atlantic security system could not easily be squared with either.

Finally, while the issue of political radicalization during the War has not yet been adequately grasped, there is no doubt that, among significant elements of the

Norwegian population, admiration of the Soviet Union and scepticism of Western capitalism and Western imperial powers ran high. This was the case well beyond the confines of the Labour and communist parties, which polled respectively 41 and 11.9% of the vote in the autumn 1945 elections. The Labour theoretical journal *Kontakt* for a period after the war featured a series of articles that were far more sceptical of American than of Soviet foreign policies. The liberal-to-radical *Dagbladet* propagated similar views from time to time, as did the government mouthpiece *Arbeiderbladet*. In June 1945 a Norwegian-Soviet Friendship Committee was formed, counting among its members such prominent Norwegians as the Prime Minister, Einar Gerhardsen, the Chief Justice and former Home Front leader, Paal Berg, as well as the trade-union leader Konrad Nordahl. When Halvard Lange took over as Foreign Minister he advised both the Labour and opposition press not to be publicly critical of the Soviet Union.[7]

By the end of the war international and domestic circumstances alike therefore pulled Norway in the direction of bridge-building. At the same time functional military ties with Great Britain were maintained. The Norwegian armed forces received training and supplies from Britain, and, based on wartime decisions, a Norwegian brigade group was stationed in the British occupation zone in Germany from 1947. These functional ties constituted the essence of the fall-back position based on the sobering lesson of 1940. Stage one of bridge-building was not a policy for all seasons.

Further complications should be added to this picture. The Swedish historian Kersti Blidberg in her study *Just Good Friends* maintains that the Norwegian Labour government bore another heritage from the turbulent inter-war period. That part of Labour which dominated the government after the war had since the late 1930s ideologically favoured collective security measures in order to maintain peace. In addition, the Labour Party drew very specific policy conclusions from the inter-war failure of the League of Nations as well as from the wartime experience of successful co-operation with the great powers. To a far greater degree than the representatives of other small powers, they were in favour of assigning to the great powers primary responsibility for maintaining the peace. At the same time they were less afraid of being dominated by the great powers.[8]

If the very fragile co-operation of the Grand Alliance were to fall apart entirely and new alliances take shape, a number of factors were likely to pull Norway to the West.

As Arne Ording observed to a British Embassy official in June 1946, should bridge-building become untenable, 'we obviously belong to "Western civilization"'.[9] However, during the first two post-war years, until the Truman Doctrine and the Marshall Plan, foreign affairs were still of secondary importance for the Labour government, as for the bourgeois opposition, let alone Labour rank and file. Issues of reconstruction, economic planning, economic growth and a more equitable distribution of income were at the top of the agenda. The Labour Party had won its position as a domestic reform party. Economic growth and transformation were overriding goals and necessities. While Britain in this context constituted a model for Norwegian policies, the United States represented an anti-model embodying the ills of unbridled capitalism. Principles, or primary goals, thus did not unambiguously pull Norway towards the West. As Ording put it in a conversation with *New York Times* journalist James Reston in early October 1947, 'We wanted socialism plus civil liberties, the American liberals were only thinking of civil liberties.'[10] Socialism in this context meant Western European social democracy, not the Eastern European and Soviet command economy. As we shall see, general foreign-policy considerations were ultimately of overriding importance for Norwegian foreign economic and economic-policy decisions, but only under very special international circumstances.[11] Those circumstances were yet to occur.

### Varieties of foreign policy: Swedish non-alignment and Danish bridge-building

Superficially there were many similarities between the respective positions of Norway, Sweden and Denmark in the immediate postwar years. As mentioned, they pursued largely the same kind of policies within the UN. They were anxious to avoid great-power conflicts or disagreements. The communist parties gained a greatly increased share of the vote in the first post-war elections: 12.4% in Denmark and 11.9% in Norway; and 10.4% in the Swedish elections in 1944. The social democratic parties were both strongly committed to economic modernization and the development of a welfare state, and very sceptical of American economic policies. Gunnar Myrdal, the prominent Swedish economist, in 1944 published the much acclaimed *Varning mot fredsoptimism* (Warning against peace optimism), predicting a major post-war economic crisis originating in the United States. Along with the governing Norwegian Labour government and Danish social democrats, the Swedes emphasized the need for planning to avoid economic turbulence and for diversifying trade to include Eastern Europe.

These similarities, noted both by contemporary and by later observers, have tended to overshadow the fact that the premises for bridge-building and non-alignment varied considerably between the three countries. Significant differences existed in geopolitical positions, historical experience, and ideological preconceptions. These very different starting points put Norway and Sweden at opposite poles in the Scandinavian security debate, with Denmark in an intermediate position.[12]

Geopolitically Norway was traditionally oriented towards the west, towards the Atlantic, Great Britain and the United States. Since the Middle Ages Norway had been heavily dependent on maritime trade for a number of vital imports, initially grain above all, subsequently coal and until recently also oil, plus industrial raw materials, capital goods and of course a wide range of consumer goods. The dominant European seapower could easily control access to Norwegian ports, as demonstrated during both the Napoleonic wars and the First World War. During the Second World War Norwegian requirements constituted a considerable drain on German resources. Profitable employment for the very large merchant navy also presumed good relations with the Western great powers. Sweden, by contrast, was a Baltic as much as a Scandinavian power, far more oriented to the East and South, less vulnerable to pressure from the dominant Western seapower, and of potentially lesser interest to the dominant continental power in a confrontation with the West. It is true that Sweden's trade was also strongly oriented towards Britain. Having avoided involvement in the Second World War, however, Sweden emerged after it with a far stronger economy than did Norway and Denmark.

For the conquest of Norway, Sweden could be bypassed, though at that time only with very considerable difficulties. At the same time Sweden emerged from the Second World War as a major military power in Europe, while Denmark and Norway until the 1950s basically had no armed forces except for the brigade groups in the British zone in Germany. All three Scandinavian nations based their defence establishments on universal military training and a mobilization army. As a consequence, occupied Denmark and Norway emerged from the War with virtually no trained manpower. Sweden on the other hand had a large pool of highly trained soldiers. Its mobilization army comprised 30 infantry and 3 armored brigades, a large number of specialist services, frontier forces and coast-guard. The air force had 15 fighter and 15 bomber squadrons; the navy was the largest in the Baltic, with one heavy cruiser, 10 destroyers, 17 submarines and 14 large minesweepers. Sweden's military strength combined with its relatively sheltered strategic position gave its political leadership good military reasons for assuming that neutrality could be maintained, and for considering Sweden the undisputed leader of the region.[13]

Since the end of the Napoleonic Wars Sweden had successfully remained at peace, its policy of neutrality vindicated by that result. Whereas the Labour leadership in Norway, operating from the premise 'never again 9 April' [1940], concluded that in case of increasing international tension Norway would need an explicit Western guarantee, Sweden's political leadership emerged from the War convinced that neutrality was a workable option. While Sweden did have to bend its principles of neutrality during the Second World War to the prevailing winds of war, she avoided actual fighting. Norway, on the other hand, managed to negotiate successfully as a small power within the Grand Alliance, maintaining its independent position, getting a hearing for its views on Allied policies regarding Norway, and in a number of instances successfully modifying these policies. Judging from the available literature, the Swedish government remained convinced that alliance meant servitude for any junior partner. In fact, for the greater part of the War the Swedish Labour government considered the Norwegian government in exile a puppet of the allied Great Powers, as it had considered the campaign in Norway in 1940 a struggle between Great Britain and Germany. While the Norwegian foreign-policy leadership to a significant degree had come to shed its small-power tradition by being occupied and allied, the Swedes maintained their doctrine of non-alignment, or more precisely 'non-alignment in peacetime with the aim of neutrality in war'. That formula dates from the late 1950s, but appears adequate to represent the fundamentals of Swedish policies since 1945. Non-alignment did not merely express Sweden's desire to remain outside the alliances in peacetime, but also signalled its resolve to stay out of a war between the great powers.[14]

We may finally speculate that Sweden's reluctance to contemplate joining the Western great powers was not based merely on its stronger defence position, its more favourable geopolitical position, its successful neutral tradition and its distrust of the great powers. Any kind of Western alignment for all or some of the Scandinavian countries would reduce Sweden's stature as the dominant Scandinavian power. This had been Sweden's position for centuries, and had been maintained after 1905 despite the loss of Norway. Having a strong economic and military position, as leader of a Scandinavian social democratic bloc Sweden would still remain a significant European actor.[15]

Sweden and Norway appear to have had their priorities worked out in case the international situation were to change dramatically. We are in retrospect able to delineate fundamentally different policy preferences behind superficially similar positions. Contemporary observers and policy-makers did not see the pattern as clearly, but leading foreign-policy makers obviously understood the problems inherent in creating a joint position if the need were to arise. In the case of Denmark, however, we may conclude that confusion was genuine. Even with the benefit of hindsight it is difficult to discern any clear hierarchy of interests on its side.

Danish historians and political scientists have shown that scepticism about the great powers was widespread in Denmark. Both the post-war, liberal-led coalition government and the subsequent social democratic cabinet that took over in 1947 wanted to mark their distance from the Western powers as well as from the Soviet Union. At the same time the Danish military maintained close contacts with the British. The functional ties in the case of Denmark appear to have been as extensive as those of Norway, and the Danes also participated with the British in the occupation of Germany. In 1947–8 the Danish military appear to have moved closer to the British than their counterparts in Norway, while their politicians still emphasized bridge-building.

Yet neutralism coupled with anti-militarism appears to have enjoyed a stronger position in Denmark than in Norway, and that combination also differentiates Denmark from Sweden. Historically the Danes had lived in fear of Germany since the war of 1864. Denmark was situated in an extremely difficult geographic position in relation to Germany and any dominant continental power. Denmark's fate would be decided by others irrespective of what she did. Thus, while neutrality as official policy had been discredited by April 1940 in Denmark as in Norway, such sentiments remained strong among the public. Furthermore, the Danish king and government remained at home during the war. The Danes thus lacked the experience of participating in the Second World War as an Allied government.

In economic terms the Danes were as dependent on Western markets as the Norwegians. Extremely efficient farmers provided the bulk of Danish exports, which were largely directed towards the British market. Thus as regards economic dependency, functional military ties and an exposed strategic position, the situation of Denmark resembled that of Norway. The strategic problem, however, complicates the comparison. The Norwegians assumed that a Western connection would be essential for purposes of deterrence as well as for actual military aid if a conflict were to break out. In the case of Denmark it could be argued that whatever its government chose to do would make little difference. This line of thought is not found in the available literature. It appears reasonable, however, to consider this as an unspoken assumption in the defence deliberations of Danish politicians.

Nikolaj Petersen has analyzed Denmark's position both before and after its accession to the North Atlantic Treaty in terms of countervailing fears of abandonment and entrapment. Close ties with the West might lead Denmark into conflicts that were not of her choosing or of relevance to the defence of Denmark. On the other hand, too great a distance from the West might cause her eventual protectors to abandon this strategically exposed nation. The Danes were thus caught in a potentially serious dilemma. The preferred escape from the dilemma was to be the Scandinavian option, that is a Scandinavian defence alliance. In that way Denmark could eschew entrapment by the West as well as abandonment. Such a policy would fit in well with traditional pro-Scandinavian sentiments. It also conformed to the extremely strong pro-Scandinavian orientation of Danish social democratic Prime Minister Hans Hedtoft.[16]

In the end defence planning in Denmark and Sweden, as in Norway, relied on the prospect of support from the West. The defence of Denmark was predicated on 'eventual armed assistance from the United Nations or from other friendly nations', meaning the Allied forces in Germany. Even Sweden's strategic defence was organized with a view to gaining time for assistance 'from the other side'.[17] Both countries assumed that the West would come to the Scandinavians' assistance if they considered it in their interest to do so; if not, prior agreements would make little difference. We shall see that such considerations played a part during the later negotiations. In one sense the Swedes and the Danes based their plans on a more cynical assessment of the West than did the Norwegians. However, they could with equal justification be considered naive in the sense that the need for peacetime preparation for wartime co-operation was disregarded, as was the deterrent effect of formal commitments. The Swedes and the Danes, in fact, established a base for military planning closely resembling the Norwegian one of the inter-war period.

### Disputed territories: peripheral areas and overseas areas

Both Denmark and Norway had overseas territories that were strongly affected by the Second World War and its attendant military and strategic innovations (see map 2). Greenland was the one remaining Danish colonial possession, a remnant of the Dano-Norwegian empire in northern waters. Greenland had been converted into an American base during the War, and the American military insisted on including the island in the far-flung system of bases they wanted to maintain. Norway had acquired Svalbard after the First World War, partly as a reward for its services as an allied neutral, but exercised only limited sovereignty. This island archipelago was open to economic exploitation by other nations, and was not to be militarized. While Svalbard was not of nearly the same strategic importance as Greenland for either great-power group, by the end of the War the Soviet Union showed considerable interest in changing the terms of the treaty in order to establish a military position there. Denmark and Norway were thus faced with potential points of friction with dominant post-war powers.

These problems were aggravated by the fact that their respective easternmost territories, in the case of Denmark the Baltic island of Bornholm, situated off the south-eastern tip of Sweden, in the case of Norway its north-eastern territory of Finnmark, were liberated by the Soviets in 1945 and 1944 respectively. Both governments feared that a Soviet withdrawal might be made conditional on concessions elsewhere, or, in the case of Bornholm, that Soviet forces might remain indefinitely. Eventually their troops pulled out of Finnmark in September 1945 and

Bornholm in March 1946. Apart from northern Iran these were the only areas that the Soviets gave up during the early post-war period. We may assume that neither area was of primary strategic importance for the Soviet Union, and that both Norway and Denmark were considered as being situated within the Western sphere of influence.[18]

The Greenland and Svalbard issues did not go away that easily. As far as the United States was concerned, the most practical solution would have been to buy Greenland, one of the so-called 'stepping stones' that were so important for United States' willingness to set up the Atlantic Alliance. As a minimum they wanted to build and maintain military facilities there. Neither party was in a hurry to find a solution, though the issue constituted a domestic problem in Denmark. When in the spring of 1947 the Danish Communist Party introduced a parliamentary resolution calling for American withdrawal, the Danish cabinet was subjected to heavy pressure to persuade the communists to withdraw the proposal. For some time in 1948–9 the Americans even considered the possibility of a special arrangement for Greenland without Denmark having to join NATO, but in the end the issue was solved by Denmark's accession to NATO.[19]

In the immediate post-war period not only the Danes and Norwegians but also the British were worried that the American demands for foreign bases would encourage the Soviets to make similar claims in Scandinavia. The Norwegians were above all concerned about the Svalbard issue. As mentioned, during the war the Soviets had proposed that the Svalbard treaty be renegotiated. In November 1944 Molotov proposed joint Soviet–Norwegian defence of the previously demilitarized islands and demanded that Norway cede Bear Island. The following April the Norwegian government in London responded by suggesting a new draft treaty, according joint military control of Spitsbergen, but this initiative did not constitute a formal proposal.

The subsequent history of the Svalbard issue until January 1947 is of a gradual Norwegian hardening of their conciliatory 1945 position. There were two main reasons for this. First, as already noted, the Soviets withdrew from Finnmark in the autumn of 1945, thereby reducing their leverage. Second, the international situation changed considerably in 1945–6. Joint military arrangements or even Soviet bases on Spitsbergen meant that Norway ran the risk of being pulled into an international conflict on the Soviet side. Nevertheless, when the dominant exile groups within the Labour Cabinet, the foreign service and the Conservative Party returned home, they were reluctant to renege on a commitment already made and thus possibly antagonize the Soviets. Conservative leader C.J. Hambro and Foreign Minister Trygve Lie both maintained that the Western powers preferred continuity in Norway's Svalbard policies. The former exiles also argued that Moscow had been reasonable to date. Lie claimed in a June 1945 meeting of the Storting (Parliament) Foreign Affairs Committee that the government had in fact 'salvaged what could be salvaged'. (C.J. Hambro even made a complimentary statement about Molotov, calling him an 'unusually pleasant man'!)[20]

The gradual retreat that was, nonetheless, made must also be seen as the outcome of a struggle in which more strongly nationalist groups in the cabinet and parliament forced the main policy-makers in exile in London on to the defensive.

Among the critics were the London premier, John Nygaardsvold, who had disliked the accommodating policy of his own foreign minister, as well as his post-war successor Einar Gerhardsen. Most of the activists, however, belonged to the liberal and agrarian parties. The otherwise vocal Labour left opposition to government foreign policy remained notably silent during these debates, while the communists supported the initial, conciliatory government stance.

In the end, the issues were peacefully shelved. The Soviets were apparently less interested than the cabinet had assumed in acquiring a military position on Spitsbergen. Without access to Soviet archives on this point we may only hypothesize that their primary interest lay in denying the West a foothold in this region of potentially great strategic importance. The stiffening of Norway's attitude, on the other hand, was not due to either American or British pressure. The cabinet had deliberately kept the Western powers in the background. Partly it was aware of Western weakness, partly it feared that the Soviets and the Americans might end up making a deal over Arctic bases at the expense of Norway and Denmark. Svalbard might even be exchanged for Iceland and Greenland. The Norwegian government vastly preferred an Arctic Ocean without great-power bases. So did the Swedes, whose foreign minister, Undén, advised his Norwegian counterpart, Lange, in a private letter in late 1946 to stand firm against Soviet pressures. The non-aligned policies of Sweden would be more difficult to maintain if Moscow were to acquire bases on formally Norwegian territory.[21] With Oslo hardening and Moscow retreating, the Svalbard issue therefore faded from international debate.

### Bridge-building and non-alignment threatened: the Marshall Plan and Western Union

These problems of a primarily bilateral nature were potentially serious. The most important threats against bridge-building and non-alignment were, however, to arise from a gradually colder climate between the victors of the Second World War. By the summer of 1946 the Norwegians were criticized by the British for sitting on the fence. Foreign-policy makers were becoming increasingly concerned that bridge-building was losing credibility with both the Soviets and the Americans. Soviet policies in Eastern and Central Europe were seen to be aggravating tensions, and the Truman Doctrine was widely considered an aggressive American move. The Scandinavian governments were not directly involved in these controversies, but the social democratic parties, the ruling parties in Norway and Sweden, had to take a position in the international socialist movement.[22]

The speech by the American Secretary of State George Marshall on 5 June 1947 created a new situation for the Scandinavian governments. They could not avoid taking a stand on an issue that would clearly widen the chasm between the two emerging power blocs. The Marshall plan created real problems for the Scandinavians. It is true that all three were, or were soon to be, facing a more or less serious dollar shortage along with the rest of Western Europe. At the same time participation in the Marshall Plan could create doubts about the credibility of both bridge-building and non-alignment. The Danes had the most serious foreign-exchange problem, and from that point of view could hardly afford to reject the

American proposal and the Franco–British invitation to go to Paris for the July 1947 conference. Sweden enjoyed the freedom of action to join the conference without committing itself fully. Its dollar problem was relatively modest – Sweden only received loans from the United States – and its non-aligned course was well established. At the present stage of research, the Norwegians seem to have been the most hesitant. Foreign Minister Lange's initial reaction on 17 June was that Norway should remain outside if it could afford to. After talks with his Swedish counterpart, Undén, in Stockholm during the last weekend of June, Lange changed his mind. The two agreed that Scandinavia had to join even if the Soviet Union declined the American offer. As Arne Ording noted in a Foreign Office memorandum on 7 July, remaining outside 'would be a demonstrative alignment with the eastern bloc'.[23]

Apart from the Soviet Union and its satellites, only Finland declined the invitation to join the Marshall Plan. Participation thus represented the smallest possible deviation from the ever-narrower path of bridge-building and non-alignment. Once inside, the Scandinavians did their best to limit the foreign-policy implications of joining. They worried that Marshall Plan co-operation might impair their national sovereignty, particularly by reducing their ability to pursue an independent economic policy. In Paris all three nations thus argued in favour of the independent 'shopping list' approach to the United States rather than the co-ordinated Europe-wide approach that the Americans demanded. In fact they supported the kind of approach that the Soviets had proposed at the great-power conference. The Scandinavians also argued in favour of dispensing aid through the UN Economic Commission for Europe, which was unacceptable to the United States, France and Britain. The Eastern bloc together with the neutrals would be able to block any Western proposals in that organization. To promote Scandinavian concepts of co-operation, Norway volunteered to represent the three Scandinavian nations on the Executive Committee of the temporary Marshall Plan organization, the Committee for European Economic Co-operation (CEEC). The CEEC was set up as a forum for planning and negotiating, and as a vehicle to channel dollars to the Europeans.

As the summer of 1947 wore on, the CEEC nations were subjected to ever-stronger American pressure to conform to American conditions for dispensing aid. The CEEC nations had to agree to a permanent organization, to scale down their initial aid estimates and to abandon 'the shopping list' approach in favour of a co-ordinated approach to European reconstruction. While a final decision on the issue of a permanent organization was postponed to the spring of 1948, the Scandinavians had to give way on most of their original positions. Considering their dollar shortage, the Danes would seem in retrospect to have had little choice. L. Dalgas Jensen in his work on Denmark and the Marshall Plan, however, emphasizes that the Danes did not feel that they had to give in to any and all American demands. By September Norway had also been hit by a severe and largely unexpected dollar shortage, which clearly contributed to its acceptance of American demands. Neither country was in a strong position to decline loans and grants, yet both considered the option of staying outside if American conditions were deemed unacceptable. However, they moderated their opposition as neither could afford to be held responsible for a possible failure of the conference. Even so the

Norwegians remained distinctively cool. Their dollar estimates of the summer, which for political reasons had been set artificially low, were therefore only inadequately increased.

The Swedish government may have felt it had the option of remaining outside the new permanent organization demanded by the United States. But in early 1948 both the Swedish and Danish governments still adhered strongly to the view that the European Recovery Program (ERP) was purely a matter of economics. They chose to downplay its general foreign-policy implications. To decline Marshall Aid at this point would have constituted an even more dramatic alignment with the Soviet bloc than initially staying outside. As all three Scandinavians had demonstrated during the First World War and the Swedes during the Second World War, some bending with the prevailing winds would be necessary for neutrals and non-aligned nations. Excepting the communists, there appears to have been no significant opposition either in Sweden or Denmark to the foreign policies of their governments.[24]

In Norway, on the other hand, the ERP was seen by supporters and opponents as posing a challenge to the country's foreign policy. Criticism of bridge-building was growing on the opposition benches in the Storting, in the non-Labour press and within the Labour Party. The international context had in fact changed to the point where the bridge-building formula was no longer valid. As stated by the Foreign Minister, if tensions were to increase between the great powers, threatening international instability, Norway would have to approach the West for protection. When the London Foreign Ministers' Meeting broke up in December 1947, great-power disagreements had progressed far beyond those of the peace settlement. Norway could no longer maintain a credible bridge-building position by not taking a stand. As early as 5 November 1947 Ording confided the dilemma to his diary: 'If we drift into isolation we cannot work for détente. The precondition for that is that we stay inside the "Western world." '[25]

Thus, when British Foreign Secretary Bevin made his plea on 22 January 1948 for greater Western co-operation, he had a ready audience in Norway. While the Swedes and Danes quickly responded by emphasizing their respective non-alignment and bridgebuilding policies, the Council of the Oslo Labour Party in a 3 February resolution came out strongly in support of the Bevin plan. Pushing the resolution in this most powerful of all Labour locals were Prime Minister Einar Gerhardsen, Secretary General of the party, Haakon Lie, and its grand old man, outstanding agitator and editor-in-chief of the party mouthpiece *Arbeiderbladet*, Martin Tranmæl. The Foreign Minister had yet to commit himself and was quite critical of the initiative. The activists in fact had to backtrack quickly, as party opinion generally was not ripe for such a definite shift westwards. At a high-level meeting in Stockholm of the Nordic (Finland added) social democratic parties soon after, the Norwegians were also rebuffed. They wanted to explore the possibilities of Nordic economic, military and political co-operation, without excluding an opening to the Western powers.[26] The first Norwegian move arising from the international changes was thus quickly immobilized.

The dramatic events of late February and early March 1948 prompted new Norwegian initiatives. The coup in Czechoslovakia brought the international crisis vividly to Norway, particularly because the Czechs were looked upon as Eastern bridge-builders, Norway's counterparts who had tried to prove bridge-building possible from the other side. Relations had been particularly close between Lange and Czech Foreign Minister Jan Masaryk. The coup evoked the spectre of internal communist subversion. The Soviet pact offer to Finland, made public on 28 February, was shortly followed by rumours, which the Norwegian Foreign Ministry had reason to take very seriously, of a similar proposal to Norway. The latter created a crisis atmosphere in Oslo, as these initiatives and rumours suggested that Stalin might also be contemplating military moves against northern Europe. Both Norwegians and Danes took steps to increase their military preparedness. Norway informed the British and United States ambassadors of the possibility of a Soviet offer of a pact, making it clear that such an offer would be rejected, and asking what kind of support might be expected in such an eventuality. Similar enquiries were made by the Danes in Washington. Swedish Prime Minister Erlander, however, appears not to have been unduly worried by the rumours.[27]

The Norwegian government reacted to this turn of events on a broad front. Norwegian initiatives were precipitated to some extent by Bevin's speech, but above all by the Czech crisis and the actual and rumoured pact proposals. Already, by the middle of February, Norwegian Marshall Plan policies were being reconsidered. The artificially low dollar estimates of the summer of 1947 were significantly increased. Secondly, as a consequence of the Czech crisis, Prime Minister Gerhardsen in a major speech branded Norwegian communists as potential fifth-columnists. Then Norwegian politicians and bureaucrats were let loose on the Americans to convince them of the necessity for awarding Norway more aid and a greater proportion of grants. To some extent the strategy succeeded. The American administration, as well as the Congress, noticed Norway's realignment.[28] It should be noted that Norway's reluctance over the Marshall Plan in the summer of 1947 and its about-face in February 1948 were both dictated by general foreign-policy considerations. Foreign economic policy played an important but clearly subsidiary role.

The main thrust of the reorientation was contained in Lange's re-assessment of Norway's security problems delivered at a secret session of the Storting in early April. In its main outline the 'lecture' was repeated in a public speech towards the end of the month. At this time Lange made it quite clear that Norway belonged to the Western community of nations. He pointed out that to be aligned with the West the Nordic countries would have to take the initiative themselves to be included in the Brussels Pact. He stated that the other Scandinavians had expressed strong reservations about adherence to the pact. The Labour cabinet clearly preferred a British-Scandinavian defence union of some sort. That would have given Norway some assurance of not being left alone, while not automatically bringing the Scandinavians into continental conflicts. The Foreign Minister at that time did not have any fixed plans apart from underlining Norway's basically Western alignment. The Norwegian initiative, however, brought the potential conflicts among the three Scandinavians out into the open. Both Norway and Denmark had made enquiries about Western support in March. Lange's April speech put defence issues at the top of the Scandinavian agenda.[29]

## *Changing perspectives: Western and Scandinavian*

The public statement by the Norwegian Foreign Minister signalled to the Western powers as well as to the Soviets and the Scandinavian neighbours that Norway was looking for protection by the West. As the Norwegian government saw it, there was no longer any room for non-aligned bridge-building. Real and assumed Soviet pressures on neighbouring states dictated a Norwegian search for a Western guarantee. Lange's speech as well as the preceding changes in Norwegian foreign and foreign-economic policies changed Norway's position considerably in the perception of the two great Western powers. American and British dissatisfaction with the Scandinavians had been growing throughout 1947 and early 1948 as Cold-War temperatures dropped further.

Among the Western Allies, the British bore the main responsibility for Scandinavia during the first few post-war years. As regards Sweden, considerable bitterness lingered in Britain as a consequence of dissatisfaction with Swedish wartime policies. The British also feared that Swedish influence over their neighbours would keep both Denmark and Norway from moving or being pulled towards a Western alignment. The British Foreign Office as well as the military clearly considered that Denmark and Norway belonged within the Western camp. Into 1947 they were getting annoyed at 'pusillanimous' Norwegians who were showing an 'increasing tendency to bury their heads in the snow in the hope of avoiding entanglement in the struggle between the Great Powers'.[30] Foreign Minister Bevin appears to have shared the views of his advisers. As early as 1946 he considered Norway 'completely preoccupied with its own affairs and out of touch with the foreign affairs situation'. Other influential policymakers were even more doubtful of Norway's position. Meeting Gunnar Jahn, President of the National Bank of Norway, British Chancellor of the Exchequer Hugh Dalton in September 1947 asked bluntly: 'Does Norway belong to Western Europe?'[31]

By the spring and summer of 1947 the British were, as Magne Skodvin has concluded, actively promoting a 'closer relationship between the Scandinavian countries and the UK; Sweden had become an interesting possibility in a partnership; Norway was held back by what to the British seemed a traditional policy of appeasement, in spite of the fact that both tradition and prognosis made the UK a natural partner for her.' Of the three Scandinavian countries the Danes were considered the most Western-oriented and co-operation-minded. The British assessment was based on the conversations of Admiral Vedel; Commander-in-Chief of the Danish Navy, with his Swedish and Norwegian counterparts, which were silently approved by the Danish cabinet. While Danish cabinets, social democrat or bourgeois, were as eager bridge-builders as the Norwegians, and probably more committed, their military was on a longer leash.[32]

The Americans were initially less interested in Scandinavia and less critical of the Scandinavians than the British. The cool Scandinavian reaction to the Truman Doctrine, the Marshall Plan and American proposals in the UN concerning Greece and Korea, however, concomitant with increasing US-Soviet tension, contributed to a distinctly tenser atmosphere. Relations between the United States and Sweden deteriorated conspicuously after the very outspoken H. Freeman Matthews was

appointed ambassador to Stockholm.[33] While Matthews was not entirely representative in his strongly anti-Swedish and anti-neutralist position, the drift of
American attitudes was unmistakable. George Kennan's irritation at the
Scandinavian reluctance to join a more permanent Marshall Plan organization in
early September of 1947 may be considered representative of informed American
opinion: 'the Scandinavians are pathologically timorous about the Russians. Finding themselves somewhat unexpectedly in a gathering denounced by Molotov as
wicked, they have the jumpy uncertainty of one who walks in pleasing but unaccus-
tomed paths of sin.'[34] All three Scandinavians were considered significantly less
Western in their orientation than Britain and the United States deemed desirable
by the summer of 1947. The Danes were considered the most Western-oriented,
because of their role in initiating defence conversations and their more forthcoming
attitude in the Marshall Plan talks. As Geir Lundestad points out, the ability of the
Danish government and Danish diplomats to argue for a policy of bridge-building
at home while conveying an image of Western orientation to the British and
Americans probably fostered a more favourable impression.[35] Sweden was clearly
the most negative in the American view. Norway was seen as closer to Denmark,
but at the same time was probably considered the most disappointing nation
bearing in mind its wartime Western record.

Lange's April 1948 speech, on the one hand, and, on the other, the previous
protestations from Undén and Danish Prime Minister Hans Hedtoft that Bevin's
Western Union address did not affect their respective non-aligned and bridge-
building policies, changed the relative position of the Scandinavians dramatically.
Norway was suddenly in the vanguard of a movement towards the West. That
change of position had already taken place behind the scenes as a consequence of
Lange's démarche to the two western ambassadors on 8 March. Lange told them
that the Norwegian government had concluded that Norway was being exposed to
a war of nerves from the Soviet Union, pledged that Norway would decline a pact
offer, and asked what the western powers could offer in terms of support. During
the following week Britain and the United States worked out their position. Both
nations declared that they were giving most urgent consideration to the question of
Norwegian security. They made it unmistakably clear to Oslo that Norway could
be catered for only within a north Atlantic framework. The British alone did not
have the military capability to protect the Scandinavians, and the other Brussels
powers lacked the interest. Apart from the risk of being rebuffed by the
Scandinavians, this lack of military strength was the reason that the Scandinavians
were not mentioned in Bevin's January proposal.

In Paris, at the meeting setting up the OEEC, Lange was informed by Bevin that
peacetime preparation in some form was a precondition for Western military
support for Norway. This, of course, tallied perfectly with Norwegian strategic
planning, and built on their common experience in the Second World War. A
neutral Scandinavian pact was not considered in the interest of the Anglo-American powers. The idea of a purely Anglo-Scandinavian defence union that Lange
had mentioned in his speech had thus been ruled out in advance. For Lange and the
Norwegian cabinet the problem of domestic consensus remained, however. There
still lingered a strong current of poorly concealed neutralism in the nation. Large

segments of the population would have preferred a Scandinavian option. They would be joined by those who saw a Scandinavian pact as a bar against Western alignment. For all of them a British guarantee or an Anglo–Scandinavian pact would have been more palatable than the north Atlantic security framework being created.

The Danes (as far as we know) made no move during February and March. They appear to have assumed that Danish security depended primarily on decisions that would be taken elsewhere. Yet Danish nerves were rattled during the so-called Easter crises. The counsellor of the Danish embassy in Washington came home to Copenhagen on 15 March to report on the situation. He warned that there was danger of Soviet action against Denmark and possibly Norway in the near future. He recommended that Denmark turn to the West, and advised that the United States was annoyed at the lack of Danish initiative. The Cabinet also was told that the Americans would need air-force bases for attacks against Moscow. When questioned, the Americans said the story was without foundation, yet they considered the communication instructive in waking up the Danes to current realities.[36]

The Americans and the British welcomed the Norwegian initiative. Norwegian and Anglo-American thinking in many respects ran on parallel tracks, even if the domestic opposition in Norway remained a significant hurdle against a north Atlantic realignment. Danish politicians leaned a little more Westward but preferred to sit on the fence while their military maintained Western contacts without committing them to paper. The dilemma of entrapment and abandonment tended to pull the Danish leadership in different directions.

These changes among the neighbours set the Swedes in motion. Their non-aligned position would be threatened if Norway and Denmark joined any kind of Western alliance. Lange had quickly informed Undén of the possible Soviet pact proposal, and the Swedish ambassador in Oslo, Johan Beck-Friis, travelled to Stockholm to brief his superiors in detail. Undén had occasion to gather further information about possible future choices during conversations with his Scandinavian colleagues and European and American leaders before and during the Paris meeting in mid-March.[37]

## A Scandinavian defence union

It took some time for the Swedes to prepare a counter-strategy to prevent the Western realignment of their neighbours. Such an eventuality could only be fore-stalled by a Scandinavian defence union. In early April Undén did not yet contemplate such a move, not least because Norwegian and Danish defences were considered too weak to make an efficient contribution to joint defence, so that the Swedes would be left to carry the major burden.[38] Subsequent internal Swedish discussions, talks with the Danes, and Lange's public speech on 18 April prodded the Swedish cabinet into action. On 22 April Undén gained the support of the parliamentary Foreign Affairs Committee for a non-binding initiative in relation to Norway. Undén then secretly travelled to Oslo on 3 May for a series of talks with Lange, Prime Minister Gerhardsen, Defence Minister Hauge and the president of Labour's parliamentary group, Oscar Torp.[39] Discussions between the three prime ministers continued at the annual conference of the Swedish Social Democratic Party the subsequent week. The basic disagreement became evident when the three parties attempted to decide on an official mandate for discussions. The Swedes wanted the defence pact to keep the Scandinavians 'outside of any grouping of other states'. The majority of the Norwegian cabinet found that unacceptable. The Norwegian counter-proposal, that the issue should be explored without any pre-condition of non-alignment, was equally unacceptable to the Swedes, though Undén at first appeared willing to consider such an option.[40]

After further deliberations and correspondence during the spring and early summer, the Norwegians eventually accepted the Swedish demands with only one caveat. By a compromise finalised in September, the Norwegian Labour government agreed to participate in a 'feasibility study' of military co-operation based on neutrality, provided that the neutrality clause was not made public. The Norwegians also agreed not to discuss defence co-operation with other states while the Scandinavian option was being investigated, though by late June Lange knew that once the north Atlantic discussions were under way Norway was likely to receive an invitation to join the West. By late September the Washington embassy informed Lange that an invitation to participate would indeed be forthcoming if Norway wanted it.[41]

By accepting these Swedish conditions the Norwegian cabinet had, at least on paper, moved a long way from its initial May position. The Swedes, on the other hand, had not compromised on their maximum demands with one exception. In spite of their misgivings about Dano–Norwegian military weaknesses, they were willing to consider taking on the defence of the whole Scandinavian area. There are a number of reasons for the Norwegian will to compromise and Sweden's stone-walling. In the first place Sweden's military and industrial might was important to Norway. Second, large groups within the Norwegian Labour Party opposed a Western alignment, and the better part of that opposition supported a Scandinavian pact. Third, the Labour Party leadership genuinely favoured some sort of a Scandinavian pact. Lange and some of his colleagues may have entertained hopes that as a consequence of the committee investigations the Swedes would see the limitations of a purely Scandinavian option and accept links with the West.[42]

The Scandinavian Defence Committee, with the aid of a number of civilian and military experts, finished its work by the middle of January 1949. The gist of the committee conclusions, however, was known to the primary policy-makers by December. The final document is still classified because of its discussion of defence plans and prospects, and only its main conclusions have been made public. The Committee assumed that a defence association would have some preventative effect against isolated action. In terms of deterrence it could not, however, be considered sufficient to 'forestall an isolated or coup-de-main attack'. The Committee concluded that a defence association did not exclude the necessity for outside support. Assistance would be required in peacetime for building and modernizing armed forces, and in case of an attack assistance would be needed already in the initial phase. The Danish and Norwegian committee members considered that, even after Scandinavian defences had been built up, already in the initial phase the three countries would need outside assistance against an armed attack. Thus peacetime preparation would be necessary. The Swedish members of the Committee, however, did not explicitly draw that conclusion. Generally speaking, the known conclusions of the Committee conformed to those already reached by the Norwegian government.[43]

At three meetings in January 1949 – in Karlstad in Sweden, in Copenhagen and in Oslo – the prime, defence and foreign ministers of the three states met to try to fashion an agreement on the basis of the committee report. In Karlstad in early January the Norwegians again showed their readiness to compromise. They were willing to consider abandoning their demands for formal links to the West if the United States were willing to give an informal or implicit promise of assistance. The Swedes in return accepted that the three nations should make a joint approach to the Western powers. The Karlstad compromise broke down at Copenhagen. The Norwegians then stated their minimum demands in the form of a question to the Swedes: if Norway agreed to a defence union that was formally and explicitly non-aligned, would Sweden then be willing to discuss with the American government some form of Western guarantee in case of war? The Swedish answer was an unequivocal 'no'. The Norwegians and the Swedes differed on one further point. Sweden as well as Norway assumed that a Scandinavian union would require military assistance from other states. While the Swedes presupposed that the Western powers would consider it in their own interest to provide such assistance, the Norwegians held that view to be unduly optimistic. A Scandinavian pact had to be established in understanding with the West.[44]

The Scandinavian union was buried at Oslo over the last weekend of January 1949. A final Norwegian draft containing guidelines for a joint Scandinavian approach to the Western powers was presented. As the proposal contained a provision allowing each of the three powers to request outside assistance if attacked, it logically implied an opening for staff talks. As such it was unacceptable to the Swedes.[45] After the debacle Norway immediately turned to the West, while Denmark made a futile attempt at concluding a bilateral defence agreement with Sweden. For Sweden a pact with Denmark would carry heavy responsibility with no obvious gain, since the West would be involved in Scandinavia under any circumstances.[46] Having failed to co-ordinate their policies, the three powers now made separate accommodations with the emerging bipolar order.

### Norway turns west

Starting out on its own, the Norwegian government first sent Lange on a fact-finding mission to Washington. He was to enquire about the conditions for accession to the Western alliance then being formed. He was also to investigate American attitudes towards the Nordic alternative, including the possibility of arms deliveries. Both the domestic situation and the ideal of a Scandinavian solution continued to weigh heavily on the government in Oslo.

Against American scepticism about the Scandinavian option Lange was to emphasize the importance of Sweden's military contribution. Lange was also to elicit American views as to the acceptable minimum that could be considered an opening to the West. The Norwegians would at least need 'an expression of their [the

Western powers'] interest in seeing the integrity of the Scandinavian states re-
spected'; and 'a certain contact between the military authorities in connection with
arms deliveries as a substitute for staff talks'.[47] The Americans were clearly sceptical of the value of such a tentative opening, and, since the Swedes would most likely
reject it, the matter was dropped.

The Americans were more flexible on the issue of arms deliveries to a
Scandinavian union. Norwegian historians as well as publicists have on different
occasions charged Lange with neglecting this possibility for resurrecting the
Scandinavian union. Such criticism appears clearly misplaced. However, the strategy chosen by the Labour government, its subsequent justification of Western
alignment, and Norwegian performance during the trip to Washington must all
take some of the blame for this misperception. The government strongly emphasized the need for cheap and high-priority arms deliveries. The issue of an opening
to the West was downplayed – for tactical reasons, we must assume. At least within
parts of the Labour party a successful push to limit defence expenditures would
count for more than the opening to the West. As far as the cabinet was concerned,
arms deliveries was a secondary issue, an acceptable opening to the West the *sine
qua non*.[48]

On the issue of Norway's accession to the North Atlantic Treaty, the delegation
raised the major question of Allied bases on Norwegian territory. Bases were
unacceptable to the Labour cabinet for internal political reasons as well as from a
desire not to provoke the Soviet Union. The Americans had previously stated that
such bases would not be required. As the Norwegian delegation was leaving Oslo
for Washington, the Soviet ambassador had asked whether Norway intended to join
the alliance, and whether accession would imply air and naval bases for foreign
forces in Norway. The Americans reiterated their previous stand, though with the
proviso that the future Atlantic council might propose that Norway should provide
facilities. Norway would then have to decide what to do.[49] These exchanges led to
the Norwegian bases declaration. Norway would accept foreign bases only in times
of war or when war threatened.

The international negotiations were thus brought to an end for the foreign and
defence ministries. The Atlantic option would next have to be carried in the
cabinet, within the Labour Party and in Parliament. Prime Minister Gerhardsen
had long been a supporter of the Scandinavian alternative, but threw his support
fully behind the Atlantic option after the Oslo meeting. The internal Labour
opposition crumbled once the Prime Minister had made his choice. The party
conference, after a divided preliminary vote, in the end resolved unanimously that
Norway should seek to solve its security problem through a 'commitment to
solidarity and cooperation with the western democracies'.[50] Yet pockets of opposition remained within the Labour party; when the motion was presented in Parliament that Norway should participate in the preparatory talks for the treaty, sixteen
Labour representatives abstained while two voted against, with the eleven communists. The same two joined the communists in opposing ratification towards the end
of March.

The Danes followed Norway reluctantly. In late February the Danish ambassador to Washington sought clarification of the modalities for Denmark's accession to

the North Atlantic Alliance. Even at that late moment, however, he was instructed to state that a Nordic defence union was the best solution for all involved. Nevertheless, once Norway had decided to go West, hardly any doubt remained that the Danes would follow suit.[51]

### Why separate ways?

We must look at several levels of explanation to understand why the Scandinavians had different security preferences, why they chose differently, and why the process was so involved. Olav Riste has stated that the real question is not why the attempt to form a Scandinavian defence union failed, but 'how it could possibly succeed?'[52] Geopolitics as well as historical experience clearly predisposed Norway and Sweden to the choices they eventually made. Denmark's orientation, as we have seen, eventually depended on the decisions of the other two. The complications and the protracted negotiations were thus functions of an intricate web of domestic politics, different perceptions of the alignment of forces at home and abroad, and tactical considerations.

Riste has pointed out that, in terms of Norway's position within the Western camp, 1949 did not represent a turning point. In long-term perspective, the continuity is striking: the implicit Western guarantee was replaced by an explicit one. The inner circle of policy-makers within the Defence and Foreign Ministries and a sprinkling of other leading Labour politicians clearly saw Norway as needing a Western guarantee in that particular international situation. Their perception was shared by the greater part of the non-Labour opposition. Seen in this perspective, Norway's alignment with the West might be considered a foregone conclusion.

On the other hand, the Labour foreign-policy leadership had to reckon with considerable opposition among rank and file members, within its parliamentary party and even within the cabinet. When the issue of Western alignment first came up, the majority of Labour parliamentarians were opposed to the north Atlantic option. Once the Scandinavian alternative was introduced, Prime Minister Gerhardsen clearly showed his preference for that.[53] The outcome of that debate cannot be considered inevitable. First of all, for domestic political reasons the Labour party had no choice but to engage in the Scandinavian negotiations. It could not afford to be blamed for splitting Scandinavia once the idea of a defence union had been launched. Second, there is no doubt that the Labour leadership itself wanted a Scandinavian pact, if it were possible to agree on a minimal opening to the West. This was partly because the leadership shared the pro-Scandinavian leanings of the rest of the party – a solution which would minimise division within the party.

A Scandinavian defence pact could also conceivably be considered less of a provocation against the Soviet Union than extending the North Atlantic Alliance to the peninsula. As was observed in the Marshall Plan discussion, it was of primary importance for Norway to maintain its connections with the West at a time of increasing tension. Reassuring the Soviets about non-aggressive Norwegian intentions was, however, an important secondary goal, as demonstrated by the bases declaration. Soviet prodding resulted in a unilateral Norwegian declaration that foreign soldiers would be stationed in Norway only in time of war or under threat of war. Being unilateral, it could be changed in the same way, but the declaration clearly signalled the purely defensive aspect of Norwegian membership.[54] Finally, as mentioned above, the strength of the Swedish defence forces and industry made Sweden very important for the defence of Norway.[55] A break with Sweden was therefore by no means a foregone conclusion for Oslo.

The Swedish situation was fundamentally different. In the first place the Swedish proposal for a Scandinavian defence union must be considered as either a diversion or a near ultimatum. The Undén proposal was launched to prevent Norway from joining the West. Negotiating the mandate for the Defence Commission, the Swedes never veered from their demand that neutrality be the basis for an eventual pact. The Swedes were determined to preserve non-alignment. They generally succeeded in pushing the Norwegians into a continuous retreat from their demand for an opening to the West. Only at Karlstad in early January 1949 did Erlander move an inch from rigid non-alignment, and he was quickly pulled back in Copenhagen.

The Swedes were in a seller's market. They possessed desirable military strength; Norway and Denmark were not likely to become military assets until the mid-1950s. Accordingly, by entering into a Scandinavian defence union Sweden would be carrying the major burden. To a significant degree that would be the case even with an opening to the West. Furthermore, in addition to perceiving themselves to be in a less exposed geopolitical position than the Norwegians, they appear to have made less of the possible Soviet threat than did the Norwegians. Neither strategic position, history nor threat perception therefore suggested strong reasons for the Swedes to compromise. They would be incurring high costs at little obvious gain. In addition, while in Norway domestic politics inclined the Labour party towards Scandinavia, in Sweden the situation was the reverse. There was considerable scepticism against compromising the straight and narrow path of non-alignment, even as regards a non-aligned Scandinavian union. Parliamentary as well as internal social democratic opposition to any opening to the West would be strong. The domestic situation in Sweden thus militated against any compromise with the Norwegians. The domestic situation in Norway offered encouragement to those who thought the Norwegian government could be forced into a total retreat.[56] We should note, however, that the Defence Commission was quite unanimous in their view that the Scandinavians could not withstand an attack from a major power. Assistance from outside, even the Swedes agreed, would be necessary for a sustained defence effort.

Danish Prime Minister Hans Hedtoft was the genuine spokesman for the Scandinavian option. For him it appears to have represented a happy marriage between the interests of his Social Democratic Party and his country. There was no significant opposition to the proposal, whether it implied an opening to the West or not. A Scandinavian union could save Denmark from abandonment by the alliance with Sweden; at the same time the Danes would not risk being embroiled in other far-away conflicts. In 1948 Sweden was a major military power in the area, while it was by no means clear that the West had much to offer in the short run.[57]

The different strategies and choices of the three nations may also be accounted for by their conflicting perceptions of the modalities for great-power support for the proposed Scandinavian union. The Danes and the Swedes were of the opinion that Britain and the United States would come to Scandinavia's aid if they deemed it in their own interest to do so, otherwise not. They thus felt that it would be perfectly sensible to create the Scandinavian union without ascertaining Western attitudes regarding an opening. Likewise they did not envisage any problems in acquiring weapons on a preferential basis. The Norwegians, in addition to emphasizing the need for peacetime military planning, were more apt to take seriously the American demands for reciprocity in a mutual security system. They did not assume that military aid would be forthcoming automatically even if it were desirable for the West to deny the Soviet Union control of Scandinavia, and were also far more disposed than the Swedes and the Danes to take at face value the American assertion that weapons and munitions were in short supply and that allies would be served first, and receive preferential treatment. Non-allies would have to wait in line and bargain for the best terms they could get.

The Swedes were generally disposed to take both a more cynical and a more naive view of how to advance their own best interests and of how the great powers viewed their own. To a degree, cynicism was appropriate. The Northern Department of the British Foreign Office under Robin Hankey in the autumn of 1948 and in January 1949 put forward different versions of what has become known as the Hankey Plan. The point for Hankey was to create an interlocking system of alliances to secure Swedish military resources for the West in case conflict embroiled the Scandinavian peninsula. The Swedes were to be tied to the Atlantic system by means of the Scandinavian alliance, the Danes and the Norwegians being members of both. Even in its most watered-down version the plan would probably have been unacceptable to Sweden; *any* version would have been unacceptable to Lange. The Gerhardsen government could not have presented an alliance proposal giving Sweden a vastly better deal than Norway. On other points, Swedish cynicism bordered on naive dogmatism. They believed to the end, in spite of all assurances to the contrary, that the Americans and the British would demand bases in Norway.[58]

A final comment on mutual perceptions and misperceptions is in order. It does appear that the object of the negotiations, a Scandinavian union, was itself conducive to creating misunderstanding among the participants as well as among some of those who have discussed the issue later. A Scandinavian union was in Swedish eyes to be wholly non-aligned; as far as the Norwegian policy-makers were concerned, there had to be some sort of opening to the West. To the Danes the precise conditions for co-operation did not really matter as long as something Scandinavian materialized. Yet for all three parties a Scandinavian union was the goal, with the neutrality issue swept under the rug in the mandate for the Commission. All three could go on for another few months hoping for an acceptable solution. The Danes were the most prone to indulge in wishful thinking. This was particularly so towards the end when they tried to resurrect the project after the Oslo meeting, even proposing a Danish-Swedish pact. They had also invested the greatest amount of prestige in a successful outcome.

To what extent the Norwegians really believed it possible to turn the Swedes around has not been fully explored. They generally seem to have had a sound understanding of the strength of Swedish non-alignment. Yet they may have been hoping that the conclusions of the Defence Commission would make a significant impact, that is primarily the argument that Scandinavian co-operation did not eliminate the need for outside assistance. In addition they may have counted on the known opposition of the Swedish military to non-alignment to pull the Erlander government around to the Norwegian point of view.[59]

Nevertheless, at the current stage of research, misperceptions appear to have played the largest role on the Swedish side. It appears that they may account in part for the protracted negotiating process and the heavy-handed Swedish pressure on Norway to accept their terms. These misperceptions were partly due to the inability of the Swedish ambassador in Oslo, Johan Beck-Friis, to report accurately on the Norwegian scene. He conveyed a misleading picture of Prime Minister Gerhardsen as an indecisive person who actually favoured the Swedish point of view when meeting the Swedes and Danes, while being totally dominated by Lange when decisions were taken in Oslo. Gerhardsen was emotionally drawn to the Scandinavian option and undoubtedly ambivalent about the United States. Yet there also seems no doubt that he accepted the need for an opening to the West. Moreover, he was very much in charge in Norway. The misperceptions of Beck-Friis should not be accorded too much weight, however; they largely mirrored those of his superior in Stockholm. There is reason to doubt that another ambassador would have made any difference. Beck-Friis, Undén, Erlander and also Danish Prime Minister Hedtoft all had quite unrealistic ideas of the strength and tenacity of the anti-Western opposition within Labour. Most likely they did not grasp that support for a Scandinavian union did not necessarily imply support for the non-aligned Swedish version.

The Stockholm cabinet does not appear to have quite accepted the reality of Norway as an independent national actor. After the Karlstad meeting Undén maintained that the Norwegians had never considered giving up their association with the Atlantic Pact. He noted that Norway had tried to drag the Swedes along: 'When they noticed that they had not succeeded, they were finished with the Scandinavian Union.' Prime Minister Erlander in a conversation with the Danish ambassador to Stockholm observed that Lange had never taken the Swedish proposal seriously, adding with bitterness: 'It is perhaps not so difficult to deceive unsuspecting friends who do not even dream of playing the game with marked cards and who are unaware that one of the partners is not following the rules of the game.'[60]

These comments are in a sense understandable from statesmen who feel they have lost a major battle. Yet, they themselves had never made any serious effort to meet the Norwegians in a compromise. They had done precisely what they blamed the Norwegians for doing and with considerably greater success. The Norwegians had watered down their demand for an opening to the West to almost nil under relentless Swedish pressure. The combination of cynicism and realism that the Swedes applied in their analysis of the acts and interests of the great powers was not applied to Swedish-Norwegian relations. In their myopic view of the Norwegian scene they were unable to grasp the degree to which the War had changed Norwegian foreign policy and politics. We may perhaps also venture the hypothesis that Erlander and Undén, as representatives of the established dominant power in the Nordic region, experienced difficulties in accepting what amounted to a reaffirmation of the Norwegian declaration of independence from Sweden. The choice in favour of the West represented the assertion of a separate Norwegian foreign policy as well as a threat against Sweden's dominant regional position. Stockholm could not view this with equanimity.

### *Epilogue: mending fences and limiting commitments*

Bitterness, however, did not lead to public recrimination. A realistic evaluation of national interests indicated that the Scandinavians would be best served by maintaining as close relations as possible, militarily and otherwise. This could be achieved in a number of ways: by strengthening military contacts among the three and between Sweden and the West, by developing other joint Scandinavian and north Atlantic organizations, and by imposing strict limitations on the implications of Danish and Norwegian NATO membership.

Contacts between the Scandinavian military had developed increasingly since 1947. These continued into the NATO period in the form of functional military co-operation. Such contacts were obviously not the equivalent of alliance partnership, but they served as means of communication between Sweden and the Western powers. Whether and to what extent there were direct contacts between the West and Sweden, we do not yet know. Nor is it clear to what extent the contacts that were established in fact altered Sweden's neutrality policies. The Norwegians certainly, and the Danes we must assume, did their best to emphasize to their allies the importance of a strong Swedish defence. For Norway that implied any possible support for Swedish arms purchases in the United States and Britain.[61]

After the outbreak of war in Korea, the United States quickly demanded that the Europeans accept West German rearmament and higher defence budgets. For both Denmark and Norway, as for other Europeans, German rearmament was a sensitive issue. Before accepting American demands, Foreign Minister Lange had to ask for a recess of the NATO meeting in New York in September 1950 to consult with the cabinet and parliamentary leaders at home. In the end both nations accepted the American demand, for general solidarity reasons as well as for reasons of more immediate self-interest. The NATO defence line on the Rhine put Denmark and southern Norway in a very exposed position outside of NATO defences. German rearmament was required to improve upon that situation.

After choosing NATO, both Denmark and Norway came to realize that serious problems attended on membership. The alliance in fact had very meagre resources with which to defend its northern flank. Thus both governments had to make a major effort to nail the allies down to their defence. They were concerned to have a credible deterrent established: thus their support for the German solution. On the other hand, they were concerned not to appear as aggressive outposts against the Soviet Union. This was a particular Norwegian anxiety: thus the Norwegian bases declaration which came to be accepted by Denmark as well. As Rolf Tamnes has emphasized, the Norwegian government was concerned with both deterrence and reassurance in its relationship with its superpower neighbour. While not the exact parallel of Petersen's entrapment and abandonment thesis for Denmark, Tamnes' pair of concepts does point to a similar double set of considerations – on the one hand, the need to be able to call on sufficient strength to deter the Soviets, while at the same time being able to reassure them of non-aggressive intentions. To present such a face to the East, Norway had to develop a double strategy towards its major alliance partners, which Tamnes has dubbed 'integration' and 'screening'. Norway would be sufficiently integrated into the NATO framework to remain a credible ally, yet would emphasize its special position as a neighbour of the Soviet Union by maintaining the ban on peacetime bases and leaving Norway's northern most county, Finnmark (the size of Denmark), a virtually demilitarized area. Such a policy served domestic purposes as well, as foreign bases would have provided the opposition with additional political ammunition. In this respect Danish policies followed closely those of Norway.[62]

In essence, what evolved may have come quite close to the British concept of interlocking alliances, though without the formal framework, with a considerably greater degree of uncertainty involved on all sides, and without the political cost for Norway. We shall obviously have to wait until Swedish and NATO military archives are opened to study this question in detail, but already accessible archives indicate not inconsiderable contact.

To what degree Nordic politicians were disappointed or satisfied with the eventual long-term outcome of the Scandinavian security debate has not been a theme for scholarly debate. Some reflections, however, are in order. The Swedes, apart from their initial disappointment at not being able to have it their own way, possibly had no reason to be dissatisfied. They were able to hang on to non-alignment, eschewing domestic political struggle. The Danes were disappointed at the outcome, but the social democratic government was generally pro-Western, and German rearmament served to quiet some of their worries. They were certainly not responsible for creating the split, and did not have to carry that onus. They would have gone along with any Swedish-Norwegian agreement.

The Norwegian body politic was strongly marked by the 1949 decision. Significant elements within Labour rank-and-file saw NATO membership as a break with the Norwegian foreign-policy tradition, as an unholy alliance with American capitalism and as implying an unacceptable level of rearmament. Very large segments of social democracy, and parts of the non-Labour opposition, kept hankering after the lost world of possible Scandinavian co-operation, of the UN as a security guarantee, and generally after a more 'positive' foreign policy. Within a fairly short time-span disaffection abated, in the sense that outright opposition to NATO membership declined dramatically. However, opposition against specific aspects of NATO policies remained strong. German rearmament, the nuclear strategy of NATO, NATO support for the French war in Indo-China all provoked protests. In 1961 the foreign-policy opposition coalesced in the Socialist People's Party, a left-wing party devoted to both foreign- and economic-policy criticism of the ruling Labour party.

The Labour party to a degree tried to bridge the chasm that had opened. Greater willingness to increase Nordic co-operation was a favourite means. The Foreign Ministry also wanted to bring Sweden closer to the West in a formal sense through its stratagems for joining the various European co-operation organizations of the post-war era with NATO. Bridging the gap was in itself desirable. Furthermore, tending to the Scandinavian dimension was also a means of pacifying at least part of the NATO opposition within the party. NATO in itself caused uneasiness on the left and among former neutralists and pacifists. Post-Korean-war rearmament intensified misgivings. Within the government, increasing international tensions and rearmament were seen to necessitate a Norwegian initiative through the UN to improve conditions in the non-European world. The outcome of these worries and plans was the Indo-Norwegian Fisheries Project, an aid project in South India destined to last for twenty years from 1952. Typically it was intended to cater for international and domestic problems at one and the same time. As Arne Ording put it in his diary on 2 February 1952: 'At Labour party headquarters. Halvard Lange presented the plan concerning a Norwegian initiative on the issue of aid to under-developed areas. An area in India under consideration. No publicity until it has all been settled. Good plan, we shall have to give people something of a positive nature in addition to the large defence appropriations.'[63]

These elements of tactical manoeuvring must not, however, be allowed to overshadow the fact that the initiatives above all were intrinsically desirable. Aid to the third world, a strengthening of Scandinavian co-operation and an extension of north Atlantic co-operation were primarily worthwhile goals in themselves. And while the Labour government wanted as far as possible to modify the international environment to suit its preferences, Norway's secure place in north Atlantic defence co-operation was the essential point of departure for any such attempts. An increasing majority of the Labour as well as the non-socialist opposition found NATO membership essential to the preservation of Norwegian security and sovereignty. While other foreign policy issues, the Common Market in particular, have proved deeply divisive in Norway, the consensus on Western alignment has grown to embrace even representatives on the new left.

The legacies of the Second World War – the lessons of April 1940 on the one hand and of successful Swedish neutrality policies on the other – have had a profound influence on post-war foreign policies in Scandinavia. Nevertheless, while appearances may have been deceptive in the early postwar period, the primacy of opposing security policy concepts never completely overshadowed the elements of regional cohesion and unity. In fact, they provided the basis for a flexible, informal arrangement. Once Swedish, Danish and NATO archives become accessible, we shall have the opportunity to study that arrangement in depth.

### Bibliographical note

The third issue of the *Scandinavian Journal of History* (henceforth *SJH*), 1985, is still the best starting point for a study of Scandinavia and the Cold War. The articles by W. Agrell, N. Petersen and H.Ø. Pharo (on Sweden, Denmark and Norway respectively) are somewhat dated but still offer the only broad historiographical surveys in English. Only a few comparative works on Scandinavian foreign and security policies deal with this period, most of which are published in English. They are all fairly detailed and largely designed for those already familiar with these issues in Scandinavian history. The most recent and comprehensive is M. Skodvin's *Nordic or North Atlantic Alliance? The Postwar Scandinavian Security Debate* (Institute for Defence Studies, Occasional Papers (henceforth *DS*), 3 (1990)). While Skodvin concentrates on 1948, K. Blidberg, in *Just Good Friends: Nordic Social Democracy and Security Policy 1945–50*, *DS*, 5 (1987), uses a longer time perspective, also emphasizing differences between Norway and the other Scandinavians towards the end of the 1930s. N. Petersen has published an article analyzing Scandinavia and Britain, 'Britain, Scandinavia and the North Atlantic Treaty, 1948–9', *Review of International Studies*, 8 (1982). G. Aalders, 'The Failure of the Scandinavian Defence Union', *SJH*, 15 (1990), is particularly concerned with Swedish policies and has been one of the first to exploit Swedish foreign ministry sources. Essential for its comprehensive treatment of the United States and Scandinavia during this period is G. Lundestad's standard work *America, Scandinavia and the Cold War, 1945–1949* (Oslo & New York, 1980). The English-language journals that most often carry articles within this field are *SJH* and primarily *Cooperation and Conflict*. The latter journal is dominated by works of political scientists rather than historians.

Among the many Norwegian historians that have analyzed this period, Olav Riste stands out in taking a long-term perspective. His seminal contribution, 'Was 1949 a Turning-Point? Norway and the Western Powers 1947–1950', in Riste, ed., *Western Security: the Formative Years* (Oslo, 1985), is crucial to understanding Norwegian policies. Riste has contributed a number of other works in English on the period, most of them published as DS Occasional Papers. N.M. Udgaard, *Great Power Politics and Norwegian Foreign Policy* (Oslo, 1973), is dated but still useful. R. Tamnes has worked particularly on the post-1949 period and his dissertation, published as *The United States and the Cold War in the High North* (Oslo, 1991), also sets out his general views on post-war Norwegian foreign policy, 1945–90. It will long remain the standard work on these issues in any language. Material in English about Swedish policy is limited, but note the John Hopkins Univ. Ph.D. by P.M. Cole, 'Sweden's Neutrality since 1945: Three Attempts to Achieve Credibility' (1990). For a useful recent collection of essays on Denmark, the Nordic countries and NATO, see C. Due-Nielsen, T.P. Noack and N. Petersen, eds., *Danmark, Norden og NATO, 1948–1962* (Copenhagen, 1991).

## Chronology of Major International Events Mentioned in the text, 1943–55

### 1943

| | |
|---|---|
| 24 Jan. | 'Unconditional surrender' doctrine promulgated by Roosevelt and Churchill at Casablanca |
| 10 July | Allied forces invade Sicily |
| 25 July | Mussolini overthrown |
| 3 Sept. | Italian armistice |
| 28 Nov.–1 Dec. | Teheran conference (Roosevelt, Churchill, Stalin) |

### 1944

| | |
|---|---|
| 6 June | Allied forces invade France (D-Day) |
| 9 Oct. | Churchill in Moscow; 'Percentages' agreement |
| 10 Dec. | De Gaulle in Moscow; Franco-Soviet treaty |

### 1945

| | |
|---|---|
| 4–11 Feb. | Yalta conference |
| 8 May | German unconditional surrender |
| 17 July | Potsdam conference opens |
| 2 Aug. | Potsdam agreement signed |
| 6 & 9 Aug. | Atomic bombs on Hiroshima and Nagasaki |
| 8 Aug. | Soviet Union enters war against Japan |
| 15 Aug. | Japan surrenders |
| 11 Sept. | Foreign Ministers Conference opens in London; ends 2 Oct. |
| 18 Nov. | Soviet troops occupy Iranian Azerbaijan |
| 16 Dec. | Foreign Ministers Conference opens in Moscow; ends 26 Dec. |

### 1946

| | |
|---|---|
| 22 Feb. | George Kennan's 'Long Telegram' |
| 5 March | Churchill's 'Iron Curtain' speech (Fulton, Missouri) |
| March | UN crisis over failure of Soviet forces to withdraw from Iran |

| | |
|---|---|
| 10–11 July | Britain and United States agree to fuse their zones in Germany from end of year |
| 7 Aug. | Soviet Union demands joint control of Turkish Straits |

## 1947

| | |
|---|---|
| 1 Jan. | Anglo-American 'Bizone' formed in Germany |
| 3 Jan. | 80th U.S. Congress: Republican majorities |
| 10 Feb. | Peace treaties signed with Italy, Hungary, Romania, Bulgaria and Finland |
| 21 Feb. | Britain notifies United States that it will end aid to Greece and Turkey on 31 March |
| 4 March | Anglo-French Treaty of Dunkirk |
| 10 March | Moscow Foreign Ministers conference opens; ends 25 April |
| 12 March | Truman Doctrine speech |
| 12 March | Belgian communists excluded from coalition government |
| 31 March | United States ends wartime Draft (conscription) |
| 4 May | French communists excluded from coalition government |
| 31 May | Italian communists excluded from coalition government |
| 5 June | Marshall's Harvard speech offering American aid to Europe |
| 27 June | Conference to draw up European Recovery Program (ERP) opens in Paris |
| 2 July | Soviet delegation withdraws from Paris |
| 12 July | East Europeans boycott Paris discussions at Stalin's behest |
| 22 Sept. | ERP report approved in Paris |
| 5 Oct. | Cominform founded to link Soviet Union and other communist parties |
| Nov. | Strikes paralyze French economy |

## 1948

| | |
|---|---|
| 1 Jan. | Benelux customs union begins |
| 22 Jan. | 'Western Union' speech by Bevin |
| 25 Feb. | Communists take power in Czechoslovakia |
| 17 Mar. | Brussels Treaty (Britain, France, Benelux states) |
| 22 Mar. | United States, Britain, Canada begin Pentagon negotiations on Atlantic security pact |
| 3 Apr. | United States-European Recovery Program becomes law |
| 5 Apr. | Soviet-Finnish friendship treaty |
| 18 Apr. | Italian elections: Christian Democratic parliamentary majority |
| 3 May | Swedes propose Scandinavian defence union |
| 17 May | Truman asks Congress to restore the Draft |
| 7 June | Western Allies announce convocation of constituent assemblies for future West German republic |
| 11 June | Vandenberg resolution passes U.S. Senate supporting Atlantic security pact |

| | |
|---|---|
| 18 June | Deutschmark introduced into Western zones of Germany |
| 24 June | Soviets blockade Berlin; Western airlift follows |
| 28 June | Yugoslavia expelled from Cominform |
| 10 Sept. | Atlantic security negotiations begin |
| 18 Oct. | Fusion of French zone with Bizone |

**1949**

| | |
|---|---|
| 29 Jan. | Scandinavian defence union talks collapse |
| 23 Mar. | Danish Parliament votes to join North Atlantic treaty |
| 29 Mar. | Norwegian Parliament votes to join North Atlantic Treaty |
| 4 Apr. | North Atlantic Treaty signed in Washington |
| 12 May | Federal German Constitution (Grundgesetz) approved by Allies |
| 12 May | Berlin blockade ends |
| 20 Sept. | Birth of Federal Republic of Germany (FRG) |
| 23 Sept. | First Soviet Atomic test made known in West |
| 7 Oct. | Birth of German Democratic Republic (GDR) |

**1950**

| | |
|---|---|
| 9 May | Schuman Plan for European Coal and Steel Community (ECSC) |
| 2 June | Britain refuses to join discussions |
| 25 June | North Korea invades the South |
| 22 Sept. | Acheson calls for German rearmament |
| 24 Oct. | Pleven Plan for European Defence Community |
| 19 Dec. | Eisenhower appointed first Supreme Allied Commander, Europe |

**1951**

| | |
|---|---|
| 4 Apr. | U.S. Senate approves 4 new combat divisions for Europe |
| 18 Apr. | ECSC treaty signed in Paris (France, FRG, Italy, Belgium, Netherlands and Luxembourg) |
| 8 Sept. | United States–Japanese peace treaty signed |
| 28 Nov. | Britain announces refusal to join EDC |

**1952**

| | |
|---|---|
| 15 Feb. | Greece and Turkey join NATO |
| 10 Mar. | Stalin note proposing German unification and neutralization |
| 27 May | EDC Treaty (Paris); related British treaty of guarantee |
| 30 June | Marshall Aid ends |
| 3 Oct. | First British atomic test |
| 1 Nov. | First American thermonuclear test |

**1953**

| | |
|---|---|
| 5 Mar. | Death of Stalin; Malenkov new chairman of Council of Ministers |
| 15 Mar. | Malenkov speaks of 'peaceful coexistence' |
| 11 May | Churchill calls for summit conference |
| June | Anti-communist disturbances in GDR |
| July | Soviet security chief Beria deposed and executed |
| 27 July | Korean armistice |
| 12 Aug. | First Soviet thermonuclear test |

**1954**

| | |
|---|---|
| Mar.–Apr. | Dien Bien Phu crisis in Indochina |
| 20 Jul. | Geneva accords on Indochina |
| 30 Aug. | French Assembly rejects EDC treaty |
| 29 Sept. | Eden promises to keep British troops in Germany until 1998 |
| 20–23 Oct. | Paris accords on German sovereignty and admittance to Brussels Pact and NATO |
| 5 Oct. | London accords divide Trieste between Italy and Yugoslavia |
| 26 Oct. | End of Allied military government in Trieste |

**1955**

| | |
|---|---|
| 8 Feb. | Bulganin replaces Malenkov as chairman of Council of Ministers |
| 5 May | Allied occupation of West Germany ends |
| 9 May | West Germany joins NATO |
| 14 May | Warsaw Pact signed by Soviet Union and seven East European states |
| 15 May | Austrian State Treaty |
| 1–3 June | Messina meeting of Foreign Ministers of 'the Six'; committee to plan further integration |
| 18–23 July | Geneva Summit: United States, Soviet Union, Britain, France |

*Principal source*: Luc Thanassecos, *Chronologie des rélations internationales, 1914–1971* (Paris, 1972)

## Table of post-war governments until 1955

(Blank spaces indicate that the previous holder was reappointed.)

### Belgium

| Assumed office | Prime Minister | Foreign Minister |
| --- | --- | --- |
| 12 Feb. 1945 | Achille van Acker | Paul-Henri Spaak |
| 13 Mar. 1946 | Paul-Henri Spaak | |
| 31 Mar. 1946 | Achille van Acker | |
| 3 Aug. 1946 | Camille Huysmans | |
| 20 Mar. 1947 | Paul-Henri Spaak | |
| 11 Aug. 1949 | Gaston Eyskens | Paul van Zeeland |
| 8 June 1950 | Jean Pierre Duvieusart | |
| 15 Aug. 1950 | Joseph Pholien | |
| 15 Jan. 1952 | Jean van Houtte | |
| 23 Apr. 1954 | Achille van Acker | Paul-Henri Spaak |

### Denmark

| Assumed office | Prime Minister | Foreign Minister |
| --- | --- | --- |
| 5 May 1945 | Wilhelm Buhl | J. Christmas Moeller |
| 8 Nov. 1945 | Knud Kristensen | Gustav Rasmussen |
| 13 Nov. 1947 | Hans Hedtoft | |
| 28 Oct. 1950 | Erik Erikson | Ole Biorn Kraft |
| 30 Sep. 1953 | Hans Hedtoft | Hans Christian Hansen |
| 29 Jan. 1955 | – – – – Hans Christian Hansen – – – – | |

### France

| Assumed office | Prime Minister | Foreign Minister |
| --- | --- | --- |
| 10 Sep. 1944 | Charles de Gaulle | Georges Bidault |
| 29 Jan. 1946 | Félix Gouin | |
| 24 June 1946 | Georges Bidault | |
| 16 Dec. 1946 | Léon Blum | Léon Blum |

| 22 Jan. 1947 | Paul Ramadier | Georges Bidault |
|---|---|---|
| 24 Nov. 1947 | Robert Schuman | |
| 27 July 1948 | André Marie | Robert Schuman |
| 5 Sep. 1948 | Robert Schuman | |
| 13 Sep. 1948 | Henri Queuille | |
| 28 Oct. 1949 | Georges Bidault | |
| 2 July 1950 | Henri Queuille | |
| 12 July 1950 | René Pleven | |
| 10 Mar 1951 | Henri Queuille | |
| 11 Aug. 1951 | René Pleven | |
| 20 Jan. 1952 | Edgar Faure | |
| 8 Mar. 1952 | Antoine Pinay | |
| 9 Jan. 1953 | René Mayer | Georges Bidault |
| 28 Jun. 1953 | Joseph Laniel | |
| 19 Jun. 1954 | – – – – Pierre Mendès-France – – – – | |
| 20 Jan. 1955 | P. Mendès-France | Edgar Faure |
| 23 Feb. 1955 | Edgar Faure | Antoine Pinay |

## Germany, Federal Republic of

| Assumed office | Chancellor | Foreign Minister |
|---|---|---|
| 20 Sep. 1949 | Konrad Adenauer | |
| 13 Mar. 1951 | | Konrad Adenauer |
| 6 Jun. 1955 | | Heinrich von Brentano |

## Great Britain

| Assumed office | Prime Minister | Foreign Secretary |
|---|---|---|
| 10 May 1940 | Winston Churchill | Lord Halifax |
| 23 Dec. 1940 | | Anthony Eden |
| 27 July 1945 | Clement Attlee | Ernest Bevin |
| 9 Mar. 1951 | | Herbert Morrison |
| 26 Oct. 1951 | Winston Churchill | Anthony Eden |
| 6 Apr. 1955 | Anthony Eden | Harold Macmillan |

## Italy

| Assumed office | Prime Minister | Foreign Minister |
|---|---|---|
| 27 Jul. 1943 | Pietro Badoglio | Raffaele Guariglia |
| 25 Dec. 1943 | | Pietro Badoglio |
| 9 Jun. 1944 | Ivanoe Bonomi | Ivanoe Bonomi |
| 12 Dec. 1944 | | Alcide De Gasperi |
| 20 Jun. 1945 | Ferruccio Parri | |
| 10 Dec. 1945 | Alcide De Gasperi | |
| 18 Oct. 1946 | | Pietro Nenni |
| 30 May 1947 | | Carlo Sforza |

| | | |
|---|---|---|
| 24 Jul. 1951 | | Alcide De Gasperi |
| 15 Aug. 1953 | Giuseppe Pella | Giuseppe Pella |
| 18 Jan. 1954 | Amintore Fanfani | Attilio Piccioni |
| 9 Feb. 1954 | Mario Scelba | |
| 18 Sep. 1954 | | Gaetano Martio |
| 6 Jul. 1955 | Antonio Segni | |

## Luxembourg

| *Assumed office* | *Prime Minister* | *Foreign Minister* |
|---|---|---|
| 5 Nov. 1937 | Pierre Dupong | Joseph Bech |
| 28 Dec. 1953 | Joseph Bech | |

## The Netherlands

| *Assumed office* | *Prime Minister* | *Foreign Minister* |
|---|---|---|
| 24 Jun. 1945 | Willem Schermerhorn | Eelco N. van Kleffens |
| 1 Mar. 1946 | | Jan-Herman van Royen |
| 3 July 1946 | Louis Beel | C.G.W.H. Baron van Boetzelaer van Oosterhuit |
| 7 Aug. 1948 | Willem Drees | Dirk U. Stikker |
| 2 Sep. 1952 | | Johan Willem Beyen |

## Norway

| *Assumed office* | *Prime Minister* | *Foreign Minister* |
|---|---|---|
| 26 June 1945 | Einar Gerhardsen | Trygve Lie |
| 1 Feb. 1946 | | Halvard Lange |
| 17 Nov. 1951 | Oscar Torp | |
| 22 Jan. 1955 | Einar Gerhardsen | |

## Sweden

| *Assumed office* | *Prime Minister* | *Foreign Minister* |
|---|---|---|
| 31 July 1945 | Per Albin Hansson | Bo Östen Undén |
| 10 Oct. 1946 | Tage Fritiof Erlander | |

## Union of Soviet Socialist Republics

| *Assumed office* | *'Prime Minister'* | *Foreign Minister* |
|---|---|---|
| | Josef Stalin | |
| 3 May 1939 | | Vyacheslav Molotov |
| 4 Mar. 1949 | | Andrei Vyshinsky |
| 6 Mar. 1953 | Georgi Malenkov | Vyacheslav Molotov |
| 8 Feb. 1955 | Nikolai Bulganin | |

## United States of America

| Assumed office | President | Secretary of State |
|---|---|---|
| 12 Apr. 1945 | Harry S. Truman | Edward R. Stettinius |
| 1 July 1945 | | James F. Byrnes |
| 10 Jan. 1947 | | George C. Marshall |
| 7 Jan. 1949 | | Dean Acheson |
| 20 Jan. 1953 | Dwight D. Eisenhower | John Foster Dulles |

*Principal source* (with amendments): Bertold Spuler, C.G. Allen & Neil Saunders (compilers), *Rulers and Governments of the World, vol. 3, 1930–1975* (London, 1977).

# *Abbreviations*

| | |
|---|---|
| ABC | atomic, biological and chemical weapons |
| ACC | Allied Control Commission |
| AVP RF | Archives of Foreign Affairs of the Russian Federation |
| BMFA | Belgian Ministry of Foreign Affairs |
| *CC* | *Cooperation and Conflict* |
| CDU | Christian Democratic Union |
| CEEC | Committee for European Economic Co-operation |
| CFM | Council of Foreign Ministers |
| CIA | Central Intelligence Agency |
| CLN | Comitato di Liberazione Nazionale |
| CPSU | Communist Party of the Soviet Union |
| *CWIHP* | Cold War International History Project |
| *DDF* | *Documents Diplomatiques Français* |
| DNW | Directie NAVO & WEU-zaken |
| *DS* | *Institute for Defence Studies, Oslo, occasional papers* |
| ECA | Economic Co-operation Administration |
| ECSC | European Coal and Steel Community |
| EDC | European Defence Community |
| ERP | European Recovery Program |
| EUI | European University Institute |
| FRG | Federal Republic of Germany |
| *FRUS* | *Foreign Relations of the United States* |
| GDR | German Democratic Republic |
| GRIT | Graduated Reduction of International Tensions |
| *IP* | *Internasjonal Politikk* |
| *IS* | *Internationella Studier* |
| KPD | Communist Party of Germany |
| MAAG | Military Assistance Advisory Groups |
| MDAP | Mutual Defense Assistance Program |
| NATO | North Atlantic Treaty Organization |
| NAW | National Archives Washington |
| NMFA | Netherlands Ministry of Foreign Affairs |
| NSC | National Security Council |

| | |
|---|---|
| OEEC | Organization for European Economic Co-operation |
| PCF | French Communist Party |
| PRC | People's Republic of China |
| PRO | Public Record Office, London |
| RPF | Rassemblement du Peuple Français |
| RTSKhIDNI | Russian Centre for the Preservation and Study of Contemporary Historical Documents |
| SED | Socialist Unity Party |
| *SJH* | *Scandinavian Journal of History* |
| SPD | Social Democratic Pary |
| SVAG | Soviet military administration in Germany |
| TSKhSD | Storage Centre for Contemporary Documentation |
| UN | United Nations |
| UNISCAN | Anglo-Scandinavian Co-operation Organization |
| WEU | Western European Union |

# Notes

## Introduction

1 Bernstein wrote in *Neue Zeit* in 1893: 'This continued arming, compelling the others to keep up with Germany, is itself a kind of warfare. I do not know whether this expression has been used previously, but one could say it is a cold war [ein kalter Krieg]. There is no shooting, but there is bleeding.' See Joseph M. Siracusa, 'Will the Real Author of the Cold War Please Stand Up?', Society for Historians of American Foreign Relations, *Newsletter*, 13: 3 (Sept. 1982), 9–11. Don Juan Manuel (1282–1348) commented: 'War that is very strong and very hot ends either with death or peace, whereas cold war neither brings peace nor gives honour to the one who makes it. . . .' Quoted in Fred Halliday, *The Making of the Second Cold War* (2nd ed., London, 1986), p. 5.

2 Walter Lippmann, *The Cold War* (New York, 1947); cf. George Orwell, 'You and the Atom Bomb', *Tribune*, 19 Oct. 1945, reprinted in Sonia Orwell & Ian Angus, eds., *The Collected Essays, Journalism and Letters of George Orwell*, vol. IV (London, 1968), pp. 9–10.

3 In the original French, détente means relaxation of tension (as, for example, relaxing the string of a bow), whereas *entente* signifies a genuine rapprochement and friendship. On the importance of this distinction for American attitudes to the Soviet Union in the 1970s, see Raymond Garthoff, *Détente and Confrontation: American-Soviet Relations from Nixon to Reagan* (Washington, 1985), p. 25: 'Much of the confusion in American understanding [of Soviet policy] seems to have stemmed from a tendency to interpret détente as though it meant entente.'

4 For examples of different periodizations, see Halliday, *Making of the Second Cold War*, ch. 1; D.C. Watt, 'Rethinking the Cold War: a Letter to a British Historian', *Political Quarterly*, 49 (1978), 405; Walter LaFeber, 'An End to *Which* Cold War?', in Michael J. Hogan, ed., *The End of the Cold War: its Meanings and Implications* (New York, 1992), pp. 13–19.

5 Some partial exceptions should be mentioned. Joseph M. Siracusa and Glen St John Barclay, eds., *The Impact of the Cold War: Reconsiderations* (Port Washington, N.Y., 1977) is an interesting but disparate collection, covering various countries, some of them European. The excellent but neglected volume edited by Olav Riste, *Western Security: The Formative Years; Europe and Atlantic Defence, 1947–1953* (Oslo, 1985) is largely concerned with Northern Europe and with defence issues. Josef Becker & Franz Knipping, eds., *Power in Europe?: Great Britain, France, Italy and Germany in a Postwar World, 1945–1950* (Berlin, 1986) deals only with these four countries and from the perspective of their continued aspirations as great powers, while Thomas G. Paterson and Robert J. McMahon, eds., *The Origins of the Cold War* (Lexington, MA, 1991) is global in scope. Charles S. Maier, ed., *The Cold War in Europe* (New York, 1991) collects some of the most useful or influential articles published in the last two decades, particularly from the United States.

6 Cf. Philip Dibb, *The Soviet Union: the Incomplete Superpower* (2nd ed., London, 1988), pp. 84–5.

7 R.W. Davies, *Soviet History in the Gorbachev Revolution* (London, 1989), pp. 3–4, 102.

8 In 1983 it was calculated that one in five of American doctoral theses on American foreign relations completed in the previous four years dealt with some aspect of the period 1945–50 (John Lewis Gaddis, 'The Emerging Post-Revisionist Synthesis on the Origins of the Cold

War', *Diplomatic History*, 7 (1983), 171). More generally, compare the figure of roughly one thousand members of the Society for Historians of American Foreign Relations cited by Stephanson with Helge Pharo's observation (ch. 8, note 2) that in all Norwegian universities and colleges there are only 80–90 tenured historians in *all* fields of history. For the state of the discipline in the United States see the essays in Michael J. Hogan and Thomas G. Paterson, eds., *Explaining the History of American Foreign Relations* (New York, 1991).

9  See also the bibliographical note to ch. 1. For surveys of this literature in French and German, see Georg Kreis, 'Le débat sur les origines de la guerre froide: état de la question', *Relations Internationales*, 47 (1986), 305–18; Wilfried Loth, 'Der "Kalte Krieg" in der historischen Forschung', in Gottfried Niedhart, ed., *Der Westen und die Sowjetunion: Einstellungen und Politik gegenüber der UdSSR in Europa seit 1917* (Paderborn, 1983), pp. 155–75.

10  On American Sovietology see Stephen F. Cohen, *The Soviet Experience: Politics and History since 1917* (New York, 1986), ch. 1.

11  Broadcast of 1 Oct. 1939, in Martin Gilbert, *Winston S. Churchill*, vol. VI (London, 1983), p. 50.

12  Robert C. Tucker, *Stalin as Revolutionary* (New York, 1973); Dmitri Volkogonov, *Stalin: Triumph and Tragedy*, ed. and transl. Harold Shukman (London, 1991).

13  Cf. e.g. Jonathan Haslam, *The Soviet Union and the Politics of Nuclear Weapons in Europe, 1969–1987* (London, 1989); George Schöpflin, 'The End of Communism in Eastern Europe', *International Affairs*, 66 (1990), 3–16; Charles Gati, *The Bloc That Failed: Soviet-East European Relations in Transition* (Bloomington, IN, 1990); Karen Dawisha, *Eastern Europe, Gorbachev and 'Reform': the Great Challenge* (2nd ed., Cambridge, 1990).

14  Quotation from 'Mr. X' article of July 1947, reprinted in George F. Kennan, *American Diplomacy* (Chicago, 1951), p. 127.

15  Quoted in Victor Rothwell, *Britain and the Cold War, 1941–1947* (London, 1982), p. 254.

16  John Lewis Gaddis, *The United States and the End of the Cold War: Implications, Reconsiderations, Provocations* (New York, 1992), p. 193. Cf. the categories of 'prudence', 'wisdom' and 'folly' used by Melvyn P. Leffler, *A Preponderance of Power: National Security, the Truman Administration, and the Cold War* (Stanford, CA, 1992), esp. pp. 498–511.

17  See especially the pioneering essays of Alan K. Henrikson, 'The Map as an "Idea": the Role of Cartographic Imagery during the Second World War', *The American Cartographer*, 2 (1975), 19–53; and 'America's Changing Place in the World: from "Periphery" to "Centre"?', in Jean Gottmann, ed., *Centre and Periphery: Spatial Variation in Politics* (London, 1980), pp. 73–100. The projection used in map 2 was a product of the cartographic revolution. It gave Americans a striking sense of their proximity to the Soviet Union across the Bering Strait from Alaska.

18  Thomas G. Paterson, *On Every Front: The Making of the Cold War* (2nd ed., New York, 1992), p. 100.

19  Though see Emily S. Rosenberg, *Spreading the American Dream: American Economic and Cultural Expansion, 1890–1945* (New York, 1982); Frank Ninkovich, *The Diplomacy of Ideas: U.S. Foreign Policy and Cultural Relations, 1938–1950* (New York, 1981); the uneven but suggestive collection of essays edited by Lary May, *Recasting America: Culture and Politics in the Age of the Cold War* (Chicago, 1989); and Stephen J. Whitfield, *The Culture of the Cold War* (Baltimore, MD, 1991).

20  Kenneth M. Jensen, ed., *Origins of the Cold War: the Novikov, Kennan and Roberts 'Long Telegrams' of 1946* (Washington, 1991); 'The Soviet Side of the Cold War: A Symposium', *Diplomatic History*, 15 (1991), 523–63.

21  Quotations from Daniel Yergin, *Shattered Peace: the origins of the Cold War and the National Security State* (London, 1978), p. 223; Hans J. Morgenthau, *Politics among Nations: the Struggle for Power and Peace* (2nd ed., New York, 1954), p. 339.

22  Robert M. Hathaway, *Ambiguous Partnership: Britain and America, 1944–1947* (New York, 1981), p. 2.

23  Geir Lundestad, 'Empire by Invitation? the United States and Western Europe, 1945–1952', *Journal of Peace Research*, 23 (1986), 263–77. This was a considerably revised and extended version of a paper originally published in the Society for Historians of American Foreign Relations' *SHAFR Newsletter*, 15/3 (Sept. 1984), 1–21. See also David Reynolds, 'The Origins of the Cold War: the European Dimension, 1944–1951', *Historical Journal*, 28 (1985), 497–515.

24  North Vietnam provides another example in the 1960s, with Ho adeptly playing on Sino-Soviet rivalry to ensure continued support from Moscow. Cf. R.B. Smith, *An International History of the Vietnam War*, vol. II (London, 1985), esp. chs. 3, 13.

25  Translated from Réné Girault and Robert Frank, eds., *La puissance française en question, 1945–1949* (Paris, 1986), p. 13.

26  William T. R. Fox, *The Superpowers: the United States, Britain and the Soviet Union – their Responsibility for Peace* (New York, 1944), p. 21.

27  Eisenhower to Gen. Alfred M. Gruenther, 26 Apr. 1954, Presidential papers, Whitman file, Administrative Series, box 16 (Dwight D. Eisenhower Library, Abilene, Kansas).

28  Cf. Ennio Di Nolfo's essay on 'Italy between the Superpowers', in Becker & Knipping, eds., *Power in Europe?*, pp. 485–500.

29  On the Italian military predicament see Leopoldo Nuti, *L'esercito italiano nel secondo dopo guerra, 1945–1950* (Rome, 1989), chs. 6–7.

30  Taking race or ideology as its defining feature. 'Asia stands on the Elbe', Konrad Adenauer stated bluntly in a letter in March 1946. See Adenauer, *Briefe, 1945–1947*, ed. Hans Peter Mensing (Berlin, 1983), p. 191. Ernst Nolte's vast, polemical survey of Germany and the Cold War from 1945 to the late 1960s depicted the two Germanies, in Hegelian vein, as incarnating the 'ideological and power-political struggle for the future structure of a united world' which had been going on since 1917 between the two 'militant universalisms' of American capitalism and Soviet communism. Ernst Nolte, *Deutschland und der Kalte Krieg* (Munich, 1974), esp. pp. 39, 57–8. See Renata Fritsch-Bournazel, *Confronting the German Question: Germans on the East-West Divide* (Oxford, 1988) for a succinct overview in English, and Josef Foschepoth, ed., *Kalter Krieg und Deutsche Frage: Deutschland im Widerstreit der Mächte, 1945–1952* (Göttingen, 1985) for some useful essays.

31  The title of Charles S. Maier's study of the late-1980s *Historikerstreit*, or historians' struggle over the Nazi era, which takes its title from the German concept of *Vergangenheitsbewältigung*, mastering the past: *The Unmasterable Past: History, Holocaust, and German National Identity* (Cambridge, MA, 1988).

32  A.J.P. Taylor, *The Course of German History* (London, 1945), p. 8.

33  Cf. Ger van Roon, *Small States in Years of Depression: the Oslo Alliance, 1930–1940* (Assen, the Netherlands, 1989). For more theoretical discussion see Michael I. Handel, *Weak States in the International System* (2nd ed., London, 1990).

34  See the discussion in Nikolaj Petersen, 'The Alliance Policies of the Smaller NATO Countries', in Lawrence S. Kaplan & Robert W. Clawson, eds., *NATO after Thirty Years* (Wilmington, DE, 1981), pp. 83–106.

35  Cf. Rolf Tamnes, 'Norway's Struggle for the Northern Flank, 1950–1952', in Riste, ed., *Western Security*, pp. 215–43; also Simon Duke, *United States Military Forces and Installations in Europe* (Oxford, 1989), chs. 3 and 9.

36  The famous phrase of Belgian diplomat André de Staercke, applied to France's involvement in NATO after the de Gaulle withdrawals. See Michael M. Harrison, *The Reluctant Ally: France and Atlantic Security* (Baltimore, MD, 1981), p. 162.

37  I develop this argument more fully in David Reynolds, 'The "Big Three" and the Division of Europe, 1945–48: an Overview', *Diplomacy and Statecraft*, 1 (1990), 111–36.

38  Quoted in Peter Hennessy, *Whitehall* (London, 1989), p. 412.

39  For a thorough analysis of the origins of the European Coal and Steel Community (ECSC) see John Gillingham, *Coal, Steel, and the Rebirth of Europe 1945–1955: the Germans and French from Ruhr Conflict to Economic Community* (New York, 1991).

40  Thomas Alan Schwartz, *America's Germany: John J. McCloy and the Federal Republic of Germany* (Cambridge, MA, 1991), p. 299.

41  Buchheim, quoted in Wolfram F. Hanrieder, *Germany, America, Europe: Forty Years of German Foreign Policy* (New Haven, CT, 1989), pp. 156–7; Wilhelm Röpke, *The German Question*, trans. E.W. Dickes (London, 1946), p. 21.

42  Ording is quoted by Pharo, above p. 201; in February 1946 Bevin depicted Britain as 'the last bastion of social democracy . . . against the red tooth and claw of American capitalism and the Communist dictatorship of Soviet Russia' (Robin Edmonds, *Setting the Mould: the United States and Britain, 1945–1950* (Oxford, 1986), p. 28). For a useful overview see Donald Sassoon, 'The Rise and Fall of West European Communism, 1939–1948', *Contemporary European History*, 1 (1992), 139–69.

43 Alfred Grosser, *The Western Alliance: European-American Relations since 1945* (London, 1980), p. 3; cf. e.g. John Lukacs, *1945: Year Zero* (New York, 1978), p. 13.

44 Cf. Charles P. Kindleberger, *The World in Depression, 1929–1939* (Berkeley, 1973); Michael J. Hogan, *The Marshall Plan: America, Britain and the Reconstruction of Western Europe, 1947–1952* (New York, 1987).

45 Josef Joffe, 'Europe's American Pacifier', *Foreign Policy*, 54 (spring 1984), 66–84.

46 Alan S. Milward, *The Reconstruction of Western Europe, 1945–1951* (London, 1984), ch. 3; see also Charles S. Maier, 'The Two Post-War Eras and the Conditions for Stability in Twentieth-Century Western Europe', *American Historical Review*, 86 (1981), esp. pp. 341–3. For a survey of recent literature, see William Diebold, Jr., 'The Marshall Plan in Retrospect: A Review of Recent Scholarship', *Journal of International Affairs*, 41 (1988), 421–35. On specific countries see Hogan, *The Marshall Plan* (on Britain); Gerard Bossuat, 'Le poids de l'aide américaine sur la politique économique et financière de la France en 1948', *Relations Internationales*, 37 (1984), 17–36; Elena Aga Rossi (ed.), *Il Piano Marshall e l'Europa* (Rome, 1983); Gerd Hardach, 'The Marshall Plan in Germany, 1948–52', *Journal of European Economic History*, 16 (1987), 433–85; and the essays in Charles S. Maier & Günter Bischof, eds., *The Marshall Plan and Germany: West German Development within the Framework of the European Recovery Program* (New York, 1991).

47 E.g. Alan K. Henrikson, 'The Creation of the North Atlantic Alliance, 1948–1952', [US] *Naval War College Review*, 32 (1980), 38, note 103; Stephen E. Ambrose, *Eisenhower: The President* (New York, 1984), pp. 505–6.

48 Walter Isaacson & Evan Thomas, *The Wise Men: Six Friends and the World They Made: Acheson, Bohlen, Harriman, Kennan, Lovett, McCloy* (New York, 1986) – 'the original best and brightest, men whose outsized personalities and forceful actions brought order to the postwar chaos' and 'forged an array of alliances' (p. 19).

49 Fitzroy Maclean in House of Commons, *Debates*, 5th series, 14 May 1952, vol. 500, col. 1506.

50 The focus in this book has been on relations between the United States and Europe, but Canada is worthy of note – poised between a British past and an American present and thereby an active participant in the early Cold War, especially in the preliminary negotiations for the North Atlantic Treaty. See Denis Smith, *Diplomacy of Fear: Canada and the Cold War, 1941–1948* (Toronto, 1988); the long essay on Canada and the Soviet Union over the same period in Lawrence Aronsen & Martin Kitchen, *The Origins of the Cold War in Comparative Perspective* (New York, 1988), pp. 148–98; the instructive memoir by Escott Reid, *Time of Fear and Hope: the Making of the North Atlantic Treaty* (Toronto, 1977). Note also James Eayrs, *In Defence of Canada: vol. 3, Peacemaking and Deterrence* and *vol. 4, Growing Up Allied* (Toronto, 1972, 1980); and John W. Holmes, *The Shaping of Peace: Canada and the Search for World Order, 1943–57* (2 vols., Toronto, 1979, 1982).

51 A guide to progress can be found in archival updates in the *Cold War International History Bulletin*, published by the Woodrow Wilson Center in Washington, from the spring of 1992. See also Odd Arne Westad, 'The Foreign Policy Archives of Russia: New Regulations for Declassification and Access', *SHAFR Newsletter*, 23/2 (June 1992), 1–10.

52 The starting point is the excellent collection of essays and documents edited by Günter Bischof & Josef Leidenfrost, *Die bevormundete Nation: Österreich und die Alliierten, 1945–1949* (Innsbruck, 1988). See also Audrey K. Cronin, *Great Power Politics and the Struggle over Austria, 1945–1955* (Ithaca, N.Y., 1986) and the dissertations by Robert G. Knight, 'British Policy towards Occupied Austria, 1945–50' (London University, 1986) and Günter Bischof. 'Between Responsibility and Rehabilitation: Austria in International Politics, 1940–1950' (Harvard University, 1989). On the central figure of Gruber see Lothar Höbelt & Othmar Huber, eds., *Für Österreichs Freiheit: Karl Gruber – Landeshauptmann und Aussenminister, 1945–1953* (Innsbruck, 1991).

53 Bischof, 'Between Responsibility', pp. 609, 807; Barbara Jelavich, *History of the Balkans*, II (Cambridge, 1983), p. 344.

54 John Barber & Mark Harrison, *The Soviet Home Front, 1941–1945* (London, 1991), pp. 206–7 (28 million); Nikolai Rudensky, 'War as a Factor of Ethnic Conflict and Stability in the USSR', in G. Ausenda, ed., *Effects of War on Society* (San Marino, 1992), pp. 187–8 (38 million), citing work of Boris Sokolov. The latter estimate includes deaths from continued Stalinist terror.

55 *Foreign Relations of the United States, 1947*, II (Washington, 1974), p. 343 (meeting of 15

April). See also Josef Foschepoth, 'Konflikte in der Reparationspolitik der Alliierten' in Foschepoth (ed.), *Kalter Krieg und Deutsche Frage*, pp. 175–97.

56 R. Michael Berry, *American Foreign Policy and the Finnish Exception: Ideological Preferences and Wartime Realities* (Helsinki, 1988); Tuomo Polvinen, *Between East and West: Finland in International Politics, 1944–1947* (Minneapolis, 1986). For fuller guidance to the historiography see Jukka Nevakivi, 'Finland and the Cold War', *Scandinavian Journal of History*, 10 (1985), 211–24. A good introductory history is D.G. Kirby, *Finland in the Twentieth Century* (London, 1979).

57 Polvinen, *Between East and West*, pp. 280–1.

58 Michael Berry, 'The Soviet-American Alliance in 1944: The Case of Finland with Reference to Romania', unpublished paper, 4th Soviet-American symposium on World War Two, Rutgers University, New Brunswick, N.J., 16–18 Oct. 1990.

59 Antony Polonsky, 'Stalin and the Poles, 1941–7', *European History Quarterly*, 17 (1987), 453–92.

60 Irène Lagani, 'Les communistes des Balkans et la guerre civile grecque', *Communisme*, 9 (1986), 60–78; see also Lars Baerentzen, John O. Iatrides & Ole L. Smith, eds., *Studies in the History of the Greek Civil War, 1945–1949* (Copenhagen, 1987), esp. the essays by John Iatrides, Elisabeth Barker and Joze Pirjevec; and Wayne S. Vucinich, ed., *At the Brink of War and Peace: The Tito-Stalin Split in a Historic Perspective* (New York, 1982), esp. the essay by Nicholas Pappas.

61 M.R. Myant, *Socialism and Democracy in Czechoslovakia, 1945–1948* (Cambridge, 1981), chs. 7–9, esp. pp. 198–202.

62 Sassoon, 'Rise and Fall of West European Communism', pp. 157–8, 165–6.

63 Robin Okey, *Eastern Europe, 1740–1980: Feudalism to Communism* (London, 1982), pp. 196–7. For some suggestive insights into events in various Central and East European countries see the uneven collection of essays in Thomas T. Hammond, ed., *Witnesses to the Origins of the Cold War* (Seattle, 1982).

64 House of Commons, *Debates*, 5th series, 12 Nov. 1940, vol. 365, col. 1617.

65 See the epigraph to this volume, quoted from François Genoud, ed., *The Testament of Adolf Hitler: The Hitler-Bormann Documents, February–April 1945* (London, 1961), p. 107.

66 A.W. DePorte, *Europe between the Superpowers: The Enduring Balance* (New Haven, 1984), p. 9; cf. Ludwig Dehio, *Germany and World Politics in the Twentieth Century* (London, 1959), e.g. p. 128. On the nineteenth century see Geoffrey Barraclough, 'Europa, Amerika und Russland in Vorstellung und Denken des 19. Jahrhunderts', *Historische Zeitschrift*, 203 (Oct. 1966), 280–315.

67 A point stressed in Gabriel Kolko's new preface to the reissue of his 1968 book *The Politics of War: the World and the United States Foreign Policy, 1943–1945* (New York, 1990), esp. pp. xix–xxiii. On this theme see also David Reynolds, '1940: Fulcrum of the Twentieth Century?', *International Affairs*, 66 (1990), 325–50.

## 1. The United States

1 Walter Lippmann, *The Cold War* (New York, 1947); George F. Kennan, 'The Sources of Soviet Conduct', *Foreign Affairs* 25 (July 1947); Anders Stephanson, *Kennan and the Art of Foreign Policy* (Cambridge, MA, 1989). Lippmann's book was actually a compilation of newspaper articles that originally appeared in September/October 1947; by November he was habitually using the concept, arguing a little prematurely that the Russians had already lost the Cold War and knew it. Hence the potential for agreement. See Ronald Steel, *Walter Lippmann and the American Century* (New York, 1980), pp. 444–7.

2 Walter LaFeber is a partial exception. See the periodization in his 'Consensus and Cooperation: a View of United States Foreign Policy, 1945–1980', in George Schwab, ed., *United States Foreign Policy at the Crossroads* (Westport, CT, 1982). John Lewis Gaddis is also interested in the periodization of the Cold War, which he does in terms of elements of *stability* (see his *The Long Peace* (New York, 1987); yet there is no real explication of the concept itself.

3 This is in part inspired by Hans Morgenthau's classic *Politics Among Nations* (New York, 1948, 1985 (with Kenneth W. Thompson)), ch. 21, and by my friend Thomas Biersteker.

4 Essentially this is the distinction between a public enemy (defined as an equal) and a private foe (to be hated) already present in classical antiquity but occluded during the middle ages,

only to be resurrected during the fully developed European state system after 1648. See Carl Schmitt, *The Concept of the Political* (New Brunswick, N.J., 1976 (first published 1927)), pp. 28–9 and passim.

5  See Michael Mann, *States, Capitalism and War* (Cambridge, 1988), pp. 177–8. Though his periodization is different from mine, see also Gaddis, *The Long Peace*, ch. 8. Gaddis usefully points to the emergence of rules of engagement; on the other hand, I think he over-emphasizes the role of nuclear weapons in creating 'stability'.

6  At last count there were 1311 members, 172 of whom were foreign.

7  Sally Marks, 'The World According to Washington', *Diplomatic History*, 11 (summer 1987).

8  Christopher Thorne, 'After the Europeans: American Designs for the Remaking of Southeast Asia', *Diplomatic History*, 12 (Spring 1988). For responses to Thorne (and Marks), see the interesting symposium in *Diplomatic History*, 14 (Fall 1990).

9  Charles S. Maier, 'Marking Time: the Historiography of International Relations', in Michael Kammen, ed., *The Past Before Us* (Ithaca, N.Y., 1980).

10  For useful introductions to the history of 'international relations', see Stanley Hoffmann, 'An American Social Science: International Relations', *Daedalus*, 106 (summer 1977) and Steve Smith, 'The Development of International Relations as a Social Science', *Millennium*, 16 (Summer 1987).

11  A representative, if uneven, collection of critical texts is James Der Derian and Michael J. Shapiro, eds., *International/Intertextual Relations* (Lexington, MA, 1989).

12  See the symposium with McMahon et al. in *Diplomatic History*, 14 (fall 1990). John Lewis Gaddis, more than any other historian responsible for bringing in neo-realist theory, has himself recently indicated broadening interests (e.g. in questions of time and space), though he maintains a basic attachment to the models of political science. See his 'New Conceptual Approaches to the Study of American Foreign Relations', *Diplomatic History*, 14 (summer 1990). I have criticized the historiographical genre of national security history in 'Ideology and Neorealist Mirrors', *Diplomatic History*, 17 (spring 1993).

13  For good overviews, see Thomas Hammond, 'Introduction' in Hammond, ed., *Witnesses to the Origins of the Cold War* (Seattle, WA, 1982); Geir Lundestad, *America, Scandinavia and the Cold War 1945–1949* (New York, 1980), ch. 1; and J. Samuel Walker, 'Historians and Cold War Origins: the New Consensus', in Gerald K. Haines & J. Samuel Walker, eds., *American Foreign Relations.* (Westport, CT, 1981). For archetypal traditionalist works, see the *oeuvre* of Herbert Feis, in particular *From Trust to Terror* (New York, 1970).

14  John W. Spanier, *American Foreign Policy Since World War II* (4th ed., New York, 1971), p. 28.

15  Louis Halle, *The Cold War as History* (New York, 1967), p. xiii.

16  See George F. Kennan, *Memoirs* (Boston, 1967). On the most straightforward realist historian, see Jerald A. Combs, 'Norman Graebner and the Realist View of American Diplomatic History', *Diplomatic History*, 11 (summer 1987).

17  Arthur M. Schlesinger, Jr., 'Origins of the Cold War', *Foreign Affairs*, 46 (Oct. 1967).

18  On American historiography in this period and generally, see Peter Novick's path-breaking *That Noble Dream: the 'Objectivity' Question and the American Historical Profession* (Cambridge, 1988).

19  See Athan G. Theoharis's useful survey, 'Revisionism', in Alexander De Conde, ed., *Encyclopedia of American Foreign Policy* (New York, 1978).

20  Ian Tyrell, *The Absent Marx* (Westport, CT, 1986); Gabriel Kolko, 'The Premises of Business Revisionism', *Business History Review*, 33 (autumn 1959).

21  Novick, *That Noble Dream*, p. 445.

22  The following account is, unless otherwise noted, based on Novick, *That Noble Dream*, Tyrell, *The Absent Marx* and Jonathan Wiener, 'Radical Historians and the Crisis in American History, 1959–1980', *Journal of American History*, 76 (Sept. 1989).

23  Apart from the preceding references, see also Lloyd Gardner, 'Consensus History and Foreign Policy' in De Conde, ed., *Encyclopedia*. Major exponents included Richard Hofstadter, Louis Hartz, and David Potter (but conspicuously not Arthur M. Schlesinger, Jr and C. Vann Woodward). Antipathy to the work of Charles Beard was dominant throughout though, as was of course anti-communism.

24  This sketch is based on remembrances offered at the Williams memorial conference, held in Washington, DC, on 10 June 1990, especially those by Wendy Williams, Lloyd Gardner,

Walter LaFeber, Gar Alperovitz and Thomas McCormick; and on subsequent interviews with McCormick and Fred Harvey Harrington in Madison, WI, May 1992.

25 On Williams's writings, see further Bradford Perkins, 'The Tragedy of American Diplomacy: Twenty-five years after', *Reviews in American History*, 12 (March 1985); J.A. Thompson, 'William A. Williams and the "American Empire"', *Journal of American Studies*, 7 (April 1973); David W. Noble, 'William Appleman Williams and the Crisis of Public History', in Lloyd Gardner, ed., *Redefining the Past* (Corvallis, OR, 1986); and idem, *The End of American History* (Minneapolis, 1985). Generally, see Charles S. Maier, 'Revisionism and the Interpretation of the Cold War Origins', *Perspectives in American History*, 1970: 4; and Stanley Hoffmann, 'Revisionism Revisited', in Lynn H. Miller & Ronald W. Preussen, eds., *Reflections on the Cold War* (Philadelphia, 1974).

26 William A. Williams, *The Tragedy of American Diplomacy* (rev. ed., New York, 1973), p. 219.

27 This was a critique from both left and right. See for example Eugene D. Genovese, 'Beard's Economic Interpretation of History', in Marvin Swanson, ed., *Charles Beard: An Observance of the Centennial of his Birth* (Greencastle, IN, 1976); Genovese, 'William Appleman Williams on Marx and America', *Studies on the Left* 6 (Jan.–Feb. 1966); and, from the opposite side, Robert W. Tucker, *The Radical Left and American Foreign Policy* (Baltimore, MD, 1971), pp. 55–7. See also Thompson, 'The "American Empire"'. There are occasional systemic formulations in Williams, e.g. his classification of the Cold War as 'the confrontation between the United States, the Soviet Union, and the People's Republic of China, between 1943 and 1971' which in turn is 'only the most recent phase of a more general conflict between the established system of western capitalism and its internal and external opponents'. Williams, *Tragedy*, p. 10.

28 William A. Williams, 'Open Door Interpretation', in De Conde, ed., *Encyclopedia*, pp. 201–2. For his most poignant statement on theoretical references, see 'A Historian's Perspective', *Prologue* (fall 1974).

29 Lloyd Gardner, *Architects of Illusion* (Chicago, 1970), p. 319. The other outstanding Wisconsin work in the area is Walter LaFeber, *America, Russia, and the Cold War* (New York, 1967).

30 Gardner, *Architects*, pp. 318–19.

31 Gabriel Kolko, *The Politics of War* (London, 1969), pp. 3–6, 619–22; Gabriel and Joyce Kolko, *The Limits of Power* (New York, 1972), pp. 2–5, 709–15.

32 Kolko, *Limits*, pp. 6–7.

33 Gabriel Kolko, *The Politics of War* (New York, 1990), p. xxii.

34 On the European point, see Maier, 'Revisionism'. See also Hoffmann, 'Revisionism Revisited' (cf. n. 25).

35 Gabriel Kolko continues this in his history of Vietnam, *The Anatomy of War* (New York, 1985), wherein the Vietnamese side receives unusual but proper attention.

36 D.F. Fleming, *The Cold War and Its Origins* (Garden City, N.Y., 1961).

37 Daniel Yergin, *Shattered Peace* (Boston, 1977); Warren Kimball, *The Juggler: Franklin Roosevelt as a Wartime Statesman* (Princeton, N.J., 1991). Yergin is scarcely a revisionist and does not claim to be one. Having published his book at the tail end of détente, he was indeed quick to deny any relation when détente was replaced by renewed Cold War. His work is better characterized as a neo-realist attack on the realist Kennan, articulator of the negative 'Riga axioms', for not being realistic. The connection with Fleming is from that angle tenuous: for Yergin, Truman is a neo-Wilsonian idealist. Interesting early critiques of his work are Carolyn Eisenberg, 'Toothless Revisionism', *Diplomatic History*, 2 (summer 1978) and Daniel F. Harrington, 'Kennan, Bohlen, and the Riga Axioms', *Diplomatic History*, 2 (fall 1978).

38 Michael Leigh's 'Is there a Revisionist Thesis on the Origins of the Cold War?', *Political Science Quarterly*, 89 (March 1974), demonstrates the internal differences but misses the unifying political theme.

39 Gar Alperovitz, *Atomic Diplomacy* (New York, 1965, rev. ed., 1985); Herbert Feis, *Japan Subdued* (Princeton, N.J., 1961).

40 J. Samuel Walker, 'The Decision to Use the Bomb', *Diplomatic History*, 14 (winter 1990), p. 111.

41 Lundestad is Norwegian but has published in the United States and intervened vigorously in the American debate. It would be pedantry, therefore, to exclude him from the purview of this essay.

42 Geir Lundestad, *America, Scandinavia and the Cold War 1945–1949* (New York, 1980), ch. 1; idem., *The American Non-Policy Towards Eastern Europe 1943–1947* (Tromso, 1978); John Lewis Gaddis, 'The Emerging Post-Revisionist Synthesis on the Origins of the Cold War', *Diplomatic History*, 7 (summer 1983).

43 Geir Lundestad, 'Empire by Invitation?', *SHAFR Newsletter*, 15 (Sept. 1984).

44 John Lewis Gaddis, *The United States and the Origins of the Cold War* (New York, 1972). The criticism for being fuzzy was evident already in some reviews of this first major work. See Barton Bernstein, 'Cold War Orthodoxy Restated', *Reviews in American History*, 1 (Dec. 1973); and Robert Schulzinger, 'Moderation in Pursuit of Truth is No Virtue; Extremism in defense of Moderation is A Vice', *American Quarterly*, 27 (May 1975). Gaddis's eclecticism was first emphasized by Warren Kimball in 'The Cold War Warmed Over', *American Historical Review*, 79 (Oct. 1974).

45 Vojtech Mastny, *Russia's Road to the Cold War* (New York, 1979); John Lewis Gaddis, *Strategies of Containment* (New York, 1982), pp. 9, 18; Gaddis, 'The Insecurities of Victory' (1984), republished in his *The Long Peace*. Gaddis ('The Emerging Post-Revisionist Synthesis', p. 176) characterizes Mastny's work, rather hyperbolically, as 'a striking and powerful new interpretation'; to me it is a useful map of Stalin's misdeeds in Eastern Europe but in a framework of old traditionalism.

46 Gaddis, *The Long Peace*, p. 34.

47 Ibid., p. 40.

48 Ibid., pp. 44, 43, chs. 2 and 8 passim. See also Gaddis, 'The Emerging Post-Revisionist Synthesis'.

49 Gaddis, *Strategies*, p. 357.

50 Stephanson, *Kennan*, ch. 4; Gaddis, *The Long Peace*, chs. 2, 3 and 8.

51 Gaddis, 'The Emerging Post-Revisionist Synthesis', p. 180.

52 The idea is not exactly new. Ronald Steel, from a more critical standpoint, referred in the mid-1960s to the 'accidental empire'. See his *Pax Americana* (New York, 1967), ch. 2, where J.R. Seeley's famous (or notorious) aside about the British Empire as a product of absent-mindedness is put to analogical use.

53 Aside from *The Long Peace*, ch. 8, see also his speculative piece 'How the Cold War Might End', *The Atlantic*, (Nov. 1987), overtaken like so many other things by the events themselves, but interesting precisely in that light. It should be compared with his 'Coping with Victory', *The Atlantic*, (May 1990), where he pleads (not unpersuasively) for the preservation of Russia as a great power. The implications of the long-peace argument have recently been drawn out with stark clarity in John J. Mearsheimer, 'Why We Will Soon Miss the Cold War', *The Atlantic*, (Aug. 1990). Leftists, primarily from the third world, express similar views from a wholly different premise, arguing something along the lines that 'the imperialist United States, in being the only remaining superpower, is now free to intervene at will in the third world'.

54 Robert A. Pollard, *Economic Security and the Origins of the Cold War, 1945–1950* (New York, 1985), pp. 3, 9, 246, 249, ix.

55 Ibid., pp. 247–8.

56 Pollard comes perilously close to 'Hurrapatriotismus', D.C. Watt's somewhat unfair description of Arthur M. Schlesinger, Jr. See Watt's 'Rethinking the Cold War: A Letter to a British Historian', *Political Quarterly*, 49 (Oct. 1978), p. 456.

57 For corporatist manifestos, see Thomas McCormick, 'Drift or Mastery? A Corporate Synthesis for American Diplomatic History', *Reviews of American History*, 10 (Dec. 1982); Michael J. Hogan, 'Corporatism: a Positive Appraisal', *Diplomatic History*, 10 (fall 1986); Joan Hoff Wilson, 'Symposium', *Diplomatic History*, 5 (fall 1981); Hoff Wilson, 'The Future of American Diplomatic History', *SHAFR Newsletter*, 16 (June 1985). To the extent that the desire for synthesis means that one thinks there are too many monographs around and not enough interpretation and periodization of the general it is of course quite praiseworthy.

58 See (aside from the preceding references) Ellis W. Hawley, 'The Discovery and Study of a "Corporate Liberalism"', *Business History Review*, 52 (autumn 1978); Martin J. Sklar, *The Corporate Reconstruction of American Capitalism, 1890–1916* (Cambridge, 1988), pp. 18–19; Michael J. Hogan, *Informal Entente: the Private Structure of Cooperation in Anglo-American Diplomacy, 1918–1928*, (Columbia, MO, 1977); Gabriel Kolko's partial *auto-critique*, 'Intelligence and the Myth of Capitalist Rationality in the United States', *Science and Society*, 44

(summer 1980); Joan Hoff Wilson, 'Economic Foreign Policy' in De Conde, ed., *Encyclopedia*. On the Wisconsin side one must also mention the influence of Thorstein Veblen.

59 On corporatism particularly see Birgitta Nedelmann & Kurt G. Meier, 'Theories of Contemporary Corporatism Static or Dynamic?' in Philippe C. Schmitter, ed., *Trends Toward Corporatist Intermediation* (Beverly Hills, CA, 1979). For the American 1920s, see Hogan, *Informal Entente*, and Ellis W. Hawley, 'Herbert Hoover, the Commerce Secretariat, and the Vision of an "Associative State", 1921–1928', *Journal of American History*, 61 (June 1974).

60 Charles S. Maier, 'The two postwar eras and the conditions for stability in twentieth-century Western Europe' (1977), an essay republished in his *In Search of Stability* (Cambridge, 1987) (quotes pp. 180, 183). See also the important companion piece in the same work, 'The politics of productivity: foundations of American international economic policy after World War II' (originally published in 1981). I have simplified, perhaps unduly, Maier's nuanced and provocative analysis.

61 Michael J. Hogan, *The Marshall Plan: America, Britain, and the Reconstruction of Western Europe, 1947–1952* (Cambridge, 1987), pp. 3, 18, 427, 429, 443.

62 Alan Milward, *The Reconstruction of Western Europe, 1945–1951* (London, 1984); Milward, 'Was the Marshall Plan Necessary?', *Diplomatic History*, 13 (spring 1989); William Diebold, Jr, 'The Marshall Plan in Retrospect: a review of recent scholarship', *Journal of International Affairs*, 41 (summer 1988).

63 For Gaddis's general assessment of the subject, see his 'The Corporate Synthesis: a Skeptical View', *Diplomatic History*, 10 (fall 1986). For a Wisconsin critique of Hogan's earlier work, see Carl Parrini, 'Anglo-American Corporatism and the Economic Diplomacy of Stabilization in the 1920s', *Reviews in American History*, 6 (Sept. 1978).

64 See Robert H. Salisbury, 'Why No Corporatism in America?', in Schmitter, ed., *Corporatist Intermediation* for an argument that agrees with this impression.

65 McCormick, 'Drift or Mastery?'; John P. Rossi, 'A "Silent Partnership"?: the U.S. Government, RCA, and Radio Communications with East Asia, 1919–1928', *Radical History Review*, 33 (1985), (quote p. 45); McCormick, 'Corporatism: A Reply to Rossi', ibid.; McCormick, *America's Half-Century* (Baltimore, MD, 1989).

66 McCormick, *America's Half-Century*, pp. 33–4, 23, 48–76, 16, and passim.

67 Peter J. Taylor, *Britain and the Cold War* (London, 1990), p. 1. Colin Gray's *oeuvre* exemplifies the geopolitical discourse of the right, e.g. his *The Geopolitics of the Nuclear Era: Heartlands, Rimlands, and Technological Revolution* (New York, 1977). The reason for the absence of the term during the post-war period was of course that it had become associated with German *Geopolitik*, i.e. with ideas of brutal territorial expansionism. 'Geopolitics' has been used variously (Gearoid O'Tuathail tells me he has found least six major usages). The common area of Wallersteinian world systems theory and neo-realism lies in the positing of the state. From the capitalist world system (his fundamental category), Wallerstein derives the functional necessity of a state system to go with it. See Immanuel Wallerstein, *Geopolitics and Geoculture* (Cambridge, 1991); and Mark Edward Rupert, 'Producing Hegemony: State/Society Relations and the Politics of Productivity in the United States', *International Studies Quarterly*, 34 (1990), pp. 427–56.

68 But see Michael J. Hogan, 'In the shadow of the left: the postrevisionist history of American economic diplomacy', *Reviews in American History*, 13 (June 1985), for a critique of any overvaluation of the strategic. For him, too, the vision is ultimately a totality; but a single element dominates.

69 Melvin Leffler, 'The American Conception of National Security and the Beginnings of the Cold War, 1945–48'. *American Historical Review*, 89 (April 1984); and 'Reply', ibid., 399, 279.

70 Ibid. Quotes from pp. 363, 371.

71 Melvyn P. Leffler, 'The United States and the Strategic Dimensions of the Marshall Plan', *Diplomatic History*, 12 (summer 1988), 278, 306.

72 Leffler, 'Reply', pp. 398–9. Gaddis's original argument, essentially that the form took over the substance, can be found in *Strategies*.

73 Melvyn P. Leffler, *The Preponderance of Power* (Stanford, CA, 1992), p. 504; idem., 'Reply', 399.

74 John Lewis Gaddis, 'Comment', Bruce Kuniholm, 'Comment', *American Historical Review*, 89 (April 1984). For Kuniholm's quotes, see pp. 387–8. He, like Gaddis, is much influenced by Mastny's notion of what are legitimate security concerns.

75  For further materials on their disagreement, see the Bruce Kuniholm's work *The Origins of the Cold War in the Near East* (Princeton, N.J., 1980); Leffler's review of it 'From Cold War to Cold War in the Near East', *Reviews in American History*, 9 (March 1981); and his 'Strategy, Diplomacy, and the Cold War: the United States, Turkey, and NATO, 1945–1952', *Journal of American History*, 71 (March 1985).

76  Gaddis, 'Comment'.

77  Leffler, *Preponderance*, p. 512. This formidably researched work exhibits a certain ambivalence. Traces of the 1984 position can be found, for example, in chapter 2; whereas the introduction and conclusion are marked analytically by, as it were, a certain *unease*. My colleague Robert Jervis first pointed out the changing nature of Leffler's argument to me.

78  Ibid., pp. 513, 512.

79  *The Long Peace* contains virtually nothing about the third world except reflections on the extent to which the United States tried to split the communist world. The long peace, of course, refers to the European and industrialized world.

80  See e.g. Ronald Steel, *Pax Americana*; Les Adler & Thomas G. Paterson, 'Red Fascism: the Merger of Nazi Germany and Soviet Russia in the American Image of Totalitarianism, 1930's–1950's', *American Historical Review*, 75 (April 1970). Among Paterson's more notable works are *Soviet-American Confrontation* (Baltimore, MD, 1973) and *On Every Front* (New York, 1979, 2nd ed., 1992).

81  Stephen F. Cohen, *Rethinking The Soviet Experience* (New York, 1985), p. 4 and ch. 1 passim.

82  Marshall D. Shulman, *Stalin's Foreign Policy Reappraised* (New York, 1966 (first published 1963)); Adam Ulam, 'Re-reading the Cold War', *Interplay*, March 1969. Later examples of a more heterodox kind could be mentioned, such as William O. McCagg, *Stalin Embattled* (Detroit, 1978) and Albert Resis, *Stalin, the Politburo, and the Onset of the Cold War* (Pittsburgh, PA, 1988). For a more mainstream (and important) work to be read alongside Mastny's, see William Taubman's *Stalin's American Policy* (New York, 1982).

83  This is an essay on the cold war in its European context and there is therefore no space to cover these other important areas. But on East Asia, which is especially important, see the survey of the literature in Robert J. McMahon, 'The Cold War in Asia: Towards a New Synthesis?', *Diplomatic History*, 12 (summer 1988).

84  Fraser J. Harbutt, *The Iron Curtain: Churchill, America, and the Origins of the Cold War* (New York, 1986).

85  See David Harvey, *The Condition of Postmodernity* (Baltimore, MD, 1988); and Richard James Blackburn, *The Vampire of Reason: an Essay in the Philosophy of History* (London, 1990).

86  See Mann, *States, War, and Capitalism*.

87  Pierre Bourdieu, *In Other Words. Essays Towards a Reflexive Sociology* (Stanford, CA, 1990), conceptualizes this phenomenon.

88  Carl Schmitt's critique of classical liberalism is worth quoting at some length here: 'In a very systematic fashion liberal thought evades or ignores state and politics and moves instead in a typical always recurring polarity of two heterogeneous spheres, namely ethics and economics, intellect and trade, education and property. . . . We arrive at an entire system of demilitarized concepts. . . . Ethical and moral pathos and materialist economic reality combine in every typical liberal manifestation and give every political concept a double face. Thus the political concept of battle in liberal thought becomes competition in the domain of economics and discussion in the intellectual realm. Instead of a clear distinction between the two different states, that of war and that of peace, there appears the dynamic of perpetual competition and perpetual discussion.' Schmitt, *The Concept of the Political*, pp. 70–2. This theme of depoliticization is somewhat similar in tenor to Maier's argument about post-war productionism. For Schmitt's analysis of the peculiarities of American foreign policy, see 'Völkerrechtliche Formen des modernen Imperialismus' (1932) in his *Positionen und Begriffe* (Berlin 1988 (first published 1940)).

89  Thus I disagree with Fred Halliday's systemic model in 'The Ends of the Cold War', *New Left Review*, 180 (Mar./Apr. 1990), which seems to be based on the capital/labour analogy.

90  Space, beyond its physical aspect, is a social construct, a product of determinate social relations; and geopolitical 'reason' is itself a form of discourse. There is no geopolitics, and certainly no account of it, that is not at the same time discursive and ideological. On geopolitics, see Gearoid O'Tuathail, 'Critical Geopolitics: the Social Construction of Space and Place in the Practice of Statecraft', Ph.D. diss. in geography, Syracuse University, 1988. See

also Henri Lefebvre, *The Production of Space* (Oxford, 1991).

91  The argument is not, of course, that third-world conflict was merely a product of the Cold War; in some instances it was, but the chief point is that various local conflicts were unnecessarily intensified and prolonged.

## 2. The Soviet Union

1  'Political report of the Embassy of the USSR in the USA for the year 1947', 25 Sept. 1948; Archives of Foreign Affairs of the Russian Federation (AVP RF), fond 0129, op. 31a, d. 1, l. 3.

2  *History of Diplomacy* (5 vols., Moscow, 1959–75); the Cold War is covered by vol. 5 in two parts.

3  Most notable were A.G. Mileykovsky, ed., *International Relations after the Second World War* (2 vols., Moscow, 1962); V.G. Trukhanovsky, *Vneshnaya politika Anglii v period 2 mirovoy voyni, 1939–1945* (Moscow, 1965), a study of British foreign policy which places the blame for the Cold War on British intrigues; G.A. Trofimenko, *SShA: politika, voyna, ideologiya* (Moscow, 1976), on the United States; and N. Sivachev & N. Yakovlev, *Russia and the United States* (Chicago, 1980).

4  O.L. Stepanova, *'The cold war': a historical retrospective* (Moscow, 1982); probably the last salvo of the old guard was in Lev Voznesensky & Valentin Falin, 'Who unleashed "the cold war"', *Pravda*, 29 Aug. 1988, 6.

5  See a rejoinder to Voznesensky & Falin by John L. Gaddis, *Pravda*, 31 Oct. 1988.

6  Attempts to identify domestic roots of American international behaviour in the activities of powerful elites always evoked a favourable response among functionaries of the old regime, including Soviet diplomats, intelligence officers and some members of the Politburo.

7  See Alexander Dallin & Gail W. Lapidus, eds., *Soviet System in Crisis: A Reader of Western and Soviet Views* (Boulder, CO, 1991), pp. 487–530.

8  Adam Ulam, Richard Pipes, David Dallin and Vojtech Mastny, among others, became spiritual guides for Soviet revisionists.

9  The Archives of the Foreign Ministry began to declassify its files in 1989–90; after the demise of the Communist Party its archives were reorganized into two separate centres open to scholars: the Russian Centre for the Preservation and Study of Contemporary Historical Documents (RTSKhIDNI) in Sept. 1991 and the Storage Centre for Contemporary Documentation (TSKhSD) in Feb. 1992. The military archives are becoming sporadically open to researchers; the KGB archives, however, are still outside a declassification process.

10  On American post-revisionist literature, see ch. 1, pp. 35–41.

11  Andrei Gromyko, *Memories* (New York, 1990).

12  Sergei Khrushchev, *Khrushchev on Khrushchev*, ed. William Taubman (Boston, 1990); Fyodor Burlatsky, *Khrushchev and the First Russian Spring* (New York, 1991); Georgi A. Arbatov, *The System: An Insider's Life in Soviet Politics* (New York, 1992).

13  Strobe Talbott, ed., *Khrushchev Remembers* (Boston, 1970), and *Khrushchev Remembers: The Last Testament* (Boston, 1974); Jerrold L. Schechter with Vyacheslav V. Luchkov, *Khrushchev Remembers: The Glasnost Tapes* (Boston, 1990). An authorized full text is being published in Russian in *Voprosy Istorii*, starting in 1991.

14  *Sto sorok besed s Molotovym: Iz dnevnika F. Chuyeva* (Moscow, 1991); see a brief review by Woodford McClellan in the *Cold War International History Project Bulletin* (henceforth *CWIHP Bulletin*), 1 (spring 1992), 17–20.

15  Thanks to Brown University's project in 1987–92. See also Oleg Troyanovsky, 'Karibski krizis – vzglyzd iz Kremlya,' *International Affairs*, Moscow, 2–3 (Mar.-Apr. 1992), 170–9.

16  Georgi Kornienko, Gromyko's former deputy, combines recollections and research in a series of articles about the origins of the Cold War, the Cuban missile crisis, and the Kennedy-Khrushchev meeting in Vienna in 1961 in *Novaya i Noveyshaya Istoriya*, 6, 1990, 105–22; 3, 1991, 77–92; 2, 1992, 97–106. On the co-ordination of policy information in Molotov's office and on Soviet German policy in general, see Viktor Yerofeyev, 'Ten Years of Secretaryship in the Foreign Commissariat', *International Affairs*, 8–9 (Aug.-Sept. 1991).

17  See Arkady N. Shevchenko, *Breaking with Moscow* (New York, 1985).

18  For an update on the Soviet archives see James G. Hershberg, 'Soviet Archives: The Opening Door', *CWIHP Bulletin*, 1 (spring 1992), 1, 12–15, 23–7.

19 Many of these are becoming available since the summer of 1992. The trial of the Communist Party of the Soviet Union (CPSU) in the Russian Constitutional Court helped to promote the process.

20 The Foreign Ministry has released some diplomatic cables from Hungary in 1956 and Czechoslovakia in 1968.

21 Among the exceptions is a collection of documents from Molotov's and Vyshinsky's secretariat in the Foreign Ministry and parts of Andrei Zhdanov's papers in the Russian Centre. Some documents from the Presidential Archives were released for an exhibition at the Library of Congress, Washington, in June–July 1992.

22 The monolithic view was held by most of the Soviet experts in the United States: see Martin Fainsod, *How Russia is Ruled* (Cambridge, MA, 1953) and William Taubman, *Stalin's American Policy* (New York, 1982). For the latter view see William O. McCagg, *Stalin Embattled, 1943–1948* (Detroit, 1978) and Robert M. Slusser, *The Berlin Crisis of 1961: Soviet-American Relations and the Struggle for Power in the Kremlin, June–November 1961* (Baltimore, MD, 1973).

23 According to Adam Ulam, Walt Rostow and others, the issue of hegemony was stimulated by the deterioration of Sino-Soviet relations, which coincided with Khrushchev's brinksmanship over Berlin and Cuba (1958–62). The theme of the tyranny of the weak has been explored for US relations with NATO by Geir Lundestad (see above, pp. 7 and 37).

24 Robert C. Tucker, *Stalin as Revolutionary* (New York, 1973), pp. 467–8.

25 Karen Horney, *Neurosis and Human Growth* (New York, 1950), p. 87.

26 Horney, *Neurosis*, p. 176.

27 Milovan Djilas, *Conversations with Stalin* (New York, 1962), p. 74.

28 *Sto sorok besed*, p. 103.

29 J.V. Stalin, *Rech na predvybornom sobranii izbirateley – Stalinskogo izbiratelnogo okruga g. Moskvy* (Moscow, 1946), p. 6.

30 *Sto sorok besed*, p. 90.

31 TSKhSD, fond 5, op. 30, d. 163, 11. 91–2.

32 From 1945 Stalin had his emissaries staying with the Chinese communists, reporting on their activities and building up 'friendly relations' – a typically Stalinist way of hedging all bets and providing levers of influence. See the interviews with one of these emissaries, Ivan V. Kovalev, by S.V. Goncharov, in *Problemy Dalnego Vostoka*, 6, 1991, and 1–2, 1992.

33 *Beseda c korrespondentom 'Pravdy' otnositelno rechi g. Cherchillya 13 marta 1946 g.* (Moscow, 1946), p. 4.

34 J.V. Stalin, *Beseda c korrespodentom 'Pravdy'* (Moscow, 1951), p. 13.

35 J.V. Stalin, *Economicheskiye problemy socialisma v SSSR* (Moscow, 1953), p. 30.

36 Ibid., p. 32.

37 Ibid., pp. 32–3.

38 Ibid., p. 34.

39 Interview with Vladimir I. Yerofeev, Stalin's interpreter and a member of Molotov's secretariat, Moscow, 14 Aug. 1992.

40 Djilas, *Conversations with Stalin*, p. 114.

41 Horney, *Neurosis*, p. 179.

42 *Sto sorok besed*, p. 14.

43 Ibid.

44 Ibid., pp. 102–3.

45 Ibid., p. 103.

46 Ibid., p. 100.

47 *Khrushchev Remembers*, p. 368.

48 *Khrushchev Remembers: The Glasnost Tapes*, p. 147.

49 Contrary to the dominant Western view of Yalta, from the Soviet standpoint it was they who made concessions – a commitment to principles of bourgeois democracy in liberated Europe, and a promise to help the United States against Japan.

50 Its name and functions changed slightly over time: Dept. of International Information (Jul. 1944–Dec. 1945), Dept. of Foreign Policy (Jan. 1946–Jul. 1948), Dept. of External Relations (Jul. 1948–Mar. 1949), Foreign Policy Commission (Apr. 1949–1953).

51 'Es wird zwei Deutschlands geben', *Frankfurter Allgemeine Zeitung*, 30 Mar. 1991, 16. Could it be that, contrary to the interpretation of the journalists, Stalin, during this meeting on 4

June 1945 talked not about a division of Germany but about the possibility of two ways of development for a future Germany: along Western lines, leading inexorably to militarism and revanchism, and along 'democratic' lines?

52  Interview with Boris Ponomarev, a veteran of the International Dept, Moscow, July 1990.
53  *Sto sorok besed s Molotovym*, p. 78.
54  Ibid., p. 76.
55  Novikov telegram, 27 Sept. 1946, in Kenneth M. Jensen, ed., *Origins of the Cold War: the Novikov, Kennan and Roberts 'Long Telegrams' of 1946* (Washington: U.S. Inst. for Peace, 1991). Although a cable from the Soviet Ambassador in Washington, Nikolai V. Novikov, this was substantially Molotov's homework. He edited the text heavily in Paris in Sept. and apparently had it up his sleeve to present to Stalin at an appropriate moment. For different views of the telegram see 'The Novikov Telegram', *Diplomatic History*, 15 (fall 1991), 523–63, and Novikov's memoirs, *Vospominaniya Diplomata: Zapiski, 1938–1947* (Moscow, 1989).
56  Woodford McClellan, 'Molotov Remembers', *CWIHP Bulletin*, 1 (spring 1992), 19; Valentin Berezhkov, 'Smertny prigovor', *Sovershenno sekretno*, 12, 1991, 13.
57  *Sto sorok besed*, pp. 100, 103.
58  AVP RF, fond 06, op. 8, p. 47, d. 794, 11. 11–12; d. 795, 11. 3, 4, 16; interview with V. Gerashenko (Soviet adviser on economic affairs, 1944–7), Moscow, June 1991.
59  Harriman saw Stalin on vacation in Oct. 1945 and agreed to accept Bulgaria and Romania as an exclusive Soviet sphere of influence. In return, Stalin renounced his claim to seek in Japan anything but token representation for Soviet interests.
60  AVP RF, fond 48'z', p. 20, d. 8, 1.172; for an American version see Adam Ulam, *Expansion and Coexistence: Soviet Foreign Policy, 1917–73* (2nd ed., New York, 1974), p. 447.
61  Until the summer of 1947 Molotov and Soviet diplomats attempted, in their usual awkward way, to maintain tactical rapprochement with the French against the British on such issues as the future of the Ruhr and Saar.
62  *Sto sorok besed*, pp. 88–9.
63  Quotations from *Khrushchev Remembers*, p. 100; and, on the economy, E. Varga to Molotov, 24 Jun. 1947, RTSKhIDNI, fond 17, op. 128, d. 408, 11. 34–8.
64  12 Dec. 1947, RTSKhIDNI, 17/128, d. 1101, 11. 184–5.
65  For more on the struggle between Zhdanovites and proponents of state interests (Malenkov, Beria, etc.) see Robert Slusser, ed., *Soviet Economic Policy in Postwar Germany* (New York, 1953) and Gavriel Ra'anan, *International Policy Formation in the USSR* (Hamden, CT, 1983), pp. 88–9.
66  It was promoted by the staff of the political adviser in Germany, V.V. Semyonov – AVP RF, fond 06, op. 9, p. 43, d. 632, 11. 16–20.
67  On this see V. Zubok, 'Soviet intelligence and the cold war: the case of the "small" Committee of Information (1952–1953)', forthcoming in *Diplomatic History*.
68  Interview with Yerofeev, 14 Aug. 1992.
69  Among recent publications in Russia on this subject see Yuri S. Aksyonov, 'Poslevoyenni stalinizm: udar po intelligentsii', *Kentavr*, (Oct.-Nov. 1991), 80–9: Ye. Zubkova, 'Obshchestvernnaya atmosphera posle voyni (1948–1952)', *Svobodnaya misl*, 9 (June 1992), 79–88.
70  G. M. Kornienko, 'U istokov "kholodnoi voiny"', *Novaya i Noveyshaya Istoriya*, 6, 1990, 105–22.
71  Deborah W. Larson, 'Crisis Prevention and the Origins of the Austrian State Treaty', *International Organization*, 41 (1987), 33–58; Robert C. Tucker, 'Research Note on Stalin's Death' (U.S.-Soviet seminar, Athens, OH, Oct. 1988); Matthew Evangelista, 'Cooperation Theory and Disarmament Negotiations in the 1950s', *World Politics*, 42 (1990), 502–29.
72  *Khrushchev Remembers: The Glasnost Tapes*, p. 73.
73  See James Richter, 'Reexamining Soviet policy towards Germany in 1953' *Europe – Asia Studies*, 45 (1993), 671–91.
74  Molotov spoke approvingly of Khrushchev at one point: 'I think that his . . . Russian nationalism helped him understand the state's interests', *Sto sorok besed*, p. 336.
75  *Khrushchev Remembers: the Glasnost Tapes*, p. 69.
76  *Sto sorok besed*, p. 104.
77  A similar phenomenon was apparent on the American side: see John L. Gaddis, *Strategies of Containment* (New York, 1982), pp. 240–3.
78  *Khrushchev Remembers: The Glasnost Tapes*, pp. 74–8.

79 13 Feb. 1948, RTSKhIDNI, fond 77, op. 3, d. 100, 1. 4. It should be noted that definitive sources on Soviet military doctrines and operational plans after 1946 are still classified.
80 Proceedings of the July 1953 Plenary Meeting of the Central Commt. of the CPSU, now available in English in D.N. Stickle, ed., *The Beria Affair* (New York, 1992).
81 TSKhSD, fond 5, op. 30, d. 126, 11. 38, 39, 41.
82 *Pravda*, 13 Mar. and 27 Apr. 1954; S.A. Kiselev, 'Yadernoye oruzhiye i vneshepoliticheskaya misl partii (1945–1955)', *Voprosy Istorii KPSS*, 8, 1991, 75.
83 Interview with Maj. Gen. Valentin Larionov, Moscow Jan. 1990.
84 Zubok, 'Soviet assessments in the cold war,' 41.
85 Interview with G.M. Kornienko, former Soviet First Deputy Foreign Minister, Moscow, 17 July 1992.
86 AVP RF fond 595, op. 6, d. 769, vol. 11, 1. 130.
87 Melvin P. Leffler, *A Preponderance of Power* (Stanford, CA, 1992), pp. 497–511.
88 Robert V. Daniels, *Russia: The Roots of Confrontation* (Cambridge, MA, 1985), p. 164.

### 3. Great Britain

1 Walter LaFeber, *America, Russia and the Cold War, 1945–1980* (New York, 1980), p. 1.
2 D.C. Watt, 'Rethinking the Cold War: a Letter to a British Historian', *The Political Quarterly*, 49 (1978), 446.
3 Joseph Frankel, *British Foreign Policy, 1945–1973* (London, 1975), p. 9.
4 F.S. Northedge, *Descent from Power: British Foreign Policy, 1945–1973* (London, 1974), pp. 357, 362.
5 Lecture of 24 Feb. 1950, quoted by Victor Rothwell, 'Britain and the First Cold War', in Richard Crockatt & Steve Smith, eds., *The Cold War Past and Present* (London, 1987), p. 67.
6 F.S. Northedge & Audrey Wells, *Britain and Soviet Communism: the Impact of a Revolution* (London, 1982), p. 200.
7 M.A. Fitzsimmons, *The Foreign Policy of the British Labour Government* (Notre Dame, IN, 1953); Leon D. Epstein, *Britain – Uneasy Ally* (Chicago, 1954); Eugene J. Meehan, *The British Left Wing and Foreign Policy: a Study of the Influence of Ideology* (New Brunswick, N.J., 1960).
8 Watt, 'Letter', 446–8.
9 David Reynolds, 'The Origins of the Cold War: the European Dimension, 1944–1951', *Historical Journal*, 28 (1985), 497–515.
10 Ian S. McDonald, ed., *Anglo-American Relations since the Second World War* (New York, 1974), pp. 181–2.
11 Michael Dockrill, *British Defence since 1945* (Oxford, 1988), p. 151; Alec Cairncross, *Years of Recovery: British Economic Policy, 1945–1951* (London, 1985), p. 278; John Baylis, *Anglo-American Defence Relations, 1939–80: the Special Relationship* (London, 1981), p. 43.
12 E.g. Wm. Roger Louis, *The British Empire in the Middle East, 1945–1951* (Oxford, 1984); David Fieldhouse, 'The Labour Governments and the Empire-Commonwealth, 1945–1951', in Ritchie Ovendale, ed., *The Foreign Policy of the British Labour Governments, 1945–1951* (Leicester, 1984), pp. 83–120; Partha Sarathi Gupta, 'Imperialism and the Labour Government of 1945–51', in Jay Winter, ed., *The Working Class in Modern British History* (Cambridge, 1983), pp. 99–124; John Kent, 'Bevin's Imperialism and the Idea of Euro-Africa, 1945–49' in Michael Dockrill & John W. Young, eds., *British Foreign Policy, 1945–56* (London, 1989), pp. 47–76.
13 Christopher Thorne, *Allies of a Kind: the United States, Britain, and the War against Japan, 1941–1945* (London, 1978). For other works in similar vein on the 1940s, see Robert M. Hathaway, *Ambiguous Partnership: Britain and America, 1944–1947* (London, 1981); Terry H. Anderson, *The United States, Great Britain, and the Cold War, 1944–1947* (Columbia, MO, 1981); Fraser J. Harbutt, *The Iron Curtain: Churchill, America, and the Origins of the Cold War* (New York, 1986); Robin Edmonds, *Setting the Mould: the United States and Britain, 1945–1950* (Oxford, 1986); Richard A. Best, Jr., *'Co-operation with Like-Minded Peoples': British Influences on American Security Policy, 1945–1949* (New York, 1986); Henry Butterfield Ryan, *The Vision of Anglo-America: The US–UK Alliance and the Emerging Cold War, 1943–1946* (Cambridge, 1987). Of these authors, only Thorne and Edmonds are not American.
14 U.S. Department of State, *Foreign Relations of the United States, 1951*, IV (Washington, 1985), pp. 981, 985–6. Henceforth cited as *FRUS*.
15 See e.g. Robert A. Pollard, *Economic Security and the Origins of the Cold War, 1945–1950* (New

York, 1985), and Deborah Welch Larson, *Origins of Containment: A Psychological Explanation* (Princeton, N.J., 1985).

16  Alan Bullock, *Ernest Bevin: Foreign Secretary, 1945–1951* (London, 1983).

17  See the essays in Anne Deighton, ed., *Britain and the First Cold War* (London, 1990); also Raymond Smith & John Zametica, 'The Cold Warrior: Clement Attlee Reconsidered, 1945–7', *International Affairs*, 61 (1985), 237–52.

18  Winston S. Churchill, *The Second World War* (6 vols., London, 1948–54), VI, pp. 498–9. On Churchill's Soviet policy see Martin Kitchen, 'Winston Churchill and the Soviet Union during the Second World War', *Historical Journal*, 30 (1987), 415–36; Warren F. Kimball, 'Naked Reverse Right: Roosevelt, Churchill, and Eastern Europe from TOLSTOY to Yalta – and a Little Beyond', *Diplomatic History*, 9 (1985), 1–24.

19  Quotations from Julian Lewis, *Changing Direction: British Military Planning for Post-War Strategic Defence, 1942–1947* (London, 1988), pp. 120, 104 respectively.

20  John Lewis Gaddis, *The Long Peace: Inquiries into the History of the Cold War* (New York, 1987), pp. 225–6.

21  Quotations from Dixon and Sir Orme Sargent in Graham Ross, ed., *The Foreign Office and the Kremlin, 1941–1945: British Documents on Anglo-Soviet Relations, 1941–1945* (Cambridge, 1984), pp. 251, 255.

22  Ray Merrick, 'The Russia Committee of the British Foreign Office and the Cold War, 1946–47', *Journal of Contemporary History*, 20 (1985), 454.

23  Lawrence Aronsen & Martin Kitchen, *The Origins of the Cold War in Comparative Perspective: American, British and Canadian Relations with the Soviet Union, 1941–1948* (New York, 1988), p. 124.

24  Memo. of 2 April 1946, in FO 371/56832, N6344/605/38 (Public Record Office, henceforth PRO).

25  Best, *'Co-operation'*, pp. 120–2.

26  Harbutt, *Iron Curtain*, p. 267.

27  Anne Deighton, *The Impossible Peace: Britain, the Division of Germany, and the Origins of the Cold War* (London, 1990), p. 74. On British policy towards Germany see also Sean Greenwood, 'Bevin, the Ruhr and the Division of Germany: August 1945-December 1946', *Historical Journal*, 29 (1986), 203–12; Josef Foschepoth, 'Grossbritannien und die Deutschlandfrage auf den Aussenministerkonferenzen, 1946/47', in Foschepoth & Rolf Steininger, eds., *Die britische Deutschland- und Besatzungspolitik, 1945–1949* (Paderborn, 1985), pp. 65–85.

28  FO memo, 3 May 1946, CAB 129/9, CP (46) 186 (PRO).

29  Deighton, *Impossible Peace*, p. 95.

30  Sir Richard Clarke, *Anglo-American Economic Collaboration in War and Peace, 1942–1949*, ed. Sir Alec Cairncross (Oxford, 1982), p. 156.

31  Anderson, *The United States*, pp. 171–5; Robert Frazier, 'Did Britain start the Cold War?: Bevin and the Truman Doctrine', *Historical Journal*, 27 (1984), 715–27; Lawrence S. Wittner, *American Intervention in Greece, 1943–1949* (New York, 1982), ch. 2.

32  *Time*, 24 Feb. 1947, p. 30.

33  Ben T. Moore to Clair Wilcox, 28 July 1947, in *FRUS, 1947*, III, p. 239.

34  See Reynolds, 'Origins of the Cold War' p. 509, n. 32.

35  Bullock, *Bevin*, p. 404.

36  Michael J. Hogan, *The Marshall Plan: America, Britain, and the Reconstruction of Western Europe, 1947–1952* (Cambridge, 1987), pp. 44–5, 51–3.

37  Bullock, *Bevin*, p. 422.

38  Quoted in Avi Shlaim, Peter Jones & Keith Sainsbury, *British Foreign Secretaries since 1945* (London, 1977), p. 48. For the new approach see esp. John W. Young, *Britain, France and the Unity of Europe, 1945–1951* (Leicester, 1984), and also the essay by Geoffrey Warner, 'The Labour Governments and the Unity of Western Europe, 1945–51', in Ritchie Ovendale, ed., *The Foreign Policy of the British Labour Governments, 1945–1951* (Leicester, 1984), pp. 61–82.

39  The debate is summarized in Bert Zeeman, 'Britain and the Cold War: an Alternative Approach; the Treaty of Dunkirk Example', *European History Quarterly*, 16 (1986), 343–67.

40  Sargent, minute, 1 Oct. 1945, FO 371/44557, AN 2560/22/45 (PRO).

41  Bullock, *Bevin*, pp. 268–9.

42  Merrick, 'Russia Committee', p. 463.

43 Quotations from CAB 129/23, CP (48) 5 and 6 (PRO).

44 Lawrence S. Kaplan, *NATO and the United States: the Enduring Alliance* (Boston, 1988), p. 1.

45 Young, *Britain, France*, pp. 84–6.

46 CAB 129/25, CP (48) 72 (PRO).

47 Minute of 5 Jan. 1949, in Clarke, *Anglo-American Economic Collaboration*, pp. 208–9.

48 Avi Shlaim, 'Britain, the Berlin blockade and the Cold War', *International Affairs*, 60 (1984), p. 14. Cf. his book *The United States and the Berlin Blockade, 1948–1949* (Berkeley, CA, 1983).

49 Sir Nicholas Henderson, *The Birth of NATO* (London, 1982), pp. vii–ix. For similar, though more muted, affirmations of the British role see Alan K. Henrikson, 'The Creation of the North Atlantic Alliance, 1948–1952', *U.S. Naval War College Review*, 32 (May–June 1980), 32; Nikolaj Petersen, 'Who Pulled Whom and How Much? Britain, the United States and the Making of the North Atlantic Treaty', *Millennium*, 11 (1982), 93–114; Best, *'Co-operation'*, ch. 6.

50 Cees Wiebes & Bert Zeeman, 'The Pentagon Negotiations, March 1948: the Launching of the North Atlantic Treaty', *International Affairs*, 59 (1983), 351–63, quoting from p. 361. See also Martin H. Folly, 'Britain and the Issue of Italian Membership of NATO, 1948–49', *Review of International Studies*, 13 (1987), 177–96.

51 CAB 129/23, CP (48) 5 (PRO).

52 Quotations from Geoffrey Warner, 'Britain and Europe in 1948: The View from the Cabinet', in Josef Becker & Franz Knipping, eds., *Power in Europe?: Great Britain, France, Italy and Germany in a Postwar World, 1945–1950* (Berlin, 1986), pp. 40–2. See also Donald C. Watt, 'Hauptprobleme der britischen Deutschlandpolitik, 1945–1949', in Claus Scharf & Hans-Jürgen Schröder, eds., *Die Deutschlandpolitik Grossbritanniens und die Britische Zone, 1945–1949* (Wiesbaden, 1979), pp. 15–28.

53 Quotation from memo by Sir Ivone Kirkpatrick, 15 Dec. 1949, in Matthias Peter, 'Britain, the Cold War and the Economics of German Rearmament, 1949–51' in Deighton, ed., *Britain and the First Cold War*, p. 277.

54 Dean Acheson, *Present at the Creation: My Years in the State Department* (New York, 1969), p. 399. Cf. Timothy P. Ireland, *Creating the Entangling Alliance: the Origins of the North Atlantic Treaty Organization* (London, 1981), ch. 6.

55 Geoffrey Warner, 'The British Labour Government and the Atlantic Alliance, 1949–1951', in Olav Riste, ed., *Western Security: the Formative Years. European and Atlantic Defence, 1947–1953* (Oslo, 1985), p. 255: Dalton quoting Attlee in Cabinet on 30 July 1951.

56 Tripartite American/British/French declaration, 14 Sept. 1951, in Denise Folliot, ed., *Documents on International Affairs, 1951* (London, 1954), p. 136.

57 John W. Young, 'German Rearmament and the European Defence Community', in Young, ed., *Foreign Policy of Churchill's Peacetime Administration*, ch. 3.

58 Sir Anthony Eden, *Full Circle* (London, 1960), p. 151; cf. Saki Dockrill, *Britain's Policy for West German Rearmament, 1950–1955* (Cambridge, 1991), esp. ch. 7; and Olaf Mager, *Die Stationerung der britischen Rheinarmee: Grossbritanniens EVG-Alternative* (Baden-Baden, 1990).

59 Quotations from Joseph Jones, *The Fifteen Weeks* (New York, 1955), p. 130; Thomas G. Paterson, *On Every Front: the Making of the Cold War* (New York, 1979), p. 23.

60 FO American Dept. memo, 21 Mar. 1944, FO 371/38523, AN 1538/16/45.

61 For this argument see David Reynolds, *Britannia Overruled: British Policy and World Power in the Twentieth Century* (London, 1991), chs. 6–7.

62 Alec Cairncross, *Years of Recovery: British Economic Policy, 1945–51* (London, 1985), pp. 44, 87.

63 See Peter G. Boyle, 'The British Foreign Office and American Foreign Policy, 1947–48' *Journal of American Studies*, 16 (1982), 377–8.

64 Ritchie Ovendale, *The English-Speaking Alliance: Britain, the United States, the Dominions and the Cold War, 1945–1951* (London, 1985), esp. ch. 7.

65 Michael Dockrill, 'The Foreign Office, Anglo-American Relations and the Korean War, June 1950–June 1951', *International Affairs*, 62 (1986), 459–76. See more generally Rosemary Foot, *The Wrong War: American Policy and the Dimensions of the Korean Conflict, 1950–1953* (London, 1985), and Peter Lowe, *The Origins of the Korean War* (London, 1986).

66 For a study of British policy, see James Cable, *The Geneva Conference of 1954 on Indochina* (London, 1986).

67  Frankel, *British Foreign Policy*, p. 198.
68  Quoted in David Dimbleby & David Reynolds, *An Ocean Apart: the Relationship between Britain and America in the Twentieth Century* (London, 1988), p. 204.
69  Martin Gilbert, *Winston S. Churchill*, VIII, 1945–65 (London, 1988), p. 831.
70  See John W. Young, 'Churchill, the Russians and the Western Alliance: The Three-Power Conference at Bermuda, December 1953', *English Historical Review*, 101 (1986), 889–912; Young, 'Cold War and Détente with Moscow', in ed. John W. Young, *The Foreign Policy of Churchill's Peacetime Administration, 1951–1955* (Leicester, 1988), ch. 2; M. Steven Fish, 'After Stalin's Death: The Anglo-American Debate over New Cold War', *Diplomatic History*, 10 (1986), 333–55; Brian White, 'Britain and the Rise of Détente', in Crockatt & S. Smith, eds., *The Cold War*, pp. 91–109 (cited in note 5).
71  Harold Macmillan, *Tides of Fortune, 1945–55* (London, 1969), p. 587.
72  Louise L'Estrange Fawcett, 'Invitation to the Cold War: British Policy in Iran, 1941–47', in Deighton, ed., *Britain and the First Cold War*, ch. 10.
73  For an example, see Daniel F. Harrington, 'United States, United Nations and the Berlin Blockade', *The Historian*, 52 (1990), 262–85. For a trenchant critique of some of the limitations of Bevin's policy see John Kent & John W. Young, 'The "Western Union" Concept and British Defence Planning', in Richard Aldrich, ed., *British Intelligence, Strategy and the Cold War, 1945–1951* (London, 1992), pp. 166–92.
74  Cf. Donald Cameron Watt, 'Britain and the Historiography of the Yalta Conference and the Cold War', *Diplomatic History*, 13 (1989), 89; Rothwell, 'Britain and the First Cold War', p. 58 (cited in note 5).
75  Bullock, *Bevin*, quoting from pp. 843, 423 respectively.
76  Deighton, *Impossible Peace* (cited in note 27).
77  John Kent, 'The Empire and the Origins of the Cold War, 1944–49', in Deighton, ed., *Britain and the First Cold War*, ch. 9.
78  Dimbleby & Reynolds, *An Ocean Apart*, p. 188.
79  Memo of 2 March 1946, in CAB 131/2, DO (46) 27. The seminal article on Attlee in 1945–7 is by Raymond Smith and John Zametica (see note 17), but see also similar claims for Attlee's neglected but 'pivotal' role in the diplomacy of the wartime coalition in Trevor Burridge, 'Great Britain and the Dismemberment of Germany at the End of the Second World War', *International History Review*, 3 (1981), 572ff.
80  Smith and Zametica, 'The Cold Warrior', p. 250.
81  Ross, ed., *The Foreign Office and the Kremlin*, p. 240 (cited in note 21).
82  Arthur J. Marder, *From the Dreadnought to Scapa Flow: The Royal Navy in the Fisher Era, vol. I: The Road to War, 1904–1914* (London, 1961), pp. 322–3. The underlined words in this official memo were omitted by Churchill when he published the quotation subsequently in his war memoirs.

## 4. France

1  The position on primary sources is as follows. French Foreign Ministry archives are now open up to December 1959. But the French official publication (*Documents Diplomatiques Français*, henceforth DDF) starts only in July 1954. For the 1947 to 1953 period one should use *Journal du Septennat* by Vincent Auriol (at that time President of the Republic) – 6 vols. already published (Paris, 1970– ). The most important manuscript collections for this topic are the papers of Georges Bidault at the National Archives and of Pierre Mendès-France at the Institut Pierre Mendès-France.
2  See Jean Laloy, *Yalta* (Paris, 1989), pp. 80–91, and Laloy's article 'A Moscou: entre Staline et de Gaulle', *Revue des Études Slaves*, LIV (1982).
3  See the unpublished dissertation of Philippe Buton, *Le Parti communiste français à la Libération, stratégie et implantation* (Paris, 1988). The author published a résumé under the same title in *L'Information Historique*, 51 (1989).
4  See the portrait of Stalin by de Gaulle in the third volume of the *Mémoires de guerre: le Salut 1944–1946* (Paris, 1959), pp. 77–9 of the Press Pocket edition. For de Gaulle's misgivings about the Soviet Union see Laloy's article, cited above, note 2.
5  I have developed this conception in 'La politique française à l'égard de la Rhénanie, 1944–1946' in Peter Hüttenberger & Hansgeorg Molitor, eds., *Französen und Deutschen am Rhein,*

*1789–1918–1945* (Essen, 1989).

6  Raymond Poidevin, 'La politique allemande de la France en 1945' in Maurice Vaïsse, ed., *8 mai 1945: la victoire en Europe* (Lyon, 1985). See also de Gaulle's speech in Baden-Baden on 5 Oct. 1945, in Charles de Gaulle, *Lettres, Notes et Carnets, 8 mai 1945–18 juin 1951* (Paris, 1984), pp. 95–8, and a note from him dated 18 Jan. 1946, ibid., p. 183.

7  Instructions to the French delegation at the San Francisco conference, April 1945, in de Gaulle, *Lettres, Notes et Carnets, juin 1943–mai 1945* (Paris, 1983), pp. 417–25.

8  *Mémoires de guerre: le Salut 1944–1946*, p. 250.

9  Général Pierre Lassale, 'Sécurité face à l'Est dans l'immédiat après-guerre', in Institut Charles de Gaulle, ed., *De Gaulle et la Nation face aux problèmes de défense, 1945–1946* (Paris, 1983), p. 111.

10  Wilfried Loth, *Sozialismus und Internationalismus: die französischen Sozialisten und die Nachkreigsordnung Europas, 1940–1950* (Stuttgart, 1977).

11  We tend to think that W. Loth exaggerates the importance of the Third Force movement in Europe after 1945 in his study *The Divison of the World 1941–1955* (London, 1989).

12  Soutou, 'La politique française à l'égard de la Rhénanie . . .', p. 52.

13  Georgette Elgey, *La République des Illusions* (Paris, 1965), p. 118.

14  Jacques Dumaine, *Quai d'Orsay 1945–1951* (Paris, 1955), p. 78.

15  Michel Margairaz, 'Autour des accords Blum-Byrnes: Jean Monnet entre le consensus national et le consensus atlantique', *Revue Histoire, Economie, Société*, 2 (1982); Jacques Portes, 'Les origines de la légende noire des accords Blum-Byrnes sur le cinéma', in *Revue d'Histoire moderne et contemporaine*, 33, avril–juin 1986. For a severe indictment of those agreements seen as French vassalage to the United States, see Annie Lacroix-Riz, 'Négociations et signature des accords Blum-Byrnes (octobre 1945–mai 1946)', *ibid.*, 31, juillet-septembre 1984.

16  Soutou, 'La politique française', pp. 55–61.

17  Ibid.

18  See my article 'Georges Bidault et la construction européenne, 1944–1954', based on the Bidault Papers at the National Archives, in *Revue d'Histoire diplomatique*, 105, 1991/3–4.

19  Wolfgang Krieger, *General Lucius D. Clay und die amerikanische Deutschlandpolitik 1945–1949* (Stuttgart, 1987), p. 220.

20  Reinhard Schreiner, *Bidault, der MRP und die französische Deutschlandpolitik, 1944–1948* (Frankfurt, 1985), pp. 91ff.

21  See a letter from Pierre-Henri Teitgen, who was deputizing for Bidault at the Quai d'Orsay during the Moscow Conference, dated 14 March, explaining to Bidault the importance of Truman's speech (Papiers Bidault, Archives Nationales, 457 AP 60) and Bidault's answer of 29 March, published in Pierre-Henri Teitgen, *Faites entrer le témoin suivant, 1940–1958: de la Résistance à Vᵉ République* (Rennes, 1988) pp. 364–5.

22  Soutou, 'La politique française', pp. 64–5.

23  Soutou, 'Georges Bidault et la construction européenne . . .', pp. 275–8.

24  Philippe Robrieux has used American archives to show that the break with the Communists happened without American pressure: 'Le PCF vu par les services spéciaux américains', *Le Monde*, 22 Nov. 1981.

25  Wilfried Loth, 'Frankreichs Kommunisten und der Beginn des Kalten Krieges', *Vierteljahreshefte für Zeitgeschichte*, 26 (1978).

26  Soutou, 'Georges Bidault et la construction européenne . . .', p. 278.

27  Service Historique de l'Armée de Terre, Fonds Ely, carton 6, dossier 2: letter of 27 July 1947, from General Humbert to Prime Minister Ramadier and note dated 23 Sept.

28  Elgey, *La République des Illusions* (Paris, 1965), p. 380.

29  Soutou, 'Georges Bidault et la construction européenne . . .', pp. 278–9.

30  Pierre Mélandri, *Les États-Unis face à l'unification de l'Europe, 1945–1954* (Paris, 1980), p. 160.

31  Soutou, 'Georges Bidault et la construction européenne . . .', pp. 284–5.

32  Ibid.; Pierre Guillen, 'La France et la question de la défense de l'Europe occidentale, du Pacte de Bruxelles (mars 1948) au plan Pleven (octobre 1950)', in *Revue d'Histoire de la Deuxième Guerre Mondiale et des Conflits contemporains*, 144 (octobre 1986). Maurice Vaïsse, 'L'échec d'une Europe franco-britannique ou comment le Pacte Bruxelles fut créé et délaisse', in Raymond Poidevin, ed., *Histoire des débuts de la construction européenne, mars 1948–mai 1950* (Brussels, 1986), pp. 369–89.

33  One should mention here the influential progressive Catholics in France, who believed in the possibility of a compromise between the Church and the communist regime, along the lines of the *Pax* movement in Poland. The important left Catholic review *Esprit* is a good example of that attitude which precluded a true understanding of what was actually taking place in Poland. See Michel Winock, *Histoire politique de la revue 'Esprit', 1930–1950* (Paris, 1975).

34  Cyril Buffet, *Mourir pour Berlin: la France et l'Allemagne, 1945–1949* (Paris, 1991).

35  Alan Bullock, *Ernest Bevin, Foreign Secretary* (Oxford, 1985), p. 536.

36  Pierre Mélandri, *L'Alliance atlantique* (Paris, 1979), pp. 45–6.

37  For all this see Soutou, 'Georges Bidault et la construction européenne . . .', pp. 280–93.

38  Pierre Guillen, 'La France et la question de la défense de l'Europe occidentale . . .'; Krieger, *Clay*, p. 492; Raymond Poidevin, *Robert Schuman* (Paris, 1986), p. 301.

39  Krieger, *Clay*, p. 333.

40  This aspect has not yet attracted much scholarly attention. See Denise Artaud & Lawrence Kaplan, eds., *Diên Biên Phu* (Lyon, 1989).

41  Poidevin, *Schuman*, pp. 304–5.

42  Soutou, 'Georges Bidault et la construction européenne . . .', pp. 287–90.

43  Poidevin, *Schuman*, pp. 208ff; Franz Knipping, 'Que faire de l'Allemagne? Die französische Deutschlandpolitik, 1945–1950', in Franz Knipping & Ernst Weisenfeld, eds., *Eine ungewöhnliche Geschichte: Deutschland-Frankreich seit 1870* (Bonn, 1988).

44  Pierre Guillen, 'Les chefs militaires français, le réarmement de l'Allemagne et la CED (1950–1954)', *Revue d'Histoire de la Deuxième Guerre mondiale et des Conflits contemporains*, 129 (janvier 1983).

45  Poidevin, *Schuman*, pp. 306–9.

46  Alain Girard & Jean Stoetzel, 'L'opinion publique devant la CED', in Raymond Aron & Daniel Larner, eds., *La querelle de la CED* (Paris, 1956).

47  For all these developments see Poidevin, *Schuman*, pp. 309ff.

48  Geneviève Rouche, 'Le Quai d'Orsay face au problème de la souveraineté allemande', *Revue d'Histoire diplomatique*, 104, 1990/1–2.

49  Georges-Henri Soutou, 'La France et les notes soviétiques de 1952 sur l'Allemagne', *Revue d'Allemagne*, 20, 3 (1988).

50  For a very good example of this programme see a note from Mendès-France's office at the Quai d'Orsay dated 21 July 1954 in *DDF, 1954* (Paris, 1987), n° 1.

51  Pierre Guillen, 'Les chefs militaires français . . .'; R. Poidevin, 'René Mayer et la politique extérieure de la France (1943–1953)', in *Revue d'Histoire de la Deuxième Guerre mondiale*, 134 (avril 1984); 'La France devant le problème de la CED: incidences nationales et internationales (été 1951 à été 1953)', *ibid.*, 129 (janvier 1983).

52  Soutou, 'Georges Bidault et la construction européenne . . .', pp. 301–5.

53  For an impassioned account of the fight against EDC see Michel Debré, *Trois Républiques pour une France, Mémoires*, II, *1946–1958* (Paris, 1988).

54  For the ideological climate in France at the time see David Caute, *Le communisme et les intellectuels français, 1914–1966* (Paris, 1967); Jeanine Verdès-Leroux, *Au service du Parti: le parti communiste, les intellectuels et la culture (1944–1956)* (Paris, 1983); Philippe Robrieux, *Histoire intérieure du parti communiste français*, II, *1945–1972* (Paris, 1981); Laurent Lemire, *L'homme de l'ombre: Georges Albertini, 1911–1983* (Paris, 1990).

55  Soutou, 'La France et les notes soviétiques', pp. 270–2.

56  Ibid, and Soutou, 'Georges Bidault et la construction européenne . . .', p. 302.

57  See Pierre Mendès-France, *Oeuvres complètes*, III, *Gouverner c'est choisir 1954–1955* (Paris, 1986); François Bédarida & Jean-Pierre Rioux, eds., *Pierre Mendès-France et le mendésisme* (Paris, 1985); René Massigli, *Une comédie des erreurs* (Paris, 1978); for the following development, unless otherwise indicated, see Georges-Henri Soutou, 'La France, l'Allemagne et les accords de Paris', in *Relations internationales*, 52 (hiver 1987); and 'Pierre Mendès-France et l'URSS' in René Girault, ed., *Pierre Mendès-France et le rôle de la France dans le monde*, (Grenoble, 1991).

58  François Joyaux, *La Chine et le réglement de la première guerre d'Indochine* (Paris, 1979).

59  See Artaud & Kaplan, eds., *Diên Biên Phu*.

60  Although the solution did have its problems: see Bruno Thoss, 'Die Lösung der Saarfarge 1954/1955', *Vierteljahreshefte für Zeitgeschichte*, 38, 1990/2.

61  Georges-Henri Soutou, 'La politique nucléaire de Pierre Mendés-France', in *Relations Internationales*, n° 59 (automne 1989).

62 Conversation between Joxe, French ambassador in Moscow, and Bulganin on 5 May, *DDF*, 1955/1, n° 249; circular telegram from 28 May, ibid., n° 305.
63 *DDF*, 1955/1, n° 305.
64 Telegram from the French High Commissar in Vienna, 11 February, *DDF*, 1955/1, n° 69. See Vojtech Mastny, 'Kremlin Politics and the Austrian Settlement', in *Problems of Communism*, July-August 1982.
65 *DDF*, 1955/1, n° 305.
66 Soutou, 'La France, l'Allemagne et les Accords de Paris', pp. 466–7.
67 Edgar Faure, *Mémoires*, II (Paris, 1984), pp. 134–41 and 151–3; letter to Eisenhower and Churchill, 22 March, in *DDF*, 1955/1, n° 139.
68 British reply, 29 March, *DDF* 1955/1, n° 157; tel. from Washington, 11 April, n° 187.
69 *DDF*, 1955/1, n° 305.
70 Note, 7 May, ibid., n° 261.
71 Note, 4 June, ibid., n° 320.
72 Conversation between Blankenhorn and Jean-Marie Soutou, 16 June, *ibid.*, n° 346.
73 Note from the Minister's Office on the tactics of the Geneva conference, 8 July, *DDF*, 1955/2, n° 21.
74 Note, 4 July, ibid., n° 7.
75 Tel. 2 August, ibid., n° 78.
76 Note, 1 August, ibid., n° 73.
77 Note from Pinay, 25 November, ibid., n° 191.

## 5. Italy

1 Albert N. Garland & Howard McGaw Smyth, *Sicily and the surrender of Italy*, in series *U.S. Army in World War II: the Mediterranean Theater of Operations* (Washington, 1965); Norman Kogan, *L'Italia e gli Alleati. 8 Settembre 1943* (Milan, 1963); Domenico Bartoli, *L'Italia si arrende. La tragedia dell'8 settembre 1943* (Milan, 1983); Giuseppe Castellano, *Come firmai l'armistizio di Cassibile* (Milan, 1945); Dino Grandi, *25 luglio quarant'anni dopo*. ed. Renzo De Felice (Bologna, 1984).
2 Elena Aga Rossi, 'La politica degli Alleati verso l'Italia nel 1943', in De Felice, ed., *L'Italia tra tedeschi e alleati. La politica estera fascista e la seconda guerra mondiale* (Bologna, 1973), 171–219; Aga Rossi, *L'Italia nella sconfitta: politica interna e situazione internazionale durante la seconda guerra mondiale* (Naples, 1985); Ennio Di Nolfo, 'Stati Uniti e Italia tra la seconda guerra mondiale e il sorgere della guerra fredda', in *Atti del primo Congresso di Storia Americana (Genova 26/29 maggio 1976)* (Genova, 1978), 123–35; Di Nolfo, 'L'armistizio dell' 8 settembre come problema internazionale', in *Otto settembre 1943: l'armistizio italiano 40 anni dopo* (Rome, 1985), 65–82; David Ellwood, *Italy 1943–1945* (Leicester, 1985); Nicola Gallerano, 'L'influenza dell'organizzazione militare alleata sulla riorganizzazione dello stato italiano (1943–1945)', *Storia contemporanea*, 115 (1974); Charles Reginald S. Harris, *Allied Military Administration of Italy, 1943–1945* (London, 1957); Michael Howard, *The Mediterranean Strategy in the Second World War* (Cambridge, 1968); James E. Miller, 'Carlo Sforza e l'evoluzione della politica americana verso l'Italia 1940–1943', *Storia Contemporanea*, 4 (1976); Antonio Varsori, 'Italy, Britain and the Problem of a Separate Peace during the Second World War: 1940–1943', *Journal of Italian History*, 1 (1978), 455–91; Varsori, '"Senior" o "Equal" partner?', *Rivista di Studi Politici Internazionali*, XLV (1978), 229–60.
3 Bruno Arcidiacono, 'The "Dress Rehearsal": the Foreign Office and the Control of Italy, 1943–1944', *Historical Journal*, XXVIII (1985), 417–28.
4 See Ennio Di Nolfo, 'L'armistizio dell' 8 settembre 1943', 65–82.
5 Mario Toscano, 'Resumption of Diplomatic Relations between Italy and the Soviet Union during World War II, in Mario Toscano, ed., *Designs in Diplomacy* (Baltimore, MD, 1970), a revised edition of Toscano's work published in Italian in 1963.
6 Bruno Arcidiacono, *'Le précédent italien' et les origines de la guerre froide: les Alliés et l'occupation de l'Italie 1943–1944* (Brussels, 1984); Ennio Di Nolfo, 'La svolta di Salerno come problema internazionale', *Storia delle Relazioni Internazionali*, 1 (1985), 5–28.
7 Ibid., 25–8.
8 Bruno Arcidiacono, 'La Gran Bretagna e il "pericolo comunista" in Italia: gestazione, nascita e primo sviluppo di una percezione (1943–1944)', *Storia delle Relazioni Internazionali*, I, (1985), (1) 29–65, (2) 239–66.

9   Paolo Spriano, *Storia del PCI*, V, *La resistenza* (Turin, 1985), 441; Francesco Catalano, *Storia del CLNAI* (Milan, 1956).
10  Ennio Di Nolfo, *Le paure e le speranze degli Italiani (1943–1953)* (Milan, 1986), p. 119.
11  David Ellwood, 'La politica anglo-americana verso l'Italia. 1945: l'anno del trapasso del potere', in Guido Quazza, ed., *L'Italia dalla liberazione alla repubblica* (Milan, 1977), 167–96; see also Antonio Gambino, *Storia del dopoguerra in Italia. Dalla liberazione al potere DC* (Bari, 1975), mostly concerned with the history of Italian post-war politics and the impact of the Cold War on the break-up of anti-fascist collaboration.
12  Norman Kogan, *L'Italia del dopoguerra* (Bari, 1977), p. 61; first published in English as *A Political History of Post-War Italy* (New York, 1966).
13  Severino Galante, 'La scelta americana della DC', in Mario Isneghi & Silvio Lanaro, eds, *La Democrazia Cristiana dal fascismo al 18 aprile* (Venice, 1978); Danilo Ardia, 'Il partito socialista italiano e gli Stati Uniti', in Ennio Di Nolfo, ed., *Italia e Stati Uniti durante l'amministrazione Truman* (Milan, 1976); Pietro Nenni, *Tempo di guerra fredda. Diari 1943–1956* (Milan, 1981); Stuart J. Woolf, ed., *Italia 1943–1950: la ricostruzione* (Bari, 1975); Antonio Varsori, 'De Gasperi, Nenni, Sforza and their role in Post-war Italian Foreign Policy', in Josef Becker & Franz Knipping, eds., *Power in Europe? Great Britain, France, Italy and Germany in a Post-war World 1945–1950* (Berlin, 1986); James E. Miller, *The United States and Italy 1940–1950: the Politics and Diplomacy of Stabilization* (Chapel Hill, NC, 1986); Roberto Morozzo della Rocca, *La politica estera italiana e l'Unione Sovietica 1944–1948* (Rome, 1985); Ennio Di Nolfo, 'Storia delle Relazioni Internazionali', in Luigi Bonanate, ed., *Studi Internazionali* (Turin, 1989), pp. 96–110.
14  Bruno Arcidiacono, *'Le précédent Italien' et les origines de la guerre froide*; Ennio Di Nolfo, ed., *L'Italia e la politica di Potenza in Europa 1945–1950* (Milan, 1988); Di Nolfo, 'La guerra fredda', in *La Storia*, IX, *L'età contemporanea: dal primo al secondo dopoguerra* (Turin, 1986), p. 665; Ilaria Poggiolini, *Diplomazia della transizione: gli Alleati e il problema del trattato italiano (1945–1947)* (Florence, 1990).
15  Giustino Filippone-Thaulero, *La Gran Bretagna e l'Italia dalla conferenza di Mosca a Potsdam 1943–1945* (Rome, 1978); Poggiolini, *Diplomazia della Transizione*, pp. 15–40.
16  Dawson Ward, *The Threat of Peace: James F. Byrnes and the Council of Foreign Ministers 1945–1946* (Kent, OH, 1979); Poggiolini, *Diplomazia della transizione*, pp. 41–73.
17  Ilaria Poggiolini., 'Italian Revisionism: Status and Security Problems (1943–1956)', in Rolf Ahmann, ed., *The Quest for Stability: Problems of West European Security 1918–1957* (Oxford, 1993).
18  Poggiolini, *Diplomazia della Transizione*, pp. 98–110.
19  Amelia C. Leiss, ed., *European Peace Treaties after World War II.* Supplementary to Documents on American Foreign Relations VIII, 1945–1946 and IX, 1947 (Washington, 1954); Giovanni Bernardi, *La marina, gli armistizi e il trattato di pace (sett.1943–dic.1951)* (Rome, 1979; Diego De Castro, *L'azione politica e diplomatica italiana dal 1943 al 1954*, 2 vols. (Trieste, 1981); Anton Giulio De Robertis, *Le grandi potenze e il confine giuliano* (Bari & Rome, 1983); Gianluigi Rossi, *L'africa Italiana verso l'indipendenza 1941–1949* (Milan 1980).
20  Alberto Tarchiani, *America-Italia: le dieci giornate di De Gasperi negli Stati Uniti* (Milan, 1947), and Tarchiani, *Dieci anni tra Roma e Washington* (Milan, 1955).
21  Gambino, *Storia del dopoguerra*; Luigi Graziano, *La politica estera italiana nel dopoguerra* (Padua, 1968); Galante, 'La scelta americana della D.C.' (cited in note. 13).
22  Di Nolfo, *Le paure e le speranze*, 239–45; Miller, *The United States and Italy*, pp. 234–6.
23  Di Nolfo, *Le paure e le speranze*, p. 244.
24  Ennio Di Nolfo, 'The United States and Italian Communism 1942–1946. World War II to the Cold War', in *Journal of Italian History*, I (1978), 74–94.
25  Elena Aga Rossi, ed., *Il Piano Marshall e l'Europa* (Rome, 1983); Pier Paolo D'Attorre, 'Guerra fredda e trasformazioni delle societa' occidentali nella storiografia americana', *Italia Contemporanea*, 140 (Sept. 1980); Charles S. Maier, 'The Politics of Productivity: Foundations of American International Economic Policy after World War II', *International Organization*, XXXI/4; Maier, 'The two Post-War Eras and the Conditions for Stability in Twentieth Century Europe', *American Historical Review*, 86 (1981), 327–52; Alan Milward, *The Reconstruction of Western Europe 1945–1951* (London, 1984); Rosaria Quartararo, *Italia e Stati Uniti: gli anni difficili (1945–1952)* (Naples, 1986); Carlo Sforza, 'Italy, the Marshall Plan and the Third Force', *Foreign Affairs*, XXXVI, 1948/3, 450–6; Egidio Ortona, *Anni d'America. La*

*ricostruzione 1944–1951* (Bologna, 1984); Federico Romero, *Gli Stati Uniti e il sindacalismo europeo 1944–1951* (Rome, 1988).

26 Giuseppe Rossini, ed., *Democrazia Cristiana e Costituente*, I, *Le origini del progetto democristiano* (Rome, 1980); Marcello De Cecco, *Economic policy in the Reconstruction Period*, in Stuart Woolf, ed., *The Rebirth of Italy 1943–1950* (London, 1972); Piero Barucci, 'La politica economica internazionale e le scelte economiche dell'Italia (1943–1947)', *Rassegna Economica*, XXXVI (1973), 669–75.

27 Pietro Pastorelli, 'L'entrata in vigore del trattato di pace e il problema della sicurezza', in Pastorelli, ed., *La politica estera italiana del dopoguerra* (Bologna, 1987).

28 'Concern of the United States for the safeguarding of the territorial integrity and internal security of Italy', report by the National Security Council, 14 Nov. 1947, in *Foreign Relations of the United States* (FRUS), 1948, III, pp. 724–6.

29 James E. Miller, 'L'ERP come fattore determinante nelle elezioni italiane del 1948', in Aga Rossi, ed., *Il Piano Marshall* pp. 139–47; *Department of State Bulletin*, 28 May 1949, 425; *Department of State Bulletin*, 25 Apr. 1948.

30 Gambino, *Storia del dopoguerra*; Di Nolfo, *Le paure e le speranze degli italiani 1943–1953*; Di Nolfo, 'The Shaping of Italian Foreign Policy during the Formation of the East-West Blocs: Italy between the Superpowers', in Becker & Knipping, eds., *Power in Europe?* pp. 485–582; Galante, 'La scelta americana della D.C.' (cited in note 13).

31 Pier Paolo D'Attorre, 'Aspetti dell'attuazione del Piano Marshall in Italia', and David Ellwood, 'Il Piano Marshall e il processo di modernizzazione in Italia', in Aga Rossi, *Il Piano Marshall*, 168–80, 149–61; Francesco Catalano, *Europa e Stati Uniti negli anni della guerra fredda* (Rome, 1972).

32 Antonio Varsori, *Il Patto di Bruxelles tra integrazione europea e alleanza atlantica* (Rome, 1988).

33 Leopoldo Nuti, *L'esercito italiano nel secondo dopoguerra 1945–1950: la sua ricostruzione e l'assistenza militare alleata* (Rome, 1989).

34 Mario Toscano, 'Appunti sui negoziati per la partecipazione dell'Italia al Patto Atlantico' in Toscano, ed., *Pagine di Storia diplomatica contemporanea*, II, *Origini e vicende della seconda guerra mondiale* (Milan, 1963), pp. 455–519; Piero Pastorelli, *La politica estera italiana*, (Bologna, 1987), pp. 209–31; Ennio Di Nolfo, 'Motivi ispiratori e genesi diplomatica del Patto Atlantico', in *Trent'anni di alleanza atlantica* (Roma, 1979), pp. 4–42; Danilo Ardia, *Il partito socialista e il Patto Atlantico* (Milan, 1973); Ardia, *Alle origini dell'alleanza occidentale* (Padua, 1983); Severino Galante, *La politica del PCI e il Patto Atlantico* (Venice, 1973); Giovanni Di Capua, *Come l'Italia aderì' al Patto Atlantico* (Rome, 1970).

35 Pierre Guillen, 'I rapporti franco-italiani dall'armistizio alla firma del Patto Atlantico', in *L'Italia dalla liberazione alla repubblica*, pp. 145–80.

36 Varsori, 'La scelta occidentale', p. 362.

37 Poggiolini, 'Italian Revisionism', pp. 343–56.

38 Poggiolini, 'Italian Revisionism', pp. 344–5; Timothy E. Smith, 'From Disarmament to Rearmament: the United States and the Revision of the Italian Peace Treaty of 1947', *Diplomatic History*, 13 (1989), 359–82.

39 Declaration by the United States, France and Britain on the Italian Peace Treaty, 26 Sept. 1951, in *FRUS*, IV, pp. 717–18; Italian Note Requesting Revision, in *Department of State Bulletin*, 24 Dec. 1951, 1011.

40 Italian Note to the Soviet Government, Feb. 1952, in Public Record Office (PRO) FO 371, WT 1071/15.

41 Antonio Varsori, 'L'Italia tra alleanza occidentale e CED (1949–1954)', *Storia delle Relazioni Internazionali*, IV (1988), 124–65.

42 From Rome (V. Mallet) to Foreign Office, 6 Feb. 1953, PRO, FO 371, WT 1022/1; from Rome (V. Mallet) to Foreign Office, 13 Feb. 1953, PRO, FO 371, WT 1022/2.

43 Bogdan C. Novak, *Trieste 1941–1954: the Ethnic, Political and Ideological struggle* (Chicago, 1970), pp. 414–17; De Castro, *La Questione di Trieste*, pp. 393–486.

44 The American Ambassador Clare Boothe Luce to the Secretary of State John Foster Dulles, 22 June 1953, in National Archives Washington (NAW), RG 59, 76500/6–2253.

45 Novak, *Trieste*, pp. 418–35; De Castro, *La questione di Trieste*, pp. 51–708.

46 *Department of State Bulletin*, 18 Oct. 1954; *FRUS*, VI, 1952–4, pp. 1565–1722.

47 Ilaria Poggiolini, 'Europeismo italiano e politica estera dell'Italia: un'ipotesi interpretativa

(1944–1949)', *Storia delle Relazioni Internazionali*, 1 (1985), 67–93; Piero Pastorelli, 'La politica estera dell'Italia negli anni cinquanta', in Pastorelli, *La politica estera italiana*, pp. 233–57.

48  Lloyd A. Free & Renzo Sereno, *Dependent Ally or Independent Partner?* (Princeton, N.J., 1956).

49  Leo J. Wollemborg, *Stars, Stripes and Italian Tricolor: the United States and Italy 1946–1989* (New York & London, 1990), p. 22.

50  Ennio Di Nolfo, 'Il caso italiano nel suo contesto internazionale' in Ennio Di Nolfo, ed., *L'Italia e la politica di potenza in Europa, 1950–1960* (Milan, 1993).

## 6. Germany

1  Cf. Jens Hacker, *Deutsche Irrtümer: Schönfärber und Helfershelfer der SED-Diktatur im Westen* (Frankfurt/M, 1992) (B). The following notes have been restricted to 'classics' and to very recent publications. Those with exceptionally useful bibliographies have been marked (B).

2  For useful wider perspectives, see the essays by Klaus Tenfelde and Heinrich A. Winkler in *Aus Politik und Zeitgeschichte* (27 Sept. 1991).

3  For reasons beyond the scope of this essay, nuclear and German issues became progressively intertwined. Various studies on this subject are under way in the Nuclear History Program for the study of the history of the nuclear arms competition (a multinational project started by Uwe Nerlich (Germany) and Ernest R. May (U.S.A.) and in part co-ordinated by this author).

4  Unfortunately Andreas Hillgruber did not live to expand his brilliant short study *Deutsche Geschichte 1945–1986: die 'deutsche Frage' in der Weltpolitik* (6th ed., Stuttgart, 1987) into a full-scale analysis of Germany and the East-West confrontation.

5  The former capital city had been divided into four occupation sectors, the three Western ones surrounded by Soviet forces.

6  For a highly readable introduction, see David Calleo, *The German Problem Reconsidered: Germany and the World Order, 1870 to the Present* (New York, 1978). The best work on the war-aims issues is now Georges-Henri Soutou, *L'or et le sang: les buts de guerre économiques de la Première Guerre mondiale* (Paris, 1989) (B). Many determinist myths about modern Germany are put to rest by Thomas Nipperdey's path-breaking new synthesis *Deutsche Geschichte 1800–1918*, 3 vols., (Múnich, 1983–92) (B).

7  Reinhard Piper (ed.), '*Historikerstreit*' (Munich, 1987); Hans-Ulrich Wehler, *Entsorgung der deutschen Vergangenheit?* (Munich, 1988); Charles S. Maier, *The Unmasterable Past: History, Holocaust, and German National Identity* (Cambridge, MA, 1988); Richard J. Evans, *In Hitler's Shadow* (New York, 1989).

8  Shulamit Volkov, 'Kontinuität und Diskontinuität im deutschen Antisemitismus 1878–1945', *Vierteljahrshefte für Zeitgeschichte*, 33 (1985), 221–43.

9  For a sweeping statement of the background, cf. Hans-Peter Schwarz, *Die gezähmten Deutschen* (Stuttgart, 1985).

10  This conclusion should not, however, lead us to disregard a point raised by professional Germany-watchers who suggest quite plausibly that the German quest for spiritual identity may not have ended with the unification of the two Germanies. Neither can a more assertive German foreign policy be categorically excluded, given the uncertainties of Europe's future.

11  Ernst Nolte, *Deutschland und der Kalte Krieg* (Munich, 1974, rev. ed. 1985); cf. the review by Felix Gilbert in *American Historical Review*, 81 (1976), 618–20. Nolte's book is still the only sweeping interpretation of this theme by a German historian.

12  Ernst Nolte, *Der europäische Bürgerkrieg 1917–1945: Nationalsozialismus und Bolschewismus* (Frankfurt/M, 1987).

13  The recently published Politbureau order of March 1941 for the killing of some 22,000 Polish officers and intellectuals demonstrates yet again the Soviet state's criminal nature, not just Stalin's. These executions included the well-known Katyn murders revealed in 1943, which the Soviets attributed to the Nazis.

14  Michael Wolffsohn, *Ewige Schuld? 40 Jahre deutsch-jüdisch-israelische Beziehungen* (Munich, 1988).

15  Some of them are quoted in: 'Deutschland, eine Supermacht?', *Der Spiegel*, 47 (20 Nov. 1989) 164ff; cf. two articles by Richard Helms, the former CIA-director, in *The International Herald*

*Tribune* (27/28 Feb. 1990); and Amnon Neustadt, 'Israelische Reaktionen auf die Entwicklung in Deutschland', *Europa-Archiv*, 11 (1990), 351–68.

16  Klaus Hildebrand, 'Geschichte oder "Gesellschaftsgeschichte"? Die Notwendigkeit einer politischen Geschichtsschreibung von den internationalen Beziehungen', *Historische Zeitschrift*, 223 (1976), 328–57.

17  Ernst Deuerlein, *Die Einheit Deutschlands: ihre Erörterung und Behandlung auf den Kriegs- und Nachkriegskonferenzen 1941–1949* (Frankfurt/M, 1957); Ernst Deuerlein, *Deutschland nach dem Zweiten Weltkrieg 1945–1955*, 2 vols, (Konstanz, 1963/1964); Richard Löwenthal, *Vom Kalten Krieg zur Ostpolitik* (Stuttgart, 1974); Wilhelm Cornides, *Die Weltmächte und Deutschland, 1945–1955* (Tübingen, 1957); Hans-Peter Schwarz, *Vom Reich zur Bundesrepublik 1945–1949* (2nd ed., Neuwied, 1980) (B); Gerhard Wettig, *Entmilitarisierung und Wiederbewaffnung in Deutschland 1943–1955* (Munich, 1967); Jens Hacker, *Der Ostblock 1939–1980* (Baden-Baden, 1983) (B).

18  Not surprisingly we find the new social history particularly entrenched in the loser nations of the Second World War, whose recent *political* history provides little support for national pride.

19  Ironically, today's pundits demand unlimited access for all refugees to Germany while the government and the general public demand more restrictive policies to stem the unprecedented influx of 300,000 to 400,000 asylum-seekers annually.

20  Cf. the 'Two-plus-Four-Treaty' of 12 September 1990. Germany remained in NATO; total German forces were limited to 370,000 (substantially below the forces of today's Ukraine, for example); and Germany completely renounced any production or ownership of atomic, biological and chemical (ABC) weapons.

21  This dilemma is reflected over and over again in the memoirs of leading officials. In hindsight they like to emphasize how they outmanoeuvred Allied officials or turned them into supporters of German interests. But private German diaries, unless edited by their authors, and government records often tell a very different story. Some of these diaries and papers are being published in the series *Biographische Quellen zur deutschen Geschichte nach 1945* (Munich, Oldenbourg).

22  In-depth studies show that opposition to Erhard's economic philosophy remained strong only until about 1952.

23  Theo Pirker, *Die blinde Macht. Die Gewerkschaftsbewegung in Westdeutschland 1945–1960*, 2 vols, (Munich, 1960); Theo Pirker, *Die verordnete Demokratie* (Berlin, 1977); Kurt Klotzbach, *Der Weg zur Staatspartei. Programmatik, praktische Politik und Organisation der deutschen Sozialdemokratie 1945–1965* (Bonn, 1982).

24  In the 1950s some 25–30% of manual workers were refugees. Their links with the traditional institutions of working-class solidarity (trade unions, workers' clubs, etc.) were comparatively weak. They tended to be more interested in improving their families' economic lot.

25  This social revolution was initially analyzed in Ralf Dahrendorf's seminal work *Gesellschaft und Demokratie in Deutschland* (Munich, 1965).

26  Lutz Niethammer, ed., *Arbeiterinitiative 1945: antifaschistische Ausschüsse und Reorganisation der Arbeiterbewegung in Deutschland* (Wuppertal, 1976). Interesting comparison can be drawn with the GDR's 'round table' movement in 1989/90. Like the Räte of 1918/19 it exemplified spontaneous local democracy when one political order had fallen and another was yet to be established. Few of their leaders later became widely-known political figures.

27  Dörte Winkler, 'Die amerikanische Sozialisierungspolitik in Deutschland 1945–1948', Heinrich A. Winkler, ed., *Politische Weichenstellungen im Nachkriegsdeutschland* (Göttingen, 1979).

28  cf. Wolfgang Krieger, *General Clay und die amerikanische Deutschlandpolitik, 1945–1949* (2nd ed., Stuttgart, 1988) (B).

29  In the Petersberg agreement of November 1949 the three Western Allies made concessions on reparations and granted certain other improvements. In return the Federal Republic became a member of the International Ruhr Authority, which meant a voluntary German recognition of Allied restriction on the Ruhr industries, a step strongly opposed by the SPD. Eventually the Coal and Steel Community (1952) and the European Economic Community (1958) were to evolve from it. Cf. Walter Lipgens, *Die Anfänge der europäischen Einigungspolitik*, vol. 1: 1945–1950 (Stuttgart, 1977) and Ludolf Herbst et al., eds., *Vom Marshallplan zur EWG* (Munich, 1990).

30 This conviction lies at the heart of the flourishing school of Adenauer historiography which in part draws on the financial support and publication outlets of the Konrad-Adenauer-Stiftung. It is closely associated with the political party (CDU) which the 'old fox' had led to unprecedented success; its Archiv has several publications series. Historical studies of a similar stripe are funded and published by the Catholic Kommission für Zeitgeschichte.

31 Bogislaw von Bonin, *Opposition gegen Adenauers Sicherheitspolitik. Eine Dokumentation* (Hamburg, 1976). Eventually the argument for a defence-only posture saw a major comeback, due to the spectacular revival of détente under Ronald Reagan and Mikhail Gorbachev.

32 German conceptual debates on defence were mostly carried on by military specialists and peace researchers rather than by historians. Even the remarkable writings from the Bundeswehr's own Militärgeschichtliche Forschungsamt (institute of military history) at Freiburg largely remained outside the university-dominated mainstream of historical writings.

33 Werner Abelshauser, *Wirtschaft in Westdeutschland 1945–1948* (Stuttgart, 1975); Werner Abelshauser, 'Hilfe und Selbsthilfe: zur Funktion des Marshallplans beim westdeutschen Wiederaufbau', *Vierteljahrshefte für Zeitgeschichte*, 37 (1989), 85–113; Christoph Buchheim, *Die Wiedereingliederung Westdeutschlands in die Weltwirtschaft 1945–1958* (Munich, 1989) (B).

34 Rolf Steininger, *Eine Chance zur Wiedervereinigung? Die Stalin-Note vom 10 März 1952* (Bonn, 1985); Hermann Graml, *Die Märznote von 1952: Legende und Wirklichkeit* (Melle, 1988).

35 Cf.: Thomas A. Schwartz, *America's Germany: John J. McCloy and the Federal Republic of Germany* (Cambridge, MA, 1991), ch. 6.

36 Jörg Friedrich, *Die kalte Amnestie: NS-Täter in der Bundesrepublik* (Frankfurt/M, 1985).

37 For a good example, see Lutz Niethammer, *Entnazifizierung in Bayern* (Frankfurt/M, 1972). John Gimbel's pioneering work of 1968 was published in German in 1971 *(Die amerikanische Besatzungspolitik in Deutschland 1945–1949* (Frankfurt/M, 1971)). GDR historians and their Western sympathizers, however, cared little for such archival evidence: cf. E. Schmidt, *Die verhinderte Neuordnung 1945–1952* (Frankfurt/M, 1970) and Ernst-Ulrich Huster et al., *Determinanten der westdeutschen Restauration* (Frankfurt/M, 1972).

38 The debates surrounding this case are highly instructive of the political mood at the time: cf. *Keesing's Archiv der Gegenwart 1978*, pp. A 22115–9 (15 Oct. 1978).

39 Ironically it was this view which had made the American national security establishment neglect Korean developments and which may have tempted Stalin into the whole adventure in the first place.

40 See Hans Günter Hockerts, *Sozialpolitische Entscheidungen im Nachkriegsdeutschland: Alliierte und deutsche Sozialversicherungspolitik 1949–1957* (Stuttgart, 1980); Martin Broszat et al., eds., *Von Stalingrad zur Währungsreform* (2nd ed., Munich, 1988); Axel Schildt & Arnold Sywottek, 'Wiederaufbau und Modernisierung: zur westdeutschen Gesellschaftsgeschichte in den fünfziger Jahren', *Aus Politik und Zeitgeschichte* (3 Feb. 1989); and Arnold Sywottek, 'Flüchtlingseingliederung in Westdeutschland: Stand und Probleme der Forschung', in *Aus Politik und Zeitgeschichte* (15 Dec. 1989).

41 For a particularly fine example see Wilhelm G. Grewe, *Rückblenden 1976–1951* (Berlin, 1979).

42 For a typical example, see Ekkehart Krippendorff, *Die amerikanische Strategie* (Frankfurt/M, 1970).

43 Paradoxically, the outstanding German centres and scholars on Soviet affairs had little influence on the wider historical (and political science) community. For an exception cf. Hannes Adomeit's book on Soviet policy during the two Berlin crises, *Soviet Risk-Taking and Crisis Behavior* (London, 1982).

44 Wilfried Loth, *Die Teilung der Welt. Geschichte des Kalten Krieges 1941–1955* (Munich, 1980).

45 Löwenthal, *Vom Kalten Krieg zur Ostpolitik* (cited in note 17 above).

46 *Akten zur Vorgeschichte der Bundesrepublik Deutschland 1945–1949*, 5 vols. (Munich, 1976–83); *Der Parlamentarische Rat 1948–1949: Akten und Protokolle*, 4 vols. to date (Boppard, 1974–89); *Die Kabinettsprotokolle der Bundesregierung*, 6 vols. to date (Boppard, 1982–9).

47 *Akten zur auswärtigen Politik der Bundesrepublik Deutschland*, 2 vols. to date (Munich, 1989–90).

48 *Anfänge westdeutscher Sicherheitspolitik 1945–1956*, 2 vols. to date (Munich, 1982–90) (B).

49 *Geschichte der Bundesrepublik Deutschland*, 5 vols. (Stuttgart, 1983–7) (B); Hans-Peter Schwarz, *Adenauer*, 2 vols. (Stuttgart, 1986–90).

50 Daniel Koerfer, *Kampf ums Kanzleramt: Erhard und Adenauer* (Stuttgart, 1987).
51 Hermann Weber, *Die DDR 1945–1986* (Munich, 1988) (B), has a useful discussion of research trends.
52 cf. Jan H. Brinks, *Die DDR-Geschichtswissenschaft auf dem Weg zur deutschen Einheit: Luther, Friedrich II und Bismarck als Paradigmen politischen Wandels* (Frankfurt/M, 1992).
53 cf. Alexander Fischer & Günther Heydemann, *Geschichtswissenschaft in der DDR*, 2 vols. (Berlin, 1988–90) (B). The debates during and after unification can be traced in *Aus Politik und Zeitgeschichte* (see particularly the issues of 9 Mar. 1990, 25 Jan. 1991, 17 Apr. 1992, 2 Oct. 1992).
54 Dietrich Staritz & Hermann Weber, eds., *Einheitsfront – Einheitspartei. Kommunisten und Sozialdemokraten in Ost- und Westeuropa 1944–1948* (Cologne, 1989); *DDR-Handbuch*, 2 vols. (Cologne, 1985) (B); Martin Broszat & Hermann Weber, eds., *SBZ-Handbuch* (Munich, 1990) (B).
55 Significant new information emerged from the files of the GDR military archives. For example, preliminary findings indicate that Warsaw Pact forces were planning, or at any rate exercising for, a military conquest of West Germany and of other NATO countries in Europe. Even 8000 'Blücher' medals were held in store with which to decorate east German soldiers for bravery (see *Frankfurter Allgemeine Zeitung*, 1 Feb. 1992, p. 1).
56 The official *DDR Handbuch*, ed. Bundesministerium für innerdeutsche Beziehungen, 2 vols. (Cologne, 1985), II, p.909, assumes that there were (in 1982) some 26,000 full-time Stasi officers of all ranks. In fact there were close to 100,000. Neither figure includes the hundreds of thousands of 'informal' collaborators of one type or another.
57 Wolfgang Leonhard, *Die Revolution entlässt ihre Kinder* (Cologne, 1955); Erich W. Gniffke, *Jahre mit Ulbricht* (Cologne, 1966).

## 7. Benelux

1 Throughout this chapter 'Benelux countries' and 'Benelux' refer especially to Belgium and the Netherlands combined, without special reference to Luxembourg. If and when necessary the special position of Luxembourg will be highlighted.
2 Nikolaj Petersen, 'The Alliance Policies of the Smaller NATO Countries', in Lawrence S. Kaplan & Robert W. Clawson, eds., *NATO After Thirty Years* (Wilmington, DE, 1981), pp. 83–106.
3 Some parts of this contribution are based on Cees Wiebes & Bert Zeeman, 'The Origins of Western Defense: Belgian and Dutch Perspectives 1940–1949', in Ennio Di Nolfo, ed., *The Atlantic Pact Forty Years Later: a Historical Reappraisal* (Berlin & New York, 1991), pp. 143–62. Important sections are derived from our forthcoming *Towards the North Atlantic Treaty: Belgium, the Netherlands and Alliances 1940–1949*.
4 Cf. the essays by Michel Dumoulin, Martine Nies-Berchem and Anjo G. Harryvan on Belgian, Luxembourger and Dutch historiography on European integration in *Historians of Contemporary Europe Newsletter*, 7 (1992), 5–16, 87–100 and 101–12.
5 For instance, in the preparation of a paper on consultation mechanisms in NATO, the Dutch foreign ministry gave the authors of this essay permission to check its files up to 1983. Cf. Cees Wiebes & Bert Zeeman, ' "I don't need your handkerchiefs": Holland's experience of crisis consultation in NATO', *International Affairs*, 66 (1990), 91–113. Richard Griffiths calls the Dutch archives 'the richest and most open to researchers in Europe' in his preface to Richard T. Griffiths, ed., *The Netherlands and the Integration of Europe 1945–1957* (Amsterdam, 1990), p. xii.
6 For the time being the only exception is Charles De Visscher & Fernand Vanlangenhove, eds., *Documents Diplomatiques Belges, 1920–1940: La Politique de Sécurité Extérieure* (5 vols., Brussels, 1964–6).
7 Cf. *Bescheiden betreffende de Buitenlandse Politiek van Nederland 1848–1919 (1st Series: 1848–1870; 2nd Series: 1871–1898; 3rd Series: 1899–1919)* (The Hague, 1957– ); and *Documenten betreffende de Buitenlandse Politiek van Nederland 1919–1945 (Series A: 1919–1930; Series B: 1931–1940; Series C: 1940–1945)* (The Hague, 1976– ).
8 Jean Stengers, 'Paul-Henri Spaak et le Traité de Bruxelles', in Raymond Poidevin, ed., *Histoire des Débuts de la Construction Européenne, Mars 1948-Mai 1950* (Brussels, 1986), pp. 119–42.

9  Based on Spaak's personal papers, Paul F. Smets edited a collection of documents on his foreign policy: *La Pensée Européenne et Atlantique de Paul-Henri Spaak (1942–1972)* (2 vols., Brussels, 1980).

10  Herman Schaper, 'The Security Policy of the Netherlands', in J.H. Leurdijk, ed., *The Security Policy of the Netherlands* (Alphen aan den Rijn, 1978), pp. 89–116, and A.E. Kersten, 'Van Kleffens' plan voor regionale veiligheidsorganisaties 1941–1943', in *Jaarboek van het Department van Buitenlandse Zaken 1980–1981* ('s-Gravenhage, 1981), pp. 157–64.

11  Cf. for instance Adrien Manning, 'Les Pays-Bas face à l'Europe', in Poidevin, *Histoire des Débuts*, pp. 419–44, and Jan Schulten, 'Die militärische Integration aus der Sicht der Niederlande', in Norbert Wiggershaus & Roland G. Foerster, eds., *Die westliche Sicherheitsgemeinschaft 1948–1950: gemeinsame Probleme und gegensätzliche Nationalinteressen in der Gründungsphase der Nordatlantischen Allianz* (Boppard-am-Rhein, 1988), pp. 89–101.

12  To a significant extent these studies are based on the important series of documents on decolonization published in the *Officiële Bescheiden betreffende de Nederlands-Indonesische Betrekkingen 1945–1950* series (17 vols. to date).

13  N.C.F. van Sas, ed., *De kracht van Nederland: internationale positie en buitenlands beleid* (Haarlem, 1991). Reviewers of this volume were quick to point to the gaps in the historiography of Dutch foreign relations. Cf. Philip Everts in *Transaktie*, 21 (1992), 301, and Bert Zeeman in *Vrij Nederland* (25 Apr. 1992), p. 88.

14  Jules Gérard-Libois & Rosine Lewin, *La Belgique entre dans la Guerre Froide et l'Europe (1947–1953)* (Brussels, 1992). Rik Coolsaet's *Buitenlandse Zaken* (Leuven, 1987) has a few chapters on post-war Belgian foreign policy (French translation: *Histoire de la politique extérieure belge* (Brussels, 1989)).

15  All three served long terms as Foreign Secretary: Bech continuously from 1926 until 1959; Spaak almost continuously from 1936 until 1949 (and again in the 1950s and 1960s); and Van Kleffens from 1939 until 1946 (see appendix 2).

16  Wiebes & Zeeman, 'The Origins of Western Defense', pp. 146–8, and Smets, *La Pensée Européenne*, pp. 51–63.

17  Cf. his memoirs: E.N. van Kleffens, *Belevenissen*, I *(1894–1940)* and II (1940–1958) (Alphen aan den Rijn, 1980–3).

18  Kersten, 'Van Kleffens' plan', pp. 157–64, and Wiebes & Zeeman, 'The Origins of Western Defense', pp. 144–6.

19  Memorandum by Van Kleffens, 28 May 1942, Legation London Secret Archives, box 21, folder 0.7/3 (Netherlands Ministry of Foreign Affairs, The Hague – henceforth NMFA).

20  Goris to Spaak, 27 Dec. 1944, File 12237 (Belgian Ministry of Foreign Affairs, Brussels – henceforth BMFA); and Loudon to Van Kleffens, 10 Sept. 1941, Collection Van Kleffens (NMFA). Young's claim that the Belgians and Dutch both hoped for British leadership of a post-war alliance system is thus only partly correct: John W. Young, *Cold War Europe 1945–1989: a Political History* (London, 1991), p. 28.

21  Albert E. Kersten, 'Nederland en België in Londen, 1940–1944: werken aan de na-oorlogse betrekkingen', in J. Art, ed., *Colloquium over de geschiedenis van de Belgisch-Nederlandse betrekkingen tussen 1815 en 1945 Acta* (Gent, 1982), pp. 495–520.

22  Jan-Willem Brouwer, 'Répondre à la Politique Européenne Française: la Belgique et le Conseil de Coopération Économique', in Michel Dumoulin, ed., *La Belgique et les Débuts de la Construction Européenne, de la guerre aux traités de Rome* (Louvain-la-Neuve, 1987), pp. 59–75. For the Tripartite Council see also Richard T. Griffiths & Frances M.B. Lynch, 'L'Échec de la "Petite Europe": le Conseil Tripartite 1944–1948', *Guerres Mondiales et Conflits Contemporains*, 38 (1988), 39–62.

23  David Reynolds, 'The "Big Three" and the Division of Europe, 1945–48: an Overview', *Diplomacy & Statecraft*, 1 (1990), 131.

24  Cf. Donald Sassoon, 'The Rise and Fall of West European Communism, 1939–48', *Contemporary European History*, 1 (1992), 139–69.

25  Luxembourger military participated in the French zone of occupation; a shortage of troops (almost all employed in Indonesia) forced the Dutch government to decline the British invitation to participate in the occupation in the British zone.

26  Already on 12 February 1947 the communist ministers resigned from the Luxembourger coalition government because of budgetary cuts. Cf. the analysis of Abraham Boxhoorn, *The Cold War and the Rift in the Governments of National Unity: Belgium, France and Italy in the*

*Spring of 1947: a Comparison* (Amsterdam, 1993).

27  H.A. Schaper, 'Het Nederlandse veiligheidsbeleid 1945–1950', *Bijdragen en Mededelingen betreffende de Geschiedenis der Nederlanden*, 96 (1981), 286–90.

28  See M.D. Bogaarts, *Parlementaire geschiedenis van Nederland na 1945. Deel II: de periode van het kabinet-Beel, 3 juli 1946–7 augustus 1948* ('s-Gravenhage, 1989), pp. 524–44. For the Belgian attitude, Ginette Kurgan-Van Hentenryk, 'La Belgique et le relèvement économique de l'Allemagne 1945–1948', *Relations Internationales*, 51 (1987), 343–63; and for Luxembourg, Paul Cerf, *Le Luxembourg et son Armée: Le Service Militaire Obligatoire au Grand-Duché de Luxembourg de 1945 à 1967* (Luxembourg, 1984), pp. 44–9.

29  Cf. Wiebes & Zeeman, 'The Origins of Western Defense', pp. 148–51.

30  Brouwer, 'Répondre à la Politique Européenne', pp. 67–75.

31  Harrison to Hoyer Millar, 10 April 1947, FO 371/67646, z 3830/50/4 (PRO).

32  Wiebes & Zeeman, 'The Origins of Western Defense', p. 150.

33  Comment, Bevin and Harvey to Sargent, 11 July 1947, FO 371/67724, z 6791/737/72G (PRO).

34  Ministry of Foreign Affairs, *Road to Recovery. The Marshall Plan, its importance for the Netherlands and European Co-operation* (The Hague, 1954), pp. 130–9 and 148–9.

35  J. Schram, 'Nederland en het Marshallplan: de Nederlandse belangen op de conferentie van Parijs, 1947', in P. Luykx & A. Manning, eds., *Nederland in de wereld 1870–1950: Opstellen over buitenlandse en koloniale politiek, aangeboden aan Dr. N. Bootsma* (Nijmegen, 1988), pp. 201–24; and A.E. Kersten, *Maken drie kleinen een grote? De politieke invloed van de Benelux 1945–1955* (Bussum, 1982), pp. 6–7.

36  Frans Govaerts, 'Belgium, Holland and Luxembourg', in Omer de Raeymaeker et al., *Small Powers in Alignment* (Leuven, 1974), p. 393.

37  Paul van Campen, 'Abandoning neutrality: how and why the Netherlands joined the Atlantic Alliance', in André de Staercke et al., *NATO's Anxious Birth: The Prophetic Vision of the 1940s* (London, 1985), pp. 130–1.

38  For the general background to Bevin's speech: Alan Bullock, *Ernest Bevin: Foreign Secretary* (London, 1983), pp. 513–18.

39  See Paul-Henri Spaak, *Combats Inachevés: De l'Indépendance à l'Alliance* (Paris, 1969), pp. 252–61 (English trans., abridged: *The Continuing Battle: Memoirs of a European 1936–1966* (London, 1971), pp. 141–8), and Stengers, 'Paul-Henri Spaak', pp. 126–32.

40  Wiebes & Zeeman, 'The Origins of Western Defense', pp. 151–2, and Schaper, 'The Security Policy', pp. 106–9.

41  All proposals in Directie NAVO & WEU-zaken (DNW) archive WEU, 999.1, box 4, folder 12 (NMFA) and file 12237 (BMFA).

42  The fullest documentation on the negotiations can be found in DNW archive WEU, 999.1, box 4, folder 13 and box 5, folder 15 (NMFA).

43  Melandri unjustly claims that Spaak 'seemed to have been charged with the task to represent the United States vis-à-vis his future allies.' See Pierre Melandri, *Les États Unis face à l'Unification de l'Europe, 1945–1954* (Lille, 1979), p. 294.

44  Van Campen, 'Abandoning neutrality', p. 131.

45  For instance Bullock, *Ernest Bevin*, pp. 513–38; John Baylis, 'Britain, the Brussels Pact and the continental commitment', *International Affairs*, 60 (1984), 615–29; and Maurice Vaïsse, 'L'Échec d'une Europe Franco-Britannique ou Comment le Pacte de Bruxelles fut Créé et Délaissé', in Poidevin, *Histoire des Débuts*, pp. 369–89.

46  Cees Wiebes & Bert Zeeman, 'The Pentagon negotiations March 1948: the launching of the North Atlantic Treaty', *International Affairs*, 59 (1983), 351–63.

47  Memo of Conversation by Achilles, 12 May 1948, and Marshall to Kirk, No. 771, 21 May 1948, RG 59, confidential files '45–'49, box C-507 (National Archives).

48  Nicholas Henderson, *The Birth of NATO* (London, 1982), p. 42.

49  Stone to Pearson, 10 Aug. 1948, File 283(s), North Atlantic Security Pact, part 2 (Department of External Affairs, Ottawa).

50  Spaak to Silvercruys, 26 June 1948, file 12071, year 1948 (BMFA). Also Vincent Auriol, *Journal du Septennat, Tome 2, 1948* (Paris, 1974), p. 298.

51  Minutes of the Second Session of the Consultative Council, 19 and 20 July 1948, Records of the Brussels Treaty Organization, DG/1/1/1 (PRO).

52  Cf. Escott Reid, *Time of Fear and Hope. The Making of the North Atlantic Treaty 1947–1949*

(Toronto, 1977), pp. 113–25, vs. Robert Rothschild, 'Paul-Henri Spaak – Future Secretary General', in De Staercke, *NATO's Anxious Birth*, pp. 114–15.

53  Spaak, *Combats Inachevés*, pp. 211–19 (reprinted in *The Continuing Battle*, pp. 117–24).

54  For all the details see Cees Wiebes & Bert Zeeman, 'United States' "Big Stick" Diplomacy: the Netherlands between Decolonization and Alignment, 1945–1949', *International History Review*, 14 (1992), 50–7.

55  Ibid., 57–70.

56  Cf. Luc De Vos, 'Ein kleines Land in der grossen Politik: Belgiens behutsamer Beitrag zum Entstehen einer militärischen Integration Westeuropas', in Wiggershaus & Foerster, eds., *Die westliche Sicherheitsgemeinschaft*, pp. 83–6, and Manning, 'Les Pays-Bas face à l'Europe', pp. 419–44.

57  Michael Cox, 'Requiem for a Cold War Critic: The Rise and Fall of George Kennan, 1946–1950', in *Irish Slavonic Studies*, 11 (1991), pp. 14–17.

58  For example: Govaerts, 'Belgium, Holland and Luxembourg', pp. 291–389; and Josef Joffe, 'The "Scandilux" Connection: Belgium, Denmark, the Netherlands, and Norway in Comparative Perspective', in Gregory Flynn, ed., *NATO's Northern Allies: the National Security Policies of Belgium, Denmark, the Netherlands, and Norway* (Totowa, NJ, 1985), pp. 224–57.

59  Kersten, *Maken drie kleinen een grote?*, p. 10.

60  See Richard T. Griffiths & Frances M.B. Lynch, 'L'Échec de la "Petit Europe": les négociations Fritalux/Finebel, 1949–1950', *Revue Historique*, 274 (1985), 159–93.

61  Alan S. Milward, 'The Belgian Coal and Steel Industries and the Schuman Plan', in Klaus Schwabe, ed., *Die Anfänge des Schuman-Plans 1950/51* (Baden-Baden, 1988), p. 437, and Emile Krier, 'L'industrie lourde luxembourgeoise et le Plan Schuman', in ibid, pp. 357–66.

62  W. Asbeek-Brusse, 'The Stikker Plan', in Griffiths, ed., *The Netherlands and the Integration of Europe*, pp. 69–92, and Richard T. Griffiths, 'The Abortive Dutch Assault on European Tariffs, 1950–2', in Michael Wintle, ed., *Modern Dutch Studies: Essays in Honour of Peter King* (London, 1988), pp. 186–201.

63  Griffiths is very negative in his evaluation of Benelux co-operation during the Schuman Plan negotiations. Cf. Richard T. Griffiths, 'Die Benelux-Staaten und die Schumanplan-Verhandlungen', in Ludolf Herbst, Werner Bührer & Hanno Sowade, eds., *Vom Marshall Plan zur EWG: die Eingliederung der Bundesrepublik Deutschland in die westliche Welt* (Munich, 1990), pp. 263–79.

64  Gérard-Libois & Lewin, *La Belgique*, pp. 151–71; Michel Dumoulin, 'La Belgique et les débuts du Plan Schuman (mai 1950–février 1952)', in Schwabe, ed., *Die Anfänge des Schuman-Plans*, pp. 271–84, and Milward, 'The Belgian Coal and Steel Industries', pp. 437–53.

65  Albert E. Kersten, 'A Welcome Surprise? the Netherlands and the Schuman Plan Negotiations', in Schwabe, ed., *Die Anfänge des Schuman-Plans*, pp. 285–304, and Richard T. Griffiths, 'The Schuman Plan', in Griffiths, ed., *The Netherlands and the Integration of Europe*, pp. 113–35.

66  Gilbert Trausch, 'Le Luxembourg face aux Traités de Rome: la Stratégie d'une Petit Pays', in Enrico Serra, ed., *Il Rilancio dell'Europa e i Trattati di Roma* (Milan, 1989), p. 425.

67  Belgium and the Netherlands both sent a small number of soldiers to Korea.

68  J. van der Harst. 'The Pleven Plan', in Griffiths, ed., *The Netherlands and the Integration of Europe*, pp. 137–64, and Albert E. Kersten, 'Niederländische Regierung, Bewaffnung Deutschlands und EVG', in Hans-Erich Volkmann & Walter Schwengler, eds., *Die Europäische Verteidigungsgemeinschaft: Stand der Probleme und Forschung* (Boppard-am-Rhein, 1985), pp. 191–219. For Stikker's own recollections: Dirk U. Stikker, *Men of Responsibility: a Memoir* (London, 1966), pp. 300–17.

69  Gérard-Libois & Lewin, *La Belgique*, pp. 205–38; Luc De Vos, 'België en het streven naar militaire integratie in West-Europa, 1945–1955', in P. Lefèvre & P. De Gryse, eds., *De Brialmont à l'Union de l'Europe Occidentale: Mélanges d'Histoire Militaire offerts à Albert Duchesne, Jean Lorette et Jean-Léon Charles* (Brussels, 1988), pp. 259–79; and Luc De Vos, 'La Communauté Européenne de Défense, une occasion manquée', in Dumoulin, ed., *La Belgique et les Débuts*, pp. 103–17.

70  Van der Harst, 'The Pleven Plan', p. 148.

71  Kersten, *In de ban van de bondgenoot*, pp. 11–12.

72  For the Luxembourger attitude: Cerf, *Le Luxembourg et son Armée*, pp. 90–1.

73 See especially Spaak, *Combats Inachevés*, pp. 268–300 (reprinted in *The Continuing Battle*, pp. 159–75).
74 Griffiths, 'Die Benelux-Staaten', p. 278.
75 See Adrian F. Manning, 'Die Niederlande und Europa von 1945 bis zum Beginn der Fünfziger Jahre', *Vierteljahrshefte für Zeitgeschichte*, 29 (1981), 14–18, and Griffiths, 'The Abortive Dutch Assault', pp. 186–208.
76 See Anjo G. Harrivan & Albert E. Kersten, 'The Netherlands, Benelux and the Relance Européenne 1954–1955', in Serra, ed., *Il Rilancio dell'Europa*, pp. 125–39.
77 Kersten, *Maken drie kleinen een grote?*, pp. 13–15.
78 In the preparation of a biography of Spaak, B. Emerson has been granted *exclusive* permission to consult Spaak's personal papers; see Dumoulin, 'L'Historiographie de la construction européenne en Belgique', *Historians of Contemporary Europe Newsletter*, 7 (1992), 14.

## 8. Scandinavia

1 N. Petersen, 'The Cold War and Denmark', *SJH*, 10 (1985), 191–209; and W. Agrell, 'Sweden and the Cold War: the Structure of a Neglected field of Research', *SJH*, 10 (1985), 239–53; on Scandinavian third-world studies, see M. Mörner, 'Research on the History of the Third World in Scandinavia', *SJH*, 11 (1986), 3–15.
2 It should be noted that there are only some eighty–ninety historians in tenured positions in Norwegian universities and colleges, a quarter of them in Oslo.
3 M. Skodvin, *Nordic or North Atlantic Alliance*, *DS*, 3 (1990), 19–57; K. Blidberg, *Just Good Friends*, *DS*, 5 (1987), 33–5; M. Skodvin, *Norden eller NATO* (Oslo, 1971); K.E. Eriksen, *DNA og NATO* (Oslo, 1972); see also the extended debate in *IP*, 1976–7.
4 *Stortingsmelding* no. 32, 1945–6, p. 3, here quoted from O. Riste, 'Was 1949 a Turning Point?', in Riste, ed., *Western Security: the Formative Years* (Oslo, 1985).
5 H.Ø. Pharo, 'Bridgebuilding and Reconstruction: Norway Faces the Marshall Plan', *SJH*, 1 (1976), 125–53; for a version published before departmental archives were generally accessible which is quite critical of bridgebuilding, emphasizing concessions to the Soviets, see N.M. Udgaard, *Great Power Politics and Norwegian Foreign Policy* (Oslo, 1973), particularly pp. 191–207; for Scandinavian bridge-building from the American point of view, G. Lundestad, *America, Scandinavia and the Cold War, 1945–1949* (Oslo & New York, 1980), particularly ch. 2–4; see also Blidberg, *Just Good Friends*; Skodvin, *Nordic or North Atlantic Alliance*; and Riste, 'Was 1949 a Turning Point?'
6 O. Riste, *'London-regjeringa': Norge i krigstidsalliansen 1940–45* (2 vols., Oslo, 1973 & 1979); and *Frå Integritetstraktat til Atompolitikk: Det stormaktsgaranterte Norge 1905–1983*, *DS*, 2 (1983), and *The Genesis of North Atlantic Defence Cooperation: Norway's 'Atlantic Policy' 1940–1945*, *DS*, 2 (1981); R. Tamnes, *Integration and Screening: the Two Faces of Norwegian Alliance Policy, 1945–1986*, *DS*, 5 (1986).
7 See note 6; see also Eriksen, *DNA og NATO*, pp. 19–28; K.E. Eriksen, 'Norge i det vestlige samarbeidet', in T. Bergh & H.Ø. Pharo, eds., *Vekst og velstand*, pp. 179–85; Pharo, 'Gjenreisning og utenrikspolitikk', in Bergh & Pharo, eds., *Historiker og veileder: festskrift til Jakob Sverdrup* (Oslo, 1989), pp. 163–202 (for an earlier English version see *Domestic and International Implications of Norwegian Reconstruction*, European University Institute (henceforth EUI) Working Paper, 81 (Florence, 1984)).
8 Blidberg, *Just Good Friends*, pp. 6–11; Eriksen, 'Norge i det vestlige samarbeidet'.
9 Arne Ording's Diaries, 27 June 1946, typescript, Oslo University Library; for a more extended treatment of this issue, see Pharo, 'Bridgebuilding and Reconstruction', 128–30.
10 Ording's Diaries, 9 Oct. 1947.
11 On the question of the primacy of foreign policy, see Pharo, 'Bridgebuilding and Reconstruction'; *Domestic and International Implications of Norwegian Reconstruction;* 'The Norwegian Labour Party', in R.T. Griffiths, ed., *Socialist Parties and the Question of Europe* (New York, 1993), pp. 201–20, and *The Third Force, Atlanticism and Norwegian Attitudes towards European Integration*, EUI Working Paper, Florence, 255 (1986).
12 U. Olsson, 'The Swedish Social Democrats', in Griffiths, ed., *Socialist Parties*, pp. 221–38; V. Sørensen, 'The Politics of Closed Markets: Denmark, the Marshall Plan, and European Integration, 1945–1963', *International History Review*, 15 (1993), 23–45; P. Villaume, 'Neither Appeasement nor Servility: Denmark and the Atlantic Alliance 1949–1955', *SJH*, 14

(1989); K. Misgeld, 'As the Iron Curtain Fell: the Coordinating Committee of the Nordic Labour Movement and the Socialist International between Potsdam and Geneva', *SJH*, 13 (1988), 49–63; L. Dalgas Jensen, 'Denmark and the Marshell Plan, 1947–48', *SJH*, 14 (1989); Blidberg, *Just Good Friends*; G. Aalders, 'The Failure of the Scandinavian Defence Union', *SJH* 15 (1990).

13   See *Svensk forsvarspolitik under efterkrigstiden*, eds. H.K. Cars, C. Skoglund & K. Zetterberg (Stockholm, 1986).

14   N. Andren, 'Svensk nøytralitetspolitikk', *IS*, 6 (1984), 34–6.

15   Blidberg, *Just Good Friends*; O. Riste, 'Nordic Union or Western Alliance?: Scandinavia at the Crossroads, 1948–1949,' in E. Di Nolfo, *The Atlantic Pact Forty Years Later: a Historical Reappraisal* (Berlin, 1991); Riste, 'Forholdet mellom den norske og den svenske regjering under krigen', *Nordisk Tidsskrift* (1989).

16   N. Petersen, 'Denmark and NATO, 1949–87', *DS*, 2 (1987); Petersen, Abandonment vs. Entrapment: Denmark and Military Integration in Europe 1948–1951', *CC*, 21 (1986); L. Dalgas Jensen, Denmark and the Marshall Plan; V. Sørensen, 'The Politics of Closed Markets'.

17   Riste, 'Nordic Union or Western Alliance?', p. 129.

18   Udgaard, *Great Power Politics*, pp. 131–6; M. Dau, *Danmark og Sovjetunionen 1944–49*, (Copenhagen, 1969); K.E. Eriksen, review of *Danmark og Sovjetunionen*, in *Historisk tidsskrift*, 50 (1971).

19   Lundestad, *America, Scandinavia and the Cold War*, where the issue of Greenland is a recurrent theme in the book; N. Petersen, 'Abandonment vs. Entrapment'; Petersen, 'The Cold War and Denmark'; N. Amstrup, 'Grønland i det amerikansk-danske forhold 1945–1948', in Amstrup & I. Faurby, eds., *Studier i dansk udenrigspolitikk tilegnet Erling Bjøl* (Aarhus, 1978).

20   T. Lie and C.J. Hambro in the Storting Foreign Affairs Committee, 26 June 1945, quoted from K.E. Eriksen, 'Svalbard-spørsmålet fra krig til kald krig', pp. 112–62, quote on p. 124, in Bergh & Pharo, eds., *Historiker og veileder*.

21   Eriksen, 'Svalbardspørsmålet', p. 144, for the Undén letter, and generally Blidberg, *Just Good Friends*, p. 40; the Spitsbergen issue is a recurrent theme in Lundestad, *America, Scandinavia and the Cold War*; Riste, *London-regjeringa*, I and II; Eriksen, 'Svalbard 1944–47 – et brennpunkt i øst-vest-rivaliseringen', *IP* (1976), 109–37; Eriksen, 'Great Britain and the Problem of Bases in the Nordic Area, 1945–1947', *SJH*, 7 (1982), 135–63; R. Tamnes, *Svalbard mellom Øst og vest. Kald krig og lavspenning i nord 1947–1953*, *DS*, 4 (1987); Riste, *Svalbard-krisen 1944–1945*, *DS*, 2 (1981).

22   Pharo, 'Bridgebuilding and Reconstruction'; Jensen, 'Denmark and the Marshall Plan'; Misgeld, 'As the Iron Curtain Fell'.

23   Norwegian Foreign Ministry Archives (UD) 44.2/26, Memorandum by Arne Ording, 7 July 1947; see generally Pharo, 'Bridgebuilding and Reconstruction'; Jensen, 'Denmark and the Marshall Plan'; Olsson, 'Swedish Social Democrats'.

24   Pharo, 'Bridgebuilding and Reconstruction'; Jensen, 'Denmark and the Marshall Plan'; Misgeld, 'As the Iron Curtain Descended'.

25   Ording's Diaries, 5 November 1947.

26   Eriksen, *DNA og NATO*, pp. 29–71; Skodvin, *Norden eller NATO*, pp. 62–89; Skodvin, *Nordic or North Atlantic Alliance*, pp. 17–30; Riste, 'Nordic Union or Western Alliance?'

27   Riste, 'Nordic Union or Western Alliance?; Skodvin, *Nordic or North Atlantic Alliance?*; Aalders, 'The Failure of the Scandinavian Defence Union'.

28   Pharo, *Domestic and International Implications of Norwegian Reconstruction*; Eriksen, *DNA og NATO*, pp. 72–94; Lundestad, *America, Scandinavia and the Cold War*.

29   Riste, 'Nordic Union or Western Alliance?'; Eriksen, *DNA og NATO*, pp. 99–101; Skodvin, *Nordic or North Atlantic Alliance?*; Skodvin, *Norden eller NATO*, pp. 113–22.

30   The quotes are from Robin Hankey of the Foreign Office Northern Department, 1 Nov. 1946, FO 371/56285; and a report from the Oslo Embassy, Oslo to FO, 8 Apr. 1947, FO 371/66061, both quoted from Skodvin, *Nordic or North Atlantic Alliance?*, p. 11, see generally pp. 10–16; K.E. Eriksen & Skodvin, 'Storbritannia, NATO og et nordisk forbud', *IP*, (1981), 449–69.

31   Bevin to Attlee, 12 June 1946, FO 371/56297, from Skodvin, *Nordic or North Atlantic Alliance?*, p. 11; Gunnar Jahn Papers, Diaries, 17 Sept. 1947, typescript, Oslo University Library.

32   Skodvin, *Nordic or North Atlantic Alliance?*, p. 14; see also K. Blidberg, *Just Good Friends*; and

K.E. Eriksen and Skodvin, 'Storbritannia, NATO og et skandinavisk forbund', pp. 449–69.

33  Lundestad, *America, Scandinavia and the Cold War*, ch. 3.

34  *Foreign Relations of the United States*, 1947, III, memorandum by Kennan, 4 Sept. 1947, p. 398; Lundestad in *America, Scandinavia and the Cold War*, p. 89, points out, however, that a CIA report on Norway from Sept. 1947 contains hardly any criticism of Norwegian foreign policy.

35  Lundestad, *America, Scandinavia and the Cold War*, pp. 100–1.

36  Skodvin, *Nordic or North Atlantic Alliance?*, pp. 41–53; K.E. Eriksen and Skodvin, 'Storbritannia, NATO og et nordisk forbund', pp. 469–81; for the domestic Norwegian situation, see Eriksen, *DNA og NATO*, pp. 72–97.

37  Blidberg, *Just Good Friends*, pp. 33–4; Aalders, 'The Failure of the Scandinavian Defence Union'.

38  Aalders, 'The Failure of the Scandinavian Defence Union'.

39  Blidberg, *Just Good Friends*, pp. 33–4; Aalders, 'The Failure of the Scandinavian Defence Union'; Eriksen, *DNA og NATO*, pp. 98–127.

40  Riste, 'Nordic Union or Western Alliance?'; Blidberg, *Just Good Friends*, pp. 34–6.

41  Riste, 'Nordic Union or Western Alliance?'; Blidberg, *Just Good Friends*, pp. 34–8, Skodvin, *Norden eller NATO*, pp. 179–83. This presentation and the following pages build very closely on Riste and to a lesser degree Blidberg.

42  Blidberg, *Just Good Friends*, p. 38.

43  Riste, 'Nordic Union or Western Alliance?', pp. 136–41.

44  Riste, 'Nordic Union or Western Alliance?', pp. 133–7.

45  Riste, 'Nordic Union or Western Alliance?'; Skodvin, *Norden eller NATO*, pp. 235–86.

46  Blidberg, *Just Good Friends*, pp. 56–7.

47  Riste, 'Nordic Union or Western Alliance?'; Skodvin, *Norden eller NATO*, pp. 288–95.

48  The issue was discussed in great detail in *IP*, 1977, in articles by Eriksen, Lundestad and Pharo. Lundestad was highly critical of Lange's neglect of this opening for a Scandinavian option. He retreated somewhat from this position in *America, Scandinavia and the Cold War*.

49  Riste, 'Nordic Union or Western Alliance?'; Skodvin, *Norden eller NATO*, pp. 228–9, 324–35.

50  Riste, 'Nordic Union or Western Alliance?'; the standard account in Norwegian is Eriksen, *DNA og NATO*.

51  Riste, 'Nordic Union or Western Alliance?'; Skodvin, *Norden eller NATO*, pp. 305–8.

52  Riste, 'Nordic Union or Atlantic Alliance?', p.135.

53  Eriksen, *DNA og NATO*, is the standard account.

54  Riste, 'Nordic Union or North Atlantic Alliance?', p. 136–7.

55  For the discussion of the pro-Scandinavian attitudes of Norway and Lange in particular, see note 30 above; see also Blidberg, *Just Good Friends*.

56  Blidberg, *Just Good Friends*; Aalders, 'The Failure of the Scandinavian Defence Union; Riste, 'Nordic Union or North Atlantic Alliance?'

57  Blidberg, *Just Good Friends*; Petersen, 'Abandonment vs. Entrapment'; Villaume, 'Neither Appeasement nor Servility'.

58  Eriksen and M. Skodvin, 'Storbritannia, NATO og et nordisk forbund'; Riste, 'Nordic Union or Western Alliance?'

59  Riste, 'Nordic Union or Western Alliance?'; Blidberg, *Just Good Friends*; Aalders, 'The Failure of the Scandinavian Defence Union.'

60  Quoted from Aalders, 'The Failure of the Scandinavian Defence Union'; see also Blidberg, *Just Good Friends*.

61  Blidberg, *Just Good Friends*, pp. 58–9.

62  R. Tamnes, 'Norway's Struggle for the Northern Flank, 1950–1952', in O. Riste, ed., *Western Security: the Formative Years* (Oslo, 1985); Tamnes, *Integration and Screening*; Petersen, 'Abandonment vs. Entrapment'; Villaume, 'Neither Appeasement nor Servility'.

63  Ording's Diaries, 2 Feb. 1952; for an analysis of the initiative, see H.Ø. Pharo, *Hjelp til selvhjelp. Det indisk-norske fiskeriprosjekts historie 1952–72* (2 vols., Oslo, 1987).

# INDEX

*Note*: The major powers, particular the USA and the USSR, are mentioned on almost every page of the book. For clarity, the main index entries for these states are brief: reference should be made to the states with which they dealt, the principal crises (e.g. 'Korean War'), to the names of policymakers, and to policy démarches (e.g. 'Marshall Plan').